THE PENNSYLVANIA GERMAN
IN THE REVOLUTIONARY WAR, 1775-1783

METALMARK BOOKS

Sincerely Yours.

H. m. m. Richards

The Pennsylvania=German

in the

Revolutionary War
1775=1783

BY

HENRY MELCHIOR MUHLENBERG RICHARDS
LATE UNITED STATES NAVY

Secretary Pennsylvania-German Society, Member Historical Society of Pennsylvania, Genealogical Society of Pennsylvania, National Geographic Society, American Academy Political and Social Science, Etc., Sons of the Revolution, Naval Order of the United States, Military Order of Foreign Wars of the United States, Naval and Military Order of the Spanish-American War, Grand Army of the Republic

A HISTORICAL SKETCH

PART XVIII. OF A NARRATIVE AND CRITICAL HISTORY
PREPARED AT THE REQUEST OF
THE PENNSYLVANIA-GERMAN SOCIETY

LANCASTER, PA.
1908

PRESS OF
THE NEW ERA PRINTING COMPANY
LANCASTER, PA.

THE author wishes to make renewed acknowledgment to Julius F. Sachse, Litt.D., of Philadelphia, for the valuable aid extended in this work and others, in the production of the excellent illustrations which have added so much to their worth and interest.

He also desires to publicly thank Dr. D. W. Nead, of Philadelphia, for his equally valuable assistance in the preparation of the index which accompanies this history, and without which it would be far from complete.

PROLOGUE.

If any excuse be needed for the pages which here follow, I trust it may be found in the fact that, until recently, no effort has been made to present to the public, even in any small degree, the great deeds done in the upbuilding of our country, from its very foundations, by those who, then and now, have formed by no means an inconsiderable portion of its population—the early German emigrants to America.

As the vast majority of these peoples came to and settled in the Province of Pennsylvania, from whence they have since radiated to the outer confines of the continent, they gradually became known as "Pennsylvania-Germans," a name of which their descendants are justly proud, and the glory of whose achievements is gradually shedding its light far and near. These achievements were well-nigh buried in oblivion until, in recent years, there came into existence the Pennsylvania-German Society, founded for the express purpose of digging away, as it were, the rubbish which had so obscured them in the past, and of uncovering them to the light of day.

There were two epochs in the history of America, both of momentous importance. One of these covered the period of the French and Indian War and the other that of our Revolutionary War. The first decided the question as to whether the Anglo-Saxon or Latin race should control and develop this newly settled land. The second was the final development of God's plan to make of it a free country and an asylum for the oppressed of all nations.

Contrary to the general belief of those who have made no exhaustive study of the subject, both of these stupendous epochs had much of their origin and culmination in the history of Pennsylvania, and success or failure, in both instances, was largely dependent upon the German settlers of Pennsylvania. It was the Pennsylvania-German who really shaped the destiny of this continent.

In my history of "The Pennsylvania-German in the French and Indian War," which has preceded this work by some two years, I have endeavored to present, rather exhaustively, their connection with that period. In this history of "The Pennsylvania-German in the Revolutionary War" I trust it will be found that I have not altogether failed in my effort to prove the important work done by our ancestors in those dark and gloomy days.

H. M. M. RICHARDS.

CONTENTS.

ILLUSTRATIONS.

CHAPTER I.

The Pioneer Exponents of Liberty.

WHEN we pause a moment to think of the large German settlements in existence, at the period of our Revolutionary War, in the Province of New York, in Virginia, in Maryland, in Carolina, Georgia and elsewhere, and of the fact that at least one third of the entire population of Pennsylvania were people of the same blood, it would be but reasonable to presume, what was in reality the case, that their deeds should correspond somewhat with their numbers, and that they, equally with their brethren of a different parentage, had performed the full measure of duty to their country.

As we turn, with expectant interest, to the pages of history, to learn somewhat of the character of these deeds, we are astonished to find them unrecorded. To such an extent has this been the case that unthinking and unreasoning persons have been led to believe that the German element of this country has been practically a nonentity in its development.   Thanks to the initiative publications of men like Dr. Seidensticker, of the University of Pennsylvania, and Governor Pennypacker, of this Commonwealth, followed by the work of the Pennsylvania-German Society and its individual members, the curtain of ignorance, which has heretofore obscured the valorous and patriotic deeds of our German ancestors, is being rolled up, from day to day, until, in the not distant future, it is to be hoped they may be revealed in all their glory and entirety.

There have been various reasons for this historical silence.   Our fathers, however educated in other languages, spoke and wrote in an alien tongue which others, too busy in recording and exploiting their own deeds and worth, had no interest in translating, and, therefore, their doings, to a certain extent, either became lost to the world or were allowed to lie hidden until the children of this generation were permitted to bring them to light.   Because of their strange tongue, and foreign derivation, they were denied the privilege of becoming the governing factors, rulers, and leaders of the nation in its early history. With but comparatively few exceptions they sought the wilderness of outer settlement, there to establish their homes, and, largely unheeded by others, to lay the foundations upon which their neighbors might build and in which they might glory.   Then, too, conservative by nature and not given to boasting, they little strove for the applause or encomiums of the world, to which they were entitled, and were well satisfied to tread the path lying open before them, leaving the future of history to right them and itself.

That future is now at hand and, as by its light we search the dark nooks and crannies of the past, even we, through whose veins courses the same blood, cannot fail to be surprised by the revelations which present themselves.

And, yet, why should there be any cause for surprise, especially in the matter of the history of our Revolutionary War, the subject now under discussion? Fleeing from persecution and warfare in the Fatherland, the men of the German Rhine sought a refuge where they might be *free*. To them liberty was all in all, because it meant an untrammeled enjoyment of their homes and the right to worship their God according to the dictates of their own conscience. When they found this liberty they clung to it most tenaciously, and, with entire unselfishness, they were willing to suffer for it, even at the risk of self-abasement, so that others, with them, might enjoy its blessing.

Had it not been for the brave stand which the Germans of Pennsylvania made against the onslaught of the savage during the French and Indian War, notwithstanding their own sad and terrible experience, there would have been no Revolutionary War and no resulting freedom.

Long years before the American Colonies dreamed of throwing off the yoke of Great Britain the German settlers of Carolina spoke out for liberty and were an important factor in the rising of that province, which terminated in the overthrow, in 1719, of its Proprietary Government. As a result of this action, though the Board of Trade was warned that " if the much greater part of the most substantial people had their choice they would not choose King George's government," and though Rhet, the receiver of the revenues, wrote from Charleston that " if the recent revolt of the people is not cropped in the bud, they will set up for themselves against his majesty "—a prophecy and warning as to the future—yet the insurrection was adopted by the Crown, and Carolina, accepting the King as an ally, received a governor of royal appointment.

With this spirit of liberty coursing through their veins is it to be wondered that, as the news of the conflict at Lexington, travelling slowly, reached the town of Charlotte, Mecklenburg County, North Carolina, where were assembled in session descendants of these same German settlers, they should have been so filled with the spirit of patriotism as to resolve upon a declaration of independence from " the authority of the King and Parliament . . . and the former civil constitution of these colonies." Two sets of resolutions exist, one much stronger than the other, but both equally strong upon the point of independence.   The dates likewise vary but both profess to have been adopted in the latter half of May, 1775, more than one year prior to the great Declaration of Independence whose birth we celebrate as of July 4, 1776.   The declaration of Mecklenburg County was communicated to the Provincial Congress of the colony, without, however, obtaining the sympathy of that assembly.   It was also forwarded to the North Carolina representatives in the Continental Congress, but so little did it move them that they did not even lay it before their colleagues.

Animated by the same spirit, and again long in advance of their English brethren, on August 1, 1775, the boards of the German Society of Pennsylvania, and of the equally German Lutheran and Reformed Churches at Philadelphia issued manifestoes declaring independence and advocating armed resistance, showing their zeal by the formation of German associations who had already begun drilling.

The first voice, raised on this continent, for individual

freedom, irrespective of color, was that of the German settlers in Germantown, in the following protest against slavery, sent to the Quakers, which is given "verbatim et literatim." The handwriting of the original appears to be that of Pastorius.

"This is to ye Monthly Meeting held at Rigert Worrells. These are the reasons why we are against the traffick of mens-body as followeth: Is there any that would be done or handled at this manner? viz. to be sold or

Seal of German Town Pa.
·1691·

made a slave for all the time of his life? How fearful & fainthearted are many on sea when they see a strange vassel being afraid it should be a Turck, and they should be tacken and sold for Slaves in Turckey. Now what is this better done as Turcks doe? Yea rather is it worse for them, wch say they are Christians for we hear, that ye most part of such Negers are brought heither against their will & consent, and that many of them are stollen. Now tho' they are black, we cannot conceive there is more liberty to have them slaves, as it is to have other white ones. There is a saying, that we shall doe to all men,

licke as we will be done our selves: macking no difference
of what generation, descent, or Colour they are.   And
those who steal or robb men, and those who buy or purchase them, are they not all alicke?   Here is liberty of
Conscience, wch is right & reasonable, here ought to be
lickewise liberty of ye body, except of evildoers, wch is
an other case.   But to bring men hither, or to robb and
sell them against their will, we stand against.   In Europe
there are many oppressed for Conscience sacke; and here
there are those oppressed wch are of a black Colour.
And we, who know that men must not commit adultery,
some do commit adultery in others, separating wifes from
their housbands, and giving them to others and some sell
the children of those poor Creatures to other men.   Oh,
doe consider well this things, you who doe it, if you would
be done at this manner? and if it is done according
Christianity?   You surpass Holland and Germany in this
thing.   This mackes an ill report in all those Countries
of Europe, where they hear off, that ye Quackers doe here
handle men, Licke they handel there ye Cattle; and for
that reason some have no mind or inclination to come
hither.   And who shall maintaine this your cause or plaid
for it!   Truely we can not do so except you shall inform
us better hereoff, viz. that christians have liberty to prac-
tise this things.   Pray!   What thing in the world can
be done worse towarts us then if men should roob or steal
us away & sell us for slaves to strange Countries, separating housband from their wife & children.   Being now
this is not done at that manner we will be done at, therefore we contradict & are against this traffick of men body.
And we who profess that it is not lawfull to steal, must
lickewise avoid to purchase such things as are stolen, but
rather help to stop this robbing and stealing if possible

and such men ought to be delivred out of ye hands of
ye Robbers and set free as well as in Europe.   Then is
Pensilvania to have a good report, in stead it hath now
a bad one for this sacke in other Countries.   Especially
whereas ye Europeans are desirous to know in what manner ye Quackers doe rule in their Province & most of
them doe loock upon us with an envious eye.   But if
this is done well, what shall we say, is don evil?

"If once these slaves (wch they say are so wicked and
stubborn men) should joint themselves, fight for their
freedom and handel their masters & mastrisses, as they
did handel them before; will these masters & mastrisses
tacke the sword at hand & warr against these poor slaves,
licke we are able to believe, some will not refuse to doe?
Or have these negers not as much right to fight for their
freedom, as you have to keep them slaves?

"Now consider well this thing, if it is good or bad?
and in case you find it to be good to handel these blacks
at that manner, we desire & require you hereby lovingly
that you may informe us herein, which at this time never
was done, viz. that Christians have Liberty to do so, to
the end we shall be satisfied in this point, & satisfie lickewise our good friends & acquaintances in our natif Country, to whose it is a terrour or fairfull thing that men
should be handeld so in Pensilvania.

"This was is from our meeting at Germantown hold
ye 18 of the 2 month 1688 to be delivred to the monthly
meeting at Richard Warrels "

"GERRET HENDRICKS

"DERICK OP DE GRAEFF

"FRANCIS DANIELL PASTORIUS

"ABRAHAM OP DEN GRAEF."

The disposition which was made of this protest appears from these notes from the Friends' records: "At our monthly meeting at Dublin ye 30 2 mo. 1688, we having inspected ye matter above mentioned & considered it we finde it so weighty that we think it not Expedient for us to meddle with it here, but do Rather comitt it to ye consideration of ye Quarterly meeting, ye tennor of it being nearly Related to ye truth, on behalfe of ye monthly meeting.

" signed, pr Jo. HART "

"This above mentioned was Read in our Quarterly meeting at Philadelphia the 4 of ye 4 mo. '88, and was from thence recommended to the Yearly Meeting, and the above said Derick and the other two mentioned therein, to present the same to ye above said meeting, it being a thing of two great a weight for this meeting to determine
"Signed by order of ye Meeting,

" ANTHONY MORRIS."

At the yearly meeting held at Burlington the 5 day of 7 mo. 1688, "A paper being here presented by some German Friends Concerning the Lawfulness and Unlawfulness of buying and Keeping of Negroes, It was adjudged not to be so proper for this Meeting to give a Positive Judgment in the case, It having so General a Relation to many other Parts, and, therefore, at present they forbear it."

The first person in America to battle for the freedom of speech, and to accomplish the liberty of the press, was John Peter Zenger (also spelled Zanger and Zinger in the records), who was born in Germany in 1697, came to this country in 1710, his father having died at sea, and, a lad of thirteen, was apprenticed to William Bradford, the New York printer. At the expiration of his ap-

A

Brief V I N D I C A T I O N

O F

T H E Purchaſſors

Againſt the P R O P R I T O R S,

I N

A Chriſtian Manner.

N E W - Y O R K.
Printed, By J. Zenger, jun. 1745·6.

prenticeship he went to Maryland and settled in Kent County, probably at Chestertown, the county seat, as early as 1720, where he was naturalized in October of said year. Shortly after he returned to New York, where he married in 1722. Here he went into business for himself as a printer, and, later, became the Collector of Taxes. About this time was started the quarrel between Governor Cosby and the Council, on the subject of salary, which waxed strong and found its way into the courts where it was decided against the Council, greatly to the indignation of the people who accused the judges of being biased. At once Zenger started a paper, the *New York Weekly Journal,* which, in its first issue, November 5, 1733, violently assailed the governor, while his former employer, Bradford, in his *New York Gazette,* espoused the governor's cause. Highly incensed, the government ordered four numbers of the *Journal* to be publicly burned by the hangman, and promptly arrested Zenger, throwing him into prison and denying him pen, ink and paper. When arraigned for trial his counsel, Smith and Alexander, began by excepting to the commissions of the Chief Justice and Justice Philipse, because they ran " during pleasure," which so enraged the Court that the advocates were at once disbarred and the case adjourned. No one else in the city dared appear for Zenger so his friends secured the services of Andrew Hamilton, long at the head of the Pennsylvania bar and without a superior in all the colonies. Hamilton's plea was a triumphant defense of his client and " the first vindication of the liberty of the Press in America." " The verdict of acquittal will stand as the first triumph of American Independence."

The first blood shed in the American battle for liberty was that of the little-known German lad, Christopher Snider (Schneider), in Boston, on February 22, 1770.

Theophilus Lillie was one of six merchants in Boston

who refused to sign association papers not to import merchandise from the mother country, thus making himself very obnoxious. One night an effigy was placed in front of his house as a mark of ridicule. In the early morning, as the people passed by, all laughed at the absurd image save Ebenezer Richardson, of unsavory record because of his employment as a spy on the actions of the Sons of Liberty. He tried to get some one to aid him in overthrowing the effigy, but without success. As a result of his efforts an altercation occurred, and the boys began calling him names, such as " Poke-nose," be-

MASSACHUSETTS.

cause always ready to spy into the business of others. This was followed by the throwing of snow-balls, to which he replied with a brick-bat. Then came more snow-balls, until, in a fit of anger, he rushed into his house, raised the window and fired a gun, wounding Samuel Gore slightly and killing Christopher Snider, a German school boy about nine years old, the only son of a widow residing in Frog Lane. It was this incident which led directly to the collision between the ropemakers and soldiers, two weeks later, resulting in the Boston massacre of March 5, 1770.

Richardson was tried, committed to jail, and sentenced to be hanged, but execution was delayed by Governor Hutchinson, and he was finally set at liberty at the outbreak of the war.

" No other incident," said John Adams, " has so stirred the people as the shooting of this boy." Never had there been such a funeral in Boston as that of Christopher Snider, on February 26, 1770. The schools were closed to allow the scholars to march in procession. Merchants put up their shutters. All tradesmen laid down their tools and made their way to the Liberty-Tree, where the procession was to form. Mothers flocked to the little cottage in Frog Lane to weep with the mother bereft of her only child. On the Liberty-Tree some one had nailed a board upon which were painted texts from the Bible:

" Thou shalt take no satisfaction for the life of a murderer. He shall surely be put to death."

" Though hand join in hand, the wicked shall not pass unpunished."

The clock was striking three when the six young men, acting as bearers, brought the coffin, from the home of the mother in Frog Lane, to the Liberty-Tree. On the velvet pall were marked the following inscriptions in Latin:

" Latet Anguis in Herba."
" Hœret Lateris lethalis Armada."
" Innocentia nusquam in tuta."

Translation.

" The serpent is lurking in the grass."
" The fatal dart is thrown."
" Innocence is nowhere safe."

All the bells were tolling. Mothers and maidens along the street were weeping. Old men uncovered their heads and bared their snow-white locks to the wintry air. School-boys, more than six hundred in number, two by two in hand; apprentices, journeymen, citizens, three thousand in number; magistrates, ministers, merchants, lawyers, physicians, in chaises and carriages, composed the throng bearing the murdered boy to his burial. What, under ordinary circumstances, would have been a trifling occurrence to be forgotten over night, became an indignant protest of an outraged community against tyranny and oppression—the enforcement of law by show of force. The first blood had been shed, the first victim had fallen, and the thoughtful asked " Where will this end? "

When Burgoyne's expedition started so auspiciously with the capture of Fort Ticonderoga, in July, 1777, the cause of independence looked dark indeed, so dark that, believing the end of the rebellion to be at hand, the king lost control of himself and rushed into the queen's apartments, clapping his hands and shouting, " I have beat them! I have beat all the Americans! " Then it was the old German veteran, General Nicholas Herkimer, with eight hundred of his fellow Palatine countrymen, brought renewed courage to the cause by defeating the enemy at Oriskany, on August 6, 1777, where men fought like demons, stabbing, cursing and dashing out each other's brains, while the vivid lightning from heaven lit up the scene in quick flashes, the rain poured in torrents, and the crashing thunder above pealed answer to the booming artillery below, and where, it is said, the carnage was more horrible than any which had ever occurred in the history of warfare.

The German Baron Steuben found Washington's army

a mob and made it a machine capable of successfully grappling with the power opposed to it.

But, fascinating as is the story of German valor in general, during our War of Independence, a story which once begun is hard to end, we are reminded that our narrative is to be confined to more narrow limits, and must embrace merely the deeds of our Pennsylvania-German ancestors. Even this subject is sufficiently vast to become almost appalling, so much so that the writer cannot claim to do more than touch upon it, leaving to abler hands, in the future, the task of filling in to make the completed whole.

The German immigration to Pennsylvania was far in excess of that to any other colony. So great was their numerical strength that they became a controlling factor which was bound to guide all movements in any desired direction, when once called into play. It is said that the greatest mistake made by the English government was its refusal to allow representation and to give an authoritative standing to the German element of the Province. It is claimed that, had such been done, so great would have been their content with the existing condition of affairs that they would never have been tempted to ask for a larger freedom, and, with non-coöperation on their part, the consent of Pennsylvania could never have been secured to a separation from the mother country, and the Declaration of Independence would have become an impossibility. With the knowledge we possess of the German character this suggestion opens up a most attractive line of thought, but, fortunately, one of no practical value.

An interesting part of our subject rests in the fact that many of the German colonists of Pennsylvania had conscientious scruples against bearing arms. Their doctrine, like that of the English Quakers, was one of non-resistance. They fled from the persecutions of the Fatherland that they might enjoy this very liberty in Pennsylvania. In spite of scoffing, fines, imprisonments and burdensome taxes, even here in their adopted country, they adhered to their doctrine of peace, to the extent even of soliciting the government to legally excuse them from bearing arms. Amongst those holding this belief, in especial, were the Moravians, Mennonites, Dunkers, Schwenkfelders, and others of like character. Even these never swerved from their duty and, in various ways which will appear later, proved their loyalty to the full measure of laying down their lives for their country in more than one instance.

In numbers, these non-resisting settlers formed no small proportion of the whole. If then the estimate, which has been made, be correct that one half of those from Pennsylvania, who served during the Revolution, had German blood in their veins, how much greater the honor to be accorded the Pennsylvania-German, who did bear arms, for his services at that time.

In the pages to follow it is proposed to show, in brief, that the Pennsylvania-Germans were the " First Defenders " of the Revolution; that, without the Pennsylvania-Germans, there would have been no Declaration of Independence; that, by his valor, the Pennsylvania-German saved the cause and its army from destruction at Long Island; that, without him, there would have been no means of holding the American army at Valley Forge nor of " bottling up " the British in Philadelphia, and that, finally, whenever and wherever called upon to do his duty he never failed to respond nobly.

CHAPTER II.

THE FIRST DEFENDERS OF THE REVOLUTION.

ON the morning of April 12, 1861, the great Civil War was begun when the troops of South Carolina, under General Robert Beauregard, fired upon the United States flag which floated over Fort Sumter, garrisoned by United States soldiers, under command of Major Robert Anderson.

On April 15, 1861, the President of the United States issued a proclamation calling for 75,000 troops. On April 16 the Ringgold Light Artillery, a company of Pennsylvania-Germans, from Reading, were already en route for Harrisburg, where they were joined by four other Pennsylvania companies, more than half of whose members were likewise Pennsylvania-Germans, and then proceeded through Baltimore, on April 18, where they were violently assaulted by a great mob, reaching Washington the same evening. They were the First Defenders of that stupendous war which struck the shackles of slavery from the limbs of millions of bondmen and bond-women. So were the Pennsylvania-Germans, of Captain George Nagel's (Nagle) company, of Reading, the First Defenders of the Revolution which gave us a free country and an asylum for the oppressed of all nations.

Somehow Pennsylvania has almost allowed the world to forget that it had any share in the operations around Boston that followed the battle of Bunker Hill, and we, of German blood, have been especially derelict in our failure to make prominent the fact that, of those Pennsylvanians, probably one half were Pennsylvania-Germans as were also fully one third of their commanding officers.

On June 14, 1775, three days before the clash of arms on Bunker Hill, and a day before the appointment of George Washington as Commander-in-Chief, Congress had already passed a resolution authorizing the raising of six companies of expert riflemen in Pennsylvania, two in Maryland and two in Virginia, to join the army near Boston so soon as completed. By a resolution, dated June 22, the " Colony of Pennsylvania " was directed to raise two more companies, which, with the six, were to be formed into a battalion, and to be commanded by such officers as the Assembly or Convention should recommend. On the 11th of July Congress was informed that two companies had been raised in Lancaster County instead of one, and, accordingly, resolved that both be taken into the Continental service. This battalion, therefore, consisted of nine companies, enlisted as follows: Captain James Chambers in Cumberland County (now Franklin), Captain William Hendricks in Cumberland, Captain Michael Doudel in York (now Adams), Captain James Ross in

Lancaster, Captain Matthew Smith in Lancaster (now Dauphin), Captain John Lowdon in Northumberland, Captain Robert Cluggage in Bedford, Captain George Nagel in Berks, and Captain Abraham Miller in Northampton.

In accordance with the resolution of Congress, on June 24 the Assembly decided "that the members of Congress deputed by this Assembly be a committee to consider of and recommend proper officers of the said battalion." The commissions to these officers are dated the next day, Sunday, June 25. The following is a copy of one of them:

"*The delegates of the United Colonies of New Hampshire, Massachusetts Bay, Rhode Island, Connecticut, New York, New Jersey, Pennsylvania, and the Counties of New Castle, Kent, and Sussex, in Delaware, Maryland, Virginia, North Carolina and South Carolina.*

" To John Lowdon, Esq.

" We, reposing especial trust and confidence in your patriotism, valor, conduct, and fidelity, do by these presents, constitute and appoint you to be a captain of a company of riflemen, in the battalion commanded by Col. William Thompson, in the army of the United Colonies raised for the defense of American liberty, and for repelling any hostile invasion thereof. You are, therefore, carefully and diligently to discharge the duty of captain, by doing and performing all manner of things thereunto belonging. And we do strictly charge and require all officers and soldiers under your command, to be obedient to your orders as captain, and you are to observe and follow such orders and directions from time to time as you shall receive from this or a future Congress of the United Colonies, or Committee of Congress for that purpose appointed, or Commander-in-Chief for the time being of the army of the United Colonies, or any other superior officer, according to the rules and discipline of war, in pursuance of the trust reposed in you. This commission to continue in force until revoked by this or a future Congress.

" By order of Congress

" JOHN HANCOCK, *President.*

" PHILADELPHIA, *June 25, 1775.*

" Attest

" CHARLES THOMSON, *Secretary.*"

The form of enlistment was, " I have this day voluntarily enlisted myself as a soldier in the American Continental Army for one year, unless sooner discharged, and do bind myself to conform in all instances to such rules and regulations as are or shall be established for the government of said army."

Each company was to consist of one captain, three lieutenants, four sergeants, four corporals, a drummer or trumpeter, and sixty-eight privates.

The pay of the officers and privates was as follows: Captain, twenty dollars per month; lieutenant, thirteen and one third dollars; sergeant, eight dollars; corporal, seven and one third dollars; drummer or trumpeter, the same; privates, six and two thirds dollars; to find their own arms and clothes.

All these men were expert riflemen. Their endurance, marksmanship and thorough scouting made them Washington's favorite troops during the war. On account of their hunting shirts and rifles the British spoke of them as " shirt-tail men with their cursed twisted guns, the most fatal widow-and-orphan-makers in the world." They turned the tide at Saratoga by their sharp-shooting, General Fraser being a victim; they were Morgan's reliance at Cowpens; British regulars were powerless against them as the rifle was unknown to the British armies, as well as to the New England and coast troops generally.

The patriotism of Pennsylvania was evinced in the haste with which the companies of Col. Thompson's battalion were filled to overflowing, and the promptitude with which they took up their march for Boston.

The exact time of arrival of each of these companies has been a subject of great interest and some little dispute. The records are more or less incomplete, and, in several instances, evidently misleading. As an example of this latter statement we have an extract from the Philadelphia *Evening Post* of August 17, 1775, publishing a New York item " that between the 28th of July and 2d instant, the riflemen, under the command of Captains Smith, Lowdon, Doudel, Chambers, Nagel, Miller and Hendricks, passed through New Windsor (a few miles north of West Point), in the New York government, on their way to Boston." The incorrectness of this item is evident when we recall the fact that several of these commands had already reached their destination prior to July 28, and that others did not pass New Windsor until August 20.

They did not march as a battalion, but each company pushed forward hurriedly by itself, when ready, to avoid all delay. With few exceptions they all touched at Bethlehem, which lay directly in the line of march to New York. The Moravian chronicles show that Captain Doudel passed through that town on July 8, Captain Cluggage, from Bedford, on August 13, and another company, unnamed, on August 10.

The journal of Aaron Wright, a member of Captain

Lowdon's company states that they were sworn in at Northumberland on June 29, 1775, where they lay until July 7, when orders were received to march; marched on board the boats the next morning; reached Reading July 13, and were there given knapsacks, blankets, etc.; left Reading July 20, and were at Bethlehem on August 1; reached North River, opposite New Windsor, August 20. On the 24th marched through Litchfield, Conn., crossed the Connecticut, near Hartford, on the 26th, and reached Dudley, Mass., on the 30th of August. On the 31st they marched to Weston, and stayed all night; thence through Framingham, Watertown, to Cambridge; thence to Prospect Hill. As, however, the regimental returns of August 18, 1775, include nine captains and twenty-seven lieutenants, the field officers, who arrived on the 17th, may have included this company, before its arrival, or Aaron Wright may have been with rear arrivals.

Henry McEwen, in his application for a pension, states that "Hendrick's company left Carlisle on the 15th of July, 1775, and arrived in camp at Cambridge on the 8th of August."

Captain Michael Doudel's company was enlisted, principally, at Samuel Getty's Tavern, now Gettysburg, June 24, 1775. They left York, for Boston, July 1, and arrived at Cambridge, Mass., July 25 at 1.00 P. M., going by the "nearest road."

Captain James Chambers writes from Cambridge, August 13, 1775, "We arrived in camp on the 7th ultimo [August 7], about twelve o'clock."

From a letter, dated at Hartford, the latter part of July, it is stated, "Yesterday came to town a number of Paxtang boys, dressed and painted in the Indian fashion, being part of a body of two hundred volunteers who are on their way to General Washington's army at Cambridge. Several of them we hear are young gentlemen of fortune." Allowing several days for the march from Hartford to Cambridge we would be warranted, therefore, in saying that Captain Smith's company reached camp about July 25 to August 1.

Captain Ross arrived in camp at Cambridge on August 18, 1775.

Because of the distance of Captain Cluggage's company, in Bedford County, it is hardly to be presumed that he could arrive at his destination until some time in August. We have no record of the time.

Neither is there any record of the time of arrival of Captain Miller's company of Northampton County, but, as they came from the further end of the county, it is probable that his company was not so promptly organized and was unable to move more quickly than did Captain Nagel, so that it is entirely unlikely that he reached Cambridge in advance of the Reading company. All records are to the contrary. Even were it otherwise they also were Pennsylvania-Germans so that our claim would still hold.

Of Captain Nagel's company a letter, dated " Camp at Cambridge, July 24, 1775," says: " The Reading company of rifles got into camp last Tuesday (18th); the rest are hourly expected and much wanted." This was barely thirty-four days after Congress had first authorized the formation of this battalion, an incredibly short period for this time in our history.

With this evidence staring us in the face, we feel justified in reiterating our claim that the Pennsylvania-Germans were truly the " First Defenders " of our country in its struggle for independence.

Thatcher, in his *Military Journal of the Revolution,* under date of August, 1775, describes the battalion as follows:

" They are remarkably stout and hardy men; many of them exceeding six feet in height.   They are dressed in white frocks or rifle shirts and round hats.   These men are remarkable for the accuracy of their aim; striking a mark with great certainty at two hundred yards distance. At a review, a company of them, while on a quick advance, fired their balls into objects of seven inches diameter, at the distance of two hundred and fifty yards.   They are now stationed in our lines, and their shot have frequently proved fatal to British officers and soldiers who expose themselves to view, even at more than double the distance of common musket shot."

They carried a green flag, with a crimson field in the center containing the device of a tiger, partly inclosed by toils, attempting the pass defended by a hunter, clad in white and armed with a spear.   The motto, on the field was " Domari Nolo."

Immediately upon arrival, though tired and worn by their long march of five hundred miles, Captain Doudel's command asked permission of Washington to capture a British transport in the Charles River.   While commending them for their patriotism, the Commander-in-Chief deemed the effort inexpedient.   On July 29, however, the out sentries, at the foot of Bunker Hill, gave notice that the enemy had cut down several large trees and were busy the previous night in throwing up entrenchments, with abattis in front.   In the evening orders were accordingly given Captain Doudel to march his company down to the advanced post on Charlestown Neck, there to endeavor to surround the enemy's advanced post and bring off some prisoners, from whom it was hoped the enemy's design might be learned.   The rifle company divided and executed their plan in the following manner: Captain Doudel, with thirty-nine men, filed off to the right of Bunker's Hill, and, creeping on their hands and knees, got into the rear of the enemy's sentries without being discovered. The other division of forty men, under Lieutenant Miller, were equally successful in getting behind the sentries on the left, and were within a few yards of joining the division on the right, when a party of regulars came down the hill to relieve the guard, and crossed our riflemen under Captain Doudel, as they were lying on the ground in an Indian file.   The regulars were within twenty yards before they saw them, and immediately fired. The riflemen returned the volley, killed several and brought off two prisoners and their muskets, with the loss of Corporal Walter Crouse (Cruise), who was then supposed to have been killed but was taken prisoner, remaining such for seventeen months, and afterwards was promoted to Captain in the Sixth Pennsylvania.

On the 23d of September Col. Hand wrote to Judge Yeates: " Day before yesterday, Lieut. McKenzie of the Bedford company, had his hat blown off by the wind of a cannon ball, and a splinter hit Dr. Hubley, and overturned him.   Morgan, Hendricks, and Smith, have left with their companies for Canada.   Seven hundred musqueteers from here are on the same expedition.   The expedition with which the York company was raised does not keep on for this misconduct; had Smith's command been better behaved they might probably have saved themselves a disagreeable jaunt.   The General refused peremptorily to take the York company."

A contemporary letter, dated September 13, says:

" On Monday last (11th) Col. Arnold having chosen one thousand effective men, consisting of two companies of riflemen (about one hundred and forty), the remainder musqueteers, set off for Quebec, as it is given out, and which I really believe to be their destination.   I accompanied on foot as far as Lynn, nine miles.   Dr. Coates,

AUTOGRAPH OF BENEDICT ARNOLD.

who goes as surgeon, Mr. Mart. Duncan, Mr. Melcher, and several other southern gentlemen as volunteers.   Here I took leave of them with a *wet eye*.   The drums beat, and away they go as far as Newburyport by land, from there go in sloops to Kennebeck river, up it in batteaux, and have a carrying place of about fifty miles, over which they must carry on their shoulders their batteaux and baggage, scale the walls, and spend the winter in joy and festivity among the sweet nuns "—*Jesse Lukens* (son of Surveyor General John Lukens, mortally wounded at Wyoming, December 25, 1775, a sad comment on his sportive letter).

In general orders, dated Cambridge, September 11, 1775, occurs:

" Col. Thompson's battalion of riflemen posted upon Prospect Hill, to take their share of all duty, of guard and fatigue, with the brigade they encamp with."   Also, September 13 : " The thirty-three riflemen of Col. Thompson's battalion, tried yesterday, by a general court-martial, whereof Col. Nixon was president, for ' disobedient and mutinous behavior,' are each of them sentenced to pay the sum of twenty shillings, except John Leamon, who, over and above his fine, is to suffer six days' imprisonment. The pay-master of the regiment to stop the fine from each man out of next months' pay, which must be paid to Dr. Church, for the use of the general hospital."

The contemporary letter above referred to supplements these orders thus:

" Our camp is separate from all others about one hundred yards.   All our courts-martial and duty was separate. We were excused from all working parties, camp guards, camp duty.   This indulgence, together with the remissness of discipline and care in our young officers, has rendered the men rather insolent for good soldiers.   They had twice before broken open our guard-house and released their companions who were confined there for small crimes, and once when an offender was brought to the post to be whipped, it was with the utmost difficulty they were kept from rescuing him in the presence of all their officers.   They openly damned them, and behaved with great insolence.   However the colonel was pleased to pardon the man, and all remained quiet; but on Sunday last the adjutant having confined a sergeant for neglect of duty and murmuring, the men began again, and threat-

ened to take him out. The adjutant being a man of
spirit, seized the principal mutineer and put him in also,
and coming to report the matter to the colonel where we
were all sitting after dinner, were alarmed with a huz-
zaing, and, upon going out, found they had broken open
the guard-house and taken the man out. The colonel and
lieutenant-colonel, with several officers and friends, seized
the fellow from amongst them, and ordered a guard to
take him to Cambridge to the main guard, which was done
without any violent opposition, but in about twenty
minutes thirty-two of Capt. Ross' company, with their
loaded rifles, swore by God they would go to the main
guard and release the man or lose their lives, and set off
as hard as they could run. It was in vain to attempt
stopping them. We stayed in camp and kept the others
quiet. Sent word to Gen. Washington, who reinforced
the guard to five hundred men with fixed bayonets and
loaded pieces. Col. Hitchcock's regiment (being the one
next to us) was ordered under arms, and some part of
Gen. Greene's brigade (as the generals were determined
to subdue by force the mutineers, and did not know how
far it might spread in our battalion). Genls. Washington,
Lee, and Greene came immediately, and our thirty-two
mutineers who had gone about a half a mile towards Cambridge and taken possession of a hill and woods, beginning to be frightened at their proceedings, were not so
hardened, but upon the General's ordering them to
ground their arms they did it immediately. The General
then ordered another of our companies, Capt. Nagel's,
to surround them with their loaded guns, which was immediately done, and did the company great honor. However, to convince our people (as I suppose, mind), that
it did not altogether depend upon themselves, he ordered

part of Col. Hitchcock's and Col. Little's regiments to surround them with their bayonets fixed, and ordered two of the ringleaders to be bound.   I was glad to find our men all true and ready to do their duty except these thirty-two rascals.   Twenty-six were conveyed to the quarter-guard on Prospect Hill, and six of the principals to the

AUTOGRAPH OF GENERAL GREENE.

mainguard.   You cannot conceive what disgrace we are all in, and how much the General is chagrined that only one regiment should come from the South, and that set so infamous an example, and in order that idleness shall not be a further bane to us, the General's orders on Monday, were 'that Col. Thompson's regiment shall be upon all parties of fatigue (working parties), and do all other camp duty with any other regiment.'

"The men have since been tried by a general court-martial and convicted of mutiny, and were only fined twenty shillings each for the use of the hospital—too small a punishment for so base a crime. Mitigated, no doubt, on account of their having come so far to serve the cause and its being the first crime. These men are returned to their camp and seem exceedingly sorry for their misbehavior and promise amendment. I charge our whole disgrace upon the remissness of our officers, and the men being employed will yet, no doubt, do honor to their Provinces. For this much I can only say for them that upon every alarm it was impossible for men to behave with more readiness or attend better to their duty; it is only in the camp that we cut a poor figure."

October 3 Hand writes to his wife:

" Capt. Ross goes for Lancaster tomorrow. Henry Fortney is well: his behavior does him credit. Mr. Henry, Junior, has followed the troops to Canada without leave. Nothing but a perfect loose to his feelings will tame his rambling desire."

Letters of Mrs. Adams, wife of John Adams, in Philadelphia *Evening Post,* 1775:

" On the 9th of November occurred the skirmish at Lechmere's Point: for their alacrity in which, Col. Thompson and his battalion were publicly thanked by Gen. Washington in general orders dated the 10th of November. The British had landed under cover of a fire from their batteries on Bunker, Breed's and Copp's Hills, as well as from a frigate which lay three hundred yards off the point. In a high tide it is an island. Col. Thompson marched instantly with his men, and though a very stormy day, they regarded not the tide nor waited for boats, but took to the water, although up to their armpits, for a quarter of a mile, and notwithstanding the regular's fire, reached the island, and although the enemy were lodged behind the walls and under cover, drove them to their boats.   Loss, one killed and three wounded; British loss, seventeen killed and one wounded."

" CAMP ON PROSPECT HILL, 10th November, 1775.
" I give you the particulars of the fun our regiment had yesterday.   About one P. M., a number of regulars, taking advantage of a high tide, landed from twenty boats on Lechmere Point to carry off some cattle.   Six men of our regiment were on the point to take care of our horses; they did their utmost, and partly effected it.   One poor fellow was taken; he was of Capt. Ross' company.   I think his name was Burke.   When the alarm was given Col. Thompson was at Cambridge.   I had gone to Water-town to receive the regiment's pay, but thanks to good horses, we arrived in time to march our regiment, which was the first ready, though the most distant of our brigade. Col. Thompson, who arrived before we had crossed the water, with thirteen men only of Ross' company, but not being supported by the musqueteers, before I could get up with the remainder of our regiment off duty, returned, and met Major Magaw and myself on the causeway; the whole then passed with the utmost diligence, up to our middles in water.   David Ziegler, who acts as adjutant, tumbled over the bridge into ten or twelve feet of water; he got out safe, with the damage of his rifle only.   As soon as the battalion had passed the defile, we divided them into two parties, part of Capt. Chambers', Capt. Miller's and Lowdon's, with Major Magaw and Col. Thompson, marched to the right of the hill, with part of Cluggage's, Nagel's, and Ross'.   I took the left, as the

enemy had the superiority of numbers, and the advantage of rising ground, with a stone wall in front, and a large barn on their right and flank, aided by a heavy fire of large grape-shot from their shipping and batteries. We had reason to expect a warm reception; but to the disgrace of British arms, be it spoken, by the time we had gained the top of the hill, they had gained their boats, and rowed off. We had but one man wounded, I believe mortally, by a swivel ball, Alexander Creighton, of Ross' company. Wm. Hamilton need not grudge the money his son cost him. His coolness and resolution surpassed his years. Billy Burd had his eyes closed, by the dirt knocked off by a cannon ball."—*Lieut. Col. Hand's letter to his wife.*

In another chapter it is proposed to take up the further services of this distinguished regiment, and to dwell, more fully, on those of some of its Pennsylvania-German officers, individually. Our present record, however, of the First Defenders of the Revolution, would be incomplete were we to omit the following petition of John Youse, an humble Pennsylvania-German private in Capt. Lowdon's company, who came from Rockland Township of Berks County, and whose services differed but little from those of many others of his countrymen which are doomed never to appear on the written pages of history:

"The petition of John Youse, a resident of Rockland township, Berks County, humbly showeth:

"That your petitioner first enlisted in the county of Northumberland, under Capt. Lowdon, in 1775, and marched to Boston in the first campaign in the Revolutionary war with Great Britain. Was in a slight engagement there, at Ploughed Hill, and in several battles and scrimmages on Long Island, and at the taking of the Hessians at the battle of Trenton, on the second Christmas day in the year.—At the battle of Brunswick, where I received a wound in the left hip (15th June, 1777), and was at the taking of Burgoyne, in the rifle corps com-

manded by Col. Morgan and Major Parr, my captain then.   I was one of the party of the corps in the expedition against the Indians at Genessee, Seneca, &c, and was one of the party of five who survived out of twenty-four in a scouting party, and forty-one days of that campaign was on half rations.   I was at the taking of Stony Point, and at the attack on the Block House (Bergen's Point, July 21, 1780), Gen Wayne our commander.   I was one of the eight hundred at Green Springs, in Virginia (July 6, 1781), in that hard engagement.   My last service was on James Island, in South Carolina, and I have never received any satisfaction for back rations to this day; and for my certificates for my pay, my indigent circumstances, obliged me to sell for fifty cents per twenty shillings, and for my said pay, it being State money, I passed for what was called silk money, which silk money went for nothing. So that I lost in a manner all my long, hard eight year earnings.   I am now unable to procure a livelihood by labor; therefore, I pray your honorable body (Legislature of Pennsylvania, March 13, 1817) to commiserate my miserable situation, and place me on the pension list, so that I may not become chargeable to the township where I live.   So that it may not be said after I am buried, ' there is John Youse's grave, who cost our township so much money.' "

FREDERICK THE GREAT AND THE SCHOOLMASTER.

CHAPTER III.

THE RESCUERS OF THE DECLARATION OF
INDEPENDENCE.

THE rejoicings over the Peace of 1763, and the close of the French and Indian War, were greatly tempered by a realization of the fact that its cost had been very great, and that a large debt had been incurred. The raising of funds for this debt was the direct cause of the American Revolution. The mother country, acting upon the specious plea that, as the debt was incurred for the benefit of her colonies, they were in duty bound to pay their share of it, proceeded to levy taxes for that purpose. This is not the place to go over the old and, more or less, familiar story of the Sugar Bill and Stamp Act, with their result and effect.

This result was widely different in the several colonies because of the diversity in character of the people who inhabited them.

The Puritan of New England was, from birth, a Republican at heart. He was never more than nominally a subject of the king. In religion, also, he was independent, so that, both from a civil and an ecclesiastical standpoint, he always insisted upon self-government. His construction of the law was based upon the contents of the Bible, and he was ever ready to dispute any emanation from Parliament or the Throne, no matter upon what legal status it may have been based, if contrary to his views or liking. It was but natural for him to become an extremist.

In Virginia the bone of contention was the Established Church which was forced upon the colony. To this the dissenters were ever opposed, and were but too ready to be ardent supporters of a revolution which would result in the suppression of their greatest practical grievance.

In New York existed the antagonism between the mass of the population and the great land-holders, between the Dutch and Scotch Presbyterians and the church people, which was felt during the whole war as it had been throughout the history of the colony.

In the Carolinas there was a spark, which had been smouldering for years, but too ready to burst into a flame whenever fanned by the right wind.

In all colonies, under the direct rule of the throne, the English government was constantly meeting with obstacles and difficulties, just as did the Continental Congress when it declared independence of the British Crown as the basis of political action.

Pennsylvania differed from every one of its sisters. With all its petty differences between Assembly and Executive, which cropped out ever and anon, these were barely ripples upon its placid stream of existence. Its government was comparatively just; its people were comparatively happy and, as it were, always at peace with each other. With such contentment and quiet why should there not be a fair degree of satisfaction with the existing condition of affairs? Rather, let us say, why should not its actions be conservative in character?

Of its three classes of inhabitants the Quakers were, by nature and religion, peaceful. They were living under a Proprietary rule which was practically controlled by themselves, under the grant of an Assembly in which they constituted the governing force. There were no parsons to rouse their passions, nor to delude them by chimerical fears of a religious revolution, whose results should be more disastrous than those by which their civil rights were threatened. The very first principle of their religion was a loyal submission to the government under which they lived, so long as it did not openly infringe their civil and ecclesiastical rights.

The Germans came to find a home and did find it. With this home they were accorded a quite full measure of freedom, which brought with it a large degree of happiness and a correspondingly kind feeling for their Quaker neighbors and rulers. This feeling continued, in spite of a certain neglect accorded them during the Indian massacres, with their resultant misery and hardship. To what an extent might it not have been strengthened had they been given proper popular representation in the governing body!

Even the Scotch-Irish, with their naturally restive dispositions and temperaments, were so well satisfied as to be little tempted to trouble, for any light cause, the peaceful waters on which they floated.

When God, in the furtherance of His plans, saw fit to harden the hearts of the King of England and his Parliament, as He did that of Pharaoh, and permitted them to do the senseless things which followed so rapidly, one after another, all colonies were equally aroused, but each one in its own way, and each according to the temperament of its own people. Massachusetts violently seized the obnoxious tea, which had been sent it, and tossed the same overboard; Pennsylvania quietly refused to receive it and allowed it to be taken, peacefully and safely, back to England. No one colony was any more loyal, nor any less patriotic, than the other, but they all differed in their manner of showing it. Some were like the babbling brook,—noisy but liable to be shallow; Pennsylvania was quiet, but none the less deep. Many wished and pleaded for violent action, from the beginning; Pennsylvania hoped to accomplish the same end peacefully and by legal enactment.

On the 4th of November, 1775, the Assembly of Pennsylvania chose, as its Delegates to the Continental

FRANKLIN ARMS.

Congress, John Dickinson, Robert Morris, Benjamin Franklin, Charles Humphreys, Edward Biddle, Thomas Willing, Andrew Allen and James Wilson, certainly the very flower of the moneyed and intellectual aristocracy of the Province, considered from an English standpoint.

On the 9th of November, 1775, the Assembly gave these delegates instructions with regard to the policy they were to pursue in Congress as representatives of Pennsylvania. They were told, "You should use your utmost endeavors to agree upon and recommend the adoption of such measures as you shall judge to afford the best prospect of obtaining the redress of American grievances, and utterly reject any proposition (should such be made) that may cause or lead to a separation from the mother country, or a change in the form of this government." (That is the charter government of the Province.)

Briefly stated, they believed that the existing government, under the charter of Penn, was ample and sufficient, and that, without going to the length of separation, all necessary redress might be legally secured from the home authorities. They foresaw the evils incident to separation, and wished to avoid them. To this plan the Assembly held, in all sincerity, to the day when the Declaration of Independence was an assured fact. It was a mistake, and proved to be the rock upon which they were finally split and wrecked, but it was only a mistake, and gives no cause for impugning the loyalty of men like John Dickinson, their leader, and others of his kind.

Opposed to this stand was the newly formed Whig party in Pennsylvania which insisted that the government, under Penn's charter, was not suited to "the exigencies of their affairs," and should be abolished in order that a popular convention might frame a new one. Again arises the question,—What might have been the result had the charter been so amended as to give true and popular representation to all classes of the citizens of the Province?

How Massachusetts, with its aggressiveness, precipitated hostilities, is known to every school boy. The same spirit of violence was permeating many of the other colonies, even though without the same result. Up to April, 1776, all the talk of independence, however, had been of a private nature. North Carolina won the honor of making the first move. On the 12th of April that

MINUTE MEN OF "76."

colony instructed its delegates in Congress "to concur with the delegates of the other colonies in declaring independence and forming foreign alliances." This was a move of the greatest importance, and it was but a short time until Rhode Island, and then Massachusetts, followed the example of their southern sister. The fourth colony, to pronounce for independence, was Virginia, which went further than all the others by instructing its delegates to propose independence to the Continental Congress. This bold resolution was sent by special messenger to Philadelphia, and, on June 7, Richard Henry Lee, one of the foremost delegates from that colony, rose to his feet and solemnly made the motion, " That these United Colonies are, and of right ought to be, free and independent states, and that they are absolved from all allegiance to the British Crown." When the resolution came up for debate, three weeks later, John Adams, of Massachusetts, delivered, in its favor, the most powerful speech made on the floor of Congress during the Revolutionary period, while John Dickinson, of Pennsylvania, unavailingly endeavored to stem the tide, by answering, as best he could, but the result was a unanimous vote, in its favor, of twelve colonies, New York not voting.

Smoothly as the proceedings may now read, the favorable result, above given, was only reached with much travail and difficulty.

Massachusetts, New Jersey, and other colonies to the north, with Virginia, Carolina, and those to the south, all wanted separation, but how would it be possible for any action, which they might take, to succeed, without not only the passive encouragement of Pennsylvania, but even its active coöperation, lying, as it did, between them and severing them in twain. To attempt anything of the sort would be worse than folly.

In spite of remonstrances, in spite of pleas, in spite of threats, in spite, even, of the refusal of the battalions of associators to obey its orders, the Assembly of Pennsylvania, the only true and legal power of the Province, would not recede from the stand it had taken. Whether this position was right or wrong, originally, it had now become an impossibility to carry it out, and it would have been the better part of judgment to bow to the inevitable, but this the Assembly was not prepared to do. Finally, by force of circumstances, on the 8th of June, 1776, that body, after much heated discussion out of doors, and several days' debate within, rescinded the instructions to its delegates, adopted November 9, 1775, and authorized them, by new instructions, to concur with the other delegates in Congress in forming contracts with " the United Colonies, concluding treaties with foreign kingdoms, and such measures as they shall judge necessary for promoting the liberty, etc., of the people of this Province, *reserving to said people the sole and exclusive right of regulating the internal government of the same."* But it was too late for even this compromise. Other events had already hastened on to other conclusions, so, when, on June 14, the resolution was to be transcribed for final passage, the Whigs of the Assembly, by a secret understanding, had withdrawn and failed to put in an appearance, thus leaving the body without a quorum. It kept up a fitful existence until the close of August, 1776, and then died of " innocuous desuetude."

In despair of converting the Assembly of Pennsylvania, and of success in any other way, John Adams, on May 10, offered a resolution in Congress recommending that the colonies should establish a " government sufficient to the exigencies of affairs." Because of objections raised to this wording, on May 15 Mr. Adams presented a preamble, which was really a substitute, to the effect that, " the respective Assemblies and Conventions of the United Colonies, where no government sufficient to the exigencies of their affairs has been hitherto established, to adopt such government as shall, in the opinion of the representatives of the people, best conduce to the happiness and safety of their constituents in particular, and America in general."

This measure was the true Declaration of Independence, because that of July 4 followed as a mere form and matter of course. It was aimed against the Charter of

Pennsylvania, which, from that hour, was doomed, together with the Assembly, not by its own act but by the greater force of Congress, which it was unable to resist. The passage of this resolution meant a popular convention, in which all classes should be represented, and a government in Pennsylvania, for the first time, " of the people, by the people and for the people." In due time delegates, from all the counties, were selected to meet in conference in the city of Philadelphia, on Tuesday, the 18th day of June. At this conference the Pennsylvania-German at last was given a voice in the governmental affairs. He held the balance of power. If his voice were uttered in favor of independence it would become a fact, if not, a failure. To his honor, be it now said, however tardily, that every man recorded his vote for freedom, and it was the Pennsylvania-German who made the Declaration of Independence possible on July 4, 1776.

CHAPTER IV.

THE PRESERVERS OF THE NEW BORN NATION.

HARDLY had the Declaration of Independence, of the newly born nation, been ushered in by the ringing of bells and firing of salvos, when the British commander decided to crush out its very life with one fell blow. To do this he determined to cut the colonies in two by the capture of New York City, and, if within his power, to annihilate the rebel army at the same time.

The battle of Long Island, the result of these movements, was, preëminently, a battle fought by the Pennsylvania-Germans. The troops engaged consisted of Col. Miles' Rifle Regiment, to which were attached at least four companies, all of whose members were practically of that blood, with many scattered throughout the other companies; Col. Atlee's Musketry Battalion had two Penn-

43

sylvania-German companies; Col. Kichlein's Associators
were all Pennsylvania-Germans, also Col. Lutz's battalion
of Associators.   No attempt has been made to learn if
there were any Germans in Col. Smallwood's battalion
of Marylanders, and among Col. Hazlet's Delaware
troops, as these constituted but a small part of the whole,
but it is likely such was the case even there.

This desperately fought battle was a loss to the Americans, it is true, but it was lost through no fault of the
troops engaged in it, and only because of the blunder of
their superior general officers.   While, on account of this
blunder, it was lost, yet the valor of the Pennsylvania-
German soldiers kept it from becoming the disaster their
enemy desired to make it; by their own sacrifice they saved
the American army from destruction, and from this fact,
became the " Preservers of the New Born Nation," of
which they represented no unworthy part.

Washington had early divined the intentions of the
British, but, while satisfied that New York City was to be
their objective point, it was impossible to foretell at which
exact spot the blow would be struck.   His whole force
consisted of but, nominally, 24,000 men, mostly militia,
of whom 7,000 were invalids, and one third of the remainder scarcely furnished with arms.   To protect all
possible points of attack the troops were disposed as
follows:

The main body on the island of New York, where it
was but natural to suppose the principal attack would come.

Two feeble detachments guarded Governor's Island
and the point of Paulus Hook.

The militia of New York Province, under Gen. Clinton,
were posted upon the banks of the sound, where they
occupied the two Chesters, East and West, and New

Rochelle, to prevent the enemy from penetrating to Kingsbridge, and thus locking up the Americans on the island of New York.

One corps only was stationed on Long Island, numbering less than 5,000 men, under the eventual command of Gen. Sullivan. Col. Miles, with his Pennsylvania Rifle Regiment, formed the extreme left of this body, in front of the village of Flatbush. The right center (and only center) was composed of Col. Atlee's Pennsylvania Musketry Battalion, with the Delaware and Maryland troops. Supporting them, somewhat to the rear, was a part of Lutz's Battalion of Pennsylvania Associators, with the Seventeenth Connecticut Regiment, and, eventually, the remnant of Col. Miles' Regiment as, while retiring, it hung on to the flank of the advancing enemy. The extreme right was held by Col. Kichlein's Pennsylvania Associators, and part of Lutz's Battalion, joined, as the fight progressed, by Col. Atlee and his men. A picket of some 200 men of Lutz's Battalion, under Major Edward Burd, was thrown out to the Red Lion Inn, near the Narrows, on the Martense Lane, leading from the old Flatbush and New Rochelle Road to the Gowanus Road, running by Gowanus Cove to the village of Brooklyn.

Opposed to the American right was the British left, 2,000 men and ten cannon, under Gen. Grant; their center consisted of 8,000 Hessians, under Gen. de Hiester, while, with 8,000 more, and a train of artillery, under Clinton, Cornwallis and Percy, the enemy planned to turn the American left. Nearly 20,000 trained and well-equipped veteran soldiers against a scant 5000, most of whom were raw recruits.

With the early morning of August 27, 1776, a force,

under Col. Dalrymple, suddenly surrounded and captured the outpost commanded by Major Burd, after a short fight. This was followed by an attack of Gen. Grant on the American right, during which much hard fighting took place. While the conflict was here ebbing and flowing, suddenly the Americans were astounded to find that the troops, which were endeavoring to circumvent Col. Miles, had succeeded but too well in the purpose, and were pouring volleys upon them both on the flank and in the rear. At the same instant the Hessians, and Grant's Highlanders, sprang fiercely upon their front. In a brief space of time the Delaware and Maryland troops were dispersed, Atlee's regiment and Lutz's battalion were broken up, and nothing remained to stem the on-rushing wave, which bade fair to annihilate everything in its course, save the associators of Col. Kichlein, together with the remnants of Lutz's battalion and Atlee's command which still held together. It was a most critical moment in the history of our nation. Unless the onslaught of the enemy could be stemmed sufficiently to allow the demoralized troops to rally under the guns of Putnam's fortifications, at Gowanus Cove, they were doomed, and, with their loss, no one could foresee the consequent train of disaster which might occur.

Bravely the Pennsylvania-Germans stepped into the very " jaws of death," and manfully they stood their ground against overwhelming foes, under the Greenwood Hills, where, to-day, a monument marks the scene of their heroism. One by one they fell, under the bullets and bayonets of their adversaries, many slaughtered in cold blood, even pinned to the trees by which they fought, until they were no more. The army was saved, the nation was preserved, but at what a cost to them. In the one company, alone, from Easton, the home of Col. Kichlein, which went into the battle with less than one hundred men, the fatalities were seventy-one.

The above outline of this unfortunate conflict has been made brief, purposely, so that its details may be given direct, as it were, from the lips of some of those who participated in it and whose records of it have been fortunately, preserved.

In this action the Rifle Regiment and Musketry Battalion were so broken up that Gen. Washington ordered the remnant to be consolidated into one regiment.

Col. Atlee was taken prisoner and remained such for twenty-six months, undergoing many sufferings. The following is an extract from his journal, in which he speaks of his command as " a regiment by whose efforts, in a great degree, was preserved our retreating troops on the 27th of August."

Extract from the Journal of Col. Atlee.

" Long Island, Tuesday, August 27th, 1776.

" This morning before day, the Camp was alarmed by an attack upon the Pickett, stationed upon the lower Road leading to the Narrows, commanded by Major Burd of the Pennsylv'a flying Camp. About day light a part of Lord Sterling's Brigade, to wit: Col. Smallwood's, Col. Haslett's, part of Lutz's & Kichline's Flying Camp, and a part of mine, in the whole about 2,300 men, under the Command of Maj. Gen. Sullivan and the Brigadiers, Lord Sterling and Parsons, march'd to support the Pickett attacked by the enemy. About ½ after seven the enemy were discovered advancing, about 2 ½ miles from the lines at Brookline, in order—their field Artillery in front. This proved the left wing of the

British Army, the 4th & 6th Brigades, composed of the following Regiments: the 17th, 23d, 40th, 42d, 44th, 46th, 55th, 57th and 64th under the Command of Major General Grant.

" I then rec'd orders from L'd Sterling, with that part of my Battalion in the Field, to advance and oppose the Enemy's passing a morass at the Foot, a fine rising Ground upon which they were drawing up, and give him time to form the Brigades upon the Heights. This order I

AUTOGRAPH OF LORD STERLING.

immediately obeyed, exposed without any kind of Cover to the Enemy's Fire of Artillery charged with Grape. We sustained their Fire until the Brigade was form'd. I then filed off to the Left and took post on a fine woody eminence on the left of the Brigade.

" My troops just posted, when I received a Reinforcement of 2 Companies from the Delawares, with orders to file off further to the Left, and prevent, if possible, a large detachment of the enemy from turning the Left of the Brigade. Upon filing off to the Left, according to the orders rec'd, I espied, at the Distance of about 300 yards, a Hill of Clear Ground, a proper situation to oppose the Regiments endeavoring to flank us; which hill,

THE PENNSYLVANIA-GERMAN SOCIETY.

BATTLE OF LONG ISLAND, AUGUST 27, 1776.

RETREAT OF THE AMERICANS UNDER GEN. STERLING ACROSS GOWANUS CREEK.

I determined, if possible, to gain before them, judging they were likewise making for it. On marching up the Hill, and within about 50 yards of the summit, we unexpectedly rec'd a heavy Fire from the Enemy taken post there before me, notwithstanding the forced march I made. Upon receiving the heavy Fire, my detachment, under a continued and exceeding warm Fire of the Enemy, formed in order.

" The 2 companies of the Delaware Reg't, excepting the Lieuts. Stewart & Harney, with about 16 privates, broke, and had nearly drawn after them the whole of my detachment. This caused a moment's Halt, but the Officers & men recovering from the surprize at receiving so rough & unexpected a salutation, upon receiving my orders to advance, immediately obeyed, with such Resolution that the Enemy, after a severe Conflict of a few minutes, left me master of the Hill, leaving behind them a Lieut. and six privates wounded, and fourteen privates killed. My troops, flush'd with this advantage, were for pushing after the flying Enemy, but perceiving at about 60 yards from the Hill we had just gained, across a Hollow way, a Stone Fence lined with wood, from behind which we might be greatly annoyed, I ordered not to advance but maintain the possession of the Hill, (which answered at this Time every necessary purpose.) The order was immediately obeyed, when we found by a heavy Fire from the Fence that it was lined as I expected. The Fire was as briskly returned by my brave Soldiers. The Enemy finding it too hott and our fire too well directed, retreated to and joined the Right of this wing of their army. In this severe conflict I lost my worthy Friend and Lt. Col. Parry, whom, in the midst of the action and immediately after he fell, I ordered to be bourn by four

4

Soldiers off the Field into the Lines at Brook Line. The
Enemies situation here was so advantageous that had they
been marksmen, and directed their Fire with judgment,
they might have cut off the greatest part of my detachment, I having left, for the security of my Right Flank
and to protect my Rear in case of Retreat, a Company
in a Wood upon my Right. After this first Attack
which continued in the whole for about 15 minutes, we
brought from the field such of their wounded whom I
judged might be assisted, and about 25 stand of Arms.
The wounded I placed in my Rear under the Shade of
some Bushes it being intencely hott; the arms I distributed
to such of my soldiers as were the most indifferently arm'd,
and the wounded Lieut. taken at our first gaining the Hill
I sent to L'd Sterling by a Drum & Fife. He died on
the way. After placing the proper Guards, I ordered
my fatigued soldiers to rest themselves. We continued
in this situation about 20 minutes, when the Enemy was
discover'd marching down to make a second attempt for
the Hill. Both officers and soldiers immediately flew to
arms, and with remarkable coolness and resolution sustained and returned their Fire for about 10 minutes, when
the Enemy were obliged once more to a precipitate flight,
leaving behind them, Killed, Lt. Col. Grant, a number of
Privates, and great many wounded. These wounded not
mortally, I likwise removed into my rear; one I sent to
L'd Sterling that had rec'd a wound in the leg. I sent
my Adjutant to his Lordship, with an acc't of my successive
advantages, to know his lordship's further orders and to
request a Re-inforcement. My Adjutant returned with
2 Companies of Riflemen of the flying Camp, who remain'd with me a few minutes, being soon order'd to
rejoin their Corps. Very luckily, after this second en-

gagement, an ammunition Cart belonging to Col. Huntington's Reg't arrived at my post, of which we stood in
great need, having entirely exhausted our ammunition
and fired many rounds from that taken from the Enemy
every time we had the good fortune to beat them off the
Field.   The officers were extremely alert, and, from the
ammunition so opportunely arrived, soon supplied their
men with sufficient Stock to sustain another attack, should
the Enemy think proper to make it.   They did not suffer
us to wait long.   In about half an Hour we were alarm'd
of their appearance the third Time.

" The eagerness of the Officers and Soldiers to receive
them deserves my warmest acknowledgments and those
of their Country.   They were received as usual, and as
usual Fled after a warm conflict of about 10 or 12 minutes.
I now determined to pursue but observed a Reg't which
proved to be the 22d or Royal Highlanders coming down
to sustain the Royal Runners who were the 23d and 44th.
I halted, prepared to receive them likewise, but the drub-
bing their Friends had so repeatedly received, I believe,
prevented them, and they seemed satisfyed with protecting
the Refugees and conducting such as were able to the
army.

" Major Burd, who was taken at the attack of the
Pickett on the Right, and was at Gen'l Grant's Quarters
during the above several attacks, informed me after each
great number of Officers and Soldiers came in wounded.

" I fully expected, as did my Officers, that the strength
of the British Army was advancing in this Quarter with
intention to have taken this Rout to our Lines, but how
greatly were we deceived when intelligence was received
that the Center, composed of the Hessians and the Right
wing, were rapidly advancing by our Rear, and that we
were nearly surrounded.

"This we were soon convinced of by an exceeding heavy Fire about a mile in our Rear, no Troops being in that Quarter to oppose the march of this Grand Body of the British Army but Col. Miles, 2 Battalions of Rifle men, Col. Willis's Reg't of Connecticut, and a part of Lutz's Battalion of Penn'a Flying Camp.

"I once more sent my Adjutant to Lord Sterling to acquaint him with my last success and for further orders, but receiving no answer and after waiting for the Enemy

THE CORTELYOU HOUSE AROUND WHICH THE BATTLE OF LONG ISLAND
WAS FOUGHT.

more than half an hour, they not approaching in Front, those in the Rear drawing very near, I judged it most prudent to join the Brigade, where I might be of more service than in my present situation. I therefore ordered a march, leaving upon the Field, Killed, Lt. Col. Grant and upward of sixty men and great number wounded, beside those taken at Sundry times into my Rear. The World may judge my surprise when coming to the Ground where our Brigade had been drawn up, to find they had gone off without my receiving the least intelligence of the Retreat or orders what to do.

"I cou'd, I doubt not, with considerable loss, have made my retreat, but perceiving at a distance, near the water, the Rear of our Troops and at the same time a Body of the Enemy advancing toward them, who proved to be the British Grenadiers, commanded by Col. Monckton, these were attacked by a few brave fellows. Not able to prevent them, I ordered my Fatigued party once more to advance and take possession of a post and Rail Fence, at the Foot of a rising Ground over which the Grenadiers were moving with great rapidity. The Timely assistance brought these few brave fellows by a party this day, often try'd and as often victorious, encouraged those already engaged and obliged the Grenadiers to quit the ground they had gain'd and retire to a fence lined with wood. Here we kept up a Close and constant Fire for upwards of a Quarter of an Hour, untill the Brigade had retreated out of our Sight. Our ammunition now again entirely spent and our Retreat after the Brigade effectually cut off, I was then obliged to file off to the Right with what men I cou'd collect and endeavor to find a way out in that Quarter.

"After various Struggles running thro' the Fire of many of the Enemy's detachments, and nearly fatigued to death, not having eat or drank since the day before about 4 o'clock in the afternoon, no alternative presenting, I was obliged to surrender to the 71st Highlanders, having with me about 40, officers included.   About 5 o'clock arrived at Gen'l Howe's Quarters, receiving as we passed thro' the right wing of the British Army, the most opprobrious and scurrulous Language.

" Thus ended this unfortunate 27th of August, during which myself and small detachment underwent inexpressable Fatigue, and escaped death in a variety of Instances; and, altho' the day terminated unsuccessfully, I have the pleasing reflection that sundry Times the entire ruin of the Troops was by my small detachment prevented; First in the three successful attacks made upon the 23d and 44th British Regiments, who were attempting to turn our left, and lastly, in preventing the Grenadiers from destroying the Rear in their retreat over the water.

" In the first, Grant fell, and in the Last was sundry officers and many soldiers killed, and Monkton wounded thro' the Body.   I, myself, several months after, was shewn the Graves of several of the Officers who fell at this time.

" I cannot here forbear testifying my acknowledgments to those brave few for their Courage this day so repeatedly Shewn.

" I think I may, without Vanity, conclude that no Regiment in this or any other service, considering the Disparity of Numbers & Discipline, has in the same time performed greater services.

" S.   J.   A.
" Exchanged Oct. 1st, 1778."

The above interesting experience of Col. Atlee is supplemented by the experience of Col. Miles, and his Pennsylvania Rifle Regiment, on the left, as recorded in his journal.

JOURNAL OF COL. SAMUEL MILES CONCERNING THE BATTLE OF LONG ISLAND.

" On the landing of the British army on Long Island, I was ordered over with my rifle regiment to watch their motions. I marched near to the village of Flat Bush, where the Highlanders then lay, but they moved the next day to Gen'l Howe's camp, and their place was supplied

COL. SAMUEL MILES.

by the Hessians. I lay here within cannon shot of the Hessian camp for four days without receiving a single order from Gen'l Sullivan, who commanded on Long Island, out of the lines. The day before the action he came to the camp, and I then told him the situation of the British Army; that Gen'l Howe, with the main body, lay on my left, about a mile and a half or two miles, and

I was convinced when the army moved that Gen'l Howe would fall into the Jamaica road, and I hoped there were troops there to watch them.   Notwithstanding this information, which indeed he might have obtained from his own observation, if he had attended to his duty as a General ought to have done; no steps were taken, but there was a small redoubt in front of the village which seemed to take up the whole of his attention, and where he stayed until the principal part of the British army had gotten between him and the lines, by which means he was made prisoner as well as myself.   If Gen'l Sullivan had taken the requisite precaution, and given his orders agreeably to the attention of the Commander-in-Chief there would have been few if any prisoners taken on the 27th of August, 1776.   As Gordon in his history of the war has charged me indirectly with not doing my duty, I will here state my position and conduct.   I lay directly in front of the village of Flat Bush, but on the left of the road leading to New York, where the Hessians were Encamped. We were so near each other, that their shells they sometimes fired went many rods beyond my camp.

" The main body of the Enemy, under the immediate command of Gen'l Howe, lay about 2 miles to my left, and General Grant, with another body of British troops, lay about four miles on my right.   There were several small bodies of Americans dispersed to my right, but not a man to my left, although the main body of the Enemy lay to my left, of which I had given General Sullivan notice.   This was our situation on the 26th of August. About one o'clock at night Gen. Grant, on the right, and Gen. Howe, on my left, began their march, and by daylight Grant had got within a mile of our entrenchments, and Gen. Howe had got into the Jamaica road, about two miles from our lines.   The Hessians kept their position until 7 in the morning.   As soon as they moved the firing began at our redoubt.   I immediately marched towards where firing was, but had not proceeded more than 1 or 200 yards until I was stopped by Colonel Wyllys, who told me that I could not pass on; that we were to defend a road that lead from Flatbush road to the Jamaica road.   Col. Wyllys bearing a Continental and I a State commission, he was considered a senior officer and I was obliged to submit; but I told him I was convinced the main body of the enemy would take the Jamaica road, that there was no probability of their coming along the road he was then guarding, and if he would not let me proceed to where the firing was, I would return and endeavor to get into the Jamaica road before Gen. Howe. To this he consented, and I immediately made a retrograde march, and after marching nearly two miles, the whole distance through woods, I arrived within sight of the Jamaica road, and to my great mortification I saw the main body of the enemy in full march between me and our lines, and the baggage guard just coming into the road. A thought struck me of attacking the baggage guard, and, if possible, to cut my way through them and proceed to Hell Gate to cross the Sound.   I, however, ordered the men to remain quite still, (I had then but the first battalion with me, for the second being some distance in the rear, I directed Major Williams, who was on horseback, to return and order Lt. Col. Brodhead to push on by the left of the enemy and endeavor get into our lines that way, and happily they succeeded, but had to wade a mill dam by which a few were drowned,) and I took the adjutant with me and crept as near the road as I thought prudent, to try and ascertain the number of the baggage guard, and I saw a grenadier stepping into the woods.   I got a tree between him and me until he came near, and I took him prisoner and examined him.   I found that there was a whole brigade with the baggage commanded by a general officer.

" I immediately returned to the battalion and called a council of the officers and laid three propositions before them : 1st to attack the baggage guard and endeavor to cut our way through them and proceed to Hell Gate and so cross the Sound; 2nd, to lay where we were until the whole had passed us and then proceed to Hell Gate; or, 3d, to endeavor to force our way through the enemy's flank guards into our line at Brooklyn.   The first was thought a dangerous and useless attempt as the enemy was so superior in force.   The 2nd I thought the most eligible, for it was evident that adopting either of the other propositions we must lose a number of men without affecting the enemy materially, as we had so small a force, not more than 230 men.   This was, however, objected to, under the idea that we should be blamed for not fighting at all, and perhaps charged with cowardice, which would be worse than death itself.   The 3d proposition was therefore adopted, and we immediately began our march, but had not proceeded more than half a mile until we fell in with a body of 7 or 800 light infantry, which we attacked without hesitation, but their superiority of numbers encouraged them to march up with their bayonets, which we could not withstand, having none ourselves.   I therefore ordered the Troops to push on towards our lines.   I remained on the ground myself until they had all passed me, (the enemy were then within less than 20 yards of us,) and by this means, I came into the rear instead of the front of my command.   We had proceeded but a short distance before we were again engaged with a superior body of the enemy, and here we lost a number of men, but took Major Moncrieffe, their commanding officer prisoner, but he was a Scotch prize for Ensign Brodhead, who took him and had him in possession for some hours, but was obliged to surrender himself. Finding that the enemy had possession of the ground between us and our lines, and that it was impossible to cut our way through as a body, I directed the men to make the best of their way as well as they could; some few got in safe, but there were 159 taken prisoners. I was myself entirely cut off from our lines and therefore endeavored to conceal myself, with a few men who would not leave me. I hoped to remain until night, when I intended to try to get to Hell Gate and cross the Sound; but about 3 o'clock in the afternoon was discovered by a party of Hessians and obliged to surrender—thus ended the career of that day."

In addition to this record of Col. Miles in direct command of the First Battalion, we have the following individual experience of Lieut. James McMichael, of the Second Battalion of the Rifle Regiment:

Extract-Diary of Lieut. James McMichael.

"*August 22.*—The enemy having landed on Long Island, our brigade was paraded and ordered thither. After leaving our camp, the order was modified—one-half to proceed to Long Island, the remainder to be in readiness to follow at a moment's notice. The First Battalion together with our musketry, and the Delaware Blues, went to the island and we were ordered to our tents.

"*August 24.*—At 10 A. M., we all marched from our encampment and crossed St. George's ferry to Long Island.

Just after we had joined the brigade, we had a heavy cannonade, with some small arms. This night we camped in the woods, without tents, in a hard rain. Sentries firing all night.

"*August 25.*—This morning we were alarmed that the enemy were about to attack us in force; we got ready and marched to meet them. Not finding them we returned to our camp.

"*August 26.*—A scouting party of 120 men, properly officered, were ordered out, but returned without making any discovery.

"*August 27.*—At sunrise we were ordered to march easterly from near Flatbush a few miles, when we discovered the enemy coming against us with 5,000 foot and 500 horse. We numbered just 400. We at first thought it prudent to retire to a neighboring thicket, where we formed and gave battle. Here my right hand man fell, shot thro' the head. We were attacked by the enemy's left wing, while their right endeavoured to surround us. Their superior numbers forced us to retire for a short distance, when we again formed and fought with fortitude until we were nearly surrounded. Having by this time lost a great number of men, we were again forced to retreat, when we found that the enemy had got between us and the fort. Then despairing of making good our retreat we resolved to die rather than be taken prisoners, and thus we were drove from place to place 'till 3 o'clock P. M., when we agreed to attempt crossing the mill-pond, that being the only way left for our escape. Here numbers were drowned, but it was the will of Providence that I should escape, and at half past three, we reached the lines, being much fatigued. The enemy advanced rapidly and endeavored to force our lines, but were repulsed with considerable loss. They afterwards marched towards the Narrows, where they found our First Battalion and the Delaware Blues under command of Col. Hazlet. These battalions were chiefly cut off, we were ordered to cover their retreat, which exposed us in open field to a heavy fire from the enemy 'till evening—the remainder of our troops brought us 23 prisoners. At dark we were relieved and ordered to St. George's ferry to take refreshments. Thus happened the memorable action on Long Island, where the enemy attacked and defeated Lord Stirling's brigade, consisting of the following regiments: Colonels Miles, Atlee, Smallwood and Hazlet. Major General Sullivan, Brig. Gen. Lord Stir-

I am Sir
(Your very hble servt)
Jno. Sullivan

AUTOGRAPH OF GENL. SULLIVAN.

ling were taken prisoners, also Col. Miles and Atlee; Lieut. Col. Piper—all of our regiment also, 19 commissioned officers, 23 sergeants, and 310 rank and file. My preservation I only attribute to the indulgent Providence of God, for tho' the bullets went around me in every direction, yet I received not a wound.

" *August 28.*—We marched to the lines at dawn of the morning and there lay under arms 'till 2 o'clock P. M., when we were alarmed that the enemy had come out to attack us. Going to the summit of the hill, we found the alarm false, and so returned to the ferry. We have had an incessant cannonade these four days past. We have the pleasing intelligence by some of our men who were captured and escaped, that the loss of the enemy is greater than ours.

" *August 29.*—Gen. Washington thinking it proper to evacuate the island, we were all ordered to march at 9 o'clock P. M. We crossed at St. George's ferry to New York with great speed and secrecy."

The next narrative contains the interesting personal experience of Capt. John Nice, a brave Pennsylvania-German Officer in Col. Atlee's Musketry Battalion:

EXTRACTS FROM DIARY OF CAPTAIN JOHN NICE.

" *August 24, 1776.*—Marched over to Long Island, to the town of Brookland [Brooklyn]; halted about two hours, then received orders to march to a place called New Utrecht to relieve Colonel Jonson's [Johnson, of New Jersey] regiment. Placed sentrys against dark; it rained very hard all night. Saw the enemy at the Plains next morning, extending from Gravesend to Flatbush. Kept to our lines and exchanged a few shots with them.

" *August 25.*—At noon we were relieved by Colonel Clark's [Seventeenth Connecticut] regiment, and marched back to Brookland, within our lines by night. Drew no provisions; it rained hard and we had no tents, subsequently we slept in a church.

" *August 26–27.*—Got part of our baggage over, drew provisions, cheerfully arranged our camp and pitched our tents, and slept comfortably until daylight, when the alarm guns from Cobble Hill fort were fired. Our drums beat and the Battalion turned out and marched, with the Delaware and Maryland Battalions in advance, down the road to the Narrows. When we got within half a mile of a place called the Red Lion, we saw the enemy advancing towards us, and the brigade was drawn up on the left of the road, by order of General Sterling. The general marched at the head of his battalion. As we came within three hundred yards of the enemy, where they were drawn up on rising ground with his field pieces in front, we received orders to file to the left, as we had the Bay close to our right, and to lay under cover of a fence, which we did for some considerable time. The enemy then began to pour grape-shot into us from his two field pieces, when our Colonel saw that it was vain for us to remain, as we could do no execution with our musketry; he therefore ordered us to retreat to the right, along the fence. In retreating we lost two men. We were next ordered to retire and incline more to the left, to keep two Battalions from surrounding us, as we observed they were filing off for that purpose. Taking post on an advantageous piece of ground, the enemy came down upon us, when we retreated from our position to the edge of a wood, where we lost our brave Lieut. Col. Parry, who was shot through the head by a musket ball, which killed him on the spot. Animated by seeing him fall, we regained our ground, repulsed and drove them back, killed Colonel Grant (Fortieth Foot), wounded a lieutenant and killed nine soldiers. They retired behind a wood, but our Colonel did not think it prudent to follow them, as we had at that time not above fifty men and they had six times our number. We held our ground near half an hour, when we observed them coming down on us with all their force. We immediately prepared to receive them, not firing a shot until they were within fifty yards of us, when we gave them such a warm reception, that they found themselves under the necessity of retreating a second time to the wood. In this attempt they left forty dead on the field, but their wounded they carried off to the wood. In all these engagements we lost not a man, but our brave Colonel seeing a party of our men engaged in a field in our rear, we went to aid them, and became engaged with a company of Grenadiers near half an hour, while our brigade crossed at the mill-dam and got in, and we made them give way and incline to their right along a thick hedge. We kept engaged until a force of Hessians came down their left and attempted to surround us, when our Colonel ordered a party of Flying Camp riflemen of Col. Lutz's Battalion to join us and break through their lines, which we could easily have done if they had joined us, but they refused and would not come up, until we were obliged to retreat back in the wood. Here the Colonel called a council of the officers he had with him, to consider what was best to be done. Before we decided, the Hessians gave us a heavy fire from the edge of the wood, which caused us to disperse and every one make the best way he could to save himself. Col. Atlee, Ensign Henderson and myself kept together in the wood, then inclined to our left until we collected about twenty men of different battalions and decided to attempt to break through their lines. Coming up a hill out of the wood we saw a Highlander coming toward us. We called to him that if he would surrender, we would give him good quarters, which he did and delivered up his arms to our Colonel. We then proceeded about fifty yards, and around the corner of a wood, came unexpectedly on a large party of Hessians, as they turned out to be; for we were deceived by their uniforms of blue and red, and taking them for our own people, allowed them to advance within fifty yards, when they fired a volley, fortunately not killing or wounding any of us. Being superior in numbers our Colonel decided not to make a stand. About one hundred and fifty yards distant we crossed a hedge, but no sooner were we over when we saw a Battalion of Highlanders drawn up with their backs to our left. Although within eighty yards, they did not see us at first, but they faced about and fired on us, and inclining to the right, we gained the point of a wood which covered us from their fire. We then ran through the wood, to the lowland, where another strong party of Hessians fired upon us, and one of them was so bold as to run into the center of our party, when one of my men fired and killed him. Finding we were pursued, we ran across a swamp where the water and mud was up to our knees, when we took up a rising piece of wood, where we were fired upon from our right. We then inclined a little to the left and still kept making for the Jamaica road, hoping that if we could cross it, we would get around the right of their lines. Advancing farther we were joined by Col. Lutz, of the Flying Camp, with a small party of his men. We now numbered twenty-five men and for half an hour lay concealed in the wood, where we held a council as to what was to be done. The Hessians were observed coming through the wood to surround us, and there being no way to retreat, we determined to push out before the Hessians and deliver ourselves up to the first British troops we met. On clearing the wood, we saw two Battalions of Highlanders drawn up on our front, and

5

the Hessians firing at us all the way, we club'd our fire-locks, followed our Colonel, and received good quarters from the Colonel of the Highlanders.   We were sent

Wappen v. Heſſen (G.-H.).

under guard to head-quarters, about one mile from our lines on the Jamaica road, where we delivered up our arms and were put in the Provost Guard, where the British officers and soldiers insulted us.   Here we continued until the 29th inst.—twenty-three officers in all—in one house, our rations consisting of Pork and Biscuit with Grog.

"*August 29.*—We were sent under a strong guard to a small town four miles down the island, called Flat Bush, and were turned over to a battalion of Hessians, who used us very well.

"*August 31.*—The Highlanders relieved the Hessians and took charge of us.   Sent all our private soldiers to Gravesend, where they were lodged in two churches.

"*September 3.*—Under guard we went on board the snow Mentor, Capt. Davis, and were placed on short allowance, ½ lb. Pork and 10 ounces of Bread per man daily.

"*September 5.*—Our men were placed on the transports Wooly and Rochford, where we lay until

"*September 22*, when we passed the Narrows and anchored between Governor's and Gallows islands.

"*September 29.*—Sailed up the North River and dropped anchor opposite Powl's Hook.

"*October 7.*—We were landed in New York and signed a second parole. The New York and New England officers were put in a house together on the Holy Ground; the Marylanders, Delewarians and Pennsylvanians were lodged in the house of Mr. Mariner, on William street, except the field officers, who had the liberty of hiring a house for themselves.

"*October 9.*—Tonight I was insulted by a number of Highland officers, who rushed into the house, abused us with bad language, and struck Lieut. Carnaghan of the Right Battalion and Ensign Farnandaz, of the Maryland Battalion, and forced them away to the guard house that night. Here they were treated very civil by the sergeant, and the next morning released by order of Gen. Robertson. We heard during the day heavy cannonading in the direction of Forts Washington and Lee.

"*November 16.*—Fort Washington was taken.

"*November 18.*—The prisoners taken at Fort Washington were brought to New York; the officers lay in the Baptist meeting house that night."

It is to be regretted that the Revolutionary rolls and records are so incomplete, or entirely lacking, as to prevent any intelligible statement as to existing conditions of regimental or company membership, losses, etc. Especially is this the case with regard to Long Island and Fort Washington. Fortunately, there has been preserved what seems to be a complete roster of the company of Captain Arndt, of Northampton County, in Col. Kichlein's Battalion, together with an account of its losses. While the record does not specifically say which were the killed, which wounded and which prisoners, yet the whole is so interesting as to make it deserving of insertion at this point as a sample of the experiences of all the Pennsylvania-Germans there engaged. The company was mustered into service on July 9, 1776.

CAPTAIN ARNDT'S COMPANY.

Captain.

*John Arndt, of Easton.

First Lieutenant.

†Joseph Martin, of Mount Bethel Township.

Second Lieutenant.

Peter Kechlein, of Easton.

Third Lieutenant.

†Isaac Shimer, of Hanover.

Sergeants.

Robert Scott; moved to Northumberland County in 1790; died in Rush Township, April 27, 1838, aged 84 years.

*Andrew Hersher, of Easton.

Philip Arndt, of Easton.

*Andrew Kiefer, of Mount Bethel Township.

---

* Killed, wounded or missing at Long Island.
† Killed, wounded or missing at Fort Washington.

Corporals.

Jacob Kechlein, of Easton.
George Edelman.
Peter Righter.
Elijah Crawford, of Mount Bethel Township.

Drummer.

†John Arndt, Jr., of Easton.

Fifer.

†Henry Alshouse, of Easton.

Privates.

†Jacob Andrew.
†Isaac Berlin.
*Peter Beyer.
†Conrad Bittenbender.
†Adam Bortz.
†Jacob Brider (or Kreidler).
*Henry Bush, Sr.
†Henry Bush, Jr.
†John Bush.
*Philip Bosh.
†Joseph Chass.
†Lewis Collins.
†Samuel Curry.
Benjamin Depue.
*Martin Derr.
Nicholas Diehl.
Robert Lyle.
Samuel McCracken.

†Henry Fretz.
*Anthony Frutchy.
*George Fry.
Michael Gress.
*John Harple.
†Christopher Harple, 1st.
†Christopher Harple, 2d.
†James Hyndshaw.
†Joseph Keller.
*Peter Kern.
John Kepler.
Michael Koehler.
Michael Kress (Gress).
†Isaac Kuhn.
*Peter Lahr.
Daniel Lewis.
Daniel Saylor.
Henry Siegel.

---

* Killed, wounded or missing at Long Island.
† Killed, wounded or missing at Fort Washington.

John McFarren.
Conrad Metz.
John Middugh.
*Barnhardt Miller.
Jacob Miller.
†Joseph Miriem (or Minem)
*Richard Overfield.
*Abraham Peter.
George Raymond.
†Frederick Reager.
†Paul Reaser.
Philip Reaser.
†Christian Roth.
†John Ross.
*Jacob Dofferd.
Jost Dornblaeser.
†George Edinger.
†Jacob Engler.
*Lawrence Erb.
George Essigh.
Adam Everets.
James Farrell.
John Falstick.
Henry Fatzinger.
†Jacob Fraunfelter.
*Peter Freas.

George Shiblin.
Isaac Shoemaker.
†John Shook.
†Henry Shoup (or Stroup).
John Smith.
Conrad Smith.
*Matthias Stidinger.
James Simonton.
Christian Stout.
*Joseph Stout.
*Thomas Sybert.
Alexander Syllyman.
Henry Unangst.
†Frederick Wagoner.
Jacob Wagoner.
†William Warrand.
†Adam Weidknecht.
†Henry Weidknecht.
*Jacob Weidknecht.
†Frederick Wilhelm.
†John Wolf.
†Henry Wolf, Sr.
Henry Wolf, Jr.
John Yent.
Valentine Yent.
Adam Yohe.

Thirty-three of this company, including the Captain and Second Lieutenant, rallied at Elizabethtown, N. J., after the battle of Fort Washington. This company was discharged December 1, 1776, having served four months and twenty-two days.

---

* Killed, wounded or missing at Long Island.
† Killed, wounded or missing at Fort Washington.

CHAPTER V.

THE PRISON SHIPS.

Wappen von
Großbritannien u. Irland.

ADDED to the terrible experiences which befell the Pennsylvania-German troops at Long Island, many of them, who survived, were unfortunate enough to be amongst those who, through another blunder, became "cooped up" at Fort Washington, where, after a useless engagement, they were forced to capitulate, on November 16, 1776, and were sent to swell the large number of their wretched comrades who, captured on August 27, at Long Island, were already suffering the misery of prison life in New York.

If the Pennsylvania-Germans were not entitled to one word of praise, from their countrymen of all generations, for deeds performed during the Revolutionary War, they deserve untold commendation and heartfelt thanks for the unswerving loyalty with which, uncomplainingly, they suffered and died in British prisons. To many of us the awful story of these prisons is an unheard tale, to others a shadowy dream, but, to the few who know somewhat of it, a horrible nightmare, to which it is difficult for the brain to give credence.

After years and generations of neglect the Long Island Society, Daughters of the Revolution, have, somewhat recently, undertaken to gather together the poor bones of these martyrs to their country's cause, and to erect over them a suitable monument. Alice Morse Earle, of their number, has eloquently written about them in the following words:

" The victory of the British army at the battle of Brooklyn in August, 1776, and the capture of Fort Washington in the following November, placed nearly 4,000 American prisoners in the possession of the British. This number was increased by the arrest of many private citizens suspected of complicity with the rebels, and by the capture of many American privateers, until the prisoners numbered 5,000 at the end of the year. New York was then in the power of the British. The only prisons at that time in the city were the ' new ' jail, which still stands, though much altered, as the Hall of Records, and the Bridewell, which was in the space between the present City Hall and Broadway. These edifices proving entirely inadequate to hold this large number of captives, the British were compelled to turn their large buildings, such as the sugar houses, several of the churches, the hospital, and Columbia College, into temporary prisons. All were soon crowded to overflowing by daily accessions of patriot prisoners, who sometimes found in their jails not even space to lie down upon the hard and filthy floors. Denied the light and air of heaven; scantily fed on the poorest and sometimes even

THE

BATTLE of BROOKLYN,

A

F A R C E

O F

T W O   A C T S:

As it was performed on

L O N G - I S L A N D,

On TUESDAY the 27th Day of August, 1776.

By the Representatives of the Tyrants of

A M E R I C A

Assembled at PHILADELPHIA.

For as a Flea, that goes to bed,
Lies with his tail above his head ·
So in this mongrel State of ours,
The rabble are the supreme pow'rs;
Who've hors'd us on their backs, to shew us
A jadish trick, at last, and throw us.
    HUDIBRAS.

N E W - Y O R K:
Printed for J. RIVINGTON, in the Year of the
REBELLION. 1776.
British Satyre on the Battle of Long Island.

uncooked food; obliged to endure the companionship of
the most abandoned criminals, and those sick with in-
fectious diseases; worn out by the groans of their suffering fellow prisoners, and subjected to every conceivable
insult and indignity by their hardened keepers, hundreds
of American patriots sickened and died.   Still, great as
was the suffering of those incarcerated within the prisons
of the city, their misery was exceeded by the wretchedness
of the unfortunate prisoners who languished in naval
prisons, the ' Prison Ships of the Wallebought.'   These
ships were originally transport vessels in which cattle and
other supplies of the British army had been brought to
America in 1776.   They had been anchored in Gravesend
bay, and to them were sent at first the prisoners taken in
the battle of Brooklyn.   But these soldiers were afterwards transferred to the prisons on shore, and the transports were devoted more especially to marine prisoners,
where numbers rapidly increased owing to the frequent
capture of American privateers by the King's cruisers.
At first these transports were anchored in the Hudson and
East rivers, and one named the *Whitby,* was the first
prison ship anchored in the Wallabout, about October
20, 1776 [the snow *Mentor* was another, which preceded
it, also the transports *Wooly* and *Rochford.*—Ed.].
She lay near Remsen's mill, and was soon crowded with
prisoners.   Many landsmen were captives on board of
this vessel.   Scant and poor rations of bad provisions
and foul water were dealt to them.   As no medical men
attended the sick, disease reigned unrelieved, and hundreds died from horrible pestilential diseases, or were
even starved on board."

General Jeremiah Johnson, an eye witness of some
aspects of these horrors, thus wrote:

" I saw the sand-beach, between the ravine in the hill and Mr. Remsen's dock, become filled with graves in the course of two months; and before May 1, 1777, the ravine alluded to was itself occupied in the same way. In the month of May, 1777, two large ships were anchored in the Wallabout, when the prisoners were transferred from the *Whitby* to them. These vessels were also very sickly, from the causes before stated. Although many prisoners were sent on board of them, and none exchanged, death made room for all. On a Saturday afternoon, about the middle of October, 1777, one of the prison ships was burned; the prisoners, except a few, who, it is said, were burned in the vessel, were removed to the remaining ship. It was reported at the time that the prisoners had fired their prison, which, if true, proves that they preferred death, even by fire, to the lingering sufferings of pestilence and starvation. In the month of February, 1778, the remaining prison ship was burned at night, when the prisoners were removed from her to the ships then wintering in the Wallabout."

Among the numerous vessels used, from time to time, as prisons, the names of the following have been preserved: *Mentor, Wooly, Rockford, Prince of Wales, Good Hope, Stromboli, Scorpion, Hunter, Jersey, John, Falmouth, Chatham, Kitty, Frederick, Glasgow, Woodlands, Scheldt, Clyde.*

Of all these the old *Jersey,* or the " Hell," as she was termed—and properly termed, from the terrible sufferings her thousands of occupants endured—won the most infamous notoriety.

The writer, previously mentioned, adds:

" This *Jersey* was an old sixty-four-gun battle ship.

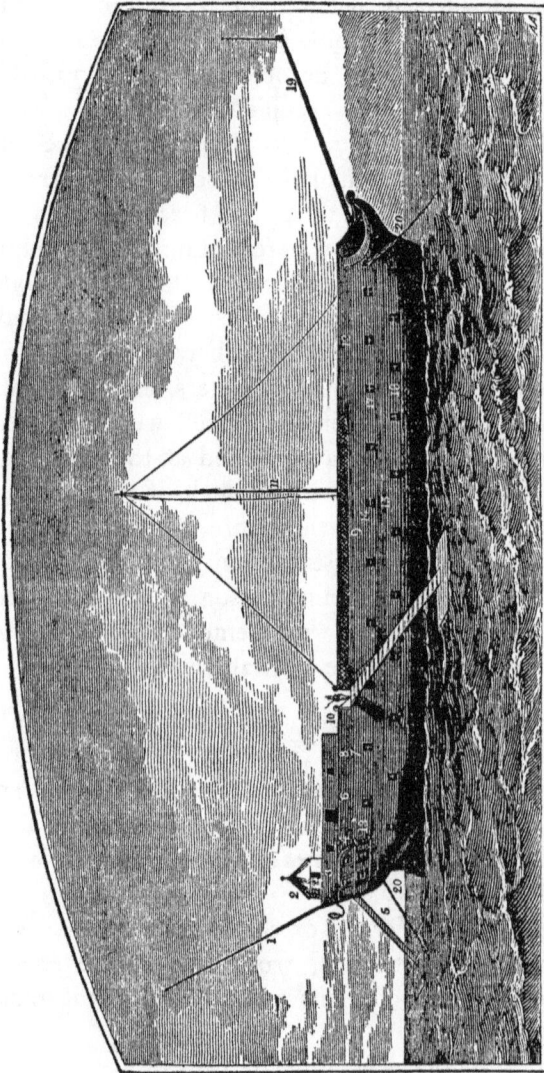

THE JERSEY PRISON SHIP.

1. Signal staff.
2. Tent for guard.
3. Quarter deck.
4. Ship officers' quarters.

5. Ladder for ship officers.
6. Sailors' quarters.
7. Cook's room.
8. Sutler's room.

9. Spar deck.
10. Gangway for prisoners.
11. Derrick.
12. The galley.

13. Gun room.
14. Hatchway to prison.
15. Hatchway to prison.
16. Foot of gang plank.

When she was anchored in the Wallabout, about 300 yards from shore, she was dismantled, even her figure-head was removed; her bowsprit was left as a derrick. Her portholes were nailed close, and four small holes twenty inches square were cut for what was, with cruel satire, termed ventilation, and were securely grated with iron cross bars. She was ' an old unsightly hulk whose dark and filthy external appearance fitly represented the death and despair that reigned within.' By day the prisoners were permitted to remain for a time on deck, but at sunset all were ordered below; the incredible sufferings at night during the summer months bore plentiful results. The brutal cry of the British soldiers down the hold each morning ' Bring up the dead,' never failed to secure active and plentiful response. The men died like rotten sheep, were carelessly sewed in blankets, and buried on the shore by their wretched survivors. Even the relief of sexton's work was so great to those miserable, pent-up creatures, that they contended eagerly for the privilege of going ashore to dig the graves.

" At the expiration of the war, the wretched prisoners who had lived and dragged through the horrors of the old *Jersey*, were liberated, and the old hulk, within whose vile walls so many had suffered and died, was abandoned where she lay. The dread of contagion prevented every one from venturing on board, and even from approaching her polluted frame. But ministers of destruction were at work. Her planks were soon filled with worms that ceased not from their labor until they had penetrated her decaying bottom with holes, through which the water rushed in, until she sank. With her went down the names of thousands of our Revolutionary patriots, for her inner planks and sheathing were literally covered with names; for few of her inmates had neglected to add their carved autograph or initials to the almost innumerable catalogue of sufferers.   Could these be known, some correct estimate might be made of the whole number who were there immured.   But the vessel was consigned to eternal oblivion, and the precise number of the martyrs who perished in the prison ships and who were buried in the loose sands of the lonely Wallabout, can never be accurately known.   It was estimated shortly after the close of the war, when the data were more easily obtainable than now, that the monstrous horror of eleven thousand died in the *Jersey* alone.   This appalling statement was never denied, either officially or by any persons then resident in New York, who, from their connection with the British commissary department, had opportunities of knowing the truth.   Certainly that estimate cannot be exaggerated if applied to the mortality, not of the *Jersey* alone, but of all the prison ships."

CHAPTER VI.

The Pennsylvania-German Continentals.

IT is probable that there will never be given to the public a full and complete record of the services of the Pennsylvania-Germans during the Revolutionary War. The task of collecting such data is made extremely difficult from the fact that so many of them were scattered, as individuals, throughout all the various regiments and battalions of the army, including those which, because of the preponderance of men of other nationalities, could hardly be ranked as German, either in whole or any material part.

The troops, named in this chapter, are those of the Regular Service which contained a reasonably large representation of men of Pennsylvania-German blood, sufficiently so, at least, to entitle them to be considered in connection with our subject.

Paradoxical as it may seem, the first of these Pennsylvania-German troops, to whom we desire to call attention, were Virginians. In the earlier part of the eighteenth century there was quite a considerable emigration of the German element of Pennsylvania into Virginia, resulting in large settlements in Loudoun County, Dunmore County, the Shenandoah Valley, and the mountain districts in general. These Germans were intensely loyal, and promptly volunteered to aid in establishing the independence of their adopted country.

EIGHTH VIRGINIA CONTINENTAL REGIMENT.

This excellent regiment was recruited by Col. Peter Muhlenberg from amongst his parishioners in Dunmore County, Virginia, in January, 1776, and was entirely German. Its first campaigns were in Georgia and South Carolina, where it behaved most gallantly at the battle of Sullivan's Island, June 29, 1776. Having been ordered north in February, 1777, it bore the brunt of the action at Brandywine, September 11, 1777, and, at Germantown, October 8, it was advanced further into the town than any other of the troops. In 1778 it was at the battle of Monmouth, and in the reserves at the storming of Stony Point in 1779; when Leslie invaded Virginia, in 1780, the regiment operated against him, and took part in the 'siege of Yorktown when Cornwallis surrendered.

Its officers were:

Col. Peter Muhlenberg.

Lieut. Col. Abraham Bowman.

Major P. Helfenstein.

They were commissioned by the Colony of Virginia in December, 1775, and in the Continental service on February 13, 1776.

GEN. DANIEL MORGAN.
B. 1736. D. 1802.

Morgan's Riflemen.

In the chapter treating of the " First Defenders " attention has already been called to the resolution of Congress, on June 14, 1775, calling for the formation of ten companies of rifle sharpshooters, of which six were appointed to Pennsylvania, two to Maryland and two to Virginia. On June 22, by additional resolution, Pennsylvania was directed to raise two more of these companies, and when, on July 11, information was received that Lancaster County, filled with patriotism, had recruited two companies instead of its quota of one, it was decided to form a battalion out of the nine companies from Pennsylvania, the command of which was given to Colonel William Thompson, of Carlisle, and which body, known as " Thompson's Rifle Battalion, or Regiment," became one of the finest organizations in the Continental army, rendering most distinguished service, as appears elsewhere in this narrative.

The two Maryland companies, thus called into existence, were commanded, respectively, by Thomas Price, who rose to the rank of colonel and whose first lieutenant, Otho Holland Williams, became a brigadier general, and by Thomas Cresap, a famous border fighter. Although stricken with a mortal ailment when his commission reached him, Cresap promptly gathered his men together, and led them to Washington's army at Cambridge, Massachusetts, where he died soon after.

Both of these Maryland companies were enlisted from Frederick County, which was settled almost exclusively by Germans who emigrated thence from Pennsylvania. They were animated by the same spirit which, in 1864, moved one of their descendants, Barbara (Hauer)

6

Fritchie, to keep flying the flag of her country in the face of the approaching Confederate invaders.

One of the Virginia companies was commanded by Captain Ericson, of whom but little is known; the other was led by Daniel Morgan, destined to become a brilliant general of the war and a personal favorite of Washington. The men were recruited from the mountaineers who resided in the vicinity of Martinsburg, and, like those of Maryland, were largely of German blood.

Familiar as most of us are with the fact that these troops were organized as a special body of sharpshooters because of the rifles they used so expertly, an arm introduced into Pennsylvania about 1700 by Palatine and Swiss immigrants and as yet unknown, save by reputation, to the rest of the colonies, it is well, however, that this same fact should be placed on record, in order that the world may not forget that the dreaded riflemen of the Revolution were mostly German mountaineers of Pennsylvania derivation whose weapon was of the same nationality although greatly improved in their own Pennsylvania-German workshops.

In like manner, it is well to describe, somewhat fully, the costume worn by these Pennsylvania-German backwoods riflemen, which was so well adapted to the warfare in which they were engaged, and which, more than once, has been suggested as a distinctively American uniform for an American army, and whose general characteristics are even now shown in our latest so-called " Khaki " uniform.

It consisted, first, of an ash-colored hunting shirt of coarse linen or linsey-woolsey. Buck-skin, which was too hot for summer weather, was worn during the winter. The shirt had a double cape and was fringed along the edges and seams. Around the waist it was secured by a belt, usually of wampum, in which were thrust the ever useful tomahawk and skinning knife, commonly called " scalping-knife." Some of the men wore buck-skin breeches; others preferred leggings of the same material, reaching above the knees, and an Indian breech-clout, thus leaving the thighs naked for better suppleness in running. Captain Morgan, himself, wore a breech-clout during the terrible mid-winter march through the Maine wilderness to Quebec, his bare thighs exposed to the elements and lacerated by thorns and bush. The head dress was a soft round hat, often made of skins, with a feather in it. On the feet were worn buck-skin moccasins, ornamented with squaw-work in beads and stained porcupine quills. Shoulder belts supported the canteen, bullet-pouch and powder-horn. The only insignia to distinguish the officers were the crimson sashes worn by them over the shoulder and around the waist. Some of the latter preferred to carry rifles, like their men, doing away with the sword to which they were entitled.

The services rendered by the riflemen at the siege of Boston were of incalculable benefit to the American cause. Many of them were detailed to take part in the expedition against Canada, and underwent all the sufferings incident to it. With the later, and more complete, organization of the troops Morgan was authorized to form a corps of rifle sharpshooters, to be selected from the entire army. This celebrated body of marksmen was generally known as " Morgan's Virginians," but, in fact, two thirds of its members were Pennsylvanians, and a very large percentage of the whole were Pennsylvania-Germans. We are told that, of the latter, a Mr. Tauk, who was with Morgan from the beginning of the war to its end, was the last survivor of the corps. When Morgan was asked, at one time, which race, of those composing the American armies, made the best soldiers, he replied: " As for the fighting part of the matter the men of all races are pretty much alike; they fight as much as they find necessary, and no more. But, sir, for the grand essential composition of a good soldier, give me the ' Dutchman '—he starves well."

The space allotted to this history makes it impossible to go into details of the services of such troops as were not a part of the regular Pennsylvania establishment, so we must be satisfied, in this instance, to say that " Mor-

I am Sir,

Your most obed. Servant

Lincoln

AUTOGRAPH OF GENERAL LINCOLN.

gan's Riflemen " were considered amongst the élite of the American forces. Their record, which is a most enviable one, covers the whole period of the war, and was especially prominent in the south at a most trying period.

After the capture of Ticonderoga by Burgoyne they were sent to the Hudson Valley by Washington, together with Generals Arnold and Lincoln, and had much to do with the results attained at Saratoga, in September, 1777, which ended with the surrender of the British general.

With a succession of deplorable calamities in the south came the cheering victory at King's Mountain, near the boundary between the two Carolinas, on October 7, 1780. To follow up this gain Morgan, with his riflemen, was promptly ordered south by the Commander-in-Chief, and Gates was replaced by Greene in December, 1780.   The first move of the latter was to send Morgan to raid the back country.   At Cowpens, not far from King's Mountain, with but nine hundred men, he met Tarleton with his eleven hundred men, and practically annihilated him, thus removing from the British forces their most brilliant cavalry leader who had literally scourged the neighborhoods which were inhabited by loyal patriots.   Cornwallis, thus weakened and operating under great disadvantages, was forced by Greene, who promptly joined Morgan, into manœuvres which finally landed him in

Yorktown, where, on October 19, 1781, he surrendered to the allied American and French armies, and the beginning of the great and long-hoped for end came.

Armand's Partisan Legion.

On May 10, 1777, Congress commissioned Charles Armand, Marquis de la Rouerie, as Colonel, and authorized him to raise a partisan corps, into which were gradually merged von Ottendorff's Corps, Capt. John Paul Schott's Company, and Pulaski's Corps. While the original intention was to have it recruited, to some extent at least, from amongst the French, yet, as a matter of fact, it was composed, nearly altogether, of Pennsylvania-Germans, from Pennsylvania itself and from Loudoun County, Virginia. It remained in service till the end of the war.

On November 26, 1777, Lafayette had a successful engagement with the enemy near Gloucester, N. J., in which it participated; it was prominent in the fight at Red Bank, in 1777, and was in Fleury's detachment at Brandywine; it was no doubt at Germantown, and probably at both Valley Forge and Monmouth.

Armand's Corps was taken into the Continental service on June 25, 1778, by order of Congress. Its winter quarters, of 1778–79, were on the upper Delaware, where, with Pulaski's Corps, it served as a protection to Pennsylvania. For some time after it was actively engaged, particularly in Westchester County, New York, against the tories.

In the summer of 1779, it was placed under the command of Gen. Robert Howe, whose duty it was to protect Connecticut, and its vicinity, from " the insults and ravages of the enemy." At this time the campaign around New York was especially active, made so by the operations of Simcoe's newly organized " Queen's Rangers." Armand's Corps, now assigned to the command of Col. Lee, was sent against this partisan and succeeded in taking him prisoner near South Amboy, N. J., on October 1, 1779. Major Baremore, another troublesome ranger, was surprised and captured by Col. Armand, on November 7, 1779, together with a Captain Cruser, of Baremore's Corps, on December 2, 1779.

A part of Armand's Corps accompanied Gen. Sullivan's Expedition, in August and September, 1779, against the Six Nations, at which time the power of this savage enemy was completely broken up.

About the beginning of 1780 this corps appears in the annals of the war down South. When Gen. Gates took command of the Southern Department the Legion did not exceed one hundred men.

At the disastrous battle of Camden, August 16, 1780, Armand's cavalry was placed in the van, and, unable to stand the assault of the enemy, broke and retreated. Much unfavorable comment was made with regard to them, but, it is only proper to say, with much injustice, as the whole trouble was more due to the arrogance and incompetency of Gen. Gates.

From lack of proper supplies and sustenance, the Legion became greatly reduced, until but forty serviceable horses were left, but these were used for scouting, by Baron Steuben, in Virginia, during the autumn of 1780, and, by Gen. Greene, later in the same year. Finally, the fragments of Armand's Corps were again united, and formed the First Battalion of the Legion Cavalry, under the Duke de Lauzun, being attached to the command of Choisy, together with a brigade of American militia. They held the investment of Gloucester Point, opposite Yorktown, and also served to prevent the retreat of Cornwallis. After the surrender, Armand's Corps went to New York with Washington's army.

Among its many officers and privates of Pennsylvania-German blood were Major George Schaffner, and Surgeon Gottlieb Morris.

VON OTTENDORFF'S CORPS.

On December 5, 1776, Nicholas Dietrich, Baron von Ottendorff, was authorized, by Congress, to raise an independent corps, consisting of one hundred and fifty men, divided into three companies, he to have the rank of Major.   By the spring of 1777 the complement of the corps was filled, all three companies being raised in Pennsylvania, and consisting of Pennsylvania-Germans. The separate record of this body is somewhat vague. One of his captains, John Paul Schott, of Philadelphia, seems to have been in command of that part of Armand's Legion which accompanied Gen. Sullivan in his expedition against the Indians, in 1779, judging from the letter written by him to the Pennsylvania Council, on November 26, 1779, from " Garrison, Wyoming," given below:

CAPTAIN SCHOTT'S CORPS.

This letter is worded as follows:

" I am a Hessian born, by Inclination, as well as duty bound, an American.   I have the Honour to be a Captn. in the Continental Army ever since the 6th day of November, 1776.   I had the Misfortune to be taken Prisoner on the 26th of June, 1777, in the Battle of Short Hills, where I suffer'd the greatest Cruelty man could Suffer.   I was struck, kick'd, abused and almost perished for Hunger; At that time I was offer'd one thousand pounds and a Majority in the Enemy's New Levies, but I despised their offer, and was determined to suffer death before I would betray the Cause I was Engaged in, Relying on the Country's Generosity to Reward me for my Grievances. When I was Exchanged I got the Command of that Corps I now command . . ."

Both of these corps were merged into that of Armand, when their history becomes the same.

PULASKI'S LEGION.

The Legion authorized by Congress, March 28, 1778, and commanded by the patriotic and brave Pole, Count Casimir Pulaski, consisted of sixty-eight horse and two hundred foot. It was recruited, largely, from among the Germans of Pennsylvania and Maryland. It was this body which carried the embroidered crimson standard made by the Moravian single sisters of Bethlehem, and purchased from them by Pulaski, while in Bethlehem between April 16 and May 18, 1778. It was not a gift, as supposed. When their gallant commander fell, mortally wounded, before Savannah, in the autumn of 1779, his Legion was also merged into that of Armand's Corps. On November 29, 1779, Congress voted a monument to the memory of the Polish patriot, which was never erected, but one was subsequently raised by the citiens of Savannah.

VON HEER'S LIGHT DRAGOONS.

This troop was organized under a resolution of Congress, May 27, 1778, as a Provost Guard to apprehend deserters, rioters, and stragglers. In battle they were posted in the rear to secure fugitives. It was composed entirely of Pennsylvania-Germans, and was officered as follows:

Captain.—Bartholomew von Heer, of Reading, from captain in Proctor's Artillery.

First Lieutenant.—Jacob Nyburger.

Second Lieutenant.—Philip Strubing.

THE PENNSYLVANIA BATTALIONS.

At the outbreak of the Revolution Pennsylvania placed in the field, exclusive of detachments of artillery and cavalry, some 6,345 regular troops, made up as follows:

One Year Men, 1775–76.

Rifle Battalion—Col. William Thompson, 839 men, commissioned June 25, 1775.

1st Pennsylvania Battalion—Col. John Philip De Haas, 652 men, commissioned October 27, 1775.

Independent Riflemen—Capt. John Nelson, 93 men, commissioned January 30, 1776.

2d Pennsylvania Battalion—Col. Arthur St. Clair, 652 men, commissioned January 3, 1776.

3d Pennsylvania Battalion—Col. John Shee, 597 men, commissioned January 5, 1776.

4th Pennsylvania Battalion—Col. Anthony Wayne, 652 men, commissioned January 3, 1776.

5th Pennsylvania Battalion—Col. Robert Magaw, 598 men, commissioned January 3, 1776.

6th Pennsylvania Battalion—Col. William Irvine, 741 men, commissioned January 9, 1776.

Two Years' Men.

Rifle Regiment—Col. Samuel Miles, 1st Battalion, 581 men, commissioned March 6, 1776.

Rifle Regiment—Col. Samuel Miles, 2d Battalion, 514 men, commissioned March 6, 1776.

Musketry Battalion—Col. Samuel J. Atlee, 426 men, commissioned March 6, 1776.

Total number of men, 6,345.

State Regiment of Foot—Cols. John Bull and Walter Stewart, commissioned April, 1777, formed from the remains of Miles' and Atlee's battalions as a nucleus.

RIFLE BATTALION.

The valuable services of this regiment have already been enumerated in the chapter on the " First Defenders." It remained in front of Boston until the evacuation in March, 1776. On the 27th of that month Lieut. Col. Edward Hand was commissioned as its colonel, Col. Thompson having been made a Brigadier General. Under date of March 11 he writes, " The enemy seems to be preparing to depart (from Boston). Our regiment is ordered to march at an hour's warning. New York is at present our destination." The regiment left Cambridge on March 14, arriving at New York on March 28. On April 12 it was moved to Long Island, where it remained until the expiration of its term of service, July 1, 1776, when the men reënlisted, and it entered upon another term of service as the First Pennsylvania Regiment of the Continental Line.

The companies of Capts. Hendricks and Smith, which participated in the Quebec campaign, under Arnold, contained very few Pennsylvania-Germans.

Those, almost entirely composed of Pennsylvania-Germans, were:

Capt. Abraham Miller, from Northampton County.

Capt. George Nagel, from Berks County.

Capt. James Ross, from Lancaster County.

Those partly composed of Pennsylvania-Germans were:

Capt. John Lowdon, from Northumberland County.
Capt. Michael Doudel, from York (Adams) County.

First Pennsylvania Battalion.

The commanding officer of this regiment, Col. John Philip de Haas, was a Pennsylvania-German, from Lebanon, as were others of its commissioned officers.

The roster of this battalion is very incomplete, but, of the companies given, one of them, that of Capt. Jonathan Jones, while raised in Caernarvon Township, of Berks County, amongst the Welsh, yet contained a fair number of Pennsylvania-Germans.

This battalion took part in the Canada expedition of Gen. Arnold. Marching to New York, they embarked in sloops, which carried them up to Albany. By February

14, 1776, five companies were reported as having passed that point. From Albany they proceeded up the Hudson to Fort Edwards, on the west bank, forty-eight miles to the north; thence to Fort William Henry (later Fort George), at the south end of Lake St. George; thence, in batteaux, to the foot of that lake; thence marched across the portage, two and one half miles, to Fort Ticonderoga, on the western shore of Lake Champlain, near the outlet of Lake George, distant about ninety-seven miles from Albany; thence sailed to Crown Point, five miles further, on the same side of the lake.

Lake Champlain stretches one hundred and twenty miles to the north, and pours its waters, through the Sorel river, into the St. Lawrence, at Sorel, which is forty-five miles from Montreal and one hundred and thirty-five from Quebec. From Sorel to Three Rivers, at the mouth of the St. Maurice river, the distance is forty-five miles down the St. Lawrence. In the early part of March the various companies of the battalion passed this point, and, on March 30, the regimental returns of troops, under Arnold before Quebec, makes the command of Col. de Haas 225 strong, being four companies.

On May 6 the army was compelled to retreat, reaching Three Rivers on the 15th, at which point the companies of Capts. Jones, Jenkins, etc., took part in an engagement where quite a number of the men were captured.

On June 14 Gen. Sullivan retreated from Sorel, and reached St. John's on the 16th, and Isle Aux Noix on the 18th. From this date the military service of the battalion corresponds with that of the battalions of St. Clair, Wayne and Irvine, to follow.

On November 13, three weeks after the expiration of its term of service, for which extra time it volunteered to remain, at the request of Gen. Gates, for the defense and security of Ticonderoga, and for which it received his thanks, the battalion was taken off duty at Ticonderoga, ordered to Fort George, and eventually discharged. A number, however, reënlisted and became the nucleus of the Second Regiment of the Continental Line, October 25, 1776.

SECOND PENNSYLVANIA BATTALION.

Of this regiment the company of Capt. Thomas Craig, of Northampton County, was, almost entirely, Pennsylvania-German, and that of Capt. Rudolph Bunner contained some.

As it was associated with the Fourth Battalion, Col. Wayne, and the Sixth, Col. Irvine, while in active service, its history mingles with that of theirs, as, at a certain point, it does also with that of the First Battalion.

On February 16, 1777, the Colonel was directed to use the utmost dispatch in getting his battalion ready, and to march the companies, so soon as ready, one at a time, to Canada. On the 20th Col. Wayne was instructed to march his battalion to New York, and to put himself under the command of Gen. Lee.

On March 13 Lieut. Col. Allen, of the Second, had arrived in New York and embarked some companies for Albany. On March 14, Col. Irvine was ordered to march his battalion to New York, and place himself under the orders of the commanding officer of the continental troops at that point.

On April 12, five companies of the Second were at Fort Edwards, and were ordered to Fort George on the 19th, fourteen miles beyond. On the 26th, the battalions of Wayne and Irvine, at New York, were ordered, by Washington, to embark for Canada. On May 10, Col. Irvine's whole battalion was at Albany, with two companies of Wayne's. On May 6, Lieut. Col. Allen, of the Second, was within three miles of Quebec, where he met Gen. Thompson, with the army, retreating. A council of war being held it was decided to continue the retreat to Sorel, which the rear of the army reached on the 24th.

Wayne's detachment, and Irvine's battalion, passed Lake George on the 24th, with Gen. Sullivan, embarked at Ticonderoga, and arrived at St. John's on the 27th.

On June 2, Gen. Thompson sent Col. St. Clair from Sorel, with over six hundred men, to attack the camp of Col. McClean, who had advanced as far as Three Rivers, with eight hundred British regulars and Canadians. Gen. Sullivan assumed command at Sorel on the 4th, Gen. Thomas having died on the 2d.

On the 6th, Gen. Sullivan ordered Gen. William Thompson to march, with the battalions of Cols. Irvine and Wayne, and the companies of Col. St. Clair then remaining at Sorel, to join Col. St. Clair at Nicolette, where he was to take command of the whole party, and, unless he found the number of the enemy at Three Rivers to be such as would render an attack upon them hazardous, he should cross the river at the most convenient place he could find and attack them. He advised him not to attack if the prospect of success was not much in his favor, as a defeat of his party at the time might prove the total loss of the country.

The following letter from Lieut. Col. Thomas Hartley to Jasper Yeates, Esq., gives a full detail of the subsequent occurrences, and contains nearly all that is known of the campaign of the Pennsylvania battalions in Canada:

" CAMP AT SOREL, June the 12th, 1776.

" Before the arrival of Col. Wayne's and Irvine's regiments, under the command of Gen. Sullivan, Col. St. Clair, with a detachment of seven hundred men, was sent down the river St. Lawrence, about nine leagues, to watch the motions of the enemy, and act occasionally.   Gen. Sullivan's arrival here was at a critical time.   Canada was lost, unless some notable exertion; the credit of our arms was gone, and no number of American troops to sustain our posts.   It was said that the taking of Three Rivers, with such troops as were on it, would be of service.   A detachment under Gen. Thompson was sent down the river.   The corps under Col. St. Clair was to join it, and if the General thought it expedient, he was ordered by Gen. Sullivan to attack the enemy at Three Rivers.

"We left this on the evening of the 5th instant, in

Autograph of Col. St. Clair.

several batteaux, and joined Col. St. Clair about twelve o'clock at night.   It being too late to proceed on to the Three Rivers, the enterprise was postponed until the next night.

"In the dusk of the evening of the 7th, we set off from the Nicolette, with about fifteen hundred rank and file, besides officers.   It was intended to attack Three Rivers about day break in four places.   Thompson landed his forces about nine miles above the town, on the north side of the St. Lawrence, and divided his army into five divisions, Maxwell, St. Clair, Wayne and Irvine, each commanding a division, and I had the honor of commanding the reserve. Leaving two hundred and fifty men to guard the batteaux, the army proceeded swiftly towards the town. I was to be ready to sustain the party which might need assistance.

" The guides proved faithless, and the General was misinformed as to the number of the enemy as well as to the situation of the town. Our men had lost their sleep for two nights, yet were in pretty good spirits. Daylight appeared and showed us to the enemy. Our guides (perhaps traitors) had led us through several windings, and were rather carrying us off from the post. The General was enraged at their conduct.

" There were mutual firings. Our people killed some in a barge. Our scheme was no longer an enterprise; it might have been, perhaps, prudent to have retreated, but no one would propose it. We endeavored to penetrate through a swamp to the town, and avoid the shipping. We had no idea of the difficulties we were to surmount in the mire, otherwise the way by the shipping would have been preferred.

" We waded three hours through the mud, about mid-deep in general, the men fasting. We every moment expected to get through and find some good ground to form on, but were deceived. The second division, under Col. Wayne, saw a part of the enemy and attacked them. Capt. Hay, of our regiment (Sixth battalion), with his company of riflemen assisted and behaved nobly. Col. Wayne advanced, the enemy's light infantry were driven from their ground, and the Indians on their flanks were silenced.

7

" The great body of the enemy, which we knew nothing of, consisting of two or three thousand men, covered with entrenchments, and assisted with the cannon of the shipping and several field pieces, began a furious fire, and continued it upon our troops in the front.   It was so heavy that the division gave way, and from the badness of the ground could not form suddenly again.   Col. St. Clair's division advanced, but the fire was too heavy. Part of Col. Irvine's division, especially the riflemen, went up towards the enemy.   I understood the army was in confusion.   I consulted some friends, and led up the reserve within a short distance of the enemy.   Capt. McClean's and Grier's company advanced with spirit; McClean's men took the best situation, and within eighty yards of the enemy, exposed to the fire of the shipping, as hot as hell.   I experienced some of it.

" Not a man of McClean's company behaved ill, Grier's company behaved well.   Several of the enemy were killed in the attack of the reserve.   Under the disadvantages, our men would fight; but we had no covering, no artillery, and no prospect of succeeding, as the number of the enemy was so much superior to ours.   Colonels Wayne and Allen rallied part of our men, and kept up a fire against the English from the swamp.   The enemy, in the meantime, dispatched a strong body to cut off our retreat to the boats, when it was thought expedient to retreat. Our General and Col. Irvine were not to be found; they had both gone up (to the front) in a very hot fire.   This gave us great uneasiness, but a retreat was necessary. This could not be done regularly, as we could not regain the road, on account of the enemy's shipping and artillery, and we went off in small parties through the swamp. Colonels Wayne and Allen gathered some hundreds together, and I got as many in my division as I could, with several others, amounting to upwards of two hundred.

" Col. Wayne, with his party, and I, with mine, tried several ways to get to our batteaux. Col. Wayne was obliged, not far from the river, to march by seven hundred of the enemy. He intended to attack them regularly, but his people were so much fatigued that it was deemed unsafe. The enemy fired their small arms and artillery on our men as loud as thunder. They returned a retreating fire. Several of the enemy were killed and wounded. We came within a mile of where our boats were but our guard [Major Joseph Wood, who commanded this guard, saved all the boats, except two—Ed.] had carried them off. The English had possession of the ground where we landed. Their shipping proceeded up the river, covering parties sent to take possession of the ferries we were to pass.

" Col. Wayne, with his party, lay near the enemy, I passed through a prodigious swamp, and at night took possession of a hill near the enemy. We were without food, and the water very bad. I mounted a small quarter guard, fixed my alarm post, and made every man lay down on the ground, on which he was to rise for action in case of an attack. I slept a little by resting my head on a cold bough of spruce.

" Morning dawned (Sunday, June 9th), and I consulted our officers and men. They said they were refreshed with sleep. It was agreed to stand together, that they would support me, and effect a passage through the enemy, or die in the attempt. A little spring water refreshed us more. The necessary dispositions were made, but we had no guides. We heard the enemy within a half mile of us, but no one seemed alarmed, so we proceeded, and luckily, fell in with Col. Wayne's track. We pursued it, and overtook him near the river Du Lac. This made us upwards of seven hundred strong, and we agreed to attack the enemy if they fell in our way to Bokie (Berthier), opposite Sorel.   We were sure they

would attempt the fort at Sorel before we could arrive; but as we came up, the English left the ferries, and drew all their forces back to Three Rivers.   By forced marches, and surmounting every difficulty, we got up, crossed the river, and arrived at Sorel Monday afternoon (June 10th).   We brought near twelve hundred men back with our party.   Many are yet missing—one hundred and fifty or two hundred.   Some scattered ones are continually coming in, so that our loss will not be so great as was first imagined.

" Col. Wayne behaved exceedingly well, and showed himself the man of courage and the soldier.   Col. Allen exerted himself, and is a fine fellow.   Col. Maxwell was often in the midst of danger.   His own division was not present to support him.   He was also very useful in the retreat, after he joined Col. Wayne.   Lieut. Edie, of the York troops, I fear is killed.   He was a fine young fellow, and behaved bravely.   He approached the enemy's works without dismay several times, and remained in the swamp to the last. He was in the second engagement, where it is supposed he was killed. Ensign Hopes, of the same company was wounded near the breast-work, when I led up the reserve. I cannot give too much commendation of him. He showed the greatest courage after he had received several wounds in the arm. He stood his ground and animated his men. He nobly made good his retreat with me, through a swamp of near eighteen miles long. The ball has hurt the bone. Several of our men were killed—I apprehend between thirty and fifty. The rest missing, have been taken, quite worn out with fatigue and hunger.

" P. S. June 13. Last night, a sort of flag of truce came from the enemy. Gen Thompson, Col. Irvine (William), Dr. McKenzie, Lieutenants Edie, Currie, and Parson McCalla (of the First) are prisoners. They were taken up by some of the rascally Canadians, in the most treacherous manner."

On the 14th, Burgoyne reached the Sorel with a column of British troops, the rear of Gen. Sullivan's army having only left a few hours before. Gen. Philips, with the right column of the British, consisting of his division and the Brunswick troops, under Gen. Riedesel, passed on up the river St. Lawrence to Longueuil, twelve miles from Chambly, where they landed on the 16th, and pushed to La Prairie, to cut off Arnold, who was retreating from Montreal. It was at Varenne, on the south bank of the St. Lawrence, fourteen miles from Montreal, that Wilkinson met this force, detained at that point by a failure of the wind, at two o'clock P. M., and hastened back with the intelligence to Arnold, without which he had been cut off, as he did not intend leaving Montreal until the morning of the 16th.

Arnold immediately ordered Wilkinson to recross the river, and traverse the country by the direct route to Chambly, twelve miles, and report the situation in which he had discovered the enemy to Gen. Sullivan, and request a detachment to cover Gen. Arnold's retreat by La Prairie.

In his memoirs Wilkinson says:

" I did not make the opposite shore and Longueuil until it was dark.   I found a public horse at the parish priest's, mounted him, and arrived at Chambly about nine o'clock at night (15th).   Here the scene presented me can never be effaced.   The front of our retreating army, overwhelmed with fatigue, lay scattered in disorder over the plain, and buried in sleep, without a single sentinel to watch for its safety.   I rode through the encampment, entered the fort by the drawbridge, dismounted, and presented myself to Gen. Sullivan, without being halted or even hailed.   The general and his companions, Colonels St. Clair, Maxwell and Hazen, all appeared astonished at my information of the near approach of the enemy to Montreal.   Maxwell, in Scottish dialect, exclaimed, ' Be the Lard, it cannot be possible ! ' to which I emphatically retorted, ' Be the Lard, sir, you know not what you say ! ' Sullivan and St. Clair, who were both acquainted with me, interposed, and corrected Maxwell's indecorum.

" It was acknowledged on all hands, that a detachment was necessary to coöperate with Arnold; but how to effect it, under the actual circumstances of the moment, was a matter of much difficulty.   The night was profoundly dark; the rain poured down in torrents; the troops at hand were fatigued, and in great disorder, and there was no officer to receive and execute orders. After some deliberation it was determined that I should proceed down the Sorel with instructions to Brig. Gen., the Baron de Woedtke, who commanded the rear, to make a detachment of five hundred men, to cover Gen. Arnold's retreat. I was directed to keep the main road on the bank of the Sorel, which Col. Hazen informed me was quite plain and unobstructed; but he deceived me, and, owing to the darkness of the night, I presently missed my way, and narrowly escaped plunging into Little River, where it was twenty feet deep. After my escape, I dismounted, and, securing my horse, groped my way in the dark, until I discovered a bridge of batteaux formed for the passage of the infantry, on which I crossed.

"I found every house and hut on my route crowded with stragglers, men without officers, and officers without men. Wet to the skin, covered with mud, exhausted by hunger and fatigue, I threw myself down on the floor of a filthy cabin and slept until dawn; when I arose and prosecuted my search in quest of the Prussian baron. The first officer of my acquaintance whom I met, was Lieut. Col. William Allen, of the Second Penn'a, who, to my inquiry for De Woedtke, replied that ' he had no doubt the beast was drunk, and in front of the army.' I then informed him of my orders for a detachment. He replied ' this army, Wilkinson, is conquered by its fears, and I doubt whether you can draw any assistance from it; but Col. Wayne is in the rear, and if any one can do it, he is the man.' On which I quickened my pace, and half an hour after met that gallant soldier, as much at his ease as if he was marching to a parade of exercise. He confirmed Allen's report respecting De Woedtke, and, without hesitation, determined to carry the order into execution, if possible.   He halted at the bridge, and posted a guard, with orders to stop every man without regard to corps, who appeared to be active, alert, and equipped. In a short time, a detachment was completely formed, and in motion for Longueuil.   The very men who only the day before were retreating in confusion, before a division of the enemy, now marched with alacrity against his main body.

"We had gone two miles when we met an express from Arnold, with verbal information of his escape from Montreal, and that he would be able to make good his retreat by La Prairie.   This information brought Col. Wayne to the right about.   We crossed Little River at a ford, and found the rear of the army not yet up to Chambly.   Our detachment was discovered advancing on the bank of the Sorel, two miles below the fort; we were taken for the enemy, and great alarm and confusion ensued, the drums beat to arms, and Gen. Sullivan and his officers were observed making great exertions to prepare for battle.   Gen. Wayne halted his column, pulled out his glass, and seemed to enjoy the panic his appearance produced.   I suggested that he would interrupt the labors of the troops on the portage of Chambly, and delay the movements of the army; on which he ordered me forward to correct the delusion.

"I reported to Gen. Sullivan, who gave orders for Wayne to march by his right, and coöperate with Gen. Arnold, if necessary, but we soon discovered Arnold had passed, and the bridge of Little River on fire; we, therefore, turned to the left, and followed him to St. John's, where we arrived in the evening (16th), and found Gen. Sullivan with the front of the army."

The rear of the army, with baggage stores, reached St. John's on the 18th, were embarked and moved up the Sorel the same afternoon. After the last boat but Arnold's had put off, at Arnold's suggestion, he and Wilkinson went down the direct road to Chambly for two miles, where they met the advance of the British division, under Lieut. Gen. Burgoyne. They reconnoitred it a few minutes, then galloped back to St. John's and stripping their horses, shot them. Gen. Arnold then ordered all on board, pushed off the boat with his own hands, and thus indulged the vanity of being the last man who embarked from the shores of the enemy. They followed the army twelve miles, to the Isle Aux Noix, where they arrived after dark.

The head of Burgoyne's column entered St. John's on the evening of the 18th, and Philips' advance guard on the morning of the 19th. On the 19th, general orders at Isle Aux Noix directed the commands of de Haas, Wayne, St. Clair, and Irvine to encamp on the east side of the island.

On the 21st, Col. Irvine's battalion met with another heavy loss, as is detailed by a letter from one of the regiment:

" Capts. McClean, Adams, and Rippey, Lieuts. Mc-Ferran, McAllister, and Hoge, and Ensigns Lusk and Culbertson, with four privates, went over from the Isle Aux Noix to the western shore of the lake, about a mile from camp, but within sight, to fish and divert themselves. Capt. McClean prudently proposed to take arms with them, but was over-ruled. Some Indians observed their motions, and while they were at a house drinking some spruce beer, the savages surrounded them, killed Capt. Adams, Ensign Culbertson, and two privates, whom they scalped in a most inhuman and barbarous manner; and carried off prisoners, Capt. McClean, Lieuts. Ferran, McAllister, and Hoge, and the two other privates. But a party coming to their relief from camp, Capt. Rippey and Ensign Lusk made their escape." The bodies of those killed were brought to the Isle Aux Noix and decently buried by Col. Wayne, who, with a party, followed the Indians and recovered the batteaux with the bodies.

Isle Aux Noix proved very unhealthy; Col. Wayne had sixty men, out of one hundred and thirty-eight, taken down with sickness, after their arrival there; and on the 24th of June, Col. de Haas and all his field officers, with a number of his men, were sick. On the 25th, Gen. Sullivan commenced moving the army to Isle la Motte. Lieut. Col. Hartley, with two hundred and fifty men of Irvine's battalion, went by land, scouring the country, traversing disagreeable swamps, destroying, on the way, the house, mills, etc., of the traitor McDonald. On June 27th, at Isle la Motte, all the army took vessels, and came to Crown Point, which they reached on the 1st of July. Gen. Gates arrived there on the evening of the 5th, superseding Gen. Sullivan, and, on the 7th, at a council of war, it was determined to remove the army to Ticonderoga. The battalions of Cols. de Haas, St. Clair, and Wayne, arrived there on the 10th, the Sixth, under Lieut. Col. Hartley, remained posted at Crown Point, where, for the balance of the summer and fall, it was the sentinel regiment of Gen. Gates' army.

On January 24, 1777, the Second Battalion left Ticonderoga, with Gen. Wayne, for their homes. Many of the privates reënlisted in the Third Pennsylvania Regiment of the Continental Line.

FOURTH PENNSYLVANIA BATTALION.

In this regiment, besides various commissioned officers and privates, scattered throughout its companies, the company of Capt. Caleb North was largely Pennsylvania-German.

Its services· were the same as those of the Second Battalion.

SIXTH PENNSYLVANIA BATTALION.

This battalion contained but a small percentage of Pennsylvania-Germans scattered throughout its several companies, more especially in that of Capt. David Grier, of York County.

Its history was merged with that of the Second Battalion.

THIRD PENNSYLVANIA BATTALION.

The Third Battalion was recruited mainly from detached parties in different parts of the State, New Jersey, Delaware and Maryland. Its officers were, principally, Philadelphians, and so incomplete are its rolls that it is difficult to arrive at any reasonable conclusion as to the nationality of its members. The few records in existence indicate a fair percentage of Pennsylvania-Germans. It was associated, in service and misfortune, with the Fifth Battalion, under which head its history will be given in detail.

FIFTH PENNSYLVANIA BATTALION.

This battalion had, in its ranks, a large percentage of Pennsylvania-Germans.

Its Major was George Nagel, of Reading, Berks County, who commanded the company of " First Defenders " in Col. Thompson's Battalion.

The following companies were composed, almost entirely, of Pennsylvania-Germans:

Capt. John Spohn, Berks County.

Capt. Peter Decker, Berks County.

While these contained a large number of the same blood:

Capt. John Miller, Germantown.

Capt. Nathaniel Vansandt, Berks and Bucks Counties.

On June 11, 1776, Congress ordered this battalion, together with the Third, Col. Shee, to New York, which they reached by the 25th, and were placed under the command of Brig. Gen. Mifflin. Both battalions were then marched towards Kingsbridge, encamped upon the ground on which Fort Washington was erected, and immediately employed in the construction of that fortress, under the direction of Col. Rufus Putnam. They remained here, undisturbed, all summer, sickness prevailing, towards fall, to so great an extent that little more than half the men were fit for duty. On August 27, during the battle of Long Island, they were marched down to New York, reaching the city on the afternoon after the battle was over. On the 28th, early, they were transported to Long Island, marched down to the entrenchments at Brooklyn, and posted on the left, extending to the Wallabout. Here, annoyed by continual rains, and without tents, they lay upon their arms, keeping up incessant skirmishing with the British. After dark, on the 29th, with the Maryland battalion, they were detached to cover the retreat of the main army from the island.

Near daybreak of the 30th they received orders to retire, and had marched nearly half-way to the river, when they were informed that they had come off too soon, and were ordered to return to their post. This order was strictly complied with, and they remained more than an hour longer in the lines before the second order came to abandon them, when they retired under cover of a thick fog, and, between 6.00 and 7.00 A. M., perhaps a little later, landed at New York.   In less than an hour after, the fog having dispersed, the enemy could be seen on the shore they had left.

On August 31st, they marched beyond Kingsbridge, towards the Sound, and, crossing the Bronx, encamped about eighteen or twenty miles from the city.   After this post was sufficiently strengthened, the two battalions re-occupied their old ground at Fort Washington.

The main army remained on the heights of Harlem a period of five weeks, the Third and Fifth Battalions constituting a part of it and doing duty accordingly. The march of the main army towards White Plains commenced on the 20th of October.

On November 16, Fort Washington was invested by Gen. Howe's army and captured.   On that day the two battalions, with some broken companies of Atlee's, Kichlein's and other battalions, principally from Pennsylvania, and nearly all Pennsylvania-Germans, were posted in the lower lines south of the fort, or towards the city.   The superiority of the British force drove them all, finally, into the fort, which was surrendered the same day, and the Third and Fifth Battalions became prisoners, almost " in toto."   Capt. Miller, of the Fifth, was killed.

The returns of the battalion, made out the day before the surrender, show a total of 280, of which 78 were sick, but present, and 202 fit for duty.   Of these 43 were killed or escaped, and 237 were taken prisoners.

The men were retained prisoners until in January, 1777, their time having then expired.   Most of the officers did not secure their release for years afterwards.

The superior officers were to blame, apparently, in not withdrawing the troops from Fort Washington in time, being aware of the danger to which they were exposed. Beyond this, however, the capture of the fort was mainly owing to the treason of William Dement, or Demont, the adjutant of the Fifth Battalion. Graydon (captain in Third Battalion), in his memoirs says: "Howe must have had a perfect knowledge of the ground we occupied. This he might have acquired from hundreds in New York, but he might have been more thoroughly informed of everything desirable to be known from an officer of Magaw's battalion, who was intelligent in points of duty, and deserted to the enemy about a week before the assault."

Graydon's suspicions were confirmed, after the lapse of a century, by the publication of Demont's letter to the Rev. Dr. Peters, in an exhaustive article on "Mount Washington and its Capture," by E. F. De Lancey, in the "Magazine of American History," for February, 1877. It is as follows:

" Rev. Sir:

" Permit me to Trouble you with a Short recital of my Services in America, which I Presume may be deem'd among the most Singular of any that will go to Upper Canada. On the 2nd of Nov'r, 1776, I Sacrificed all I was Worth in the World, to the service of my King & Country, and joined the then Lord Percy, brought in with me the Plans of Fort Washington, by which Plans that Fortress was taken by his Majesty's Troops the 16th instant, Together with 2700 Prisoners and Stores & Ammunition to the amount of 1800 Pounds. At the same time, I may with Justice affirm from my knowledge of the Works, I saved the Lives of many of His Majesty's Subjects,—these Sir are facts well-known to every General Officer which was there—and I may with Truth Declare from that time I studied the Interests of my Country and neglected my own—or, in the language of Cardinal Woolsey, 'had I have Served my God as I have done my King he would not thus have Forsaken me.'"

. . . .

"Your most obedient and Most Hum'l Serv't
" Rev'd Sir with Dutiful Respect
" WILLIAM DEMONT "
" London, Jan'y 16, 1792."

MILES RIFLE REGIMENT.

The Pennsylvania Rifle Regiment of Col. Miles, and the Pennsylvania Battalion of Musketry, under Col. Atlee, were embodied strictly for the defense of the Province of Pennsylvania, by the prudent foresight of its House of Representatives, at the suggestion of the Committee of Safety.

On March 5, 1776, the House resolved to levy 1,500 men, officers included, to serve until January, 1778, and, on the 6th, decided that 1,000 of these levies should be riflemen, divided into two battalions of 500 each, the remainder to be a battalion of musketmen.

Nearly the whole of the rifle regiment was raised in about six weeks, and rendezvoused at Marcus Hook. It was made up, largely, of Pennsylvania-Germans. The following companies were nearly all such:

Capt. Lewis Farmer, from various counties, Capt. Henry Shade, Northampton County, First Battalion; Capt. Peter Grubb, Jr., Lancaster County, Capt. Henry

Christ, Jr., Berks County, Second Battalion; with a considerable number in nearly all the other companies.

On July 16, the regiment had marched to Amboy and joined Gen. Mercer. It was followed by Atlee's musketry battalion on the 21st.

On August 12 the three battalions were brigaded under the command of Lord Stirling.

Their gallant stand at the Battle of Long Island has already been given in full.

These three battalions were so broken up in this battle that they were consolidated into one regiment, by order of Gen. Washington, under command of Lieut. Col. Brodhead.

This consolidated regiment became " The Pennsylvania State Regiment of Foot."

On November 16, part of the musketry battalion was in Fort Washington and was captured. On the 22d, the regiment was in Hand's brigade at headquarters, now New Brunswick. It was engaged in the capture of the Hessians at Trenton, December 26, 1776; in the Battle of Princeton, January 3, 1777; lay part of the winter at Philadelphia, and moved down to Billingsport in March, 1777.

With the defeat on Long Island and the loss of New York, followed by the fall of Forts Washington and Lee, resistance, on the part of the colonies, seemed almost crushed out, and the future appeared dark indeed. Then came, with Trenton and Princeton, the unexpected ray of light which was but the forerunner of a more glorious dawn.

Confronted by a powerful and victorious army, Washington turned towards the Delaware as the Mecca of his hopes. He reached Trenton, with the main body of

WASHINGTON CROSSING THE DELAWARE PREVIOUS TO THE BATTLE OF TRENTON.

SAFE CONDUCT, ISSUED BY HESSIAN COMMANDER, SIGNED BY LIEUT. HINRICHS.
(Original in J. G. Rosengarten Collection.)

8

his army, on December 3, 1776, went to Princeton on the 6th, but, learning that the enemy was manœuvring to get in his rear, fell back to Trenton, and immediately began the passage of the river, a short distance below the present railroad bridge.   He crossed, in person, with the rear-guard, on Sunday morning, the 8th.   About eleven o'clock, the same morning, the British came marching down the river, expecting to cross also, but were disappointed to find no boats within reach, Washington having secured them all and carefully retained possession of them.   The two armies now faced each other, with Washington master of the situation.

The Rifle Regiment, under Lord Stirling, was stationed near Robert Thompson's mill, the commanding officer being quartered in Thompson's house, in the west room upstairs, still standing, and recently belonging to the estate of the late John T. Neely.   The regiment, under Major Eunion Williams, was almost naked, and their sufferings were intense.   The authorities failed to send them supplies, and the County Committee of Safety, in pity, gathered "old clothes" from the neighboring inhabitants, to aid in relieving their necessities.

Reinforcements, brought by Gates and Sullivan from New England and Virginia, raised the number of troops under Washington to 6,000, but, of these, only 2,400 men were strong enough for the march and assault which he had planned against his foe.

Active preparations were now made for this dangerous undertaking.   The most trusted battalions were selected, those from Pennsylvania, New England and Virginia, amongst them Lord Stirling's brigade.

Meanwhile, everything was pleasant and serene within the enemy's lines.   The Hessian officers, and their 1,200 men, had a very merry Christmas at Trenton. Col. Rahl, their commanding officer, with his boon companions, were invited to supper at the house of Abraham Hunt, a suspected tory, where cards and wine, with their accompanying hilarity, occupied the night. They dreamed of no surprise, deeming it impossible. Gen. Grant, at Princeton, had received some warnings of the fact, and so notified Rahl, but to these the infatuated officer paid no attention. It is even known that a Bucks County tory, at the risk of his life, crossed the river, carrying a note, giving all information on the subject, for the Hessian commander. With much difficulty he succeeded in placing it in his hands, only to see it thrust, unopened, into his pocket, where it was discovered the morning after his death.

On Christmas afternoon, at three o'clock, the troops left their quarters for the crossing. Their march was marked by the bloody foot-prints of the Pennsylvania-German riflemen in particular, as they trod the icy road with their nearly naked feet. The crossing was begun about sunset, and, with the river full of ice, was most difficult. Men were stationed in the bows of the boats, with boat-hooks, to keep off the floating cakes of ice, while the roar of the waters and crash of ice nearly drowned the words of command. It was three o'clock in the morning before the crossing was fully accomplished, and four o'clock before the troops were able to take up their line of march. Silence was enjoined upon all by their commander, who said, " I hope you will all fight like men." Two divisions were formed, the one led by Washington in person, who was accompanied by Lord Stirling, Greene, Mercer and Stephen, the other by Gen. Sullivan. That under Washington turned to the left, marched up

To his Excellency General Howe express
orders that no harm humane or else
to molest or injure John: Roberts ——
house or property —— By order of his Excellency
Head Quarters .... Donop ....
.... Heister
adjutant

SAFE CONDUCT, SIGNED BY COUNT DONOP AND ADJT. HEISTER.

the cross-road to the Bear Tavern, a mile from the river, turned into the Scotch, and then into the Pennington, road. In this division were the Pennsylvania-Germans. Sullivan marched by the river road.

The morning was bitter cold, and it began to hail as the troops started on their march. The snow and hail on the ground deadened the foot-falls of the men, as well as the noise of the artillery wheels. Fearing that the storm had rendered useless many of the muskets, Sullivan sent an aide to his chief to report and ask what was to be done, to whom Washington replied, " Tell your general to use the bayonet, and penetrate into the town; for the town must be taken, and I have resolved to take it."

Washington's column reached the enemy's outpost exactly at eight o'clock, and within three minutes he heard the firing of Sullivan's division. " Which way is the Hessian picket? " he inquired of a man chopping wood at his door, and the surly reply came back, " I don't know." " You may tell," said Capt. Forrest, of the artillery, " for that is General Washington." The aspect of the man changed in a moment. Dropping his axe, and raising his hands to heaven, he exclaimed, " God bless and prosper your Excellency! The picket is in that house, and the sentry stands near that tree there."

So silent was the march of the American troops that their presence was unnoticed until they approached the enemy's outpost, on the outskirts of the town. One of the sentries called out to David Lanning, of near Trenton, the guide, who was some little in advance of Washington's column, "Who is there?" Lanning replied, " A friend." " A friend to whom? " queried the sentry. "A friend to General Washington," was the answer, when the sentry fired and retreated.

As soon as the alarm was given, both divisions of the American army rushed into the town. The enemy made but a feeble resistance, and the fruit of the morning's work was nearly a thousand prisoners, the same number of arms, and several cannon.

The moral effect of this victory can hardly be realized, even now. It was simply tremendous. It infused new life into the cause and the country, and its quickening influence was felt from Massachusetts Bay to Georgia. It was really the turning point of the Revolution.

The army returned, with its prisoners, and recrossed the river at McKonkey's ferry. Washington then inaugurated the skillful campaign which followed, and which nearly relieved New Jersey of the enemy.

Cornwallis, on hearing of the American victory, gave up his visit to England and hastened towards Trenton, where Washington had again established his quarters, with even a larger, and certainly more hopeful, army than before. The terms of enlistment of a large number of men, amongst the Americans, expired with the year 1776, but they were induced to remain. The British commander, having reached Princeton, began his march on Trenton, January 2, 1777, with 8,000 of his best troops, which they reached late in the afternoon. Cornwallis was now determined to throw his entire force against Washington, crowd him to the bank of the Delaware, and capture his whole army. But his men were weary and it was evening so he decided to wait till the next morning. He retired in high spirits, saying, " At last we have run down the old fox, and will bag him in the morning." The fox, however, was too wily to be caught. Realizing his inferiority in numbers he decided not to risk a battle. Keeping his fires burning brightly all night, and a few men busily engaged in throwing up entrenchments within sound of the British, he silently removed his army, around the left wing of the enemy, to his rear, and, by daylight, was happily marching toward Princeton. As the army neared the town a detachment, under Gen. Mercer, encountered some 2,000 British, under Col. Mawhood, marching to join Cornwallis. An immediate conflict ensued. After a fierce volley, the British charged with the bayonet, which the Americans could not withstand and fled, leaving their gallant commander upon the field, mortally wounded.

As the enemy pursued the fugitives they came to the brow of a hill, where they met the main army, under Washington, hastening to the rescue. The battle became general but the foe was soon routed, and Cornwallis was amazed to discover, on the morning of January 3, that his prey had again escaped him. He broke camp and made a dash for Brunswick to save his stores collected there, while Washington moved northward to Morristown, and went into winter quarters in a strong position, having done a marvelous work for liberty, and achieved a most brilliant campaign, within the short period of three weeks.

From *The Phenix,* of March 24, 1832, published at Wellsborough, Pennsylvania, the following interesting personal narrative of Sergeant R—— is taken. His name is not given, nor his regiment, but he seems to have been under command of Gen. Mercer:

DIARY OF SERGEANT R—— AT PRINCETON.

" Three or four days after the victory at Trenton, the American army recrossed the Delaware into New Jersey. At this time our troops were in a destitute and deplorable condition.   The horses attached to our cannon were without shoes, and when passing over the ice they would slide in every direction, and could advance only by the assistance of the soldiers.   Our men too, were without shoes or other comfortable clothing; and as traces of our march towards Princeton, the ground was literally marked with the blood of the soldiers' feet.   Though my own feet did not bleed, they were so sore that their condition was little better.   While we were at Trenton, on the last of December, 1776, the time for which I and most of my regiment had enlisted expired.   At this trying time General Washington, having now but a little handful of men and many of them new recruits in which he could place but little confidence, ordered our regiment to be paraded, and personally addressed us, urging that we stay a month longer.   He alluded to our recent victory at Trenton; told us that our services were greatly needed, and that we could now do more for our country than we ever could at any future period; and in the most affectionate manner entreated us to stay.   The drums beat for volunteers, but not a man turned out.   The soldiers worn down with fatigue and privations, had their hearts fixed on home and the comforts of the domestic circle, and it was hard to forego the anticipated pleasures of the society of our dearest friends.

" The General wheeled his horse about, rode in front of the regiment, and addressing us again said: ' My brave fellows, you have done all I asked you to do, and more than could be reasonably expected; but your country is at stake, your wives, your houses, and all that you hold dear.   You have worn yourselves out with fatigues and hardships, but we know not how to spare you.   If you will consent to stay only one month longer, you will

SURRENDER OF COL. RAHL AFTER THE BATTLE OF TRENTON, DECEMBER 26, 1776.

THE PENNSYLVANIA-GERMAN SOCIETY.

render that service to the cause of liberty, and to your country, which you probably never can do under any other circumstances.   The present is emphatically the crisis, which is to decide our destiny.'   The drums beat the second time.   The soldiers felt the force of the appeal.   One said to another, ' I will remain if you will.' Others remarked, ' We cannot go home under such circumstances.'   A few stepped forth, and their example was immediately followed by nearly all who were fit for duty in the regiment, amounting to about two hundred volunteers [about half of these were killed in the battle of Princeton or died of the small-pox soon after.—Ed.]. An officer inquired of the General if these men should be enrolled.   He replied, ' No! men who will volunteer in such a case as this, need no enrolment to keep them to their duty.'

"When we were about commencing our march for Princeton, Lord Cornwallis left that place with the intention of attacking, and at one blow cutting off the rebel army.   He appeared near Wood creek or the Assanpink river, where a skirmish took place at the bridge over the creek.   The Hessians were placed in front of the British troops, and endeavored to force the bridge.   They retired, and we were left undisturbed for the night.

"Leaving our fires kindled to deceive the enemy, we decamped that night, and by a circuitous route took up our line of march for Princeton.   General Mercer commanded the front guard of which the two hundred volunteers composed a part.   About sunrise of the 3d January, 1777, reaching the summit of a hill near Princeton, we observed a light-horseman looking towards us, as we view an object when the sun shines directly in our faces.   Gen. Mercer observing him, gave orders to the riflemen who

were posted on the right, to pick him off.   Several made
ready, but at that instant he wheeled about, and was out
of their reach.   Soon after this as we were descending a
hill through an orchard, a party of the enemy who were
entrenched behind a bank and fence, rose and fired upon
us.   Their first shot passed over our heads cutting the
limbs of the trees under which we were marching.   At
this moment we were ordered to wheel.   As the platoon
which I commanded were obeying the order, the corporal who stood at my left shoulder, received a ball and
fell dead on the spot.   He seemed to bend forward to
receive the ball, which might otherwise have ended my
life.   We formed, advanced, and fired upon the enemy.
They retreated eight rods to their packs, which were laid
in a line.   I advanced to the fence on the opposite side
of the ditch which the enemy had just left, fell on one
knee and loaded my musket with ball and buckshot.   Our
fire was most destructive; their ranks grew thin and the
victory seemed nearly complete, when the British were
reinforced.   Many of our brave men had fallen, and we
were unable to withstand such superior numbers of fresh
troops.

"I soon heard Gen. Mercer command in a tone of distress, 'Retreat!'   He was mortally wounded and died
shortly after.   I looked about for the main body of the
army which I could not discover—discharged my musket
at part of the enemy, and ran for a piece of wood, at a
little distance where I thought I might shelter.   At this
moment Washington appeared in front of the American
army, riding towards those of us who were retreating, and
exclaimed, 'Parade with us, my brave fellows, there is
but a handful of the enemy, and we will have them directly.'   I immediately joined the main body, and marched
over the ground again.

" O, the barbarity of man! On our retreat, we had left a comrade of ours whose name was Loomis, from Lebanon, Ct., whose leg was broken by a musket ball, under a cart in a yard; but on our return he was dead, having received several wounds from a British bayonet. My old associates were scattered about groaning, dying

CONTINENTAL CURRENCY IN WHICH THE AMERICAN SOLDIERS WERE PAID.

and dead. One officer who was shot from his horse lay in a hollow place in the ground rolling and writhing in his blood, unconscious of anything around him. The ground was frozen and all the blood which was shed remained on the surface, which added to the horror of this scene of carnage.

" The British were unable to resist this attack, and retreated into the College, where they thought themselves safe. Our army was there in an instant, and cannon were planted before the door, and after two or three discharges, a white flag appeared at the window, and the British surrendered. They were a haughty, crabbed set of men, as they fully exhibited while prisoners, on their march to the country. In this battle, my pack, which was made fast by leather strings, was shot from my back, and with it went what little clothing I had. It was, however, soon replaced by one which had belonged to a British officer, and was well furnished. It was not mine long, for it was stolen shortly afterwards.

" Immediately after the battle an officer observing blood on my clothes said ' Sergeant R—— you are wounded?' I replied 'No,' as I never expected to be injured in battle. On examination I found the end of my forefinger gone, and bleeding profusely. When and how it happened I never knew; I found also bullet holes in the skirts of my coat, but, excepting the slight wound of my finger, was not injured.

" In this battle and that of Trenton, there was no ardent spirits in the army, and the excitement of rum had nothing to do in obtaining the victories. As I had tried powder and rum on Long Island to promote courage, and engaged here without it, I can say that I was none the less courageous here than there. The army retreated to Pluckemin mountains. The weather was extremely cold, and we suffered greatly from its severity. We stayed three or four days and then marched through New Jersey towards New York. The inhabitants manifested very different feelings towards us, from those exhibited a few weeks before, and were now ready to take arms against the British. At Morristown I was sick of the small-pox and many of our little army died there of that disease.

" Such were some of the hardships and self-denials en-

dured in securing the blessings now enjoyed by this free
and happy country. But the old soldiers have been
almost forgotten, until they have nearly all gone to their
graves. Many never received a cent of compensation
for some of the most trying services, as I am sure I never
did for the month for which I volunteered."

Atlee's Musketry Battalion.

The interesting record of this battalion at Long Island
has already been given. After that it was merged into
the Rifle Regiment, with its history.

A large number of its members were Pennsylvania-
Germans, including, almost in whole, the following companies, with a fair representation in others:

Capt. Thomas Herbert—Lancaster County.
Capt. Abraham De Huff—Lancaster County.

Pennsylvania State Regiment of Foot.

In April, 1777, the Pennsylvania State Regiment of
Foot was formed upon the remains of Miles' Rifle Regiment and Atlee's Musketry Battalion as a nucleus, and
supplied with field and staff officers. It, of course, contained many Pennsylvania-Germans.

On June 2, the regiment was stationed at Fort Mercer,
under Col. Bull. Col. Walter Stewart took command
on July 6, 1777, and commanded it at Brandywine and
Germantown, where its losses were sixteen killed and
missing, and twenty-two wounded.

Having been transferred by the State Assembly, on
June 10, 1777, from State control to that of the Continental Congress, by resolution of the latter body, November 12, 1777, Col. Stewart's regiment was annexed
to the Pennsylvania Line in Continental service, and
formed the Thirteenth Regiment.

CHAPTER VII.

The Pennsylvania Line.

ITH the expiration of the term of service of the Pennsylvania State Battalions, in January, 1777, a reorganization of the troops was made. Thirteen regiments of infantry, besides some small bodies of cavalry and artillery, were enlisted in Pennsylvania directly for the Continental service, for a period of "three years or the war." Many of the members of these new regiments had belonged to the old State battalions. They were all, at this time, in Washington's army, and formed what was known as "The Pennsylvania Line."

These troops were formed into two divisions, commanded, respectively, by Gen. Wayne and Lord Stirling, and were made up as follows:

Division of Brig. Gen. Anthony Wayne—Nov. 1, 1777.

First Brigade.

1st Pennsylvania Regiment—Col. James Chambers.
2d Pennsylvania Regiment—Col. Walter Stewart.

126

7th Pennsylvania Regiment—Lieut. Col. Morgan Connor.

10th Pennsylvania Regiment—Liet. Col. Adam Hubley.

Second Brigade.

4th Pennsylvania Regiment—Lieut. Col. William Butler.

5th Pennsylvania Regiment—Lieut. Col. Francis Johnston.

8th Pennsylvania Regiment—Col. Daniel Brodhead.

11th Pennsylvania Regiment—Col. Richard Humpton.

DIVISION OF GEN. LORD STIRLING—July 1, 1777.

Conway's (formerly Mifflin's) Brigade.

3d Pennsylvania Regiment—Col. Thomas Craig.

6th Pennsylvania Regiment—Lieut. Col. Henry Bicker.

9th Pennsylvania Regiment—Col. George Nagel.

12th Pennsylvania Regiment—Col. William Cooke.

De Borre's Brigade.

German Regiment—Col. Nicholas Haussegger.

WAYNE'S DIVISION—1778.

First Brigade—April 11, 1778.

1st Pennsylvania Regiment—Col. James Chambers.

2d Pennsylvania Regiment—Col. Henry Bicker.

7th Pennsylvania Regiment—Col. William Irvine.

10th Pennsylvania Regiment—Col. George Nagel.

Second Brigade—April 19, 1778.

4th Pennsylvania Regiment—Lieut. Col. William Butler.

5th Pennsylvania Regiment—Col. Francis Johnston.

8th Pennsylvania Regiment—Col. Daniel Brodhead.

11th Pennsylvania Regiment—Col. Richard Humpton.

First Brigade—*October 24, 1778.*

1st Pennsylvania Regiment—Col. James Chambers.
2d Pennsylvania Regiment—Col. Walter Stewart.
7th Pennsylvania Regiment—Col. William Irvine.
10th Pennsylvania Regiment—Col. Richard Humpton.

Second Brigade—*October 24, 1778.*

3d Pennsylvania Regiment—Col. Thomas Craig.
5th Pennsylvania Regiment—Col. Francis Johnston.
6th Pennsylvania Regiment—Lieut. Col. Josiah Harmar.
9th Pennsylvania Regiment—Col. Richard Butler.

MAJOR GENERAL ARTHUR ST. CLAIR'S DIVISION—October 15, 1779.

First Brigade—*Gen. Anthony Wayne.*

1st Pennsylvania Regiment—Col. James Chambers.
2d Pennsylvania Regiment—Col. Walter Stewart.
7th Pennsylvania Regiment—Lieut. Col. Morgan Connor.
10th Pennsylvania Regiment—Col. Richard Humpton.

Second Brigade—*Gen. William Irvine.*

3d Pennsylvania Regiment—Col. Thomas Craig.
5th Pennsylvania Regiment—Col. Francis Johnston.
6th Pennsylvania Regiment—Lieut. Col. Josiah Harmar.
9th Pennsylvania Regiment—Col. Richard Butler.

PENNSYLVANIA LINE (*Six Regiments*)—*January 17, 1781.*

1st Pennsylvania Regiment—Col. Daniel Brodhead.
2d Pennsylvania Regiment—Col. Walter Stewart.
3d Pennsylvania Regiment—Col. Thomas Craig.

4th Pennsylvania Regiment—Lieut. Col. William Butler.
5th Pennsylvania Regiment—Col. Richard Butler.
6th Pennsylvania Regiment—Col. Richard Humpton.

With the reorganization of the army, in 1777, a large number of new recruits were sent to it, which, added to the confusion of a formative period, made it, naturally, weak and unfit to operate, offensively, against a trained and seasoned foe. Washington's policy, therefore, was of a Fabian character. His success, at Trenton and Princeton, enabled him to assume an excellent defensive position on the high ground near Morristown, which he strengthened by entrenchments, and thus, on the right flank of his foe, prevented him from making any hostile movement looking to the capture of Philadelphia, while still permitting himself to so manœuvre as to intercept the British commander, should he endeavor to form a junction with Burgoyne up the Hudson river.

During the month of June, Washington's army was encamped at Middlebrook, near the Raritan, strongly entrenched. Various efforts were made by Sir William Howe to coax the Americans away from this admirable position into the open field, but without avail. Finally, despairing of success, he determined to approach Philadelphia by sea, and, accordingly, embarked his troops at Staten Island, immediately upon the evacuation of New York.

While there was much uncertainty as to the destination of the English, whether it was to reinforce Burgoyne or to capture Philadelphia, yet Washington felt assured that the latter was the case, and promptly sent Gen. Wayne to organize the Chester county militia, which were then placed under command of Gen. John Armstrong, a veteran of the French and Indian War.

9

On August 23 the American army marched through Philadelphia, and took post near Wilmington. While here a very thorough reconnoissance was made of the route by which the enemy was advancing, and it was finally decided to take post on the eastern side of the Brandywine, and there meet him in open battle.

In the formation of the army, at this engagement, the division of Wayne and artillery of Proctor (also from Pennsylvania), with the Third Virginia regiment, were posted on the left of the American line, on the east bank of the Brandywine. This creek was fordable in front of the position, at a place called Chad's Ford, and here Wayne's division was stationed, in the rear of a redoubt containing Proctor's artillery; Green's division was in the rear, and to the north of Wayne, acting as a reserve; Maxwell, with some light troops, was on the west side of the stream, to skirmish with the enemy as they advanced; the Pennsylvania militia guarded the fords below Chad's Ford; while above Chad's Ford were posted the divisions of Sullivan, Stirling and Stevens. On the 10th of September the British were a few miles west of Kennett Square, and every one realized that the conflict must take place the next day.

At daybreak Howe's army was in motion. Knyphausen, with from 7,000 to 10,000 men, marched through Kennett Square towards Chad's Ford, and another division, 7,000 strong, under Cornwallis, accompanied by Howe, took a road running to the north, and leading to Jefferi's Ford, to turn the right flank of the Americans, while Knyphausen engaged their attention at Chad's Ford.

While the fighting, between Maxwell and Knyphausen, at times became fierce, yet, by alternately advancing and retreating, the latter succeeded in preventing a general engagement which he was most desirous of avoiding.

In the meantime, rumors reached Washington of the British movements, in a despatch, received through Sullivan, from Lieut. Col. Ross, dated Great Valley Road, 11 a. m., giving minute information on the subject, and the American commander was just on the point of ordering forward his whole available force across Chad's Ford, to crush Knyphausen before the arrival of Cornwallis,

THE BRANDYWINE BATTLEGROUND, DELAWARE COUNTY, PENNA.
From an old print.

when another despatch was received from Sullivan to the effect that, during the morning, Major Spear, of the militia (no such officer has ever been located, notwithstanding many efforts to that end), had ridden over the road upon which Cornwallis was reported to be advancing without seeing any trace of the enemy, and the order was countermanded, Washington feeling assured that, in such case, the whole British force lay before him.

Greene, who had already crossed the stream, was recalled, and scouts sent out for additional information.   Before they had a chance to report, however, a man dashed up to where the general and his staff were stationed, and insisted upon speaking to Washington.   He told him that Cornwallis had turned his flank and was but two miles distant.

Sullivan was at once ordered to take his division, with those of Stirling and Stevens, and defend the right of the army, by taking position on the high ground to the west. It was half-past two when this order was received.   Cornwallis, from Osborn's Hill, watched Sullivan forming his men.   Taking a final glance at the Americans, and remarking, with an oath, as he closed his glass, "Those rebels form well," he ordered his men to advance.   It was a splendid sight as they gathered on the crest of Osborn's Hill and swept down the southern slope, their bright uniforms, and flashing arms, placing them in strong contrast with the Continental troops that stood on the opposite hill, awaiting their attack.   Of these, no two were dressed alike; the best wore hunting shirts, the others were almost naked.   Every variety of arms could be seen in a single company.   Their tactics were of the most primitive character.   They were unable to wheel by company, or by platoon, into line, and, to change position on the field, they were obliged to make a continuous countermarch; but Lafayette said they were bold and resolute.

The first shots were fired by the Americans from an orchard on the Jones property, at the corner of the Street Road and the road to the Birmingham Meeting House. It was not until the British reached the former that they returned the fire.   Then they sprang upon the bank at the side and fired at the Americans through the fence.

While Sullivan was attempting to close the distance between his divisions, the British were upon him. His troops, thrown into confusion, were swept past the Meeting House to the south. It was there Lafayette was wounded, while endeavoring to rally the men. Another stand was made but Sullivan was again obliged to fall back, fighting desperately. For fifty-one minutes the hill was disputed, almost muzzle to muzzle, and Conway, who had seen service in Europe, said he never before witnessed so close and severe a fire.

Washington heard the sound of battle drawing closer and closer to him, and understood too well what it meant. He ordered Greene to take the reserve and reinforce the right wing, while he, with a guide, mounted on the horse of one of his aids, rode in the direction of the firing. The guide's horse took all the fences as they were reached, but, the man said subsequently, that the head of Washington's horse was always at the flank of his own, and the words, "Push on, old man, push on!" were continually ringing in his ears.

Washington arrived as Sullivan was about retreating from his second position. Encouraging the troops, he sent back additional orders to Greene, who, with the brigades of Weedon and Muhlenberg, hurried to the scene of conflict. Weedon was ordered to form across a defile commanding the road over which the enemy was approaching. With the remaining forces he pressed on to hold Cornwallis in check while Sullivan's men passed to the rear. This he did and fell back slowly, followed by the enemy. As the latter reached the road commanded by Weedon, they received a withering fire which threw them into confusion. The position then taken by the Americans was stoutly disputed, the conduct of the brigades of Muhlenberg (Virginian) and Weedon (Virginian), and the regiments of Stevens and Walter Stewart (2d Pennsylvania), being especially brilliant. This last stand of the Americans was made near Dilworthtown, and when we recall that it took from half-past three o'clock until night-fall for the British to force them back this short distance, of less than two miles, some adequate idea may be formed of the desperate character of the fighting.

When Knyphausen heard that Cornwallis was engaged, he attempted to cross Chad's Ford and force the American left, but Wayne, although outnumbered three or four to one, held him back until the retreat of the right wing enabled Knyphausen to turn his flank, when he, too, was obliged to retire, doing so in good order. In the retreat one howitzer was left behind but, through the bravery of Col. Chambers (1st Pennsylvania), assisted by Capt.

Wappen von Ansbach.

Buchanan and Lieuts. Simpson and Douglass, it was recovered. Night finally ended the battle, and the Americans retreated to Chester, thence marching to their old camp near the Falls of the Schuylkill. The British loss, in killed, wounded and missing, is reported to have been about 600, that of the Americans 1,000.

At that time the battle was felt to be a humiliating defeat, and Washington was blamed for having undertaken it. Why, then, was it fought? Because the country demanded it, as an unreasoning public, in all future wars, have demanded advance movements at most inopportune times. The people were tired of a Fabian policy. Even John Adams wrote, on August 29, complaining that other commanders had been able to strike aggressive blows, and wondering why Washington did not act. He ended up by saying: " I am weary, I own, with so much insipidity. I am sick of Fabian systems in all quarters. The officers drink ' A long and moderate war,' by toast is ' A short and violent war.' " In the face of such sentiments, and with the capitol of the nation threatened, the Battle of Brandywine became a political necessity.

Instead of a totally routed and disorganized force, after the battle, as many suppose, Washington found it to be, in his own words, " in good spirits and nowise disheartened by the recent affair, which it seemed to consider as a check rather than a defeat." Under the conditions, he determined to make another effort to save Philadelphia, so he recrossed the Schuylkill at Conshohocken, with Wayne's division in the advance, found the enemy near Warren Tavern, about twenty-two miles from Philadelphia on the Lancaster road, and prepared to attack, but a deluge of rain separated the combatants. On the 19th, the Americans, save Wayne's and Smallwood's divisions, crossed to the east side of the river, at Parker's Ford (Lawrenceville), to intercept the British, but Sir William Howe, after having deceived his adversary by a feint, gained possession of an open road to Philadelphia, which he entered in all the panoply and pomp of war.

Meanwhile Wayne's division had been ordered to take post between Paoli and Warren Tavern (on the Lancaster road, about two miles apart), in order to attack the rearguard of the British, then encamped in the Great Valley

THE OLD MONUMENT AND ENCLOSURE MARKING THE BATTLEGROUND AT PAOLI, CHESTER COUNTY, PENNA.

between him and the Schuylkill, and, if possible, to capture the baggage train under its charge, as soon as it moved towards the river. Although the greatest secrecy was observed yet the position of his camp was betrayed to the English commander by tory spies, and, on the night of September 20, 1777, he was attacked by an overwhelming force of the very troops he was preparing to assail the next day, a force so large that two of the British regiments, of which it was composed, were not engaged in the horrible work in which the rest were so conspicuous, their services not being required. This was the affair known as the "*Paoli massacre.*"

There has been much common misapprehension with

regard to this fight, which has been termed a "massacre," under the supposition that the Americans were taken entirely by surprise. This was not the case. Alarmed, about eleven o'clock, by the firing of his pickets, Wayne immediately formed his division, and, when the British had approached within ten yards "a well-directed fire *mutually* took Place, followed by a charge of Bayonet—numbers fell on each side. We then drew off a little Distance and formed a Front to oppose to them. They did not think Prudent to push matters further. Part of the Division were a little scattered but are Collecting fast—We have saved all our Artillery, Ammunition & Stores except one or two waggons belonging to the Commissary Department—. . ."

The whole number of Wayne's detachment was about twelve hundred men, of whom but sixty-one were killed, so that, however bloody the fight, the term "massacre" is unquestionably a misnomer.

Wayne was so stung by the criticism passed upon him that he prompty asked for a court-martial which fully exonerated him from any negligence of duty.

Sir William Howe's army having reached Germantown, and Washington's army being encamped in the White-

GERMANTOWN.

marsh Valley, it was determined to attack the British as soon as practicable.

Having learned that Howe had despatched a considerable portion of his force to reduce the works on the Delaware at Billingsport, Mud Island and Red Bank, it was deemed a most opportune time to carry out the proposed plans, accordingly, on October 3, Washington moved his army, of about eleven thousand men, from his camp, between the Perkiomen and Skippack Creeks, towards the enemy's line at Germantown.

According to Washington's plan of the battle, Sullivan was to command the right wing, composed of his own division and that of Wayne, flanked by Conway's brigade. They were to march down the main road from Chestnut Hill to Germantown, sometimes called the Skippack Road. They were supported, on the right, by the Pennsylvania Militia, under Gen. Armstrong, who were to fall down the Manatawney road, by Van Deering's mill, and get upon the enemy's left and rear. On the left were the divisions of Greene and Stephen, flanked by McDougall's brigade, who were to enter, by taking a circuit by way of the Limekiln Road, at the Market House, and attack the enemy's right wing, while the militia of Maryland and New Jersey, under Generals Smallwood and Forman, were to march by the old York Road and fall upon the rear of their right. Lord Stirling, with the brigades of Nash and Maxwell, was to form a reserve corps. The official order further explains that "General McDougall is to attack the right wing of the enemy in front and rear; General Conway to attack the enemy's left flank, and General Armstrong to attack the left wing in flank and rear."

On the evening of October 3 the army left its encampment on Metuchen Hills, by the routes prescribed in the order of battle. It was a hard march in the darkness over rough roads, and, at daybreak of a dark, foggy morning, the right wing, with Washington, after such a halt as the time allowed, reached Chestnut Hill. As it descended into the valley, approaching Mount Airy, the sun rose, but soon buried itself in a bank of clouds. Conway's brigade led the column, with Sullivan's division following, and Wayne's in the rear of Sullivan's, the whole under Sullivan's command. Here one regiment from Conway's brigade, and one from the Maryland brigade, were advanced in front, and a detachment, under Captain Allen McLane, of Delaware, was sent forward to take the enemy's picket at Allen's house, on Mount

BIRTHPLACE AND HOME OF GENL. ANTHONY WAYNE, NEAR PAOLI, PENNA.
From an old print.

Airy. He fell upon and killed the double sentries with the loss of one man, but the alarm was given, and the outpost, after discharging their two six-pounders, fell back upon the battalion of light infantry that was already forming in line of battle upon the east of the road at Mount Pleasant. Conway thereupon formed his brigade to sustain the attacking regiments, while Sullivan drew up his own division on the right of the road, at Allen's Lane. For some minutes the ground was hotly contested, but the enemy at length gave way. Wayne's division, having by this time come up, Gen. Sullivan formed it upon the east of the road, and directed Conway to file off to the extreme right, sending also one regiment from Wayne's and one from his own division, with Moylan's regiment of light horse, to further protect his right flank. These dispositions made, he advanced his line, the light infantry leaving the field, and, with it, their encampment, but making "a stand at every fence, wall, and ditch they passed, which were numerous," the General explained, adding that "we were compelled to remove every fence as we passed, which delayed us much in the pursuit."

It was with peculiar spirit that Wayne's division advanced against the British light infantry, for it was that body which had made the cruel attack on the camp at Paoli, and Lieut. Hunter, writing a few days afterwards, says: "When the first shots were fired at our pickets, so much had we all Wayne's affair in our remembrance, that the battalion were out and under arms in a minute. At this time the day had just broke, but it was a very foggy morning, and so dark we could not see a hundred yards before us. Just as the battle had formed, the pickets came in and said the enemy were advancing in force. They had hardly joined the battalion when we heard a loud cry, 'Have at the bloodhounds! revenge Wayne's affair!' and they immediately fired a volley." Wayne himself gives a similar account, and writes: "Our people, remembering the action of the night of the 20th of September, near the Warren, pushed on with their bayonets, and took ample vengeance for that night's work. Our officers exerted themselves to save many of the poor wretches, but to little purpose; the rage and fury of the soldiers were not to be restrained for some time, at least not until great numbers of the enemy fell by their bayonets."

Sullivan continued his advance, having sent word back to Washington that he had engaged the enemy's left, and asking that Wayne be advanced against the right, seemingly not aware, in the fog, that Wayne was already moving forward.

The morning was very dark; the thick fog, rendered more dense by the smoke of cannon and musketry, ob-

THE CHEW HOUSE, GERMANTOWN.
From an old print.

scured everything, and it was impossible for the soldiers, marching over ground broken by roads and houses, to see clearly what was before them as they advanced upon the two sides of the town. Sullivan, however, pushed on past the present Washington Lane, and Wayne as far as the Green Tree Tavern. When Washington, who followed with the reserves, arrived at the top of the hill marking the entrance into the town, he found that Col. Musgrave, with six companies of the Fortieth Regiment, had boldly thrown himself into Chew's house, and, having barricaded the doors and windows, was prepared for a vigorous defense.

In the presence of the Commander-in-Chief a group of officers discussed the wisdom of disregarding this impudent obstacle and continuing the advance, but Gen. Knox, chief of artillery, was greatly opposed to such action, and his voice finally prevailed. The garrison was first summoned to surrender. Lieut. Col. Smith, a gallant young Virginia staff officer, volunteered to carry the flag of truce but was shot down as he advanced across the lawn. Gen. Maxwell, with his brigade and four pieces of artillery, was, thereupon, ordered to attack the house, resulting in an ineffectual siege, many brave individual actions, and much loss of life.

Gen. Greene, meanwhile, had made the circuit of the Limekiln Road, and, half an hour from the time of the attack on Mount Airy, had engaged the enemy's right. The first troops he encountered was the First Battalion of the Light Infantry. He formed his army in line, with Stephen's division upon the west of the road and his own division, composed of Muhlenberg's and Scott's brigades, under the immediate command of Gen. Muhlenberg, on the east, with McDougall's brigade on the extreme left flank.

The hilly character of the country, and the multitude of fences, with other obstructions, soon broke the line, and Woodford's brigade, whose brave commander was, at the time, lying ill of wounds received at Brandywine, bore away to the left, and, led by the sound of firing, pressed towards Germantown, quickening their pace as they advanced, and coming out opposite Chew's house. Here they halted and, while Maxwell was attacking on one side, they opened fire on the other. The remainder of Stephen's division, upon the retreat of the enemy, pushed on in a similar direction, and thus came upon the flank of Wayne's troops, already disturbed by the firing in their rear, and became entangled with them. Taking them for the enemy Wayne's men fell back two miles, in defiance of every exertion of their officers, before the mistake was discovered. This confusion ended the efforts of Sullivan's column upon the east side of the town.

Greene, with the remainder of his command, continued to advance, maintaining the line of battle, until, as Lieut. Col. Heath explains, "that the order was found impracticable, which, from the number of post and rail fences, thickets, and in short everything that could obstruct our march, threw us frequently into the greatest disorder."

The account of the movements of this wing of the army now becomes exceedingly obscure, and cannot be described with accuracy. Col. Walter Stewart writes: "I happened to be detached and fell on the left of the whole, when I engaged the Fifth and Thirty-eighth; they both ran lustily, and I took a little flush redoubt (at Luken's mill), with three pieces of cannon, from them. I had cursed hot work for it before they left them." Stewart then pushed forward to the Market House, where he found the Ninth Virginia Regiment, but became so closely engaged that he was unable to extricate himself, in the retreat which followed, and was taken prisoner, with his command, on Kelly's Hill.

By this time the American army, because of all the facts just stated, had become greatly disorganized, while, on the contrary, the British troops were reforming and getting into better shape. When, therefore, General Grey advanced to the attack the confused Americans were unable to resist him. General Agnew, following immediately after, increased the rout. Washington, seeing the failure of all his well-laid plans, was forced to order a retreat, and returned that night to Pennybacker's Mills, where the army resumed its camp.

The entire loss sustained by the combatants, in this engagement, was never accurately ascertained. According to the returns, collected afterwards by the Board of War, the casualties in Washington's army were thirty officers and one hundred and twenty-two men killed, one hundred and seventeen officers and four hundred and four men wounded, and about four hundred prisoners. Included in this last number were some fifty officers and Col. Matthew's regiment. The British loss was reported to be thirteen officers and fifty-eight men killed, and fifty-five officers and three hundred and ninety-five men wounded. An aggregate of 1,157, killed and wounded, out of the comparatively small forces engaged on either side shows that the Battle of Germantown was no child's play.

After the battle of Germantown the first subject to claim the attention of Washington was the strengthening of the posts at Billingsport, on the Jersey side of the Delaware, and of Forts Mifflin and Red Bank, on opposite sides of the river just above. This was done, but, while the importance of retaining these positions was fully realized, the Commander-in-Chief did not consider his force sufficiently strong to detach any portion of it for the relief of

WASHINGTON AND LAFAYETTE AT VALLEY FORGE WINTER OF 1777-78.

their garrisons. Thus, left to themselves, with the aid of the Pennsylvania navy they held out during more than six weeks, with a bravery as heroic as any displayed during the war, but the force of superior numbers gradually obliged them to abandon one post after the other until, on November 10, a combined attack, made by the English naval and land forces, so terrible in character and overwhelming in force, on Fort Mifflin, caused it to be evacuated, and the river lay open to the enemy.

On October 17, thirteen days after the battle at Germantown, the country was electrified by the surrender of

THE VALLEY FORGE HILLS, FROM THE WEST.
From an old print.

Burgoyne, and, on the 19th of December, Washington, with his half-clad army of 11,000 men, went into winter quarters at Valley Forge, where he could best watch and hold in check his foe.

The sad story of Valley Forge need not be told here. On reaching its bleak hills the soldiers found it shelterless, and, for two weeks, toiled in the bitter weather, building huts in which to spend the winter. Many were without blankets and were forced to sit by the fire all night to keep from freezing. Washington informed Congress, on December 23, that he had in camp 2,898 men "unfit for duty because they are barefoot, and otherwise naked." The rudely-built hospitals were soon crowded with the sick and dying. Some died for want of straw to make a bed on the frozen ground, others from want of sufficient nourishment. "The unfortunate soldiers were in want of everything," wrote Lafayette years afterwards; "they had neither coats, hats, shirts, nor shoes, their feet and legs froze till they became black, and it was often necessary to amputate them."

For whole days the army frequently remained without provision. Horses starved to death by the hundreds. The petty jealousies, which had sprung up in Congress amongst its members, because of sectional feeling, prevented them from being united on any one point save a greater jealousy of Washington and his army. In vain did he call on them to trust him; in vain did he urge them to let their patriotism embrace the whole country, instead of merely that small part which they represented individually; in vain did he plead for a properly organized army. They continued to adhere to their own selfish and imperfect plans. The consequence could be naught else than a poorly equipped, and worse managed, quartermaster and commissary department. Large quantities of material were allowed to go to waste within a short distance of thousands of naked and starving men.

With lack of food, and lack of clothing, came lack of health. Sickness and mortality spread through the quarters to an astonishing degree. The small-pox broke out. Notwithstanding the diligence and care of the physicians and surgeons the sick and dead list increased one third in the course of one week, and bade fair, with the inclement weather which was experienced, to grow in a much greater proportion.

Thus that long and drear winter was spent, and the fewness of the desertions, in that trying hour, attest the depths of the patriotism of those who won for us the independence of our country.

The Pennsylvania troops, under Conway, were stationed to the rear of Washington's headquarters in Pott's House, behind an abattis and between the brigades of Huntington (Connecticut) and Maxwell (New Jersey).

THE WASHINGTON HEADQUARTERS AT VALLEY FORGE.
From an old print.

Wayne's brigade lay in the advance of the right center, and Muhlenberg's Virginians at the corner of the entrenchments by the river, on the extreme left.

On the 4th of May, 1778, came the cheering news of the French alliance, which was gladly celebrated on the 6th. On May 18, Lafayette took post at Barren Hill, from which he escaped so brilliantly two days later.

On June 18, six brigades were put in motion, followed by the remainder of the troops on the 19th, when Valley Forge was left alone with its dead and their glory, and the army was on its march to Monmouth.

Early in June, 1778, it became apparent that the British were preparing to evacuate Philadelphia, as it was feared by them that a French fleet, in pursuance of the treaty of alliance made with France, February, 1778, would soon appear and blockade the English fleet in the Delaware.

On June 18 the enemy, 12,000 strong, left Philadelphia, crossed the Delaware, and took the route eastward across Jersey, followed by Washington, who crossed above Trenton on the 21st, and pursued on a parallel route. The Commander-in-Chief decided to attack, as soon as possible, at least the English rear-guard, by which the train of baggage, etc., was escorted. Fearing to delay longer, on the 27th Lafayette was directed to take five thousand troops, "picked and selected men," to attack the English rear so soon as it began to move the next morning. A considerable portion of this detachment was composed of Wayne's troops. Charles Lee, who had opposed this aggressive movement through fear of the vast superiority of the British troops, at first declined to command the detachment, but, shortly after, thinking better of this step, claimed to lead it, and was, unfortunately, permitted to do so. Lee's command marched about five miles in advance of the main army, his orders being to attack vigorously the rear-guard, and he was expressly told that he would be supported by the rest of the troops.

Having arrived within striking distance, near Freehold, Wayne was directed by Lee, the next morning, to take with him, from his division of about twelve hundred men, seven hundred, to lead the advance and attack the left rear of the English. He was told by Gen. Lee that he held the post of honor, and it soon turned out that he held, at least, the post of imminent danger. The enemy did not wait to be attacked, but a party of Simcoe's Rangers, or Dragoons (American Loyalists), charged upon a portion of Col. Richard Butler's Pennsylvania Regiment, of about two hundred men (9th Penn.). They were repulsed and driven back but could not be followed for want of cavalry.

While Wayne's force was thus engaged with Simcoe's Dragoons, the main English force, from having been on the defensive, now became the assailants. At first the force in front of Wayne was simply a covering party, supposed by him to have consisted of about two thousand men, but it rapidly increased in numbers. Wayne looked around for the reinforcements which had been promised him, but was surprised to find that the rest of Lee's command was in full retreat, leaving him to shift for himself, and placing him in great danger of being surrounded. With much difficulty he made his way through the swamp and the woods until he reached the parsonage, just in advance of the "Tennent Church," and on the southern side of the road leading to Freehold, where he found all the troops, which were to have supported him, falling back by Gen. Lee's orders. They were met by Washington, amazed at the retreat of the advance corps, and angry beyond restraint with Gen. Lee who had ordered it.

The enemy, whose whole force by this time had faced about, were in full pursuit, and the Commander-in-Chief had, it is said, but a quarter of an hour to make such disposition of his troops as would check them. Washington's presence and example at once stopped the retreat. Danger seemed to have aroused all his energies. With the true instinct of a great general he rallied his troops at once, directing Wayne, who was near him, to form two trusty regiments instantly and check the assault of the enemy, while he would hasten to the rear and bring forward the main portion of the army to support him.

The regiments, which were called upon at this critical moment—one of the most critical in the history of the Revolution—were those of Col. Walter Stewart, 13th Pennsylvania, Col. William Irvine, 7th Pennsylvania, and Col. Thomas Craig, 3d Pennsylvania, aided by a Maryland and a Virginia regiment. These held the advance post, the well-known orchard of Monmouth, until the reinforcements, which made up the second line, appeared.

There were hills on each side of this orchard, which were at once occupied by these reinforcements; that on the right was held by Greene, with Knox's artillery; that on the left by Stirling. The batteries on both these hills enfiladed the English army on the right and the left, while the withering fire of Wayne's command, in front, rendered further advance well-nigh impossible.

The British Grenadiers, with their left on Freehold and the Guards on their right, had driven Lee's advance to the position near the parsonage, which Wayne now occupied. Crossing a fence, in their front, they advanced to the attack of Wayne's position with dauntless courage, first on the right and then on the left, but were repulsed, in both cases, with great loss. Finally, the

Guards, officered by the sons of the noblest English families, who had, for more than eight months, given the tone to fashionable dissipation while Philadelphia was occupied by the British army, and had taught their admirers, among the ladies in that city, to look with contempt upon the brave yeomen who were suffering the pains of nakedness and hunger at Valley Forge, were, at last, to meet foemen worthy of their steel. Their commanding officer, Col. Monckton, the brother of Lord Galway, was fully convinced that the task assigned to this *corps d'élite* was one that would test, to the utmost, those soldierly qualities for which the grenadiers and guards had gained so great renown.

The Guards having been formed for a bayonet charge, their colonel made them a short speech, in which he urged them, by all the motives which appeal to a soldier's pride and his *esprit de corps,* to charge home. So near were they to the American line that, it is said, every word of his speech was heard there, and, probably, it did as much to inspire Wayne's men with courage and determination as it did those to whom it was addressed.

They then rushed on with a furious charge, hoping to drive their enemies back by the bayonet. Without waiting until they approached quite closely, they were met with a withering fire of musketry, which killed not only the colonel, who bravely led them on, but many of his officers. The column was driven back in the utmost confusion. How complete was this repulse is shown by the inability of the Guards to rescue from Wayne's men the lifeless body of their commander, although they made the most frantic efforts to recover it.

The battle raged for hours after this fruitless attempt to penetrate Wayne's column, and, at last, the enemy, finding that they could make no impression upon the American army, and utterly exhausted by the heat of the day, retired in confusion and with great loss.

The repulse of the bayonet charge of the British Guards and Grenadiers, forming the *élite* of their infantry, and regarded by their countrymen, ever since the days of Crécy and Agincourt, as the most formidable warriors in the world when armed with such a weapon, by a body of American yeomen, most of whom were Pennsylvanians, and not a few Pennsylvania-Germans, under a Pennsylvania general—men who were inferior in numbers and imperfect in discipline, who had just been rallied after an ignominious retreat—must be regarded, in the progress of the Revolution, as a prodigious historical event.

The only thing to mar the rejoicings of the day was the conduct of General Lee. He was brought before a court-martial and tried for both disobedience of orders and for misbehavior before the enemy in making an unnecessary retreat, being found guilty on both charges.

The duty of the army, for nearly eighteen months after the battle of Monmouth, consisted in ingloriously watching the enemy at New York, lest they should sally forth and make destructive raids in Jersey, or should attempt to recover possession of the Highlands of the Hudson.

To that end the American army was drawn up in the form of a segment of a circle. extending from Middle-brook, in New Jersey, to the Delaware on the south, and, on the north, to Long Island Sound.

The winter of 1778–79 was passed in camp at Middle-brook, where the Pennsylvania Line suffered almost beyond endurance, not only from a want of clothing and supplies of all kinds, but also from the payment of their wages in money of merely a nominal value.

BATTLE OF MONMOUTH, JUNE 28, 1778.

In June, 1779, Gen. Washington was extremely desirous of recapturing two forts,—one at Stony Point, on the western side of the Hudson River, and the other at Verplanck's Point, opposite on the eastern side—which guarded the approach to King's Ferry, and which the British had forced the Americans to evacuate on the first of June. The forts were regarded as important, not only because they commanded King's Ferry, the only convenient line of communication between the New England and the Middle Colonies, but also because, standing as they did at the southern extremity of the Highlands, they gave control, in the hands of the enemy, over West Point and its dependencies to the northward.

The fort at Stony Point was built on a rocky promontory, on the west side of the Hudson, about one hundred and fifty feet high. Three sides of this promontory were surrounded by water, and, on the fourth, a swamp or morass, which was not passable at high tide, separated it from the land. It was guarded by three redoubts, and protected by a double abattis of logs, which extended across the peninsula. The cannon were so arranged as to enfilade any approach to the inner works supposed to be practicable. It had a garrison of about five hundred men, under the command of Col. Johnston, who was regarded as a highly capable officer.

The troops selected for the storming of this apparently impregnable position were the men of the Light Infantry Corps, under command of Gen. Wayne, consisting, on July 1, 1779, of two regiments, or four battalions, supposed to form the pick of Washington's army. They were commanded, respectively, by Col. Richard Butler, the Pennsylvanian, whose coolness in action in many previous severe engagements, especially in Morgan's

Rifle Regiment, fitted him for any emergency, by Cols. Putnam and Meigs, of Connecticut, and Col. Christian Febiger, of Virginia, the latter a Dane by birth.

The plan of attack, outlined by Washington himself, is shown in the following letter, of July 10, from the Commander-in-Chief to Wayne. With but a slight modification, made necessary during the assault, this plan was fully carried out:

"My ideas of the enterprise in contemplation are these:

"That it should be attempted by the Light Infantry *only,* which should march under cover of the night, and with the utmost secrecy, to the enemy's lines, securing every person they find to prevent discovery.

"*Between one & two hundred chosen men & officers* I conceive fully sufficient for the surprise, and apprehend that the approach should be along the water on the south side, crossing the beach and entering at the abattis.

"This party is to be preceded by a van guard of prudent and determined men well commanded, who are to remove obstructions, secure the sentries and drive in the guard. They are to advance (the whole of them) with fixed bayonets and muskets unloaded. The officers commanding them are to know precisely what batteries or particular parts of the line they are respectively to possess so that confusion & the consequences of indecision may be avoided.

"These parties should be followed by the main body at a small distance for the purpose of support. . . . Other parties may advance to the works by the way of the causeway & the River on the north if practicable, as well for the purpose of distracting the enemy in their defense as to cut off their retreat. . . .

"If success should attend the enterprise measures

should be taken to prevent the retreat of the garrison by water, or to annoy them as much as possible should they attempt it. The guns should be immediately turned against the shipping and Verplanck's point, and covered, if possible, from the enemy's fire.

" Secrecy is so much more essential to these kind of enterprises than numbers, that I should not think it advisable to employ any other than light troops. If a surprise takes place they are fully equal to the business, if it does not numbers will avail little."

Wayne promptly made his arrangements. His " order of battle " directs the regiments to move forward in absolute silence; no one, on any pretense, to leave the ranks (to preserve secrecy), on penalty of being at once put to death by the officer in charge. That this was no vain threat is evidenced by the fact that one unfortunate soldier did step out of ranks, to load his musket, and was at once run through by one of the officers. Arrived at the foot of the hill, Col. Febiger was to form his regiment in a solid column of half-platoon front, Col. Meig's to follow immediately after Febiger, and Major—afterwards General—Hull (in the absence of Col. Putnam, on duty at Constitution Island), in the rear of Meigs. These were to form the right column of attack. The left column was formed in the same way, under Col. Richard Butler, with Major Murfrees, of North Carolina, in the rear.

Each column was to be preceded by a detachment of one hundred and fifty " picked and determined men," that on the right to be commanded by Col. Fleury (a French officer who had done much gallant service during the war), that on the left by Major Jack Stevens, of Maryland. Each was to send forward, on his march, an officer and twenty men, a little in advance, whose business it should be to secure the sentries and remove the abattis and obstruction for the column to pass through. These parties of twenty men were the "forlorn hope," and were led, respectively, by Lieut. Knox, of the Ninth Pennsylvania, on the right, and Lieut. Gibbons, of the Sixth Pennsylvania, on the left. As the left column reached a certain point Murfrees was to separate from it, and open a furious fire on the front of the works, in order to draw the attention of the enemy from the flanking column. The right and left columns were to capture the outlying pickets, and, attacking the defenders, force their way over and around the abattis, and enter the interior of the fort by the sally-port, driving the enemy before them.

Gen. Muhlenberg was placed in reserve. With regard to him, Wayne reports: " Previous to my marching I had drawn General Muhlenberg into my rear, who, with three hundred men of his brigade, took post on the opposite side of the marsh, and was to be in readiness either to support me, or cover a retreat in case of accident; and I have not the least doubt of his faithfully and effectually executing either, had there been an occasion for it." To the reserves was also added Major Henry Lee's battalion of light horse, and Col. Ball's regiment of infantry.

At 11.30 P. M., on July 15, the formation being completed, the word to advance was given. The right column diverged to the south for the purpose of passing the swamp and reaching the beach at the foot of the hill, and, at the same time, the left, under Col. Butler, crossed the creek for the purpose of seizing the post of a picket of the enemy and assaulting the right flank of the fortification. Major Murfrees, between these two columns, advanced up the slope. The right, or column led by Wayne in person, was obliged, in order to reach the abattis, to wade through water two feet deep, and this somewhat delayed the movement. Meantime, Murfrees began, as a feint, a tremendous firing of musketry. This, of course, aroused the garrison, who, in a very short time, were at their stations, striving to repel the assault with grape and musketry. This was the crisis of danger for the assailants. The forlorn hope of each column rushed forward to perform the duty assigned it, that of cutting away the abattis and removing the obstruction which stood in the way of the advance of their comrades. So fierce and terrible was the fight at this point that, of the twenty men detailed for this service on the left, under Lieut. Gibbons, seventeen were killed or wounded in the assault, and yet, it is worthy of remark, that, so many had volunteered for this dangerous duty, it became necessary to select their numbers by lot.

The double row of abattis on the right seems to have been more readily disposed of than that on the left, where, as we have seen, resistance was overcome only after a terrible slaughter.

The first abattis was turned by the column of Col. Febiger moving along the beach, under the immediate direction of Gen. Wayne, "spear in hand." Just as the column had climbed over this obstruction a musket shot, coming from a body of men on the hill above, who were taunting the assailants and shouting imprecations on "the rebels" as they advanced, struck Wayne and inflicted a scalp wound about two inches long. He immediately fell, and was for a short time dazed and stunned. Quickly recovering his senses, however, he raised himself on one knee and shouted, "Forward, my brave fel-

lows, forward!" and then, turning to his aides, Capts.
Fishbourne and Archer, he begged them to carry him to
the interior of the fort, where he wished to die should his
wound prove fatal. The men, hearing that their commander had been mortally wounded, dashed forward,
climbing the rocks with bayonets ready to charge, and bore
down all further opposition.

Col. Fleury, who led the right column, soon reached
the flag-staff on the bastion and hauled down the English
standard. He was the first to enter the fort, being
quickly followed by two sergeants of the Virginia and one
of the Pennsylvania regiments, all of whom had been
severely wounded.

So accurately had the movements for storming the
works been timed, and so perfectly had the plans and
orders been carried out, that both columns of assault, as
well as Major Murfree's two companies, met almost at the
same time in the interior of the fort. They encountered,
as they advanced, a persistent fire of grape and musketry.
Not a shot was fired by the assailants (except Murfree's
command, as noticed). All those killed by the Americans, and they amounted to sixty-three (the same number
as had been killed by General Grey at the so-called Paoli
massacre), were dispatched by the bayonet. As soon as
the attacking columns met each other in the fort, Col.
Fleury, feeling that the resistance was at an end, shouted in
broken English, "The fort is ours!" the watchword
previously agreed upon.

The triumphant shout of the advancing party was
taken up by the troops as they rushed on, crushing all
hope of resistance on the part of the garrison. With
this shout were mingled the cries of the soldiers, especially
of the New York Loyalists, who, a short half-hour

before, had defied their assailants to come on, "Mercy, dear Americans, mercy!" Although no such cry had been heeded at Paoli, Wayne made use of his returning strength to stay the arm of vengeance as soon as resistance had ceased, and, it is said, not a man was killed who begged for quarter.

Two flags and two standards were captured, the latter those of the Seventeenth Regiment. The total number of prisoners taken was five hundred and forty-three. The British lost sixty-three killed, the number of their wounded is not given. The American loss was fifteen non-commissioned officers and privates killed, and eighty-three officers and privates wounded.

The successful assault on Stony Point made a prodigious sensation throughout the country. The immediate material gain was slight, as the post was abandoned not long after, but its moral effect, in strengthening the tone of public feeling and the army, was incalculable.

The campaign of 1780 began under conditions even more gloomy and discouraging than that of 1779. The Pennsylvania troops had dwindled away in the most extraordinary manner. By the monthly returns of September, 1780, there were present, in the eleven regiments of foot, two thousand and five, and absent two thousand, five hundred and eleven; in other words, more than half of their strength was not present with the colors, and those who were present formed about two thirds of Washington's army. This condition was mainly owing to the financial poverty of the authorities, which prevented them from paying the troops, clothing them decently, or even feeding them properly.

With this small force Washington was obliged to

march and countermarch between Morristown and West
Point, so as to meet any assault which might be made
by the British at New York, on any point of this long line.

It was determined, during the summer, to capture a

WASHINGTON'S HEADQUARTERS, MORRISTOWN.

block-house behind Bergen Heights, which had been made
a place of deposit, by the armed refugees, of stolen horses
and other property, the spoils of the neighborhood.
Wayne, with the First and Second Pennsylvania Brigades,
and four pieces of artillery, was sent to attack it.

The following account of this expedition is given, in
his letter to President Reed:

"TATOWAY, 26th July, 1780.

"*Dear Sir:*

"You have undoubtedly heard of our *tour* to Bergen
but it is a duty which I owe to you, the troops I command
& to myself, to make you acquainted with the Objects of
that expedition—lest envy, Malice, or the tongue of

Slander, should attempt to misrepresent that affair—One was to take all the stock out of Bergen Neck, to prevent the Enemy from receiving constant supplies from the Inhabitants out of that Quarter—and in Case of a siege to secure to our own use those Cattle that they would Inevitably carry into New York. Another was the destruction of a post near Bulls ferry—consisting of a Block House surrounded by a strong stockade and Abbattis, Garrisoned by the Refugees & a wretched banditti of Robbers, horse thieves, &c—

"But the Grand Object was to draw the Army which S'r Henry Clinton brought from Charlestown into an Action in ye Defiles of the Mountain in the Vicinity of Fort Lee, where we expected them to Land in order to succour the Refugee post, or to endeavor to cut off our retreat to the Liberty pole & New Bridge; the apparent object to them was great, and the *lure* had like to take the wished effect—three thousand men Consisting of the flower of the British Army were embarked from Phillips—and stood down the river hovering off the land'g near Fort Lee—where the 6th & 7th Penn'a Regiments lay concealed with directions to let them land unmolested (giving me Intelligence of the attempt) & then to meet them in the Gorge of the Defile and with the point of the Bayonet to dispute the pass at every expense of Blood, until the arrival of the first & second Penn'a Brigades when we should put them between three such forces as no human fortitude could withstand—and I may now with safety mention, that it was also designed to divert their attention from a meditated attempt upon Rhode Island, by a Combined attack by Land and Water on the French fleet & Army in that Place; this has had the effect, by retarding them four days after they had actually em-

11

barked upwards of six thousand men for that purpose, it will therefore be too late to attempt anything at this period as the French will be prepared against it. . . ."

The enemy, not discerning the real object of the movement, most annoyingly asserted that the Americans had been repulsed from the block-house by a small garrison composed of Tory refugees only, and, in some scurrilous verses, called "The Cow Chase," which were widely distributed, and had been written by the unfortunate Major André a short time before his capture and execution, the exploits of Wayne, and the other American officers, are ridiculed with a kind of pitying contempt which is very noteworthy. "The Cow Chase" closes with this significant verse, significant indeed when we recall the sad fate of the author:

> "And now I've closed my epic strain,
>   I tremble as I shew it,
> Lest this same warrior-driver, Wayne,
>   Should ever catch the poet."

The gloomy campaign of 1780 was made still more gloomy, at its close, by the memorable treason of Arnold, in September of that year. The details of this attempt (which had so well-nigh succeeded) to betray the garrison at West Point, and its dependencies, into the hands of the enemy, are too well known to need recapitulation.

The part taken by Gen. Wayne, and the Pennsylvania Line, in defeating this treasonable scheme, however, is not so well known, and some account of it may well be in order.

His division was then stationed near Haverstraw, and, in those days when there seemed a disposition to suspect the loyalty of everyone, and when even Arnold could prove a traitor, it is satisfactory to find that implicit trust was placed not only in Wayne but in the men who commanded his regiments,—Chambers, Walter Stewart, Craig, W. Butler, Harmar, Richard Butler, with true and staunch Gen. William Irvine at their head. On their arrival at West Point, "having marched over the mountains sixteen miles in four hours without losing a man," they were placed by General Washington in charge of the post, he being well assured that they would prove its most trustworthy safeguard amidst the threatening dangers by which it was surrounded. The choice of the Pennsylvania regiments for such a duty, at such a time, has a significance which was very apparent at that crisis, but which has been singularly overlooked by historians.

Towards the close of the year a growing feeling of discontent arose in the Pennsylvania Line, owing to three causes. They were, first, the non-payment of the men, or, rather, their payment in a nominal currency far depreciated beyond what they had agreed to receive; second, an insufficient supply of provisions and clothing, with its accompanying suffering; and, thirdly, the conviction that it was the intention of the authorities to hold all those soldiers, who had enlisted for "three years or the war," for the latter period.

It is not to any sufficient extent within our province to discuss, in detail, the events which led to the unhappy occurrence, between nine and ten o'clock on the evening of January 1, 1781, called "The Revolt of the Pennsylvania Line," when, with but few exceptions, the men rushed from their huts, paraded under arms without their officers, supplied themselves with ammunition and provisions, seized six pieces of artillery, took the horses from the general's stables, and killed or wounded many officers who attempted to suppress the uprising. Wrong as was their action, we must recall the sufferings of these brave men and their many just complaints which they had to offer.

Suffice it to say that, through the efforts of Gen. Wayne and others, peace was finally restored, many wrongs were righted by the authorities, and the men once more returned to their allegiance.

The British, misunderstanding the motives which prompted the revolt, promptly undertook to induce the insurgents to join them, offering many inducements to that end, but, to the lasting honor of Pennsylvania soldiery, these offers were promptly spurned and the bearers of the proposals arrested as spies, to be turned over to Wayne.

The Pennsylvania Line was almost wholly dissolved by the revolt, and it was a long time before the people recovered from the panic produced by it. Finally, measures were taken to recruit the regiments and reorganize the division. It was decided to reduce the number of regiments to six. Of the men who were retained many were veterans, having served continuously for five years. No greater proof could be given of their confidence in Wayne, and their officers, than that shown by the eagerness with which the old soldiers pressed forward to serve again under him. There seems to have been no effort made to exclude the former mutineers from reënlistment. Two thirds of those whose time had expired, and who had been discharged, were desirous of reëntering the service under Wayne's command, and, in his own language, "were as importunate for service as they had been for their discharge." The trouble was not with the service, nor with the officers, but with the broken promises of the State and of Congress with regard to their pay and clothing.

On February 26, 1781, Wayne was ordered to command a detachment of the Pennsylvania Line, which it had been determined to send as a reinforcement to Gen. Green, then in charge of military affairs in South Caro-

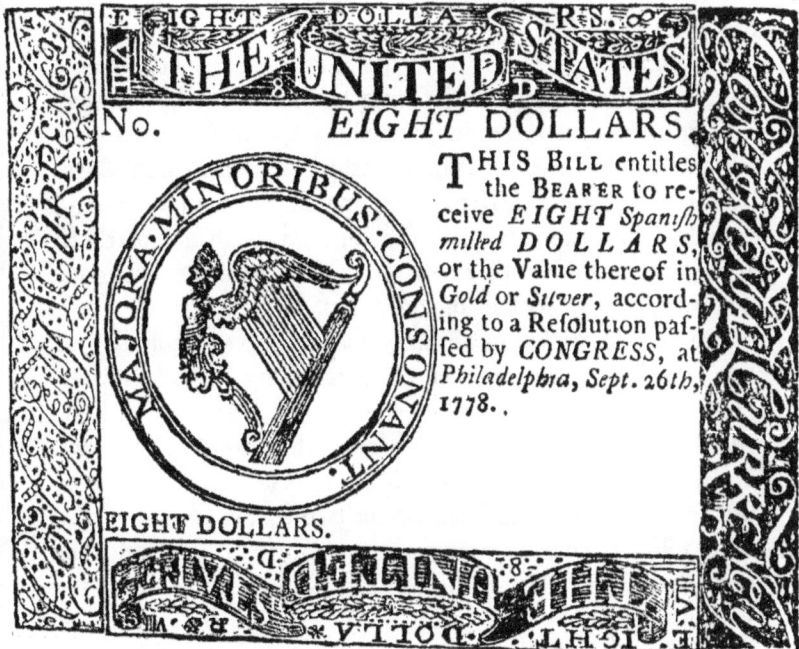

EIGHT DOLLARS

THE UNITED STATES

No.

EIGHT DOLLARS.

THIS BILL entitles the BEARER to receive *EIGHT Spanish milled* DOLLARS, or the Value thereof in *Gold* or *Silver*, according to a Refolution paffed by *CONGRESS*, at *Philadelphia, Sept. 26th,* 1778.

MAJORA·MINORIBUS·CONSONANT

EIGHT DOLLARS.

CONTINENTAL CURRENCY, WHICH WAS CHIEFLY RESPONSIBLE FOR THE REVOLT OF THE PENNSYLVANIA LINE.

lina. The detachment was to consist of details from each of the six regiments, in number about eight hundred, and the rendezvous and headquarters were established at York, Pa. It was only with much difficulty that this body could be so organized and equipped as to enable it to march southward, from York, on May 20.

Wayne joined La Fayette, on June 7, at Fredericksburg, where he formed his men into two battalions, the first commanded by Walter Stewart, the second by Richard Butler. These battalions, with one from Virginia under Col. Gaskin, formed a brigade, and acted as such, under Wayne's command, until the surrender of Yorktown.

During the autumn of 1781 La Fayette and Wayne were busily engaged in checking the raids of the English detachments sent into the interior, and also preventing the retreat of Cornwallis from Portsmouth into North Carolina, it being essential that the British commander should be held where he was until Washington, with his northern army, could join with the French fleet in completing his discomfiture by blockading his army.

This mode of campaigning was most wearisome. At last, on July 6, it seemed as if the long-looked for opportunity of attacking the enemy to advantage had arrived. Cornwallis, moving down the James River, on his way to Portsmouth, sent a portion of his force across the river, thus cutting his army in two by a wide river, and giving his adversary a favorable chance of attacking the rear, as it remained on the left bank and north side of the James.

La Fayette directed Wayne to move forward at once and attack that portion of the force which had not yet crossed. Upon arriving at Green Spring, near the enemy, Wayne discovered that the intelligence, that any considerable portion of the army had passed the river, was false. He and La Fayette, leading the advance, in order to make a more complete reconnoissance, had crossed a swamp by a causeway, with a force of about eight hundred men, before they ascertained that they had a large portion of Cornwallis' army in their front, and they soon found this force formed in battle array.

La Fayette at once sent back to the main American army, a distance of five miles, for reinforcements, ordering those left behind to join them with all speed. "Meanwhile," says Wayne, "the riflemen in the advance commenced and kept up a galling fire upon the enemy, which continued until five in the afternoon, when the British began to move forward in column, upon which Major Galvan (a French officer in the continental service) attacked them, and, after a spirited, though unequal contest, retired upon our left. A detachment of light infantry, under Major Willis, having arrived, also commenced a severe fire upon the enemy, but it was obliged to fall back. The enemy, observing our small force, began to turn our flanks—a manœuvre in which had they persevered they must have inevitably surrounded our advanced corps, and taken position between this corps and the other portion of the army, comprising the reinforcement about to join them. At this crisis Colonel Harmar and Major Edwards, with part of the 2d and 3d Penn'a regiments under Colonel Humpton, with one field piece, having joined, it was determined, among a choice of difficulties, to advance and charge the British line, although it numbered more than five times our force."

In other words, Wayne, perceiving that he was confronted by the entire force of the enemy, whose lines overlapped and endangered his flanks, decided instantly that the proper move to make was a vigorous charge. A sudden retreat might have ended in a panic. To await the shock of the approaching army might be ruinous. "With the instinct of a leader and the courage of a lion," says Professor Johnston, "he determined to become the assailant—to advance and charge."

Within seventy yards of the enemy, and for fifteen

minutes, a sharp action took place.   All the horses of the
American artillery were either killed or disabled.   In
danger of being outflanked all the time, the Pennsylvania
Line was steady, and retreated through the woods and
across the swamp to Green Spring, where it reformed.
It is worthy of note, in this connection, to say that Wayne
was materially aided, in his efforts to extricate himself, by
the timely arrival and assistance of Gen. Muhlenberg,
who, without orders, advanced his brigade to the support
of his brother officer.

After the engagement at Green Spring Cornwallis retired to Portsmouth, on the south side of the James, and
began to fortify himself there.   Shortly after, in accordance with instructions received from Sir Henry Clinton,
but contrary to his own judgment, he took position at
Yorktown, which he fortified.

On September 26, Washington's army, with the French
auxiliaries, under Rochambeau, reached Williamsburg,
where the officers of each army vied in their efforts to
entertain, worthily, those of the other.

On October 19, 1781, came the surrender of Cornwallis, and, with it, the beginning of the end.

There was nothing especially noteworthy in the part
taken by the Pennsylvania Line, under Wayne, at Yorktown.   His brigade formed a portion of the division
under Von Steuben.   The third battalion of Pennsylvanians, under Col. Craig, arrived too late to take part in
the siege, as did also Gen. St. Clair.   The storming and
capture of the two redoubts, the only operation attended
with serious danger, was not assigned to the Pennsylvanians, although two of their battalions supported the
attack.

Even though the Pennsylvania Line were not so fortunate as to be selected to lead the storming party on that occasion, the honor was accorded to Gen. Muhlenberg, a son of Pennsylvania, and a Pennsylvania-German, who had immediate command of it, and whose brigade composed it.

With the surrender of Cornwallis the main service of the Pennsylvania regular troops came to a practical end, save for Wayne's expedition down south, which hardly needs any extended description.

These services have been presented in the form of a continuous narrative, as in no other way is it possible for the student of history to get any adequate idea of the operations of the Pennsylvanians. Having before us the record, as a whole, it remains to consider the connection of each regiment, as a unit, with it, and, especially, to decide as to the part our Pennsylvania-German ancestors had in these trying but glorious deeds.

This latter is a matter of exceeding difficulty, so much so as to make it almost an impossibility. With the reorganization of the army, from July 1, 1776, to January 1, 1777, when the State Battalions went out of service and the Continental regiments came in, or, rather, when the former were largely merged into the latter, much of the identity of the several county organizations became lost. Men, formerly in the same company, reënlisted into different organizations, officers became scattered, and still more scattered, as the war progressed. The Pennsylvania-German, instead of being, frequently, a separate and distinct factor, to be found in certain battalions, was now spread throughout the whole, and, as a consequence, not easily defined as to his nationality.

Added to this, we are confronted with very incomplete and exceedingly meager company and regimental records,

as regards most of the Pennsylvania Continentals.   The
writer, after no little research, no slight advantages, and
no ignorance, at least, of the subject, has been unable
to find, anywhere, such data as would enable him to furnish
the full account of the Pennsylvania-Germans, who formed
the component parts of the several Pennsylvania Continental regiments, which he would like to here give.   He
does not believe it will ever be furnished, or that the data
are in existence which will enable any one to furnish it at
any future time.

The only manner in which the subject can be at all
treated is to take each regiment separately, to consider
which battalion of the preceding State troops was its
nucleus at the time of reorganization, to scan its available
rolls, and, from these, to adduce the probable membership
of Pennsylvania-Germans in its ranks.   This plan will be
followed.   With the aid of a few comments the reader
will then be in a position to study, by consulting the narrative just ended, the part taken by each command in the
general operations.   As time passes by items and records
may be brought to light, here and there, which, joined
to this necessarily incomplete account, will tend to add to
the grandeur of the structure even though it should never
become complete.

CHAPTER VIII.

FIRST PENNSYLVANIA REGIMENT.

Wappen von Braunschweig.

T HIS regiment was made up from the reënlistment of Col. William Thompson's gallant "First Defenders," the Pennsylvania Battalion of Riflemen, who, upon the expiration of their term of service, June 30, 1776, reënlisted into the Continental service as the First Pennsylvania Regiment. The following companies contained many Pennsylvania-Germans: Captain James Ross; Captain Charles Craig; Captain David Harris; with no small number scattered throughout the others.

On July 1, 1776, it began its new term of service in camp on Long Island.

For its part in the battle of Long Island, on August 27, 1776, we quote the following letter of Lt. Col. James Chambers to his wife:

"On the morning of the 22d August, there were nine

thousand British troops on New Utrecht plains. The guard alarmed our small camp, and we assembled at the flag-staff. We marched our forces, about two hundred in number, to New Utrecht, to watch the movements of the enemy. When we came on the hill, we discovered a party of them advancing towards us. We prepared to give them a warm reception, when an imprudent fellow fired, and they immediately halted and turned toward Flatbush. The main body also moved long the great road toward the same place. We proceeded along the side of them in the edge of the woods as far as the turn of the lane, where the cherry trees were, if you remember. We then found it impracticable for so small a force to attack them on the plain, and sent Captain Hamilton, with twenty men, before them, to burn all the grain, which he did very cleverly, and killed a great many cattle. It was then thought most proper to return to camp and secure our baggage, which we did, and left it in Fort Brown. Near twelve o'clock, the same day, we returned down the great road to Flatbush, with only our small regiment and one New England regiment sent to support us, though at a mile's distance.

"When in sight of Flatbush, we discovered the enemy, but not the main body. On perceiving us, they retreated down the road, perhaps a mile. A party of our people, commanded by Captain Miller, followed them close with a design to decoy a portion of them to follow him, whilst the rest kept in the edge of the woods alongside of Captain M. But they thought better of the matter, and would not come after him, though he went within two hundred yards. There they stood for a long time, and then Captain Miller turned off to us, and we proceeded along their flank. Some of our men fired upon and killed several

Hessians, as we ascertained two days afterwards. Strong guards were maintained all day on the flanks of the enemy, and our regiment and the Hessian Jägers kept up a severe firing, with a loss of but two wounded on our side. We laid a few Hessians low, and made them retreat out of Flatbush. Our people went into the town, and brought the goods out of the burning houses.

"The enemy liked to have lost their field-pieces. Capt. Steel, of your vicinity, acted bravely. We would certainly have had the cannon had it not been for some foolish person calling retreat. The main body of the foe returned to the town, and when our lads came back, they told of their exploits. This was doubted by some, which enraged our men so much that a few of them ran and brought away several Hessians on their backs. This kind of firing by our riflemen and theirs continued until two o'clock on the morning of the 26th, when our regiment was relieved by a portion of the flying camp, and we started for Fort Green to get refreshment, not having lain down the whole of the time, and almost dead with fatigue. We had just got to the fort, and I had only laid down, when the alarm guns were fired. We were compelled to turn out to the lines, and, as soon as it was light, saw our men and theirs engaged with field-pieces.

"At last the enemy found means to surround our men there upon guard, and then a heavy firing continued for several hours. The main body, that surrounded our men, marched up within thirty yards of Forts Brown and Greene, but, when we fired, they retreated with loss. From all, I can learn, we numbered about twenty-five hundred, and the attacking party was not less than twenty-five thousand, as they had been landing for days before. Our men behaved as bravely as ever men did, but it is surprising that with this superiority of numbers, they were not cut to pieces. They behaved gallantly, and there are but five or six hundred missing.

"General Lord Stirling fought like a wolf, and is taken prisoner. Colonels Miles and Atlee, Major Burd, Captain Peebles, Lieutenant Watt, and a great number of other officers, also prisoners. Colonel Piper missing. From deserters we learn that the enemy lost Major General Grant and two brigadiers and many others, and five hundred killed. Our loss is chiefly in prisoners.

"It was thought advisable to retreat off Long Island, and, on the night of the 30th, it was done with great secrecy. Very few of the officers knew it until they were on the boats, supposing that an attack was intended. A discovery of our intention to the enemy would have been fatal to us. The Pennsylvania troops were done great honor by being chosen the *corps de reserve* to cover the retreat. The regiments of Colonels Hand, Magaw, Shee and Hazlett were detached for that purpose. We kept up fires, with outposts stationed, until all the rest were over. We left the lines after it was fair day, and then came off.

"Never was a greater feat of generalship shown than in this retreat—to bring off an army of twelve thousand men, within sight of a strong enemy, possessed of as strong a fleet as ever floated on our seas, without any loss, and saving all the baggage. General Washington saw the last over himself."

With the organization of the Continental troops, in the spring of 1777, the First Pennsylvania was placed in the First Brigade of General Wayne's Division.

At the battle of Brandywine this regiment rendered distinguished service. Col. Chambers makes the following mention of it:

"As there were no troops to cover the artillery in the redoubt, the enemy was within thirty yards before being discovered; our men were forced to fly, and to leave three pieces behind. Our brigade was drawn into line, with the park of artillery two hundred yards, in the rear of the redoubt. The enemy advanced on the hill, where our park was, and came within fifty yards of the hill above me. I then ordered my men to fire. Two or three rounds made the lads clear the ground.

"The General sent orders for our artillery to retreat —it was on my right—and ordered me to cover it with part of my regiment. It was done, but to my surprise the artillery men had run and left the howitzer behind. The two field pieces went up the road, protected by about sixty of my men, who had very warm work, but brought them safe. I then ordered another party to fly to the howitzer and bring it off. Captain Buchanan, Lieutenant Simpson, and Lieutenant Douglass went immediately to the gun, and the men followed their example, and I covered them with the few I had remaining. But, before this could be done, the main body of the foe came within thirty yards, and kept up the most terrible fire I suppose (was) ever heard in America, though with very little loss on our side. I brought all the brigade artillery safely off, and I hope to see them again firing at the scoundrels. Yet we retreated to the next height in good order, in the midst of a very heavy fire of cannon and small arms. Not thirty yards distant, we formed to receive them, but they did not choose to follow."

This gallant soldier was wounded in this action, in the side, by a Hessian bullet, which he carried to his grave. At the battle of Monmouth, he states:

.   .   .   .

"Our Division was in front of our artillery, in a small hollow; while the enemy's artillery was placed on an eminence in front of our brigade.

"Of course we were in a right line of fire, both parties playing their cannon over our heads, and yet only two killed of our men, and wounded four of my regiment with splinters of rails. . . . They fled in all quarters, and, at sunset, we had driven them near to Monmouth town. . . .

"I rode over the whole ground, and saw two hundred of their dead. It is surprising that we lost not more than thirty . . ."

In a letter to his wife, dated "Camp at New Bridge, Hackensack, September 5, 1780," he says, of the attack on the Bergen Block House:

"The 1st regiment was ordered to attack a Block House, built on the bank of the North River, on the point that runs down to Bergen, Six or Seven miles from that town. My regiment was ordered to advance, and commence the attack and to cover the Artillery, which was done with unparalleled bravery. Advancing to the abattis, which was within twenty yards of the house, several crept through and then continued under an excessive fire; until ordered away. They retreated with reluctance. The foe kept close under shelter, firing from loop-holes. Our men and artillery kept up a galling fire on the house, but at last were obliged to fall back, as our field pieces were too light to penetrate. There were twelve killed of the 1st Regiment, and four of them in the abattis; in all, forty men were killed, wounded and missing,—three of those in Ben's platoon. You may depend your son is a good soldier. All the officers say he behaved exceedingly well.

THE PENNSYLVANIA-GERMAN SOCIETY.

MOLLY PITCHER AT THE BATTLE OF MONMOUTH.

I had not the pleasure of seeing it, as I lay very sick at the time."

SECOND PENNSYLVANIA REGIMENT.

This regiment was organized from the First Pennsylvania Battalion as a nucleus, whose rolls were very incomplete, but contained one company (Capt. Jonathan Jones) from Berks county, in which were a number of Pennsylvania-Germans. A scrutiny of the rolls of the Second Pennsylvania Continentals indicates that about eighteen per cent. of its members were of the same blood, Lieut. Col. Henry Miller's company being largely made up of such.

The Second Pennsylvania was organized October, 1776, and was connected with Wayne's division, First brigade, during its entire service.

The regiment did valiant duty at both Brandywine and Germantown, suffering heavily, six lieutenants, besides its commander, being either killed or wounded. In the latter engagement it was commanded by Major Williams until he fell, wounded, and was taken prisoner. Captain Howell then assumed command.

By the arrangement, which took place July 1, 1778, the Thirteenth Pennsylvania was incorporated with the Second Pennsylvania, and Col. Walter Stewart became its Colonel. This was due to the fact that the enlistments of the men in Miles' Rifle Regiment and Atlee's Musketry Battalion, who were consolidated into the Thirteenth Regiment, had then expired, thus causing the disbandment of the latter organization.

THIRD PENNSYLVANIA REGIMENT.

Recruited in December, 1776, January and February, 1777, it was arranged in the Continental service March

12

12, 1777, having been formed on the basis of the Second
Pennsylvania Battalion. This Battalion had contained the
company of Capt. Thomas Craig, from Northampton
county, which was almost entirely Pennsylvania-German,
and that of Capt. Rudolph Bunner, which contained some.

Such lists of the members of the Third Pennsylvania
Continentals, as are in existence, indicate that about ten
per cent. of them were Pennsylvania-Germans.

During 1777 the regiment was in Conway's brigade,
of Lord Stirling's division, and under command of Col.
Thomas Craig. They were with La Fayette at Brandywine, who, in his Memoirs, speaks of the brilliant manner
in which "General Conway, Chevalier of St. Louis, ac-
quitted himself at the head of his brigade of eight hundred
men in the encounter with the troops of Cornwallis near
Birmingham Meeting House."

On October 24, 1778, the regiment was in the Second
brigade of Wayne's division. On October 15, 1779, it
was in Irvine's Second brigade of St. Clair's division.

At Monmouth, when Lee had retreated and the success
of the battle was at stake, the Third was one of the regiments selected by Wayne, at the command of Washington, to stem the onset of the enemy. It was here that
Lieut. Col. Bunner was killed, after having greatly distinguished himself on the field.

A letter, dated April 17, 1780, has the following account of the death of Major Thomas Langhorne Byles:

"Yesterday morning, a detachment of 200 Continental
troops, under the command of Major Byles, stationed at
Paramus, was suddenly attacked by a party of the enemy,
consisting of 200 horse and 400 foot. The attack commenced a little after sunrise. Major Byles, besides his
usual patrols, had that morning sent out two parties, each

with a commissioned officer, but such is the situation of
that part of the country, intersected with roads and inhabited chiefly by disaffected people, that all precautions
failed. The sentinels, near the quarters, were the first
that gave notice of the enemy's approach. He immediately made the best disposition the hurry of the moment
would permit, and animated his men by his exhortation
and example. The house he was in was surrounded.
Some of the men began to cry for quarters; others, obeying the commands of the officers, continued to fire from
the windows. The enemy upbraided them with the per-
fidy of asking for quarters, and persisting in resistance.
Major Byles denied, in a determined tone, that he had
called for quarter but his resolution did not avail. A
surrender took place, and, in the act, the Major received
a mortal wound, with which he expired. . . . The
enemy made their boasts that as Major Byles did not
present the hilt of his sword in front when surrendering,
they shot him."

In July, 1778, the Twelfth Pennsylvania, which had
been reduced to a skeleton by exposures as a picket regiment, being largely composed of riflemen, was incorporated with the Third, and, on January 17, 1781, the Third
was then reorganized, under Col. Craig, and, after recruiting at Easton, accompanied Gen. Wayne upon the
southern campaign, or, at least, the largest portion of it,
being detached for that purpose.

FOURTH PENNSYLVANIA REGIMENT.

Col. Shee's Third Pennsylvania Battalion, under Col.
Cadwalader, by reënlisting, formed the Fourth Pennsylvania Continental Regiment, but, as nearly the whole of
the Third Battalion was captured at Fort Washington,

November 16, 1776, it became, largely, a new regiment, recruited in January and February, 1777.

One company, that of Capt. Edward Scull, of Berks county, contained a large percentage of Pennsylvania-Germans. From the incomplete returns available I have estimated that the Pennsylvania-Germans formed some ten per cent. of the whole command.

During the whole of its active service the Fourth was under the command of Lieut. Col. William Butler, Col. Cadwalader being a prisoner on parole.

It was in the Second brigade of Wayne's division in 1777. During the short campaign of that summer it lost half of its effective force, its Major, Lamar, having been killed, and six of its lieutenants wounded, at Paoli. The last words of Major Lamar, on receiving his death wound, were, "Halt, boys! Give these assassins one fire!"

Shortly after the battle of Monmouth, June 28, 1778, Col. Butler was ordered to Schoharie, New York, with his regiment, and a detachment from Morgan's Rifles, to defend the frontiers of New York and Pennsylvania, and to chastise the Indians, which was done very effectually by various punitive expeditions, during which much of their material and stock was either captured or destroyed.

On May 26, 1781, the regiment marched south with Wayne.

FIFTH PENNSYLVANIA REGIMENT.

By the reënlistment, to a large extent, of the Fourth Pennsylvania Battalion, Col. Wayne, under its old officers, the Fifth Pennsylvania Continental Regiment was formed, the beginning of 1777.

The best calculation which can be made would indicate a Pennsylvania-German percentage, in the whole, of about fifteen.

The regiment was under Wayne's command, that is in his brigade or division, during most of its service. After the promotion of Wayne, the regimental command devolved upon Col. Francis Johnston, until January 17, 1781, when he was retired and succeeded by Col. Richard Butler, under whose charge it was during the southern campaign which followed.

At the battle of Brandywine Col. Johnston was taken prisoner, and its lieutenant-colonel, Frazer, with the adjutant, Harper, were captured the next day. One captain was made prisoner at Germantown, and the major, with two lieutenants, were wounded.

Sixth Pennsylvania Regiment.

This regiment was organized, January, 1777, on the basis of Col. Magaw's Fifth Pennsylvania Battalion, which, with all its records, was captured in the disaster at Fort Washington, November 16, 1776, so that data concerning it are scarce. As Col. Magaw remained a prisoner, Lieut. Col. Henry Bicker took command, until succeeded by Lieut. Col. Josiah Harmar, under whose charge it was during most of its military career.

With the Third, Ninth and Twelfth regiments it was in Conway's brigade of Lord Stirling's division, during 1777; on October 24, 1778, it was attached to the Second brigade of Wayne's division; on October 15, 1779, it was in Irvine's Second brigade of St. Clair's division; in 1781 it went south with Wayne.

The old Fifth Battalion contained a large number of Pennsylvania-Germans, and such was the case with the new Sixth Pennsylvania Continentals. The roll of the company of Capt. Jacob Moser, from Berks county, which is given, shows the entire company to have been Pennsylvania-German, while some twenty per cent. of the regiment, as a whole, were of like blood.

SEVENTH PENNSYLVANIA REGIMENT.

The Seventh regiment was organized January, 1777, by the reënlistment of Col. Irvine's Sixth State Battalion. Col. Irvine, then a prisoner, was exchanged April, 1778, and, the following year, made brigadier-general. Major David Grier had charge of the regiment until this time, when Lieut. Col. Morgan Conner was assigned to the command.

The regiment did not return to Carlisle, from Ticonderoga, until March, 1777.

The Sixth State Battalion contained a comparatively small number of Pennsylvania-Germans. In the new Seventh Continentals about six per cent. were Pennsylvania-Germans, scattered throughout the various companies.

During its entire service it was under the direct command of Gen. Wayne, and shared, with him, all the vicissitudes of his brigade and division.

The experience of the Seventh Pennsylvania at Paoli is given in the following letter from Maj. Hay to Col. Irvine, dated " Camp at Trappe, September 29, 1777 ":

" *Dear Colonel:* Since I had the pleasure of seeing you, the Division under the command of General Wayne has been surprised by the enemy, with considerable loss. We were ordered by his Excellency to march from the Yellow Springs down to where the Enemy lay, near the Admiral Warren, there to annoy their rear. We marched early on the 17th instant, and got below the Paoli that night. On the next day fixed on a place for our camp. We lay the 18th and 19th undisturbed, but, on the 20th,

GEN. ANTHONY WAYNE.

B. EASTTOWN, PA., JAN. 1, 1745. D. PRESQUE ISLE, DEC. 15, 1796.

at 12 o'clock at night, the Enemy marched out, and so unguarded was our Camp that they were amongst us before we either formed in any manner for our safety, or attempted to retreat, notwithstanding the General had full intelligence of their designs two hours before they came out. I will inform you in a few words of what happened. The annals of the age cannot produce such a scene of butchery. All was confusion. The enemy amongst us, and your Regiment the most exposed, as the Enemy came on the right wing. The 1st Regiment (which always takes the right) was taken off, and posted in a strip of woods, stood only one fire and retreated. Then we were next the Enemy, and, as we were amongst our fires, they had great advantage of us. I need not go on to give the particulars, but the Enemy rushed on, with fixed bayonets, and made the use of them they intended. So you may figure to yourself what followed. The party lost 300 Privates in killed, wounded and missing, besides commissioned and non-commissioned officers. Our loss is Col. Grier, Captain Wilson and Lieutenant Irvine [who received seventeen bayonet stabs, from which he never entirely recovered.—Ed.] wounded (but none of them dangerously), and 61 non-comm⁴ and privates killed and wounded, which was just half the men we had on the ground fit for duty. The 22ᵈ, I went to the ground to see the wounded. The scene was shocking— the poor men groaning under their wounds, which were all by stabs of Bayonets, and cuts of Light-horsemen's swords. Col. Grier is wounded in the side by a bayonet, superficially slanting to the breast bone. Captain Wilson stabbed in the side, but not dangerous, as it did not take the guts or belly. He got also a bad stroke on the head with the cock-nail of the lock of a musket. Andrew

Irvine was ran through the fleshy part of the thigh with a bayonet. They are all laying near David Jones' tavern. I left Capt. McDowell with them to dress and take care of them, and they all are in a fair way of recovery. Major La Mar, of the 4th Regiment, was killed, and some other inferior officers. . . ."

At Monmouth, the Seventh Pennsylvania was one of the three Pennsylvania regiments selected for the post of honor.

After the revolt of the Pennsylvania Line, in 1781, the remains of the regiment were drafted into the Fourth, subsequently the Fourth into the Third, and, finally, in 1783, into the First.

EIGHTH PENNSYLVANIA REGIMENT.

Under authority of a resolution of Congress, dated July 15, 1776, for the defense of the western frontier, to garrison the posts of Presqu' Isle, Le Boeuff and Kittaning, to consist of seven companies from Westmoreland, and one from Bedford county, the Eighth Pennsylvania was raised. Its first colonel was Aeneas Mackey, July 20, 1776, who died in service February 14, 1777, and was succeeded by Col. Daniel Broadhead.

It contained a very small number of Pennsylvania-Germans, so small as not to warrant the insertion of its interesting services.

NINTH PENNSYLVANIA REGIMENT.

The Ninth regiment was organized October 25, 1776, in accordance with a resolution of Congress dated September 16, under Col. James Irvine, who was transferred to the Second Pennsylvania March 12, 1777, when Lieut. Col. George Nagel succeeded him, serving until February 17, 1778, when made colonel of the Tenth Pennsylvania. Col. Richard Butler then took command.

Under Col. Nagel it was a part of Conway's brigade of Lord Stirling's division, under command of Gen. Sullivan, and did its full duty at Brandywine and elsewhere.

In 1778–9, under Col. Butler, it formed a part of the Second brigade of Wayne's division, and, later, of the Second brigade, Gen. William Irvine, in St. Clair's division.

It took a prominent share in the capture of Stony Point. Lieut. George Knox led the forlorn hope of the right column in the assault, and was the second man inside of the works, for which he received four hundred dollars; this he directed to be distributed amongst his men; for his gallantry he was breveted Captain, by resolution of Congress.

After the revolt in the Pennsylvania Line, in 1781, the Ninth Pennsylvania was pretty generally reënlisted, under their old colonel and his captains, into the Fifth Pennsylvania.

Of the couple company rolls in existence that of Capt. John Davis shows quite a number of Pennsylvania-Germans. Out of the total number given a percentage of some fifteen is indicated as of German blood.

Tenth Pennsylvania Regiment.

The Tenth Pennsylvania was also raised under the resolution of Congress of September 16, 1776. During its entire service it was in the brigades and division commanded by Gen. Wayne.

Its first active head was Lieut. Col. Adam Hubley, then Col. George Nagel, February 7, 1778–July 1, 1778, then Col. Richard Humpton.

A regimental return, of November 1, 1777, gives, besides some other details, the following account of casualties:

> Taken at Bound Brook, April 13, rank and file..15
> Taken at Princeton...................... 7
> Missing at the battle at Brandywine, Paoli and
>   Germantown, etc. 38
>   Total 60

The lists in existence, of various companies, indicate a considerable number of Pennsylvania-Germans in each of them. About twenty to twenty-five per cent. of the entire regiment were Pennsylvania-Germans.

ELEVENTH PENNSYLVANIA REGIMENT.
(The "Old Eleventh.")

This regiment came into existence by resolution of Congress September 16, 1776. Its colonel was Richard Humpton. Its service lasted from October, 1776, to July 1, 1778, during which it was continually attached to Gen. Wayne's division. It lost very heavily at the battle of Brandywine, and, on the date last named, was incorporated with the Tenth Pennsylvania.

About ten per cent. of its members were Pennsylvania-Germans.

TWELFTH PENNSYLVANIA REGIMENT.

Congress authorized this regiment to be raised in the counties of Northampton and Northumberland. Its organization began October 1, 1776.

The greater part of the regiment was recruited upon the West Branch of the Susquehanna. On December 18 it left Sunbury, in boats, for the battle-fields of New Jersey. Being composed of good riflemen and scouts, it was detailed on picket and skirmish duty. Its colonel was William Cooke. With the Third, Sixth, and Ninth Pennsylvania regiments, it was in Conway's brigade of Lord Stirling's division. Its headquarters were at the five cross-roads at Metuchin, between Quibbletown and Amboy, where its companies were engaged in the various skirmishes which there took place; at Bound Brook, April 12, 1777; Piscataway, May 10, where Joseph Lorentz, and twenty-one others, were made prisoners by the British, Wendell Lorentz making his escape by running in among a flock of sheep; at Short Hills, June 26, and Bonhamton. In June Col. Daniel Morgan's rifle command was formed, and a detachment from the Twelfth Pennsylvania, under Capt. Hawkins Boone, placed in it.

In the battle of Brandywine the Twelfth was under Sullivan, at the Birmingham Meeting House, where it lost heavily. At Germantown, Conway's brigade led the attack on the left wing of the British, and the regiment was in the hottest of the fight, again losing heavily. It wintered at Valley Forge, and its remnant was nearly destroyed at Monmouth. By July 1, 1778, it was incorporated into the Third Pennsylvania.

Its rolls are very few in number, but the meager data in existence would indicate that about ten to fifteen per cent. of its members were Pennsylvania-Germans.

Thirteenth Pennsylvania Regiment.

It will be recalled that the remnant of Miles' Rifle Regiment and Atlee's Musketry Battalion were incorporated into the State Regiment of Foot. With the reorganization of the army these brave men were taken, November, 1777, by resolution of Congress, into the Continental service as the Thirteenth Pennsylvania Regiment, under command of Col. Walter Stewart.

It was attached to the command of Gen. Sullivan at both Brandywine and Germantown, and, in the latter engagement, penetrated to the Market House. At Monmouth it was one of the three Pennsylvania regiments which was given the post of honor and danger, by Gen. Wayne.

By July 1, 1778, the Thirteenth was incorporated into the Second Pennsylvania, the term of enlistment of its original members having expired.

From the origin of this command it is evident that it contained many Pennsylvania-Germans, but its rolls are so utterly lacking that it would be impossible to attempt to fix upon any definite percentage.

ADDITIONAL REGIMENTS.

On December 27, 1776, Congress authorized Gen. Washington to raise sixteen battalions of infantry in addition to those already voted. On January 11, 1777, Washington issued commissions and authority to raise two of these regiments, to Lieut. Col. Thomas Hartley, of the Seventh Pennsylvania, and Major John Patton, of Miles' Rifle Regiment.

COL. THOMAS HARTLEY'S REGIMENT.

Hartley's regiment was in Wayne's First brigade at Brandywine and Germantown. It was ordered to Sunbury, about July 14, 1778, and remained in service on the West Branch until incorporated with the new Eleventh, on January 13, 1779.

Practically no rolls of this command are in existence.

It seems to have contained a very small percentage of Pennsylvania-Germans.

COL. JOHN PATTON'S REGIMENT.

Probably a number of its men were recruited from New Jersey and Delaware. Practically no records exist concerning it. It was merged into the new Eleventh on January 13, 1779.

ELEVENTH PENNSYLVANIA REGIMENT.
(The " New Eleventh.")

The new Eleventh came into existence, as already stated, on January 13, 1779, and was commanded by Lieut. Col. Adam Hubley. It went out of service January 13, 1781, with the reorganization which then took place.

It was attached to the western army of Gen. Sullivan, an account of which will be given later.

About eight or nine per cent. of its members were Pennsylvania-Germans.

CHAPTER IX.

The German Regiment.

Wappen von Bayern.

AS its name implies this regiment was composed entirely of Pennsylvania-Germans. It was first under the command of Col. Nicholas Haussegger, who, after the battle of Monmouth, returned to his farm, near Lebanon, Pa., and was succeeded by Lieut. Col. Ludwig Weltner. The regiment was engaged both at Trenton and Princeton. In May, 1777, it was attached to De Barre's brigade, Sullivan's division, and took part in all the operations of that division, a narrative of which has already been given. In 1779 it was a part of Sullivan's expedition against the Indians, a more detailed record of which will be given in a succeeding chapter. In the spring of 1780 it was stationed on the frontiers of Northumberland county. By resolution of Congress the regiment was reduced in October, and ended its organization January 1, 1781.

The following orders given Major Burchardt, by Gen. Hand, are interesting as showing its movements while on the way to Wyoming, also those of Armand's and Schott's Corps:

"MINISINK, 5th April, 1779.

"*Sir:* Agreeable to the orders you yesterday rec^d, you will proceed to Wyoming, on the Susquehanna River, with the Regiment under your Immediate Command, Col. Armand's and Capt. Schott's corps, the former is commanded at present by Major Lomaign & the latter by Captn Selin. These corps will join you at or before you reach Col. Stroud's, at Fort Penn (site of Stroudsburg— Ed.) as you will see by their Orders, left open for your perusal, & which you will have delivered. You must take with you from here all the flour now left in store, and Beef sufficient to carry the Detachment thro' to Wyoming; you will receive an additional supply of Flour at Col. Stroud's. Take care that each corps takes with them the provisions they have respectively drawn. You will receive a few Camp Kettles for the Detachment at Col. Stroud's, and may draw 20 Axes for your Regiment, 6 for Armand's & 3 for Schott's here.

"It will take you four days from Col. Stroud's to Wyoming; you will, therefore, regulate your Provision accordingly. Captn Alex^r Patterson, A. D. Q. M., will send express to Col. Zebulon Butler, commanding at Wyoming, with notice of your approach. From Fort Penn you will march to Lardner's; thence to an Incamping Place in what is Commonley cal'd the Great Swamp; the third day to Bullock's, which is within five miles of Wyoming Garrison, where for the present you will put yourself under Col. Butler's directions.

"I am thus Particular, as It will be necessary to make easie marches in order to reconnoitre the Country well and examine every thicket & hollow way, or swamp, before you enter it, which I desire you may be very particular in doing to prevent being Surprised or led into an Ambuscade or attack'd without previous knowledge of the Enemy's being near. You will be particularly attentive to keep the Body of the Troops compact. Suffer no straggling on any account; keep a proper advance & rear Guard, tho' not at too great a distance, and also small parties on your Flanks, observing the same caution. Should any enemy appear, you must take care not to advance on them precipitately before you know their numbers, or until you have sufficiently extended your front to prevent being out-Flanked.

"By a steady adherence to the above directions, you will have little danger to apprehend—double your attention as you approach the Fort. As the badness of the Roads at present and the scarcity of horses will prevent your carrying your heavy Baggage, you must leave it at Fort Penn with a Guard until you have a more favorable opportunity."

Because of the fact that this one regiment was entirely German the writer feels justified in giving its roster in full, as of September, 1778, in the succeeding chapter.

PENNSYLVANIA ARTILLERY.

Capt. Thomas Proctor's artillery company originated from a resolution of the Committee of Safety, dated October 16, 1775, for raising an artillery company to be placed at Fort Island, to consist of one captain, one lieutenant, one drum and fife, and twenty-five privates, to serve the Province twelve months.

Early in April, 1776, while stationed on Fort Island, the company was increased to one hundred and twenty men, and, on August 14, to two hundred men.

The company, having reënlisted October 30, 1776, remained on Fort Island until about December 25, when a portion were ordered to New Jersey and took part in the capture of the Hessians at Trenton, also in the battle of Princeton where Major Proctor captured a brass six-pounder.

On February 6, 1777, it was resolved to increase this force to a full regiment, to the command of which Col.

REFERENCES.—*A*, Pennington Road; *B*, Hessian Picket; *C*, Hand's Rifle Corps; *D*, Battery opened by Washington on King Street; *E*, Hessians, who were obliged to surrender at this spot; *F*, Virginia troops; *G*, King Street; *H*, Gen. Dickinson's house; *I*, Water Street; *J*, Ferry; *K*, Blooms-bury; *L*, Morrisville.

Proctor was assigned, and it then became a part of the Continental service.

It had its first disaster at Bound Brook, N. J., April 13, 1777, where Lieuts. Ferguson and Turnbull were captured, with twenty privates and pieces of artillery.

13

At the battle of Brandywine Proctor bravely maintained his position at Chad's Ford, until the defeat of the right wing forced his retreat, with the loss of some guns and ammunition, the former being recaptured by the infantry.

At Germantown a portion of the regiment was engaged opposite Chew's house.

From its necessarily detached service very little of the detailed history of this body of troops has survived, but detachments from it were engaged in nearly all of the operations of the main army, subsequently, notably at Monmouth and in Sullivan's campaign of 1779. In 1780, part of the regiment, under Major Isaac Craig, were ordered to Fort Pitt, with stores and cannon. They left Carlisle May 23, arriving at their destination on June 25.

The artillery corps contained quite a number of Pennsylvania-Germans, not less than fifteen per cent. of the whole.

GERMANTOWN DUNKER CHURCH AND PARSONAGE.

CHAPTER X.

ROSTER OF THE GERMAN REGIMENT.

COLONEL.

HAUSSEGGER, NICHOLAS, from Fourth battalion, July 17, 1776; retired from the army in 1778, and died on his farm near Lebanon, Pa., in July, 1786.

Wappen von Anhalt.

LIEUTENANT COLONELS.

Stricker, George, July 17, 1776.
Weltner, Ludwig, from major, April 9, 1777.

MAJORS.

Weltner, Ludwig, of Maryland, June 17, 1776; promoted lieutenant colonel.
Burchardt, Daniel, from captain, April 9, 1777.

CAPTAINS.

Burchardt, Daniel, of Philadelphia, July 8, 1776; promoted major, April 7, 1777.

Hubley, George, of Lancaster, July 8, 1776.

Bunner, Jacob, July 8, 1776; retired January 1, 1781.

Weiser, Benjamin, July 8, 1776; resided after the war at Selinsgrove.

Woelpper, John D., July 17, 1776; transferred to Invalid corps, June 11, 1778.

Boyd, Peter, of Philadelphia, May 9, 1777; from first lieutenant; retired January 1, 1781.

Rice, Frederick William, from first lieutenant, January 4, 1778; retired January 1, 1781.

Hubley, Bernard, from first lieutenant, February 24, 1778; retired in 1781; brigade inspector of Northumberland county, etc.; in 1807, published his first volume of his History of the Revolution; died in 1808.

CAPTAIN LIEUTENANT.

Shrawder, Philip, February 8, 1778, from lieutenant; retired January 1, 1781.

FIRST LIEUTENANTS.

Rowlwagen, Frederick, July 12, 1776.

Boyer, Peter, July 12, 1776; promoted captain, May 9, 1777.

Rice, Frederick William, July 12, 1776; promoted captain, January 4, 1778.

Bower, Jacob, July 12, 1776.

Hubley, Bernard, August 15, 1776; promoted captain, February 24, 1778.

Shrawder, Philip, of Philadelphia, May 13, 1777; promoted captain lieutenant, February 8, 1778.

Weidman, John, from first lieutenant, May 14, 1777; retired January 1, 1781; died June 9, 1830, aged seventy-four; buried in Lutheran cemetery, Reading.

Cremer, Jacob, from second lieutenant, January 8, 1778; retired January 4, 1781.

Swartz, Christopher Godfried, February 12, 1778; retired January 1, 1781.

Young, Marcus, March 12, 1778; retired January 1, 1781.

SECOND LIEUTENANTS.

Hawbecker, George, July 12, 1776.

Landenberger, John, July 12, 1776.

Schaffer, George, July 12, 1776.

Yeiser, Frederick, July 12, 1776.

Shrawder, Philip, August 12, 1776; promoted second lieutenant, May 13, 1777.

Smith, Adam, resided in Huntingdon county, in 1835, aged eighty-one.

Cremer, Jacob, from ensign, May 13, 1777; promoted first lieutenant, January 8, 1778.

Swartz, Christopher Godfried, from ensign; promoted first lieutenant.

ENSIGNS.

Weidman, John, July 12, 1776; promoted lieutenant, May 14, 1777.

Helm, Christian, July 12, 1776.

Cremer, Jacob, July 12, 1776; promoted second lieutenant, May 15, 1777.

Swartz, Christopher Godfried, July 12, 1776; promoted second lieutenant.

Cleckner, Christian, Philadelphia, July 23, 1778; retired January 1, 1781.

Diffenderfer, David, of Lancaster, July 23, 1778; resided in Lancaster county, in 1832, aged eighty.

ADJUTANTS.

De Linkensdorf, Lewis, August 9, 1776; formerly lieutenant in one of the king of Sardinia's Swiss regiments.

Weidman, John, lieutenant, June 20, 1779; captured and exchanged in 1780.

PAYMASTERS.

Michael, Eberhard, 1776–7; died in Lancaster, Pa., July 16, 1778.

Hubley, George, captain, 1778.

Boyer, Peter, captain, June 20, 1779.

QUARTER-MASTERS.

Myle, Jacob, October 24, 1776.

Raybold, Jacob, of Maryland, July 24, 1778.

SURGEON.

Peres, Peter, of Philadelphia, September 1, 1778–1781; retired January 1, 1781.

SURGEON'S MATE.

Smith, Alexander, of Maryland.

SERGEANT MAJOR.

Francis, George, Lancaster, December 15, 1777.

SERGEANTS.

Benickler, John, from Thompson's.

Gabriel, Peter, Philadelphia, July 13, 1776; transferred to First Pennsylvania, 1781.

Gleim, Philip, Lancaster; Rice's company, August 7, 1776; wounded at Germantown, through left shoulder.

Hauss, Michael, Philadelphia, August 2, 1776; transferred to Invalid corps, 1780.

Johnston, John, Philadelphia, October 21, 1776.

Linderman, Frederick, August 20, 1776; resided at Limerick township, Montgomery county.

Luff, George, Philadelphia, July 10, 1777.

Moser, Henry, Philadelphia, July 10, 1776; died February 21, 1825, aged sixty-eight, at Philadelphia.

Mulls, Francis, 1776 to November 1, 1780; transferred to Invalid corps.

Reichley, Lewis, Philadelphia, August 26, 1776.

Shrider, Israel, Philadelphia, November 13, 1779.

Weissert, Jacob, Capt. Bunner's company, July 20, 1776.

Wentz, Jacob, Philadelphia, July 23, 1776.

Wiand, John, Lancaster, Bunner's company, August 24, 1776.

CORPORALS.

Brownsburgh, Lewis, Germantown, July 14, 1776.

Cypril, Frederick, Philadelphia, August 18, 1776.

Deal, Adam, July 16, 1776; transferred to Invalid corps, October 16, 1779.

Fesmire, John, Philadelphia, September 4, 1776; died September 2, 1821, in Philadelphia, aged sixty-nine.

Funk, George, Reading, October 19, 1776; resided in Lancaster county, 1835, aged eighty-three.

Gohoon, James, Berks county, August 6, 1776.

Kline, Philip.

Rifferts, Christian, Philadelphia, July 25, 1776; residing in Philadelphia, 1835, aged eighty-five.

Shrider, Philip, Philadelphia, July 20, 1776.

Sipperel, Frederick, Philadelphia, August 18, 1776.

Wilhelm, Frederick, Lancaster, August 3, 1776; resided in Philadelphia, 1835.

DRUM MAJOR.

Hart, John, Philadelphia, July 2, 1776.

FIFERS.

Alexander, Joseph, Philadelphia, July 12, 1776.
Brown, John, Philadelphia, November 12, 1779.
Borgignon, Francis, Philadelphia, October 4, 1776.
Fortner, Peter, Philadelphia, May 11, 1779; Burchardt's
company.

PRIVATES.

Baker, Christian, October 12, 1776.
Banig, Dedrick.
Bantzer, Detmar, or Bonsa, Betmire, October 12, 1776;
transferred to Second Pennsylvania.
Belcher, Benjamin.
Beyerly, Christopher, Lancaster, enlisted September,
1776.
Bloom, David, Berks county, August 8, 1776; for three
years.
Botamer, Jacob, Berks county, August, 1776; of Captain
Peter Boyer's company; wounded at Trenton, New
Jersey, January, 1777; resided in Westmoreland county,
in 1813.
Bowers, George, died November 24, 1827, in Allegheny
county, aged sixty-seven.
Briningen, Frederick, Philadelphia, December 29, 1776.
Brodbach, Michael, Philadelphia, February 25, 1779.
Brookhaus, Rudolph, August 20, 1776.
Brunner, John, Burchardt's company; Philadelphia; Au-
gust 18, 1776.
Calhoun, James.
Cantwell, Richard, Boyer's company; deserted November,
1780.

Carles, Frederick, January 1, 1777.
Casner, Christian, October 20, 1779–1781.
Christman, Charles, July 28, 1776.
Clifton, Thomas, died in Ross county, Ohio, September 30, 1832, aged eighty-seven.
Cline, Philip, Germantown, August 18, 1776.
Cockendorf, John.
Cook, Philip, Philadelphia, September 30, 1776–1781.
Coon, Christian, Lancaster, August 23, 1776.
Coon, John, October 23, 1776.
Coppas, Peter, December 10, 1776.
Copple, Daniel, July 28, 1776.
Crane, John, Baltimore, October 23, 1776.
Deetz, Frederick, Philadelphia, July 20, 1776.
Deperung, Henry, July 28, 1776.
Dillinger, Frederick, Chester, August 21, 1776.
Dominick, Henry, Philadelphia, October 23, 1776.
Donahoo, Robert, October 21, 1776.
Doyle, Maurice, March 3, 1780; deserted.
Drank, Peter.
Drexler, David, October 10, 1776.
Dunkin, James, Capt. Weiser's company; blacksmith; served three years; resided Huntingdon county, 1818, aged sixty-seven.
Eirich, Michael, April 15, 1776–1781.
Ferraugh, Michael, Philadelphia, July 20, 1776.
Fleish, Christian, August 15, 1776.
Flock, Matthias, Philadelphia, October 23, 1776.
Flowers, Philip, killed October 4, 1777.
Gable, Henry, Northampton county, February 26, 1779.
Gerhart, Abraham, Philadelphia, 1777–1781.
Gerhart, Charles Conrad, Philadelphia, January 20, 1777.
Gerlinger, Lewis, July 20, 1776.

Gruber, George.

Haag, Christian, Philadelphia, October 23, 1776.

Hagar, Andrew, Berks county, December 9, 1776.

Halfpenny, James, Philadelphia, December 27, 1776.

Hammereich, Henry, July 17, 1776; Bunner's company; resided in Philadelphia in 1835, aged ninety-four.

Hantzel, George, Philadelphia, October 24, 1776; transferred to Invalid corps.

Hargood, Henry, Lancaster, December 29, 1776.

Harper, Jacob, Philadelphia, August 2, 1776.

Hartman, Michael, resided in Armstrong county in 1835.

Hartman, Theodore, Bunner's company, July 15, 1776.

Hawke, Andrew.

Heffner, Jacob, resided in Richland county, Ohio, 1834, aged seventy-seven.

Heidler, Martin, Philadelphia, August 20, 1776.

Heims, William, Philadelphia, July 16, 1776.

Herts, Frederick, Philadelphia, July 20, 1776.

Hess, Michael, Philadelphia, December 29, 1776.

Hess, Tobias.

Higgens, Patrick, Lancaster, August 18, 1776.

Hiles, Conrad, died May 17, 1821, in Fayette county, aged sixty-one.

Hilter, Philip.

Huhn, John.

Isaloo, Casper, August 8, 1776.

Janson, Jacob, resided in Greenwood township, Columbia county, 1828.

Johnston, Hugh, Sunbury, October 20, 1779; paid at Carlisle in April, 1781.

Judy, Martin, Philadelphia, October 4, 1776.

Kappais, Peter, January 1, 1777.

Keen, Thomas, Philadelphia, February 1, 1777.

Keyser, John, Philadelphia, July 27, 1776.

Keppard, John, Philadelphia, October 23, 1776.

Kerhart, Conrad, January 1, 1777.

Kerls, Frederick, July 21, 1776.

Kerls, William, Philadelphia, August 10, 1776.

Kerstetter, George, Burchardt's company, July 29, 1776; in the battles at Brunswick, Trenton, Brandywine, and Germantown; in Sullivan's expedition; discharged at Northumberland, 1779; resided in Perry township, Union county, in 1821.

Kettle, Cornelius, Sunbury, February 25, 1779.

Kettle, Jonas.

Kleich, Cornelius, January 1, 1777-1781.

Knowland, Joseph.

Kochenderfer, John, Lancaster, August 26, 1776.

Kremer, Jacob, Boyer's company, July 19, 1776-1779; resided in York county, 1818, aged sixty-two.

Lash, Philip, Philadelphia, July 14, 1776; died February 8, 1822, aged seventy-nine, in Philadelphia.

Leaf, M., July 11, 1776.

Lehman, William, Philadelphia, July 29, 1776.

Lehr, Henry, Philadelphia, July 21, 1776.

Leidy, Christopher, Philadelphia, July 20, 1776; deserted November, 1780.

Leonard, John, Philadelphia, October 23, 1776.

Lynn, George, Philadelphia, October 23, 1776.

McClean, Jacob, February 25, 1779; Captain Weiser's company; died February 18, 1824, in York county, aged sixty-six.

Mandeville, Philip, September 1, 1778-1781.

Marsh, John, Lancaster, August 15, 1776; Bunner's company; left the army September, 1780.

Mast, Joseph, Lancaster, July 24, 1776.

Mayer, Eberhart, Philadelphia, February 25, 1777.

Myer, Philip, Philadelphia, September 3, 1776.

Menges, Christian.

Meyer, Peter, Heidelberg, Berks county, March 17, 1780.

Miley, Jacob, resided in Lancaster county, 1835, aged seventy-eight.

Miller, Mark, Philadelphia, August 18, 1776.

Moore, Thomas, Northumberland, May 7, 1780.

Myer, Jacob, Philadelphia, July 16, 1776.

Nuble, Adam, Germantown, October 23, 1776.

Ottenberger, George, Philadelphia, July 28, 1776.

Phile, Philip, transferred to Invalid corps, July, 1778.

Pifer, Henry, Philadelphia, August 18, 1776–1781; resided in Philadelphia, 1835, aged seventy-nine.

Portner, John, February 25, 1779.

Price, Abraham, Easton, February 25, 1779.

Price, George, Berks county, July 12, 1776.

Rankey, Frederick, Philadelphia, July 23, 1776.

Rauch, Conrad, Philadelphia, July 17, 1776.

Refferts, Christian, promoted corporal.

Reigel, Michael, resided in Mifflin county, 1835, aged eighty-four.

Richcreek, John, Dover township, York county; Capt. George Hubley's company; wounded at Germantown, and transferred to Invalid corps.

Rinehart, George S., resided in Cumberland county, 1835, aged eighty-six.

Rively, Frederick, Philadelphia, July 21, 1776; resided in Delaware county, 1835.

Roop, Nicholas, of Capt. B. Hubley's company.

Rummell, Michael, Philadelphia, April 9, 1776.

Rybaker, John, August 17, 1776; shot through the hand and shoulder at Germantown.

Sailor, Jacob, died February 25, 1833, in Philadelphia, aged eighty-one.

Saine, John, Philadelphia, August 20, 1776.

Schroyer, Matthias, resided in Butler county, 1835, aged eighty-two.

Shearer, Philip, Philadelphia, July 21, 1776.

Sheppard, Jacob, Philadelphia, August 10, 1776.

Sherrick, Jacob, Lancaster, October 23, 1776.

Shiers, Peter, resided in Tuscarawas county, Ohio, in 1835, aged eighty-eight.

Shudy, Martin, Philadelphia, September 4, 1776.

Shuler, Henry, Philadelphia, July 21, 1776; died in Mifflin county, January 10, 1820, aged sixty-nine.

Shirk, Joseph, died in Franklin county, February 19, 1826, aged sixty-seven.

Smiltzer, John, Tulpehocken, February 13, 1780; paid at Carlisle in April, 1781.

Smith, George, transferred to Invalid corps.

Smith, John, Philadelphia, December 2, 1776.

Snider, John, October 23, 1776, wounded in the head at Germantown.

Snyder, Henry, Reading, July 25, 1776.

Specht, Adam, Schafferstown, 1776; discharged at Northumberland, 1779; shoemaker; died at New Berlin, Union county, October 4, 1824.

Stonebreaker, Adam, Hagerstown; Capt. Weiser's company; died in Franklin township, Huntingdon county, November 1, 1827, aged seventy-seven.

Stoll, Adam, July 21, 1776.

Stover, Nicholas, July 20, 1776.

Stoule, Henry.

Stroad, Philip, October 21, 1776.

Stroub, Henry.

Strouss, George, Philadelphia, September 5, 1776; died in Philadelphia, February 10, 1820, aged seventy-five.

Sunliter, John, August 17, 1776.

Swetzgay, Henry, died July 20, 1825, aged seventy-seven, in Berks county.

Sybert, Henry, Lancaster, July 27, 1776; Bunner's company; died July 27, 1830, in Philadelphia, aged seventy.

Teats, Frederick, Philadelphia, July 20, 1776.

Treartz, Conrad, Capt. Weiser's company, August 15, 1776; discharged January, 1781; resided in Union county, 1822.

Turnbelty, John, Northumberland; Burchardt's company, February 27, 1780.

Turner, Thomas, Kensington, October 23, 1776; resided in Philadelphia, in 1835.

Wagoner, Jacob, died in Clarke county, Ohio, November 4, 1823, aged sixty-eight.

Waggoner, Henry, wounded in leg at Germantown.

Wagner, Casper, Philadelphia, November 9, 1776.

Weidman, John, Berks, August 10, 1776.

Weigel, Christopher, Weiser's company; wounded in the ankle; discharged at Valley Forge, 1778; resided in Berks county, 1835, aged seventy-nine.

Weisler, Jacob, Reading, October 23, 1776.

Wheeler, Frederick, Philadelphia, August 10, 1776.

Wheeler, Thomas, Philadelphia, August 10, 1776.

Wilhelm, George, died June 21, 1821, in Fayette county, aged sixty-six.

Williams, Frederick, resided in Philadelphia, 1835, aged eighty.

Williams, William.

Wincher, Christian, Germantown, October 23, 1776.

Winckler, John Henry, Philadelphia, August 1, 1776; died in service.

Yaple, Henry, of Northampton, February 25, 1777.

Yackle, Philip, of Northampton, February 25, 1777.

Yiesely, Michael, served eighteen months in Capt. Weiser's company, resided in Union county, 1822.

ROLL OF CAPTAIN BENJAMIN WEISER'S COMPANY OF THE GENERAL BATTALION OF CONTINENTAL TROOPS, COMMANDED BY COLONEL NICHOLAS HOUSEAKER, ESQ., IN THE SERVICE OF THE UNITED COLONIES. IN BARRACKS, PHILADELPHIA, OCTOBER 3, 1776.

Captain.

Weiser, Benjamin.

First Lieutenant.

Bower, Jacob.

Second Lieutenant.

Yeiser, Frederick.

Ensign.

Kreamer, Jacob.

Sergeants.

1. Glichner, Charles, July 10, 1776.
2. Herbert, Stewart, July 15, 1776.
3. Benkler, John, August 15, 1776.
4. Miller, Joseph, August 19, 1776.

Corporals.

1. Waldman, Nicholas, July 10, 1776.
2. Price, George, July 14, 1776.
3. Rahn, Conrad, August 15, 1776.

Drummer.

Marx [or Mara], William, July 25, 1776.

Fifer.

Bush, Adam, July 12, 1776; discharged September 16, 1776.

Privates.

Barnheisell, John, July 22, 1776.
Bishop, John, July 28, 1776.
Christman, John, August 6, 1776.
Derr, John, August 25, 1776.
Fick, George, July 10, 1776.
Heier, John, July 25, 1776.
Henry, John, August 12, 1776.
Kealer, Caspar, August 23, 1776.
Killman, Philip, July 14, 1776.
Lesher, Peter, August 15, 1776.
Lorash, Jacob, August 6, 1776.
Mast, Joseph, July 19, 1776.
Maurst, John, August 15, 1776.
Mayer, Eberhart, August 27, 1776.
Mickley, Jacob, September 1, 1776.
Newfang, Baltzer, July 15, 1776.
Portner, John, August 3, 1776.
Price, Abraham, August 9, 1776.
Razor, John, July 24, 1776.
Regel, Michael, July 20, 1776.
Reiskell, Martin, August 6, 1776.
Romick, Joseph, August 6, 1776.
Rosemeisell, Adam, July 12, 1776.
Schiffer, Peter, July 12, 1776.
Survey, Benjamin, July 19, 1776.
Seyffert, Henry, July 22, 1776.
Smith, Jacob, July 21, 1776.
Snyder, John, August 16, 1776.

Spire, Frederick, July 15, 1776.
Stoll, Adam, July 20, 1776.
Toney, Peter, August 2, 1776.
Trester, Frederick, July 26, 1776.
Treywitz, Conrad, August 18, 1776.
Tudro, John, July 15, 1776.
Wallman, William, July 27, 1776.
Warby [or Warley], Philip, July 22, 1776.
Weigle, Christopher, July 28, 1776.
Williams, Frederick, August 9, 1776.
Williams, Vincent, August 19, 1776.
Yeisley, Michael, August 9, 1776.

ROLL OF CAPTAIN CHARLES BALTZEL'S COMPANY, GER-
MAN REGIMENT, COMMANDED BY LIEUTENANT
COLONEL WELTNER, SEPTEMBER 9, 1778.

Sergeants.

Henry Speck, July 15, 1776.
Willim Trux, July 21, 1776.
John Cole, July 16, 1776.
John Hering, July 30, 1776.

Corporals.

Philip Beam, July 30, 1776.
John Trux, July 21, 1776.
Patrick Kelley, July 30, 1776.

Drummer.

Benja. England, July 15, 1776.

14

Fifer.

John Brown, July 28, 1776.

Privates.

Peter Kneise, July 16, 1776.
John Miller, July 24, 1776.
Jacob Waggoner, July 21, 1776.
Conrad Beam, July 24, 1776.
Jacob Shitz, August 12, 1776.
Lewis McColough, August 2, 1776.
James Burk, July 28, 1776.
Michel Crush, July 15, 1776.
Christo'r Settlemyer, July 17, 1776.
Peter Engel, August 30, 1776.
Conrad Reily, July 21, 1776.
Daniel Bailor, August 5, 1776.
John Shirk, August 7, 1776.
Fred'k Mongall, July 22, 1776.
Godfrid Lawly, July 28, 1776.
Matias Shroyer, July 21, 1776.
Christ. Smith, October 1, 1776.
John Bower, July 23, 1776.
Adam Shaffer, August 5, 1776.
John Casess, —————.
John Franklin, —————.
John Kendrick, May 20, 1778.
James Champness, May 6, 1778.
George Buch, May 4, 1778.
Adam Muller, April 30, 1778.
William Vincent, May 20, 1778.
Stephen McGrough, April 24, 1778.
William Neving, May 19, 1778.
Thos. Woolford, May 15, 1778.

James Stites, May 13, 1778.
Peter Bartholomay, May 20, 1778.
Richard Hazlip, April 24, 1778.
Rotard Porter, May 15, 1778.
Will'm Mumart, April 25, 1778.
Hugh McKay, May 19, 1778.
John Amesley, April 27, 1778.
John Staton, May 2, 1778.
John Bennet, May 18, 1778.
John Rouch, April 1, 1778.
Thomas Hazelwood, May 2, 1778.
Benj. Ellett, May 20, 1778.
Cornelius Quinlin, February 26, 1778.
Philip Fitzpatrick, May 28, 1778.
Francis Carnes, June 1, 1778.
Charles Tone, May 22, 1778.
James Enery, July 18, 1776.
Samuel Bartes, April 25, 1778.
Jacob Haflick, July 8, 1776.

Charles Baltzel, *Capt.*

ROLL OF CAPTAIN JACOB BUNNER'S COMPANY, GERMAN
REGIMENT OF CONTINENTAL TROOPS, COMMANDED
BY LIEUTENANT COLONEL WELTNER.

Sergeants.

Peter Gabrial.   Jacob Wisert.
Henry Winkler.

Corporals.

Philip Shreder.   Rich'd Shibler.
Henry Moser.   Andw. Deal.

Drummer.

F. Multz.

Privates.

Henry Hammick.	Lenr'd Garlinger.
Fredk. Deats.	Rich'd Stoner.
Theodore Hartmand.	Pedro Ronsey.
Henry Snider.	Con'd Rank.
Martin Hydler.	Jacob Myer.
F. Rankey, July 16, 1776.	Geo. Platenberger.
Philip Shaw.	Jno. Keiser.
Wm. Hymes.	Philip Kerr, May 21, 1778.
Fredk. Hirsh.	Geo. Reyball, May 12, 1778.

Bernard Hubley, *Lieut.*

ROLL OF CAPTAIN PETER BOYER'S COMPANY, GERMAN
REGIMENT, CONTINENTAL TROOPS, COMMANDED
BY LIEUTENANT COLONEL WELTNER.

Sergeants.

Christ'n Kleckner.	Geo. Luft.

Corporals.

Jacob Wentz.	Jacob Mayer.

Drummer.

John Hart.

Fifer.

Jos. Alexander.

Privates.

Fred'k Rively.
Henry Shuler.
Jacob Harper.
Henry Lear.
Ch'n Riffit.
Fred'k Kerle.
Fred'k Delinger.
Math's Rinehart.
Jacob Botomer.
Philip Lach.
Wm. Kerle.
Ch'n Leidy.
Rud. Brookhouse.
John Weidman.
Jacob Grumly.
Nich's Werner.
 P. Boyer, *Capt.*

Thos. Wheler.
Jno. Firmire.
Con'd Gerhart.
Ch'n Fleish.
Dan'l Coppt, July 18, 1776.
James Gohoon, August 13, 1776.
Mich'l Firmick.
Peter Coppus.
Dav'd Drexler.
Martin Shudy.
Henry Deberring, July 13.
Jno. Sanliter, July 16, 1776.
Dav'd Bloom, July 30.
Geo. Keretiter.
Ch's Christman, July 30.

ROLL OF CAPTAIN GEORGE HUBLEY'S COMPANY OF CONTINENTAL FORCES IN THE SERVICE OF THE UNITED STATES OF AMERICA, COMMANDED BY LIEUTENANT COLONEL WELTNER.

Sergeant Major.

Geo. Francis, November 4, 1776.

Sergeants.

John Johnstone, November 4, 1776.
Lewis Reiskly, August, 1776.

Corporals.

Lewis Brownsbery, July 21, 1776.
Geo. Funk, July 20, 1776.

Drummer.

Israel Jenkins, October, 1776.

Privates.

Mathias Flough, July 13, 1776.
Geo. Linn, July 24, 1776.
Jacob Visler, July 27, 1776.
Adam Neble, July 23, 1776.
Christ'n Mencher, July 25, 1776.
John Leonhard, August 4, 1776.
Jacob Thirk, August 5, 1776.
John Kuhn, August 7, 1776.
Christ'n Hake, August 28, 1776.
Thos. Turner, September 1, 1776.
Henry Dominick, September 4, 1776.
Christ'n Baker, November 5, 1776.
Geo. Hansel, November 2, 1776.
John Crane.
Robert Stroud.
Philip Donochor.
John Rysbecker.
John Kephard.
John Snyder, August 13, 1776.

Mathias Leaf.
Casper Isralo, August, 1776.
Burchardt Hand, July 10, 1776.
Christn. Byerly, September 5, 1776.
    Geo. Hubley, *Capt.*

Roll of the First Vacant Company, German Regiment, Commanded by Lieutenant Colonel Weltner.

Sergeant.

George Price, June 2, 1776.

Corporal.

Fred'k Wilhalm, August 3, 1776.

Privates.

John Partner, August 3, 1776.
John Smith, May 1, 1776.
Philip Gilman, June 8, 1776.
Everhart Myer, September 1, 1776.
Patrick Higgins, November 1, 1776.
John Christman, August 5, 1776.
Henry Capple, October 1, 1776; on cattle guard.
Philip Cakel, August 1, 1776.
Henry Sivert, June 10, 1776.
Jacob McLain, June 29, 1776.
Abraham Price, August 9.
    Henry Maag, *Ensign.*

[Endorsed] Company Roll of the First Vacant Company, German Regiment Commanded by Lieutenant Colonel Weltner.

ROLL OF THE SECOND VACANT COMPANY IN THE GER-
MAN REGIMENT OF CONTINENTAL FORCES
COMMANDED BY LIEUTENANT COLONEL
LUDWIG WELTNER.

Sergeants.

Jacob Low, August 6, 1776.
Henry Hean, July 26, 1776.
John Leather, August 3, 1776.

Corporals.

Jesey Honshitt, July 27, 1776.
John Shatz, July 29, 1776.
Christofiel Standly, July 19, 1776.

Privates.

John Washtel, July 30, 1776.
Peter Amrick, July 25, 1776.
Peter Cuntz, July 25, 1776.
Jacob Miller, Jr., July 25, 1776.
Andrew Roberson, July 25, 1776.
John Cline, August 11, 1776.
Ben. Corley, August 22, 1776.
Levi Arron, April 22, 1776.
Henry Herrin, July 25, 1776.
Philip Stoter, August 11, 1776.
Edward Roberson, July 25, 1776.
Michel Moser, July 30, 1776.
Jacob Crammer, July 19, 1776.
John Abel, July 19, 1776.
Martain Walzkins, July 19, 1776.
Michel Moser, July 26, 1776.
Jacob Smadron, April 21, 1776.

Rudolph Marole, July 21, 1776.
Camer Hill, February 27, 1778.
Wm. Taylor, August 20, 1776.
Bertel Engel, July 31, 1776.
Peter Huber, July 31, 1776.
Robert Dill, July 31, 1776.
Philip Fisher, August 4, 1776.
Thomas Mehoney, April 2, 1778.
John Dalton, April 22, 1778.
Michel Hardman, April 20, 1776.
Jacob Miller, July 19, 1776.
Jacob Ricknogel, August 1, 1776.
John Snider, August 1, 1776.
Henry Cronise, August 1, 1776.
Lennerd Lodwick, August 3, 1776.
Ludwick Wisinger, August 4, 1776.
John Zimerman, July 25, 1776.
Conrad Housman, July 25, 1776.
Adam Kintner, July 19, 1776.
Michel Stoner, July 19, 1776.
Henry Fisher, April 21, 1778.
Fredk. Shoemaker, May 8, 1778.
James Dayler, April 27, 1778.
John Matodey, May 2, 1778.
James Johnston, May 20, 1778.
Charles Follen, April 23, 1778.
Thos. Mehoney, May 13, 1778.
Alex'r Smith, May 20, 1778.
John Wade, May 5, 1778.
John Humore, May 12, 1778.
John Timbler, April 20, 1778.
Christofiel Keplinger, June 18, 1778.
Philip Henkel, June 18, 1778.

Thos. Colhons, June 18, 1778.
Abraham Miller, June 18, 1778.
Parnham Rednour, June 18, 1778.
Jacob Alexander, January 28, 1778.
   William Rick, *Lieut.*

ROLL OF THE THIRD VACANT COMPANY IN THE GERMAN REGIMENT OF CONTINENTAL FORCES IN THE SERVICE OF THE UNITED STATES, COMMANDED BY LIEUTENANT COLONEL LEWIS WELTNER.

Sergeants.

Wm. Rumelson, July 12, 1776.
Fred'k Sollars, July 29, 1776.
Geo. Stauffer, July 30, 1776.

Corporals.

Joseph Hook, July 31, 1776.
Jacob Etter, July 15, 1776.
Wm. Krafft, July 27, 1776.

Drummer.

Adam Mattrell.

Fifer.

Mich'l Smith.

Privates.

Mich'l Crowley, August 15, 1776.
John Shlifl, July 20, 1776.
Fred'k Wm. Haller, July 18, 1776.
John Shafer, July 29, 1776.
Wolfgang Elzberger, July 17, 1776.
Vendle Lorantz, July 20, 1776.

Geo. Lightherser, August 26, 1776.
Jacob Meiley, August 11, 1776.
John Schryock, July 16, 1776.
Joseph Stricter, July 17, 1776.
Henry Rumfelt, July 17, 1776.
Rudolph Crower, July 15, 1776.
Ferdinant Lorantz, July 15, 1776.
Jacob Myers, July 20, 1776.
Philip Kantz, July 20, 1776.
Henry Smith, July 25, 1776.
Paul Estin, July 30, 1776.
Geo. Crethorn, August 2, 1776.
David Fink, August 7, 1776.
Jos. Williams, August 23, 1776.
John Smith, August 15, 1776.
John B. Dyche, July 14, 1776.
Thos. Laramot, August 25, 1776.
Martin Lanz, July 15, 1776.
Geo. Rittlemys, September 10, 1776.
Jacob Ruppert, July 15, 1776.
Godlieb Danroth, August 2, 1776.
Geo. Good, June 19, 1778.
Mathias Smith.
Wm. Rider.
Wm. Mallins.
Benj'n Cole.
Timothy Cahill.
Robert Smith.
Cornelius Vaughan.
Christian Castner.
Wm. Pope.
Jacob Kauffman, April 10, 1778.
Thos. Proctor, April 16, 1778.

Rich'd Gaul, April 16, 1778.
John Shiveley, May 1, 1778.
Thos. Halfpenny, April 22, 1778.
Wm. Johnston, May 16, 1778.
John Richards, June 2, 1778.
Albert Hendricks, June 18, 1778.
Philip Bates, June 18, 1778.
Geo. Arnold, June 18, 1778.
John Fennell.
Jacob Feymiller, July 15, 1776.
Mich'l Kershner, July 16, 1776.
John Harley, July 19, 1776.
David Mumma.
Abr'm Frantz.
Anthony Miller, July 20, 1776.
James Murphy.

Martin Shugart, *Lieut.*

[Endorsed] Return of Third Vacant Company in the German Regiment, Commanded by Lieutenant Colonel Lewis Weltner, Esq.

Roll of the Fourth Vacant Company in the German Regiment of Continental Forces, Commanded by Lieutenant Colonel Lewis Weltner.

Sergeants.

Jacob Hose, August 11, 1776.
John Jaquit, July 21, 1776.
William Lewis, July 16, 1776.

Corporals.

Barned Frey, July 26, 1776.
John Breecher, July 17, 1776.
John Michael, July 16, 1776.
Adam Stonebreaker, August 22, 1776.

Drummer.

Moses McKensey, April 2, 1778.

Fifer.

Joshua McKensey, April 20, 1778.

Privates.

Henry Stroam, July 17, 1776.
John Flick, August 2, 1776.
Henry Michael, August 22, 1776.
Melcher Binner, July 17, 1776.
Jacob Klein, August 1, 1776.
Jonathan Hacket, July 18, 1776.
Michael Camlee, July 26, 1776.
Thomas Clifton, August 3, 1776.
Michael Boward, July 17, 1776.
John Crofft, July 27, 1776.
John Kibler, August 8, 1776.
Christ. Wagner, August 10, 1776.
John Smith, July 27, 1776.
Patrick Flemming, August 9, 1776.
Mathias Keiser, August 10, 1776.
Michael Weaver, July 19, 1776.
George Riggleman, August 18, 1776.
John Haltfield, August 13, 1776.
Conrad Hogle, July 20, 1776.
Christ. Reaser, July 27, 1776.

Henry Panther, July 27, 1776.
James Duncan, July 16, 1776.
George Wilhelm, July 17, 1776.
John Etnier, July 16, 1776.
Philip Timothy, August 2, 1776.
Jacob Bishop, July 26, 1776.
Alexander Sailor, July 28, 1776.
Jacob Heefner, August 18, 1776.
John Smithley, August 2, 1776.
Frederick Locher, August 5, 1776.
Michael Yockley, July 22, 1776.
Henry Quir, July 18, 1776.
John Cropp, August 11, 1776.
Henry Stattler, August 4, 1776.
George Gitting, July 28, 1776.
Jacob Beltzhoover, July 26, 1776.
Jacob Masser, May 12, 1778.
Richard Oquin, May 1, 1778.
James Ashley, April 25, 1778.
James Smith, May 20, 1778.
Thomas Rowlands, June 18, 1778.
George Bantz, June 18, 1778.
Philip Fisher, August 9, 1778.
Frederick Filler, July 9, 1778.
Francis Cavin, August 4, 1778.
James Furnier, July 26, 1778.
Frederick Sweitzer, July 16, 1778.
John Armstrong, July 27, 1778.
Henry Tomm, July 27, 1778; wounded.
Jacob Hoover, July 16, 1778; wagoner.
Henry Wagner, August 5, 1778.

   Christian Myer, *Lieut.*

[Endorsed] Roll of the Fourth Vacant Company in

the German Regiment, Commanded by Lieutenant Colonel Weltner.

ROLL OF THE FIFTH VACANT COMPANY, GERMAN REGIMENT, COMMANDED BY LIEUTENANT COLONEL LEWIS WELTNER.

First Lieutenant.

Michael Boyer.

Sergeants.

Michael Haus, August 16, 1776.
Fred'k Lindeman, August 21, 1776.
David Diffenderfer, August 25, 1776.

Corporals.

John Weyand, August 25, 1776.
Fred'k Siperil, August 19, 1776.

Drummer.

Geo. Facundus, May 4, 1777.

Fifer.

Francis Bordignon, October 2, 1776.

Privates.

Francis Mulz, August 5, 1776.
Philip Cline, August 6, 1776.
Michael Rummel, August 9, 1776.
Marc Miller, August 19, 1776.
John Soene, August 21, 1776.
Ch'n Kuhn, August 24, 1776.

John Kochenderfer, August 26, 1776.
Philip Moyer, September 3, 1776.
James Halfpenny.
Ditrick Banick.
Geo. Keller.
Thomas Keen.
Geo. Smith.
Henry Swethe, April 27, 1777.
Adam Stoll, April 27, 1777.
Tobias Hess, April 27, 1777.
Peter Moyer, May 24, 1777.
Adam Spect, April 27, 1777.
Geo. Gruber.
Henry Herrgood.
Michael Hess.
Casper Wagoner.
Philip Helter, August 9, 1776.
Abram Dutton, August 4, 1776.
Henry Shaub, May, 9, 1777.
Andrew Hawke, April 27, 1777.

Michael Boyer, *Lieut.*

HOUSE ON THE SCENE OF THE BATTLE OF GERMANTOWN.

MUSTER ROLL OF CAPTAIN WILLIAM HEYSER'S COM-
PANY OF THE GERMAN REGIMENT, COMMANDED BY
BARON ARENDT, COLONEL; QUIBBLE TOWN,
MAY 22, 1777.

Captain.

William Heyser, July 12, 1776.

Lieutenants.

Jacob Kotz, July 12, 1776.
Adam Smith, July 12, 1776; resigned May 4, 1777.

Sergeants.

David Morgan.   John Jaquet.
Jacob Hose.   Jacob Miller.

Corporals.

Andrew Tiller, discharged   Bernard Frey.
   by the Surgeon.   William Lewis.
Philip Reevenacht.   John Breecher.

Privates.

Henry Stroam.   Melchoir Benner.
Adam Stonebreaker.   John Fogle.
John Flick.   Francis Myers.
Henry Michael.   Jacob Kliene.
Philip Fisher.   John Micheal; on com-
Jonathan Hacket.   mand with Paymaster.
Henry Tomm.   Simon Fogler.
Jacob Hoover.   John Robinson.
Michael Camler.   Jacob Beltzhoover.
Henry Wagner.   Peter Sheese.

15

George Harmony.
Michael Bawart.
John Croft.
Frederick Filler.
John Kibler.
John Smith.
Math's Keyser.
Michael Weaver.
Nicholas Beard.
John Hatfield.
Conrad Hoyle.
Christian Reaver.
Adam Lower.
Ph. Greechbaum.
James Duncan.
John Etnier.
Philip Smithly.
Christian Sides.
Jacob Bishop.
Alexander Saylor.
John Smithley.
Frederick Locher.
Michael Yockley.
James Fournier.
Henry Quir.
John Cropp.
H'y Statler.
George Gitting.
Thomas Clifton; sick in hospital.
George Riggleman; on command with Commissary.

Thomas Burney.
John Metz.
John Shoemaker.
Tobias Friend.
Adam Leiser.
Jacob Greathouse.
Robert Hartness.
Martin Piffer.
George Miller.
Christopher Wagner.
Mathias Dunkle.
John Roth.
Jacob Piffer.
George Bouch.
Henry Panthar.
Jacob Grass.
George Wilhelm.
George Wise.
Jacob Heffner.
Everhard Smith.
John Armstrong.
Godfried Young.
Peter Gitting; died March 18, 1777.
Archibald Fleegert; died in Philadelphia.
Wentle Strayley; died January 15, 1777.
Balzer Fisher; died March 15, 1777.
Frederick Switzer; missing at Bonumstown, May 10, 1777.

May 22, 1777, mustered; then Capt. Wm. Heyser's Company, as specified in the above Roll.

Will Bradford, Jr., *D. M. M. G.*

MUSTER ROLL OF THE THIRD VACANT COMPANY OF THE GERMAN REGIMENT COMMANDED BY LIEUTENANT COLONEL LEWIS WELTNER FOR THE MONTH OF MARCH, 1778.

Captain.

Philip Graybill; resigned March 12, 1778.

Lieutenants.

1st. William Rice.   2d. Martin Shugart.

Sergeants.

1. William Rumelson.
2. Frank Sollars; on furlough.
3. Geo. Stauffer.

Corporals.

1. Joseph Hook.   2. Jacob Etter.

Privates.

1. Ferdinant Lorantz.
2. Mich. Crowlcy.
3. Anthony Miller; on furlough.
4. John Schlife.
5. John Eysell; on furlough.
6. Mich'l Thershner; on furlough.
7. John Harley; on furlough.

8. Frank Wm. Haller.
9. Jacob Myers; on guard.
10. John Schaffer.
11. Philip Shantz.
12. Wolgong Ebeberger; on command.
13. Wendle Lorantz.
14. Henry Smith.
15. Nichl. Keyser; on guard.
16. Joseph Williams.
17. Abrm. Frantz.
18. Geo. Sighheiser; on furlough.
19. David Muma; on command.
20. James Caple; on command.
21. Peter Baker; on furlough.
22. Jacob Meily; on command.
23. John Schryock; sick at present.
24. Wm. Krafft; on command.
25. Joseph Striter.
26. Jacob Frymiller.
27. Paul Esling.
28. Geo. Cretho.
29. David Fink.
30. John Smith; on command.
31. Henry Rumfelt; on command.
32. Rudolph Crower.
33. Mich. Huling; died 2d February.

VALLEY FORGE, April 3d.

Mustered there the Third Vacant Company as specified in the above Roll.

A. Dickey, *D. M. M.*

A Return of the Names of the Officers, Non-commissioned Officers, and Privates, of the Five Companies Belonging to the State of Pennsylvania in the German Regiment Commanded by Lieutenant Colonel Ludwig Weltner, and the States, Counties and Towns in which they were Commissioned and Enlisted, with the Dates of their Appointments, Enlistments and the Terms Enlisted for.

			ENLISTED.	
Daniel Burchardt,	Major,	Phila.,	April 9, 1777,	During War.
Jacob Brunner,	Captain,	do.	July 8, 1776,	do.
Peter Boyer,	Captain,	do.	May 9, 1777,	do.
William Rice,	Captain,	Kensington,	Jan. 4, 1778,	do.
Bernard Hubley,	Captain,	Lanc.,	Feb. 24, 1778,	do.
Philip Shrawder,	1st Lieut.,	Phila.,	May 13, 1777,	do.
John Weidman,	1st Lieut.,	Lanc. Co.,	May 14, 1777,	do.
Jacob Cramer,	1st Lieut.,	Phila.,	Jan. 8, 1778,	do.
Godfried Schwartz,	1st Lieut.,	do.	Feb. 24, 1778,	do.
Marcus Young,	1st Lieut.,	Lanc.,	March 12, 1778,	do.
John Weidman,	Ensign,	Phila.,	Aug. 16, 1777,	do.
David Diffenderfer,	Ensign,	Lanc.,	July 23, 1778,	do.
Christian Glickner,	Ensign,	Phila.,	July 23, 1778,	do.
Peter Peres,	Surgeon,	Penn.,	Oct. 1, 1778,	do.
Fred'k Teats,	Private,	Phila. Co.,	July 20, 1776,	do.
William Heims,	do.	Phila.,	July 16, 1776,	do.
Philip Shearer,	do.	do.	July 21, 1776,	do.
Fred'c Hersh,	do.	do.	July 20, 1776,	do.
Lewis Gerlinger,	do.	do.	July 20, 1776,	do.
Henry Shnider,	Private,	Reading,	July 25, 1776,	During War.
Thomas Bontzy,	do.	Phila.,	Oct. 16, 1776,	do.
Martin Heidler,	do.	do.	Aug. 20, 1776,	do.
Conrad Rauch,	do.	do.	July 17, 1776,	do.
Jacob Shepherd,	do.	do.	Aug. 10, 1776,	do.
John Marsh,	do.	Lanc.,	Aug. 15, 1776,	do.
Henry Ammerich,	do.	Phila.,	July 17, 1776,	do.
Theodore Hartman,	do.	do.	July 15, 1776,	do.
Frederick Rankey,	do.	do.	July 23, 1776,	3 years.
Jacob Myers,	do.	do.	July 16, 1776,	During War.
George Ottinberger,	do.	do.	July 28, 1776,	do.
John Keyser,	do.	do.	July 27, 1776,	do.
William Lehman,	do.	do.	July 29, 1776,	do.
Nicholas Stover,	do.	do.	July 20, 1776,	do.
Frederic Rively,	do.	do.	July 21, 1776,	do.

ENLISTED.

Henry Shuber,	Private,	Phila.,	July 21, 1776,	During War.
Fred'c Kerls,	do.	do.	July 21, 1776,	do.
Mich'l Ferrick,	do.	do.	July 28, 1776,	do.
Charles Christman,	do.	do.	July 28, 1776,	do.
Christian Leidy,	do.	do.	July 20, 1776,	do.
Martin Shudy,	do.	do.	Sept. 4, 1776,	do.
George Kersteter,	do.	do.	July 29, 1776,	do.
Peter Coppus,	do.	do.	Dec. 10, 1776,	do.
Charles Gerhard,	do.	do.	Jan. 20, 1777,	do.
John Weidman,	do.	Berks Co.,	Aug. 10, 1776,	do.
Henry Lear,	do.	Phila.,	July 20, 1776,	do.
Christian Riffet,	do.	do.	July 25, 1776,	do.
Frederic Delinger,	do.	do.	Aug. 21, 1776,	do.
Jacob Bottomer,	do.	Berks Co.,	Aug. 9, 1776,	do.
Philip Lash,	do.	Phila.,	July 14, 1776,	do.
Rudolph Brookhaus,	do.	do.	Aug. 9, 1776,	do.
Jacob Grumley,	do.	do.	Aug. 20, 1776,	do.
Fred'c Wheeler,	do.	do.	Aug. 10, 1776,	do.
John Fesmire,	do.	do.	Sept. 4, 1776,	do.
David Drexler,	do.	do.	Oct. 10, 1776,	do.
Christian Fleish,	do.	do.	Aug. 15, 1776,	do.
Philip Cook,	do.	do.	Sept. 30, 1776,	do.
William Kerls,	do.	do.	Aug. 10, 1776,	do.
David Bloom,	do.	Berks Co.,	Aug. 8, 1776,	3 years.
Jacob Harper,	do.	Phila.,	Aug. 2, 1776,	During War.
Henry Deperwing,	do.	do.	Aug. 3, 1776,	3 years.
Daniel Copple,	do.	do.	July 28, 1776,	do.
John Sunliter,	do.	do.	July 20, 1776,	do.
Philip Gillman,	do.	Lanc. Co.,	Aug. 17, 1776,	3 years.
John Smith,	do.	Phila.,	Dec. 2, 1776,	During War.
Eberhard Myer,	do.	do.	Feb. 25, 1779,	do.
Jacob McLane,	do.	do.	Feb. 25, 1779,	do.
Mich'l Broadback,	do.	do.	Feb. 25, 1779,	do.
Joseph Mast,	do.	Lanc. Co.,	July 24, 1776,	3 years.
Henry Cybert,	do.	do.	July 27, 1776,	do.
John Portner,	do.	do.	Feb. 25, 1779,	During War.
Henry Yaple,	do.	Northampton Co.,	Feb. 25, 1779,	do.
Philip Yackel,	do.	Phila.,	Feb. 25, 1779,	do.
Christian Haag,	do.	Phila.,	Aug. 28, 1776,	do.
Jacob Wheasler,	do.	Reading,	Oct. 23, 1776,	do.
John Kipart,	do.	Phila.,	Oct. 23, 1776,	do.

ENLISTED.

Jacob Sherrick,	Private,	Lanc.,	Oct. 23, 1776,	During War.
John Coon,	do.	Phila.,	Oct. 23, 1776,	do.
Henry Dominick,	do.	do.	Oct. 23, 1776,	do.
Matthew Leaf,	do.	do.	July 11, 1776,	do.
George Lynn,	do.	do.	Oct. 23, 1776,	do.
John Leonard,	do.	do.	Oct. 23, 1776,	do.
Christian Winger,	do.	German-town,	Oct. 23, 1776,	do.
John Crane,	do.	———,	Oct. 23, 1776,	do.
Matthias Flock,	do.	German-town,	Oct. 23, 1776,	do.
Thomas Terner,	do.	Kensing-ton,	Oct. 23, 1776,	do.
Adam Nebel,	do.	German-town,	Oct. 23, 1776,	do.
George Hansel,	do.	Phila.,	Sept. 29, 1776,	do.
Christian Baker,	do.	do.	Oct. 12, 1776,	do.
Casper Isaloo,	do.	do.	Aug. 8, 1776,	3 years.
John Rybaker,	do.	do.	Aug. 7, 1776,	During War.
Philip Stroad,	do.	do.	Oct. 21, 1776,	do.
Robt. Donahoo,	do.	do.	Oct. 21, 1776,	do.
John Snider,	do.	do.	Oct. 23, 1776,	do.
Peter Fortner,	do.	do.	May 11, 1779,	do.

Daniel Burchardt, *Major.*

CHAPTER XI.

The Pennsylvania-German Emergency Men.

Wappen von Heſſen-Naſſau.

NOT only did the Pennsylvania-German loyally serve his country in its regular Continental regiments, and take part in their years of weary marches, terrible hardships, and glorious, even though at times unfortunate, battles, but, on all other occasions, when the emergency arose, and the call came to those whom age, family ties and cares, even health, forbade their attempting a lengthy enlistment, he likewise performed his full duty.

Here, again, the historian is prevented from doing justice to these people, and recounting all their deeds, not alone because of the absence of all but the most meager data on the subject, but because, in addition, as was the case with the Continentals, the Pennsylvania-Germans, as individuals, were scattered, more or less numerously, throughout *all* the different counties and their various militia battalions.

PLAN OF THE BATTLE OF PRINCETON, FOUGHT JANUARY 3, 1777.

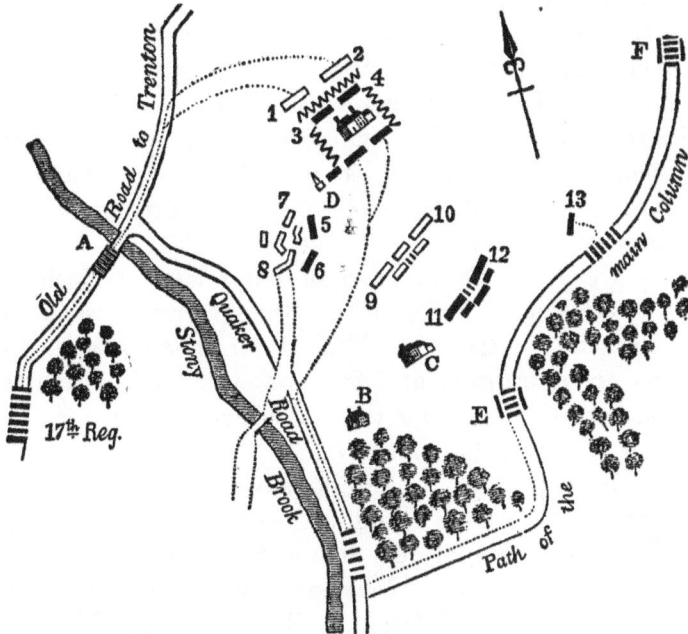

REFERENCES.—*A*, Bridge on the old Trenton road; *B*, Friends meeting-house; *C*, T. Clark's house, in which Gen. Mercer died; *D*, The place where Gen. Mercer was mortally wounded; *E*, Head of column when first seen by the British; *F*, Head of column after Mercer's engagement; 1, 2, The British 17th Regiment; 3, 4, Mercer's detachment, commencing the action; 9, 10, The 17th Regiment, formed to dislodge Moulder; 11, 12, The Pennsylvania Militia under Washington; 13, Hitchcock's regiment; 5, 6, Pursuit of the Americans; 7, 8, Retreat of the British.

The one, and only, feasible way of treating the subject, with some degree of fairness, is to take the Pennsylvania-German counties, well known as such, and portray the part taken by each one of them, as a whole, in the emergency operations of the war.

These counties were Northampton (practically entire), Berks (practically entire), Lancaster (practically entire), Philadelphia (especially that part now called Montgomery), Cumberland (in part), York (in part), Northumberland (in part), Bedford (in smaller part).

Under the head of Northampton county is included the present Lehigh county, with parts of the present Monroe and Schuylkill counties; under that of Lancaster is included the present Lebanon and Dauphin counties; under that of Philadelphia is taken the present Montgomery county.

Shortly after the adoption of our immortal Declaration of Independence came the British army to strike a deadly blow at the life of this same independence, by means of the capture of New York city, and, with this threatened invasion, came the first emergency call for volunteers to aid in its defence.

On June 3, 1776, Congress resolved "that a Flying Camp be immediately established in the middle colonies, and that it consist of ten thousand men . . .," to be raised in Pennsylvania, Maryland, and Delaware, and, on the same day, "*Resolved,* That thirteen thousand eight hundred militia be employed to reinforce the army at New York."

The several counties at once began, enthusiastically, the formation of their " Associators " into battalions for this " Flying Camp."

The troops of the Flying Camp were placed under command of Gen. Hugh Mercer (killed at Princeton, January 3, 1777); and stationed at Perth Amboy and points north of that place, opposite the west side of Staten Island, where the British forces were encamped. Prior to July 15, some two thousand of its men were sent to

College of New Jersey, Princeton.

Washington, at New York, where many of them did noble duty in the battle on Long Island, August 27. Parts of the Flying Camp took part in the later movements about New York city, especially in the battle and capture of Fort Washington; and, when the dark days came, prior to Trenton (where, by order of Washington, the Pennsylvania militia supported Gen. Mercer), and Princeton, the cause was saved, and these battles gained, merely because of the presence of other parts of the same emergency volunteers.

The testimony of Washington is as follows: "The readiness with which the militia of Pennsylvania have shown in engaging in the service of their country at an inclement season of the year, when my army was reduced to a handful of men, and our affairs were in the most critical situation, does great honor to them."

The promptness with which the militia of Pennsylvania responded to the demands upon them "enabled General Washington," wrote John Cadwalader, "to strike a blow which has greatly changed the face of our affairs."

Says another, high in command, "their behavior at Trenton in the cannonade, and at Princeton, was brave, firm and manly; they were broken at first in the action at Princeton, but soon formed in the face of grape-shot, and pushed on with a spirit that would do honor to veterans, besides which they have borne a winter's campaign with soldier-like patience."

LANCASTER COUNTY.

In Lancaster a meeting was called, on the memorable 4th of July, 1776, for the purpose of choosing two brigadier-generals, consisting of delegates from the fifty-three battalions of Associators. There were present:

First Battalion,—Col. George Ross, Lieut. Col. Adam Reigart. Privates,—Christ. Wirtz, Francis Baily.

Second Battalion,—Col. Curtis Grubb, Major Philip Marstaller. Privates,—James Sullivan, Lodwick Ziering.

Third Battalion,—Lieut. Col. Robert Thompson, Major Thomas Smith. Privates,—John Smith, Isaac Erwin.

Fourth Battalion,—Capt. Joseph Sherer, Capt. James Murray. Privates,—Abraham Darr, William Leard.

Fifth Battalion,—Col. James Crawford, Capt. James Mercer. Privates,—Henry Slaymaker, John Whitehill.

Sixth Battalion,—Lieut. Col. Alexander Lowry, Major James Cunningham. Privates,—John Bealy, John Jameson.

Seventh Battalion,—Col. M. Slough, Lieut. Col. Leonard Raudfang. Privates,—Christian Bough, Simon Snider.

Eighth Battalion,—Col. Peter Grubb, Capt. Henry Weaver. Privates,—William Smith, George Ury.

Ninth Battalion,—Lieut. Col. Christian Wegman, Major Michael Till. Privates,—Michael Diffenbaugh, Anthony Debler.

Tenth Battalion,—Col. John Ferree, Lieut. Col. Andrew Little. Privates,—George Line, Joseph Whitehill.

Eleventh Battalion,—Col. Timothy Green, Lieut. Col. Peter Heddricks. Privates,—William Barnet, George Little.

The meeting elected Daniel Roberdeau and James Ewing as the two brigadiers, and resolved:

"That we will march under the Direction & Command of our Brigadier Generals to the assistance of all or any of the free, independent States of America."

On July 8, the Committee of Safety appointed Dr. Adam Kuhn (son of Dr. Adam Simon Kuhn, of Lancaster) as physician and director-general of the hospital for the provincial troops under orders for New Jersey.

The record for the Lancaster county troops in the Flying Camp is not sufficiently complete to allow of a detailed account, but, from the minutes of the Committee of Safety, the following interesting items have been gleaned.

Col. Matthias Slough's Second Battalion.—Clothing and arms furnished May 25; same to command of Capt. Jacob Glotz (Klotz). Col. Slough's battalion was amongst the first to join the camp, some of its companies, if not all, reporting about July 8. It was in the battle of Long Island, and, after performing its tour of duty in the vicinity of New York, returned home, and was subsequently employed in guarding prisoners of war at Lancaster and Lebanon. The middle of December it was ordered to march immediately to Philadelphia.

Col. George Ross' Battalion.—Rifles furnished July 15. Mention is made of the companies of Capt. Hoofnagle and Capt. Andrew Graff. The date is not given when the battalion marched to New Jersey. Capt. Mercer's company was ordered to march immediately to Philadelphia the middle of December.

Col. James Crawford's Battalion.—Arms, etc., furnished August 5.

Col. Bartram Galbraith's Battalion.—Arms, etc., furnished August 13. Mention made of Capt. Robert McCallen's company.

Col. Thomas Porter's Battalion.—Arms furnished August 29. Mention made of Capts. William Ross, John Boyd, John Eckman and John Patton.

Col. John Ferree's Battalion.—Arms furnished in August. Mention made of Capts. John Rowland, Jacob Carpenter, ———— Bowman, Alexander Martin, Robert McKee, Andrew Bean, John Withers.

Col. Peter Grubb's Battalion.—Arms delivered August 22. Mention made of Capts. Alexander Martin, Henry Weaver, ———— Adams, ———— Morgan.

Col. James Burd, and Col. Timothy Green.—Made up principally of men living in what is now Dauphin county. Reference is made to the companies of Capts. James Murray, James Cowden, Joseph Sherer, William Bell, Richard Manning, Jacob Fridley, John Reed and Allbright Deibler, of Burd's battalion, and Capts. Richard McQuown, William Brown, Thomas Koppenheffer and James Rogers, of Green's battalion.

Mention is also made of a company commanded by Capt. Paul Zantzinger, of Lancaster. Other companies named are those of Capt. Joshua Evans, Eighth battalion, Capt. Wm. Parey, Capt. John Jones, Capt. Matthew Hand, Capt. Matthew Smith.

The Pennsylvania Archives contain the following list of captains "whose companies of militia went to Jersey in August, 1776, and were absent till Jan. and Feb., 1777."

Adams, Isaac.	Musser, George.
Boyd, John.	Peden, Hugh.
Boyd, Samuel.	Reed, John.
Brown, William.	Ross, James.
Campbell, Robert.	Sherer, Joseph.
Cowden, James.	Steele, William.
Crawford Christopher.	Page, Nathaniel.
Doebler, Albright.	Parry, Wilson.
Evans, Joshua.	Rutherford, John.

Fridley, Jacob.
Graff, Andrew.
Hollinger, Christian.
Hoofnagle, Peter.
Johnston, ———.
Jones, John.
Krug, Jacob.
Koppenheffer, Thomas.
Manning, Richard.
McCallen, Robert.
McQuown, Richard.
McKee, Robert.
Morgan, David.
Murray, James.
Morrison, James.
Martin, Alexander.

Tweed, John, Lieut. Commandant.
Watson, James, company commanded by Lieut. John Patton.
Weaver, Henry.
Whiteside, Thomas.
Wilson, Dorrington, commanded by Lieut. John Eckman.
Withers, John.
Wright, Joseph.
Yeates, Jasper.
Zantzinger, Paul.
Ziegler, Frederick.
Zimmerman, Bernard.

These companies were distributed in the battalions as follows. The dates are those of the muster rolls.

Col. James Burd's Battalion.

Capt. James Cowden.

Capt. Joseph Sherer—in active service during the whole of the spring and summer campaign of 1776, a number of the men being wounded in a skirmish with a party of British cavalry near Amboy, N. J.

Capt. James Murray—this company went into service, with others, in November or December, and were present at the battles of Trenton and Princeton.

Capt. William Bell.

Capt. Richard Manning—from Upper Paxtang and Hanover.

Capt. Jacob Fridley—from near Hummelstown; served

in the campaign and were present at Trenton and Princeton.

Capt. John Reed—in service until after Trenton and Princeton.

Capt. Albright Deibler—in active service for nearly a year, returning home in January, 1777. A portion of the command was captured at Long Island, and not released until the year 1778. During that and the following year, the company was commanded by Capt. John Hoffman, and, under him, they were on the frontiers, protecting the defenceless inhabitants from the encroachments of the Indians and Tories, who had their headquarters in southern New York, and against whom Gen. Sullivan's army was successfully sent in 1779.

Col Timothy Green's Battalion.

Capt. Thomas Koppenheffer. August 12, 1776.

Capt. Richard McQuown. August 31, 1776.

Capt. William Brown. August 31, 1776.

Capt. James Rogers. June 6, 1776.

Capt. John Reed. July 24, 1776.

Col. Thomas Porter's Battalion.

Capt. James Watson. August 13, 1776, under Lieut. John Patton, in Col. James Cunningham's battalion (Flying Camp), commanded by Lieut. Col. William Hays, in battle of Long Island.

Capt. Thomas Whiteside. August 13, 1776.

Capt. John Boyd. August 13, 1776.

Capt. James Morrison. August 15, 1776.

Capt. William Steel. August 15, 1776, under Ensign Samuel McIntire.

Capt. Dorrington Willson.   August 15, 1776, under Lieut. John Eckman.

Capt. Robert. Campbell.

Capt. ——— Ross, detachment, under Lieut. Joshua Anderson.

Capt. ——— Johnston, detachment, under Lieut. John Tweed.

Capt. ——— Paxton, detachment, under Lieut. John Ramsey.

Col. John Ferree's Battalion.

Capt. John Withers.   August 19, 1776.
Capt. Samuel Boyd.   August 14, 1776.

Col. M. Slough's Battalion.

Capt. Jacob Krug.   September 9, 1776.
Capt. Jasper Yeates.   September 9, 1776.
Capt. Frederick Sigler.   September 5, 1776.
Capt. Barnard Zimmerman.   September 10, 1776.
Capt. Nathaniel Page.   September 11, 1776.
Capt. Joseph Wright.   September 11, 1776.

Col. Peter Grubb's Battalion.

Capt. Alexander Martin.   August 15, 1776.
Capt. Isaac Adams.   August 15, 1776.
Capt. John Jones.   August 15, 1776.
Capt. John Huver.   Ordered for defense of Philadelphia, June 24, 1776.
Capt. David Morgan.   Ordered for defence of Philadelphia, June 1, 1776; ordered to Jersey, August 16, 1776.
Capt. Robert Good.   Ordered for defence of Philadelphia, June 24, 1776.
Capt. Joshua Evans.   August 17, 1776.

Capt. William Parry. August 19, 1776.
Capt. Henry Weaver. August 20, 1776.
Capt. Christian Hollinger. August 26, 1776.

Col. Galbraith's Battalion.

Capt. Robert McCallen. August 20, 1776.
Capt. Hugh Pedan. August 12, 1776.
Capt. Robert McKee. August 13, 1776.
Capt. Andrew Graff. July 16, 1776, at Philadelphia.

Col. Ross' Battalion.

Capt. Lieut. Christopher Crawford, standing guard at Lancaster, July, 1776; commanding detachment of First battalion, containing his own company with those of Capts. Samuel Boyd, Andrew Graff, John Henry, Peter Hofnagle.

First Battalion—Flying Camp.

(In the Long Island Campaign.)

Colonel, James Cunningham.
Lieut. Col., William Hay.
Major, Thomas Edwards.

First Company.

Captain, Robert Clark.
1st Lieut., William Steel, promoted captain.
2d Lieut., James Turner.
3d Lieut., William Nelson.

Second Company.

Captain, James Watson.
1st Lieut., Thomas Lindsay.

2d Lieut., Robert Coleman.
3d Lieut., Matthew Swan.

Third Company.

Captain, Jacob Klotz, promoted.
1st Lieut., Thomas Robinson, promoted.
2d Lieut., John Campbell.
3d Lieut., Andrew Boggs, discharged on account of wounds received at Long Island.
3d Lieut., Thomas Whitmore, promoted from sergeant.

Fourth Company.

Captain, George Graeff.
1st Lieut., Conrad Connor.
2d Lieut., Dorrington Wilson.
3d Lieut., William Calhoun.

Fifth Company.

Captain, John Reed.
1st Lieut., James Collier.
2d Lieut., John Gilchrist, discharged August 14, 1776, on account of wound in right arm.
3d Lieut., Thomas Johnston, promoted 2d Lieut.
3d Lieut., John Cochran, promoted from sergeant.

Sixth Company.

Captain, Daniel Oldenbruck.
1st Lieut., Ludwig Meyer, promoted to Klotz's company.
2d Lieut., William McCullough.
3d Lieut., Benjamin Fickle, discharged on account of wound.
3d Lieut., John Rohrer, promoted from sergeant.

Seventh Company.

Captain, Joseph Work.
1st Lieut., Patrick Hays, discharged for disability.
2d Lieut., William Patterson, reported killed or taken prisoner at Long Island.
3d Lieut., Richard Keys, discharged for disability.
3d Lieut., James Barker, promoted from sergeant.

Eighth Company.

Captain, Timothy Green.
1st Lieut., William Allen, wounded at Long Island.
2d Lieut., ——— Weiser.
3d Lieut., John Barnett.

Ninth Company.

Captain, John McKown.
2d Lieut., John Bishop.
3d Lieut., Henry Buehler.

Fifth Battalion.

At the call for additional reinforcements a part of this battalion turned out, on December 19, 1776, and marched to Philadelphia, but were ordered back on the 26th, by Major General Putnam, to bring up the rest of the battalion, which they did, returning to Philadelphia January 20, 1777.

We have the following officers given:

Colonel, James Crawford.
Major, George Stewart.
Captain, Robert Boyer.

BERKS COUNTY.

The quota of Berks county Associators, to be furnished the Flying Camp, was 666 men, to which was voluntarily added one extra company. On Tuesday, July 2, 1776, a meeting was called in the court-house at Reading to select officers for this battalion, which resulted as follows:

Colonel, Henry Haller.

Lieut. Col., Nicholas Lutz, prisoner at Long Island, August 26, 1776, discharged September 10, 1779.

Major, Edward Burd, prisoner at Long Island.

Captains, Joseph Hiester, of Reading, prisoner at Long Island; Jacob Graul, of Reading; George May, of Reading; Jacob Maurer, of Maidencreek, prisoner at Long Island; John Ludwig, of Exeter; John Old, of Amity; George Douglass, of Amity; Peter Decker, of Reading, prisoner at Long Island.

Under the command of Lieut. Col. Lutz (Col. Haller remaining behind to complete other organizations) these troops joined Washington's army at New York city, hence are generally known as "Lutz's Battalion." They did noble duty in the battle of Long Island and lost heavily, a more detailed account of which has already been given. They lost, in the engagement, their lieutenant colonel, major, three captains and one lieutenant.

Besides this battalion other men were hurried forward to reinforce the American army.

Major Hiester's First Battalion.

On duty at Newtown, Bucks county, January 2, 1777. The only names given in connection with this organization are:

Lieut. Col., Henry Haller.
Major, Gabriel Hiester, December 10, 1776, in command.
Captains, George Will, John Diehl, Nicholas Scheffer.

Col. Mark Bird's Second Battalion.

At South Amboy, N. J. He reported to the Council of Safety, on August 7, 1776, that about three hundred of his men would be ready to march in several days, he having supplied them with provisions, tents and uniforms, at his own expense. He was a prominent iron-master at Birdsboro, but residing in Reading.

Lieut. Col. Lutz's Third Battalion.

This battalion had already proceeded to Long Island, where it arrived in time for the battle.

Col. Balzer Geehr's Fourth Battalion.

This battalion was also in active service.

Col. Patton's Fifth Battalion.

It was stationed at South Amboy on September 5, 1776, and officered as follows:
Lieut. Col., John Patton.
Majors, Joseph Thornburgh and Christian Lower.
Captains, John Lesher, Michael Furrer, George Miller, Michael Wolf.

They were collected together at Womelsdorf, and the following interesting itinerary of their march to Perth Amboy is given:

" At Womelsdorf from August 1st to 9th, getting cloth for tents and making tents. August 11th marched at 12 M. from Womelsdorf to Sinking Spring, 9 miles. Au-

gust 12th to Reading, 5 miles, and detained there by
Committee 13th & 14th.   August 15th, marched to
Levan's (Kutztown) 18 miles.   August 16th, to Bethlehem, 24 miles.   August 17th, to Straw's Tavern, 15 miles.
Next day, Sunday, remained there, raining all day.   August 19th, marched to South Branch of Raritan River, 20
miles.   August 20th, to 'Punch Bowl,' 20 miles.   August
21st, to Bonnamtown, 17 miles, and on 22d arrived at
Perth Amboy, 7 miles.   Total distance marched, 135
miles."

The Moravian Archives, at Bethlehem, contain the
following interesting items relative to the movements of
the Berks county troops through Bethlehem to the Jerseys,
in which we notice the company of Captain De Turk,
without being able to assign him to his proper command.

August 4, 1776.—Arrival of Capt. Old's company at
9 A. M.   Attended divine service, Rev. Ettwein presiding.

August 16.—Four companies of militia from Tulpehocken (Col. Patton's battalion), who lodged over-night
at the Sun Tavern.

August 23.—Capt. Will's company, who attended
evening service.

August 26.—Two companies arrived, one being from
Oley, under Capt. Daniel De Turk, who attended evening
service.

August 28.—A company from Reading, under Capt.
George May, arrived.

September 1.—The fourth battalion of Berks county
militia, under Col. Balser Geehr, arrived at noon, and,
at 4 P. M., Rev. Ettwein preached to them in the chapel.

NORTHAMPTON COUNTY.

Amongst the first to join Washington at New York were the Pennsylvania-German Associators from Northampton county. So rapidly did the recruiting progress that they were able to report early in August.

They were promptly stationed on Long Island, and it was these noble men who bore the brunt of the battle on August 27, and whose self-sacrifice saved the army from destruction. The Moravian records, at Bethlehem, contain this interesting item, under date of September 2–6:

" In these days, parties of militia on their return from New York, passed, bringing the intelligence that a battalion from the county (First battalion, Lieut. Col. Kechlein), had suffered severely at the engagement with the British on Long Island, on the 27th of August last, having left most of its men either dead or wounded."

The remnant of the regiment, left from that fight, was practically wiped out of existence at the battle and capture of Fort Washington, on November 16, 1776.

The details of the part taken by the Northampton county Flying Camp, in these two engagements, has been given heretofore, as well as a record of the losses sustained by Capt. Arndt's company.

At the close of the year 1776, the most dismal in the history of the war, a further requisition for troops was made on the county by the Pennsylvania Council of Safety, through Gen. Washington. Here, again, action was taken so promptly and energetically that some of the men, furnished upon this requisition, reached the army in time to participate in the battle of Trenton, and that of Princeton which followed.

The following data are in existence relative to these battalions, of which four were in active service:

First Battalion.

(Lost very heavily at Long Island and Fort Washington.)
Colonel, ——— Hart.
Lieut. Col., Peter Kechlein, July 17, 1776, in command
  at Long Island.
Major, Michael Probst, July 17, 1776.
Sergeant Major, John Spangenberg, July 17, 1776. The
  company officers were commissioned July 9, 1776.

First Company.

Captain, John Arndt.
1st Lieut., Joseph Martin.
2d Lieut., Peter Kechlein, Jr.
Ensign, Isaac Shimer.   Total number of men, 92.

Second Company.

Captain, Henry Hagenbuck.
1st Lieut., John Moritz.
2d Lieut., Godfrey Meyer.
Ensign, Jacob Mumma.   Total number of men, 120.

Third Company.

Captain, Nicholas Kern.
1st Lieut., Enoch Beer.
2d Lieut., Peter Baagley.
Ensign, William Daniel.   Total number of men, 57.

Fourth Company.

Captain, Timothy Jayne.
1st Lieut., Peter Middaugh.
2d Lieut., Benjamin Ennis.
Ensign, Abner Everitt.   Total number of men, 49.

This regiment, being practically wiped out of existence, was no longer in service after the battle at Fort Washington.

With the call for additional troops, in the fall, Northampton county sent out four battalions, of which we have these records:

First Battalion.

Colonel, George Taylor, December 10, 1776.
Captain, John Nelson (Mount Bethel company).

Second Battalion.

Colonel, Henry Geiger, October, 1776.
Captains, George Losch, Michael Snyder, ———— Rider.

Third Battalion.

Colonel, Yost Dreisbach, December 14, 1776.
Lieut. Col., John Siegfried, December 14, 1776, in command.
Captain, Alexander Brown, December 14, 1776; Roberts Hays from January 6, 1777.

Fourth Battalion.

Colonel, Jacob Stroud, October, 1776.
Major, John Van Camp.
Captains, ———— Schoonhaver, ———— Mead, Samuel Drake.

In addition to the names just given the following companies are mentioned, which cannot be properly located as to their battalions, but were a part of the Flying Camp of 1776:

Captain, ———— Miller (Hamilton company).
Captain, ———— Dull (Plainfield company).

Captain, —— Santee (Eighth company).
Captain, —— Sayler (Captain Adam Stahler).

YORK COUNTY.

The records of York county, unfortunately, are but fragmentary.

The following list is given of "Officers in Service, 1776."

Colonels.

William Rankin, June, 1776.
James Smith, August, 1776.
Matthew Dill (Fifth), August, 1776.
William Smith, December, 1776.
Robert McPherson, August, 1776.
Richard McAllister, August, 1776.
Joseph Donaldson, August, 1776.

Lieutenant Colonel.

Francis Holton (Fourth), August, 1776.

Majors.

Adam Vance, August, 1776.
John Dill (Fifth), August, 1776.
John Andrews, August, 1776.

Captains.

John McDonald, August, 1776.
—— Reed, August, 1776.
Simon Vanarsdalen (McA.), December, 1776.
William Ashton (Dill's), August, 1776.
Thomas Fisher (McA.), August, 1776.
William Smith, August, 1776.

Nicholas Bittinger (Fifth), September, 1776.
Michael Hahn (First), December, 1776.
Jacob Dritt (First), December, 1776.
John Harbeson (First), December, 1776.
Samuel Wilson (Fifth), December, 1776.
James Agnew (Second), December, 1776.
William Mitchell (Fifth), December, 1776.
Benjamin Savage (First), December, 1776.
James McCandless (W. Smith's), December, 1776.
———— McNary (W. Smith's), December, 1776.
William Rowan (Fourth), December, 1776.
Lewis Williams (Dill's), December, 1776.
Michael Smyser (First), July, 1776.
Hugh Campbell (Second), July, 1776.
George Dill, September 11, 1776.
Jost Herbach, September 11, 1776.
Samuel Nelson, September 11, 1776.
Daniel May, September 11, 1776.
John Paxton, September 11, 1776.
Robert McConaughy, September 11, 1776.
George Long, September 11, 1776.
Rudolph Spangler (First), July, 1776

Lieutenants.

Samuel Farra (Fifth), August, 1776.
William Rowan (Fourth), August, 1776.

Ensign.

Laurence Oats (Fifth), ————, 1776.

In July, 1776, five battalions of the York county emergency men were enrolled for duty with Washington. Two of these battalions saw active service. The Second battalion was commanded by Col. Richard McAllister, but did not contain a large element of Pennsylvania-Germans.

The First battalion, commanded by Col. Michael Swope, was almost entirely German. It suffered very severely at Long Island and Fort Washington. Capt. Graeff's company was captured in the former battle, only eighteen men returning to join the command; Capt. Stake's company lost many in the latter engagement. Ensign Jacob Barnitz, of York, was wounded at Long Island, and lay for fifteen months in prison. The following is its roster:

Colonel, Michael Swope.
Lieut. Col., Robert Stevenson.
Major, William Bailey.

First Company.

Captain, Michael Schmeiser.
1st Lieut., Zachariah Shugart.
2d Lieut., Andrew Robinson.
Ensign, William Wayne.

Second Company.

Captain, Gerhart Graeff.
Lieut., ——— Kauffman.
Ensign, Daniel McCallom.

Third Company.

Captain, Jacob Dritt.
1st Lieut., ——— Baymiller.
2d Lieut., ——— Clayton.
Ensign, Jacob Mayer.

Fourth Company.

Captain, Christian Stake.
1st Lieut., Cornelius Sheriff.
2d Lieut., Jacob Holzinger.
Ensign, Jacob Barnitz.

Fifth Company.

Captain, John McDonald.
1st Lieut., William Scott.
2d Lieut., Robert Patten.
Ensign, ———— Howe.

Sixth Company

Captain, John Ewing.
Ensign, John Paysley.

Seventh Company.

Captain, William Nelson.
1st Lieut., ———— Todd.
2d Lieut., Joseph Welsh.
Ensign, Alexander Nesbit.

Eighth Company.

Captain, ———— Williams.

Later in the fall the other battalions were in active service, containing many Pennsylvania-Germans, but no rolls are on hand to make clear the details, except that of Capt. Daniel Eyster's company of Pennsylvania-Germans, which served in Jersey from September, 1776, to January, 1777.

NORTHUMBERLAND COUNTY.

Northumberland county placed four battalions in service from February to October, 1776, more especially for its own frontier defense. Probably one fourth of these were Pennsylvania-Germans.

Under date of January 30, 1777, however, we have the muster roll of one company, all Pennsylvania-Germans, commanded by Capt Benjamin Weiser, who had recently commanded a company in the German Continental Regiment. It was then at or near Philadelphia. It is as follows:

Captain, Benjamin Weiser.
1st Lieut., Christopher Snider.
2d Lieut., Adam Shaffer.
3d Lieut., Joseph Van Gundy.
1st Sergeant, Marx Haines.
2d Sergeant, George Markel.
1st Corporal, Philip Moyer.
2d Corporal, Frederick Eisenhauer.
Drummer, Will. Thompson.

Privates.

Peter Hosterman.
John Levenguth.
Thomas Kitch.
John Meysor.
Philip Heitz.
John Stroup.
John Hauser.
Christian Shaffer.
George Moyer.
John Faust.

Adam Leffler.
Matthias Witmer.
Jacob Snider.
John Henter.
Henry Groninger.
George Troutner.
Christian Furst, sick at present.
Nicholas Shaffer.
Conrad Furst.
Henry Kaufman.

George Brossius.

Andrew Reitz.

Adam Herstetter.

Nicholas Brossius.

John Heim.

George Peifer.

Martin Kerstetter.

Zacharius Spengle.

Michael Newman.

Peter Weis.

BEDFORD COUNTY.

As in the case of Northumberland county so did Bedford place in the field two battalions of Associators whose duties seem to have been that of ranging its frontiers. The first battalion was under command of Col. John Piper, and the second of Col. George Wood, both going into service July, 1776. A fair number of Pennsylvania-Germans were scattered throughout the various commands.

The roll of Capt. Jacob Hendershot's company is given and shows a large proportion of Pennsylvania-Germans. Its record is that it "marched to camp under the command of Capt. Jacob Hendershot, and inroled 9th January; discharged 10th March and allowed pay until the 25th March, 1777."

JERSEY CAMPAIGN OF 1776.

Return of Pennsylvania Militia and Flying Camp, under command of Brigadier General Hugh Mercer, Perth Amboy, October 8, 1776.

Militia.	*Officers and Men.*
Lieut. Col. Tea, at South Amboy	181
Col. Allison, at Perth Amboy	144
Col. Savitz, at Perth Amboy	68
Col. Henderson, at Perth Amboy	31
Col. Slough, at Elizabeth	219

Flying Camp.

Col. Moore, at Perth Amboy.................. 382
Col. Richard McAllister, at Perth Amboy....... 522
Col. Klotz 150
Lieut. Col. Lawrence, at Elizabethtown......... 91
Col. Swope, at Fort Constitution.............. 440
Col. James Cunningham, at Fort Constitution.... 167
Col. William Montgomery, at Fort Constitution.. 363
Col. Frederick Watts, at Fort Constitution....... 500

Return of Pennsylvania Militia at Trenton, December 1, 1776.

Gen. James Ewing's Brigade.

Col. William Montgomery's battalion.......... 330
Col. Frederick Watt's battalion................ 273
Col. Richard McAllister's battalion............ 169
Col. Klotz's battalion 198
Major James Moore's battalion................ 300

Gen. Edward Hand's Brigade.

Col. Henry Haller's battalion................. 315
Col. James Cunningham's battalion............ 507

The next emergency, following that of Trenton, arose when it was apparent to the Commander-in-Chief that the British general was about to attempt the capture of Philadelphia by a movement up the Chesapeake Bay. At once the call was sent out for all the available militia to join the American army, in preparation for the battle which Washington had determined to risk for the preservation of the capital.

The troops thus gathered were placed under command of Gen. Armstrong, and, at the battle of Brandywine, were stationed at the fords below Chad's. The movement of the enemy being to turn the American flank, by crossing at the upper ford, the militia were not enabled to take a very active share in that memorable conflict.

With the unfortunate defeat which was incurred came the necessity for a further call to the remaining battalions of militia to repair to the field.

All these men took part in the further movements of the American army during the entire campaign, until the encampment at Valley Forge, when they were permitted, once more, to return to their homes. The services they performed were, by no means, light, and were faithfully done. Without their aid it would have been impossible for Washington to have held his ground, and the only remaining alternative would have been to retire towards the mountains of Pennsylvania, leaving the whole country, his own store-house of supplies, open to the incursions of the enemy.

It is well, then, that we should sketch the operations of the army embracing the period between Brandywine and Valley Forge, so that we may have an understanding of them in their entirety, after which we will better be able to consider the aid extended by each county individually.

On the night of the battle of Brandywine, September 11, Washington retreated to Chester, a distance of about twelve miles, and reached a safe encampment about ten o'clock. Starting early the next morning he marched to his old camp near the Falls of the Schuylkill, a distance of at least sixteen miles. Recrossing the river at Conshohocken, the Pennsylvanians in the van, he moved to Germantown, but, after a day's rest, he again crossed the Schuylkill and advanced to Warren's Tavern, in Chester county, with the intention of giving battle to Gen. Howe, who had moved leisurely forward to that point. A deluge of rain, with accompanying floods, separated the combatants.

When it was learned that the British were pressing up the Schuylkill Valley, intent, as was supposed, in getting possession of the abundant stores of ammunition at Reading, Gen. Washington once more crossed to the east side of the river at Parker's Ford (near Linfield), five miles east of Pottstown, on the nineteenth, hoping to intercept the enemy, but Sir William Howe, after having by a feint, induced Washington to suppose that he would take one of the upper fords, by a rapid countermarch, during the night, fell back to Fatland Ford, just below Valley Forge, and crossed the river, whence he had an unopposed route to the city.

While Howe was moving leisurely towards Philadelphia his troops burned Col. Dewees' Forge, Col. Thompson's Inn at Jeffersonville, and Col. Bull's dwelling and mills at Norristown. Part of them encamped, for the night, on the banks of Stony (creek) run (now) Norris-

AUTOGRAPH OF GENERAL PUTNAM.

town. At this time some of them visited Henry Rittenhouse's home. It was day-time. On seeing the red-coats approach, the Rittenhouse boys, who were home, took flight and hid in the bushes, leaving the house in charge of the women. A lass, then on a visit to them, became greatly frightened, when Mother Rittenhouse, noticing her condition, pushed the girl into a closet and then shoved a large cupboard in front of the door, completely hiding it from view. The soldiers were soon on the scene, and commenced ransacking the house. Finding nothing of importance, they became gruff and impatient, and demanded that the cupboard door, then locked, be opened. As no quick response was given to their demands they split the door with an axe. Finding that it contained nothing of interest to them they secured something to eat and left, taking with them a quantity of wearing apparel belonging to the family, after which the captive was released, the boys returned from the woods, and peace and quiet once more reigned supreme.

Under date of Friday, September 19, Washington wrote to the President of Congress:

"I am repassing the Schuylkill at Parker's Ford with the main body of the army, which will be over in an hour or two, though it is deep and rapid. . . . As soon as the troops have crossed the river I will march them as expeditiously as possible towards Fatland, Swedes and other fords where it is most probable the enemy will attempt to pass."

Pastor Muhlenberg's Journal of September 19, 1777, says:

"The army marched southward from Parker's Ford, on the east side of the river, by way of the Trappe (a village on the Reading road, twenty-five miles from Philadelphia) as far as Perkiomen creek, when it encamped.

"His Excellency, General Washington, was with the

troops in person, who marched past here (the Trappe) to the Perkiomen. The procession lasted the whole night, and we had numerous visits from officers, wet breast high, cold and damp as it was, and to bear hunger and thirst at the same time."

On the twentieth the American army seems to have gone by the "Church Road," and other roads, to their encampment on the Perkiomen and Skippack, with head-

THE OLD LUTHERAN CHURCH, AT TRAPPE, MONTGOMERY COUNTY, PENNA.
From an old print.

quarters at Fatland, where the men were rested, and thence, on the 21st, by the Egypt road to near its junction with the Ridge road, with headquarters near Thompson's tavern.

The British, finding they were checked from crossing the lower fords of the river, made use of the feint already mentioned and began to move rapidly up its west bank. Fearing for his stores at Reading Washington was forced to follow them, on the other bank, to within four miles of Pottsgrove (now Pottstown), eight miles above the Trappe. Here is the gate to the Crooked Hills, so named by the Continentals, which a part of the troops entered.

The Crooked Hill Hotel is an old landmark, well known by that name for generations, but, of late years, it has assumed the name of Sanatoga Hotel, from the Sanatoga Creek which has its source in these hills. The village of Sanatoga extends west of the hotel, along the Reading turnpike, for at least half a mile, to the post-office in a country store, where the main crossroad leads off northeast to the Continental Camp Ground at Fagleys-ville. The army did not enter Camp Pottsgrove at Fagleysville by the Crooked Hill road, but they traveled up the Great road to Limerick Square, and then took the road to the right that leads into Falkner Swamp Valley by the "Old Swamp Tohr."

The British commander having given him the slip, Washington remained at this camp from September 22 to 26.

The army occupied the Fagley and Brand farms, on both sides of the road. The Artillery division was en-camped on farms west of Fagleysville, from the Speck (Specht) Creek Valley to the top of the first elevation.

The militia and army stores were located southwest of Fagleysville, on the Sanatoga Valley slope, also on the Speck Creek Valley (Speck, or fat, creek, so called be-cause the offal of slaughtered cattle was dumped into it), and on Col. Frederick Antes' farm, then known as Philip Brand's farm, on which Prospect Hill is located.

The troops were in wretched condition when they reached Pottsgrove, almost starved, poorly clad, and nearly dead from fatigue. The old folks of the vicinity were wont to tell how they went out in companies and squads, from the hillsides to the valley, to find something to eat. They went among the farmers, took possession of the farms, ran things to their own liking, consumed all the farmers' grain and crops, and killed all their cattle.

The immediate need of the men is shown by an appeal made to the people, and to the farmers' wives for each to

AUTOGRAPH OF GENERAL MIFFLIN.

bake a full oven of rye bread, as was then in use, and also for coffee, which was of the home-made rye variety, potatoes, beans, ham, or any other kind of meat, and all kinds of vegetables.

Appeals were also made for clothing and shoes, of every description. The army teams were commanded to follow up the order, given the previous day, to collect the bread and such articles as could be spared by the people.

On September 25, while the army was preparing to leave Pottsgrove, Muhlenberg (the Lutheran Patriarch) entertained at breakfast Lord Stirling, Gen. Wayne, their aids and officers, at his Trappe home. That night his barn was occupied by soldiers, and the little hay, which he had reserved for winter, was scattered and spoiled.

The next day, at 9 A. M., the American army moved from Pottsgrove toward Trappe, but, at Limerick Square, turned off and proceeded to Schwenksville. Gen. Armstrong, however, with three or four thousand Pennsylvania militia, continued down the Great Road and took up his headquarters in the Lutheran Augustus Church and school-house. On the following morning, September 27, Pastor Muhlenberg went to the church to bury the child of one of his vestrymen but found it filled with officers and soldiers, with their arms stacked in one corner. The choir loft was full of soldiers, one playing on the organ and the rest singing lustily. Straw and filth were scattered everywhere, and, on the altar, the soldiers had piled their provisions. He entered calmly, without a word, but some began to mock and others called to the player at the organ for a Hessian march. He sought out Col. Dunlap and asked him if this was the promised protection to civil and religious liberty, but the latter excused himself by saying that, as the militia was composed of all nations, it was difficult to maintain strict discipline. The soldiers, in the meantime, had turned their horses into Muhlenberg's blossoming buckwheat-field of three acres, near the church, and, what was not consumed was trampled to ruin.

On October 2 the militia, under Armstrong, left the Trappe, marched to Philadelphia, after joining the main army, and, on the 4th the battle of Germantown took place. After the battle the army returned to the old camp, the militia again quartering at the Trappe. The old church was now transformed into a hospital. On October 5, Washington rode up to the southwest entrance of the church, on his white charger, and, dismounting, entered the building and spoke words of cheer to the wounded and dying.

While the Pennsylvania militia remained in camp at the Trappe, the main army encamped at Pennypacker's Mills (Perkiomen and Skippack township), where they arrived at four o'clock on the afternoon of Friday, September 26, a cold, rough and windy day. Before night every fence upon the place was carried away for camp fires. The hay and straw in the barns, and on stacks, disappeared, and every fowl perished save one old hen, which, as it chanced, was trying to hatch a late brood. These depredations, however, were stopped by order of Gen. Washington, who informed the officers that they must prevent such infringement of discipline.

The Commander-in-Chief made his headquarters at the home of Samuel Pennypacker, the owner of the mills. The house, a two-story stone building, is still standing.

On Saturday, the 27th, Gen. Smallwood joined the army with a reinforcement of 1,000 Maryland militia.

Sunday, September 28, was an eventful day about the mills. In the morning came the glad news that Gen. Gates had defeated Burgoyne at the battle of Stillwater, which was at once announced to the soldiers. To celebrate this success the troops were paraded at four o'clock in the afternoon, and served with a gill of rum per man, while eighteen pieces of artillery were discharged.

The American army now consisted of some 8,000 Continental troops, rank and file, and 3,000 militia. At a Council of War, held the 28th, it was decided not to risk an immediate attack on the enemy, but to move to a proper camp, some twelve miles further, there to await reinforcements and a more fitting opportunity for attack.

On Monday, September 29, Washington led his army from " Pennypacker's Mills " down to Skippack, within twenty-five miles of Philadelphia. On Tuesday, the 30th, the main army advanced still further on the Skippack road.

The Pennsylvania militia, meanwhile, remained quietly at the Trappe. The next morning (October 1), however, the scene was changed. Before sunrise everything was preparation for the march and coming battle. At 10 o'clock several regiments started, with flying colors, to join the main army at Skippack, the greater portion remaining until the morrow. On the morning of October 2, the balance of the militia, under Gen. Armstrong, marched down the Great Road towards Philadelphia.

On October 2 the army marched about five miles further down on the Skippack road to Worcester township. It was from "Methacton Hill" that the army started, at seven o'clock on the evening of October 3, to attack the enemy at Germantown.

During the night of Friday, October 3, the American troops, in several divisions, marched silently towards Germantown. The roads were rough, and the different columns reached the British outposts at irregular intervals, in the midst of a thick fog, which, eventually, was the cause of the disaster which followed on the 4th.

The movements of the American army at the battle of Germantown, have already been narrated, except those of the Pennsylvania militia. While the divisions of Sullivan and Wayne, flanked by Conway's brigade, were to enter the town by way of Chestnut Hill, the Pennsylvania militia, under Gen. Armstrong, were directed to proceed down the Manatawny road by Van Deering's Mill, and get upon the enemy's left flank and rear. The official order explains that "General McDougall is to attack the right wing of the enemy in front and rear; General Conway to attack the enemy's left flank, and General Armstrong to attack their left wing in flank and rear." The pickets were to be "taken off"—not driven in—those at Van Deering's Mill by General Armstrong, those on

Mount Airy by Sullivan, and those at Lucan's Mill by Greene.

In addition to the troops above mentioned, a detachment of militia, under Gen. James Potter, was sent down the west side of the Schuylkill, with orders to make a demonstration at the Middle Ferry, at Market Street, to engage the attention of the enemy and prevent reinforcements being sent from the city. This movement appears to have received but little attention from historians. While no especial result was attained the demonstration was a part of the battle. Robert Morton, in his diary, has this to say of it:

"I went this morning to the plantation, from thence to the middle ferry, where I saw a number of the citizens, with about 30 of the Light Dragoons on Foot, watching the motions of the enemy on the other side. I waited there about an hour, during which time there were several shots from both sides without much execution, when 3 columns of the Americans with 2 field pieces appeared in sight marching tow'ds the River. The Dragoons were order'd under arms and an express sent off for a reinforcement immediately, after which the Americans fired a field piece attended with a volley of small arms. I thought it most advisable to leave the Ground, and rode off as fast as possible. The Americans afterwards came down to the River with 2 Field Pieces, which they fired with some small arms and run and left them; soon after they returned and brought them back without any considerable loss 1 man being wounded on their side and none on the other."

Major Jno. Clarke, Jr., wrote to Washington (October 6, 1777) that one of his friends told him that "if the troops had arrived at the middle ferry earlier 'twould have prevented the enemy's reinforcement from the city joining the main body."

In accordance with his orders Gen. Armstrong proceeded down the Ridge Road, with his column of Pennsylvania militia, to attack the enemy's left. The extreme left of the British line was held by the Hessian Yägers, under Colonel von Wurmb, who, apprised of the attack, as were many of his brother officers, was more vigilant than most of them, and kept up a continuous watch throughout the night, whereby the approach of the militia was discovered at daybreak. There followed a brisk interchange of shots, but no real engagement. "We cannonaded from the heights on each side of the Wissahickon," says Armstrong, "whilst the riflemen on opposite sides acted on the lower grounds." About nine o'clock, he continues, he was called off to join the General, but left a party, under Colonels Eyers and Dunlap, who, shortly after, were obliged to retreat, bringing off their field-piece and a second one which Armstrong had left "in the horrenduous hills of the Wissahickon." The militia went up the stream to Cresheim Creek, which led them across above Germantown, "directed by a slow fire of cannon," and there fell in front of a body of the enemy, whom they engaged for some time. "Until then," says Gen. Armstrong, "I thought we had a victory, but to my great disappointment soon found out our army had gone an hour or two before, and we last on the ground."

One episode of the battle still remains to be told. In the midst of the confusion, into which Sullivan's division had been thrown, he was attacked by Gen. Grey and obliged to retreat. General Agnew, following in the rear of Grey, entered the main street and rode forward at the head of his column. As he ascended the hill he received a sudden volley from a party of citizens who were concealed behind the Mennonite Meeting House, and fell mortally wounded. He was carried into a house, near the spot, where he died, and his remains were removed to his former quarters, the present residence of Charles J. Wister. The man who shot General Agnew is said to have been Philip Boyer, a Pennsylvania-German.

With victory almost in their grasp the Americans, confused and disorganized by the dense fog which prevailed, were obliged to retreat from the field of Germantown and return to their old encampment at Pennypacker's Mills.

Says Pastor Muhlenberg, on October 5, another Sunday:

" From early in the morning until noon the troops who marched from here on the 2nd inst. are returning in companies and singly with their wagons, tired, hungry and thirsty, and have taken possession of their old quarters, to consume completely what was left previously."

In Pickering's Journal is contained this statement:

" After the army were all retreating, I expected they would have returned to their last encampment, about twelve or thirteen miles from the enemy at Germantown, but the retreat was continued upwards of twenty miles; so that all those men, who retired so far, this day marched upwards of thirty miles without rest, besides being up all the preceding night without sleep."

Also the following:

" Sunday, October 5. At Pennebecker's Mills; this day the stragglers generally joined the army over Perkiomen Creek. After remaining here a few days, the army removed to Towamensing township."

The encampment in Skippack was quite large and occupied territory on both sides of the Perkiomen. On the west side the camping ground included, among others, farms then owned by Henry Keely and Peter Pool.

A large number of wounded and dying were brought back with the troops, and placed in the churches at Evansburg and Trappe, which were converted into hospitals, where many died and were buried. Others were taken to the encampment at Pennypacker's Mills and placed in private houses, amongst which were the homes of Henry Keeley and William Pennebecker.

The army remained at this encampment until October 8, when it marched to Towamensing township, stopping at the Mennonite Meeting-House, near Kulpsville, where Brig. Gen. Nash, who died from his wounds, was buried with military honors, in the grave-yard attached to the meeting-house, at 10 o'clock on October 9, all officers attending his funeral as a mark of respect to his memory.

Washington's headquarters, in this township, were at the farm-house of Frederick Wampole, about a mile above Kulpsville.

Amongst the other homes of the vicinity, which opened their hospitable doors on this occasion, was that of John Jantz, or Johnson, Sr., a Pennsylvania-German who lived near the Skippack. Several wagon loads of the wounded were placed in his house, with a nurse to care for them. Besides these he boarded ten officers or soldiers, of the regular army, for a while, during the time Washington had his quarters on the Wampole farm, about one and one half miles south of Jantz's place. To accommodate these soldier boarders, who did a great deal of writing, he had made for them a fine cherry table, with carved legs, by Hans Jakob Hagey, an ingenious carpenter near by, which is still in possession of the family.

Another private house, whose doors stood wide open, was that of the Pennsylvania-German, Adam Gotwals, about one and one quarter miles southwest of the Mennonite Meeting-House, to which General Nash was carried on a litter, or bed, of poles, as well as Colonel Boyd and Major John White, both of Philadelphia, and Lieut. Matthew Smith, of Virginia, all wounded, and all of whom died here.

The camp at Towamensing was occupied until October 16, and extended from Towamensing into Lower Salford, occupying fields on the farms of Jacob Bossert and his neighbor, Mr. Getz, northwest of the Skippack Creek. It covered about 300 acres, the northern section being on Frederick Wampole's farm, where were the headquarters, the western section on Jacob Bossert's farm, and the most southerly section on Benj. Fuller's farm.

On Thursday, October 16, the army moved to Worcester township for the second time, where headquarters were at the house of Peter Wentz.

It was here the Commander-in-Chief had the pleasure of announcing, on Saturday, October 18, the complete surrender of Gen. Burgoyne and his army, on the fourteenth of the same month.

The army remained in Worcester township until October 21, when it removed its quarters to Whitpain township, and from thence, on November 2, to Whitemarsh township, where the Commander-in-Chief made his headquarters at the Emlen mansion. The main body were quartered on Camp Hill, while the militia, seven hundred strong, occupied the heights of Militia Hill (whence its name), a spur, or continuation, of Camp Hill, running

BATTLE OF GERMANTOWN, OCTOBER 4, 1777.

ATTACK ON THE CHEW HOUSE.

from east to west, and extending from the Wissahickon Creek at St. Thomas' Church to the village of Cold Point. The neighborhood still shows traces of the occupation of the army. On its northern slope of Militia Hill are to be seen the spaces and ditches marking the location of the tents, in a well defined line near the summit.

With the approach of cold weather a Council of War was here convened, on the last day of November, to decide upon the location of winter quarters. Many divergent opinions prevailed but Washington finally decided to take a position where he could watch the movements of the enemy, hold them in Philadelphia and prevent them from foraging on the rich surrounding country.

Gen. Howe, in the meanwhile, had planned to surprise his antagonist. On the night of Thursday, December 4, he slipped out of Philadelphia, with a force of some 12,000 effective and well-equipped men, passed beyond Chestnut Hill and halted in the vicinity of Flourtown to reconnoitre. Warned of the British approach by Capt. McLane, and his light-horsemen, alarm guns were fired, and the Americans paraded their troops at 3 A. M. on the sixteenth, which brought the enemy to a halt.

In this state of affairs Brig. Gen. Irvine, with 600 Pennsylvania militia, was sent forward by Washington to skirmish with the British light advanced parties on Chestnut Hill, but, unfortunately, fell in with them before reaching the foot of the same, a trifle over two miles from camp. A conflict ensued, but the men gave way before superior numbers, leaving the general wounded, with four or five others, who were taken prisoners, the enemy having also suffered fully to this extent.

During the night the British moved towards the northeast, approaching within a mile of the encampment, the

18

valley and stream of Sandy Run intervening, where, on Edge Hill, they remained all day of the 6th, apparently at a loss as to their next movement.

At one o'clock on Sunday morning, December 7, they advanced still further to the American left, or northeast. Realizing that their purpose was to attack him, and learning that they were extensively plundering the neighborhood, Washington decided to check them. He, accordingly, ordered Col. Morgan and his Rifle Corps (containing many Pennsylvania-Germans), supported by Gen. Potter's brigade of Pennsylvania militia, Col. Gist's Maryland militia, and Col. Webb's Continental regiment, to move forward for that purpose. A sharp and severe conflict ensued. To stand their ground the British were compelled to concentrate their forces. Owing to a decided superiority of numbers, the militia fell back near sunset, as Washington did not desire to bring on a general engagement. All arrangements were made in anticipation of an attack during the night or following morning, but it did not occur, the enemy withdrawing. The losses in these two engagements at Edge Hill, in Whitemarsh township, were quite severe, especially on the part of the British, but the actual number was not obtained.

The increasing severity of the weather decided Washington to leave Camp Hill, and its vicinity, for the more comfortable winter quarters which he had selected on the west side of the Schuylkill.

At four o'clock, on the morning of December 11, the whole army marched from Whitemarsh, by way of Broad Axe, towards Matson's Ford, where Washington had planned for it to cross, and, by passing through one of these narrow valleys, to reach its destination a mile or so beyond the river. The first division, under Gen. Sullivan, with a part of the second, passed over the ford on a bridge constructed of thirty-six wagons, placed end to end, across which rails were laid to facilitate the passage.

It happened also, on the same day, that a large body of British, under Cornwallis, had left Philadelphia, by the Middle Ferry, on a foray. Col. Edward Heston, learning of their purpose, hastened to Merion to appraise Gen. James Potter, upon whose staff he was serving.

Gen. Potter had been assigned the particular duty of protecting the Delaware and Schuylkill, with a brigade of Pennsylvania militia. On receiving Heston's warning, he hastily placed the militia in position on the hills through Lower Merion, himself taking post at " Harriton," then the home of Charles Thomson, Secretary of the Continental Congress, situated to the north of the present village of Bryn Mawr, and now known as the Morris Farm.

Potter's advance guard met Cornwallis' men near the Black Horse tavern, on the Lancaster road, a few miles west of the city, and engaged the enemy. The militia were forced back, defending desperately but losing, in turn, each position, until their retreating column reached the valley and slopes of the Gulph hills, leading to the Schuylkill at Matson's Ford. Though bravely contested to this point, and within reach of assistance, here the battalions broke and fled in panic, leaving the Gulph, and its flanking hillsides, in possession of the British.

Sullivan, who had crossed the river, and was on his way to the proposed encampment, now found himself confronted by the victorious red-coats, assembled on the heights on either side of the valley road leading to the Gulph, and discovered them to be in such force that he was obliged to order, promptly, the retreat of his division to the east side of the river to enable him to rejoin the main body, which, having learned the state of affairs that existed, was now on the move towards Swedes' Ford, a crossing three miles higher up, where the whole army encamped for the night.

After recrossing the Schuylkill, Gen. Sullivan destroyed his bridge of wagons to prevent any attempt at pursuit, upon which, however, Cornwallis did not seem inclined to enter.

On December 12, at sunset, the army finally crossed the river at Swedes' Ford, and, in the midst of a blinding snow-storm, marched down on the west side, bivouacking amongst the sheltering boulders on the pine-clad slopes at Gulph Mills, at three o'clock on the morning of December 13.

The snow, which began on the night of the twelfth, ended with rain on the sixteenth, when, for the first time, the tents were pitched, and some slight degree of comfort secured for the men, who were in a most miserable condition.

December 18 was the day set apart by Congress for thanksgiving and prayer, when the troops remained in their quarters and the various chaplains held divine service.

While at Whitemarsh Washington had reached a general conclusion with regard to the location of his winter quarters, without selecting any definite spot. On December 17 the final decision was arrived at to encamp at Valley Forge.

On December 19, 1777, the American army went into winter quarters at Valley Forge, where it remained until June 19, 1778.

Practically the entire force of militia were then sent to their homes. A small force, however, remained on duty to guard the Delaware-Schuylkill peninsula, and prevent supplies from reaching the enemy. This body of four hundred Pennsylvania militia was placed under command of Brig. Gen. John Lacey, who entered upon his duties in January, 1778.

He was a constant thorn in the side of Gen. Howe who determined upon his defeat and dispersion. To that end, Lt. Col. Abercrombie, with Major Simcoe's command of the Queen's Rangers, a tory corps, to which was added a considerable body of cavalry and light infantry, was ordered to surprise Lacey on May 1, at Crooked Billet (Hatboro), where he was then expected to be.

The movements of the British were so well timed and arranged that they came within two hundred yards of the American camp before being discovered. Lacey was in bed, but dressed in a hurry, mounted his horse and joined his command. It is charged that he carried part of his clothing in his hands. The enemy, sheltered by the houses and fences, opened fire on his front and rear at the same time. Seeing that his force was surrounded, Lacey ordered a retreat, moving by column to the left, in the direction of a wood, across open fields, the wagons following. Coming in full view of the British his flanking parties were soon hotly engaged.

Upon reaching the wood his situation became so critical, and the engagement so severe, that he was obliged to abandon his baggage and force his way through his opponents. The retreating Americans were pursued for a couple miles, skirmishing with the enemy, an occasional man falling. They passed across the farm of Thomas Craven, and by the present Johnsville to near the Bristol road, when they turned to the left into a wood, and the pursuit was relinquished.

The loss of the Americans was not as heavy as might have been expected, under the circumstances, 26 being killed, 8 or 10 wounded, and several taken prisoners.

The British are charged with extreme cruelty to the American wounded at Crooked Billet. Several of the fatigued militiamen having crept into a large pile of buck-wheat straw on the Craven farm, the British were informed of the fact by a tory and set fire to the straw while the men were sleeping, some of whom were consumed at once, and others so badly burned that they died shortly after. Others, wounded by musket balls, were hacked with swords and stabbed with bayonets. An eye witness states: "When the firing ceased we continued on and found three wounded militiamen near the wood; they appeared to have been wounded by a sword and were much cut and hacked. When we got to them they were groaning greatly. They died in a little while and I understood were buried on the spot. They appeared to be Germans."

On April 25, 1777, the Pennsylvania militia were called out, and it was determined that the counties of Philadelphia, Bucks, Cumberland, Berks and Northampton, should send their proportion to Bristol to form a camp, while the counties of Chester, Lancaster and York were to form another camp at or near Chester.

CHAPTER XII.

PHILADELPHIA COUNTY.

OUT of the large number of emergency men furnished by Philadelphia county, during the Revolution, it is naturally most difficult to select entire organizations which were distinctively Pennsylvania-German. Many of this blood were scattered throughout all of the various companies. The following are especially noticeable.

Light Dragoons, County of Philadelphia.

Lieut., David Snyder.   *Cornet*, Casper Dull.

Col. John Eyre's Artillery Battalion.

(As of August 25, 1777.)

Fifth Company.

Captain, Andrew Summers, September 6, 1777.
Capt. Lieut., Christian Bartling, September 6, 1777.
1st Lieut., Jacob Diegal, September 11, 1777.
2d Lieut., Baltzer Steinford, September 11, 1777.
3d Lieut., Samuel Sivert, September 11, 1777.
Capt. Engineer, Benjamin Davis, September 11, 1777.

Philadelphia County Associators. *April 22, 1777.*

First Battalion.

Upper Salford, Lower Salford, Franconia, Towamensing, Hatfields and Perkiomen and Skippack.

Colonel, Daniel Hiester, Jr.   *Lieut. Col.,* Jacob Reed.
Major, Jacob Markley.

Sixth Battalion.

Limerick, Douglas, Marlborough, New Hanover, Upper Hanover and Frederick.

Colonel, Frederick Antes. *Lieut. Col.,* Frederick Weiss.
Major, Jacob Bishop.

Captains, John Brooke, Benjamin Brooke, Peter Lower, Philip Hahn, Peter Richards, Michael Dotterer, Andrew Reed, ———— Childs.

The following men were in Capt. Dotterer's company from Frederick: Peter Acker, Francis Bast, Jacob Belts, Samuel Bertolet, Conrad Bickhart, Henry Boyer, Philip Boyer, Valentine Boyer, William Boyer, Jacob Christman, Jacob Detweiler, Conrad Diffenbacher, John Dotterer, John Geist, Matthias Geist, John Hiltebeitel, Henry

Hollobush, Yost Hollobush, Daniel Krause, Henry Krause, Michael Krause, Michael Kuntz, Francis Leidig, Leonard Leidig, John Lay, George Michael, Zacharias Nyce, Gottfried Saylor, Henry Sassaman, Charles Solner, Jacob Stetler, Henry S. Stetler, Christian Stetler, George Smith, George Swanck, Jacob Swanck, Jacob Reimer, John Reimer, Ludwick Reimer, Jacob Undercuffler, Henry Warner, Jeremiah Weiser, Jacob Zieber and John Zieber.

The following were in Capt. Hahn's company from New Hanover: John Bitting, Peter Bitting, Yost Bitting, Philip Brandt, George Buchert, Peter Dehaven, Jacob Denny, John Detier, Michael Egolf, George Emhart, *Ensign,* John Fagley, Lewis Frankenberger, John Freed, Jacob Freese, Bernard Freyer, John Freyer, Adam Gerver, John Grove, Michael Hieber, Jacob Hill, *Corporal,* Michael Hoover, Jacob Kern, *Corporal,* Sebastian Koch, Adam Krebs, Philip Krebs, Michael Krebs, David Lessig, Peter Loch, Benjamin Markley, Joseph Maybury, Frederick Miller, Martin Miller, Benedict Mintz, Alexander McMichael, Adam Neidig, Jacob Neighman, George Polsgrove, Henry Polsgrave, John Richards, John Sackman, Christian Sackriter, George Sheffer, *Corporal,* Jacob Sheffy, John Sheffy, John Shuler, Christian Slonaker, George Adam Slonaker, Henry Slonaker, John Smith, Henry Snider, Jr., Jacob Snider, John Snider, Ludwick Starck, Jacob Strouse, Adam Warthman, John Walter, John Willower, Philip Yawn, Adam Yerger, Andrew Yerger, Martin Yerger, Philip Young and Christian Zoller.

Fourth Battalion—1777.

First Company.

Captain, Christian Dull.
1st Lieut., Peacock Major.
2d Lieut., John Troxel.
Ensign, John Shelmire.

First Battalion—Col. William Bradford.

(As of June 25, 1777.)

Second Company.

Captain, Charles Lyng.
1st Lieut., Jacob Graff.
2d Lieut., Adam Sichler.
Ensign, William Redisher.

Third Company.

Captain, George Esterly.
1st Lieut., Theobald Scheibel.
2d Lieut., Andrew Burkhardt.
Ensign, John Geyer.

Third Battalion—Col. Morgan.

Colonel, Jacob Morgan.
Lieut. Col., William Wills.
Major, Joseph Kerr.

First Company.

Captain, George Esterly.
1st Lieut., Theobald Shei-
bald.
2d Lieut., Martin Fiss.
Ensign, Godfrey Baker.

Fifth Company.

Captain, Williamson Tolbert.
1st Lieut., James Pickering.
2d Lieut., Joseph Franklin.
Ensign, Jacob Schweighouser,
Jr.

Second Company.

Captain, Peter Merlin.
1st Lieut., Henry Hay.

Sixth Company.

Captain, George Reinhard.
1st Lieut., Alexander Quarrier.

2d Lieut., Michael Gilbert. *2d Lieut.*, Andrew Foster.
Ensign, Matthias Gilbert. *Ensign*, John King.

Third Company.

Captain, Conrad Rush.
1st Lieut., Ezekiel Merriam.
2d Lieut., And. Burkhard.
Ensign, Charles Deshler.

Seventh Company.

Captain, Jacob Weidman.
1st Lieut., Henry Meyer.
2d Lieut., John Ecky.
Ensign, Andrew Young.

Fourth Company.

Captain, Elijah Weed.
1st Lieut., Jacob Bender.
2d Lieut., Ezekiel Worrell.
Ensign, John Guyer.

Eighth Company.

Captain, John Linnington.
1st Lieut., Thomas Heston.
2d Lieut., John Peter, Jr.
Ensign, Leonard Fisher.

Fourth Battalion—Col. Bayard.

Sixth Company.

Captain, Christian Shaffer.
1st Lieut., John Everhard.
2d Lieut., Edward Glascow.

Sixth Battalion—Col. Knox.

Second Company.

Captain, Jacob Synk.
1st Lieut., Adam Pole.
2d Lieut., Conrad Lube.

Seventh Company.

Captain, Christian Grover.
1st Lieut., Godfrey Shesler.
2d Lieut., William Lasher.
Ensign, William Folkner.

Second Battalion—Col. Sharpe Delaney.
(As of June 25, 1777.)

First Company.	Third Company.
Captain, Charles Syng.	*Captain*, Peter Mehrling.
1st Lieut., John Pollard.	*1st Lieut.*, Henry Horne.
2d Lieut., Evan Cook.	*2d Lieut.*, Ezekiel Worrel.
Ensign, Thos. Cummings.	*Ensign*, Charles Deshler.

Third Battalion—Col. Jonathan Bayard Smith.
(As of August 2, 1777.)

Captain, Conrad Rush.	*Captain* Adam Foulk.
1st Lieut., Jacob Bender.	*1st Lieut.*, John Barker.
2d Lieut., Martin Fiss.	*2d Lieut.*, Thomas Millard.
Ensign, Matthias Gilbert.	*Ensign*, Henry Ritter.

Captain Anthony Lechler.
1st Lieut., Henry Brustarr.
2d Lieut., John Cauffman.
Ensign, George Lesher.

Fourth Battalion— Lieut. Col. Wm. Will.
(As of September 9, 1777.)

Captain, Philip Wagener.
1st Lieut., Isaac Warner.
2d Lieut., William Beating.
Ensign, William Rush.

All other companies in this battalion contained many Pennsylvania-Germans.

Sixth Battalion—Col. Robert Knox.
(As of September 11, 1777.)

Captain, Christian Grover. *Captain,* Christian Shaffer.
Lieut., Thomas Thomson. *1st Lieut.,* John Everhart.
Ensign, John Lare. *2d Lieut.,* Andrew Foster.
        Ensign, John McCartney.

Captain, John Bergman. *Captain,* Jacob Weidman.
1st Lieut., Fred'k Meyer. *1st Lieut.,* James Pickering.
2d Lieut., Wm. Kensher. *2d Lieut.,* John Peters, Jr.
Ensign, John Painter. *Ensign,* Andrew Young.

Col. Cowperthwaite's Battalion.
(As of September 11, 1777.)

Captain, Geo. Reinhardt. *Captain,* William Bower.
1st Lieut., Alex'r Quarries. *1st Lieut.,* John Sobers.
2d Lieut., John Ecky. *2d Lieut.,* Conrad Miller.
Ensign, John King. *Ensign,* George Krouscop.

LANCASTER COUNTY.

Lancaster county sent the following battalions:

First Battalion.

Colonel, Philip Greenawalt.
Lieut. Col., Philip Marsteller.
Major, Samuel Jones.

First Company.   *Fifth Company.*
Captain, Casper Stoever. *Captain,* Mich'l Holderbaum.
1st Lieut., Andrew Fickes. *1st Lieut.,* George Nagle.

2d Lieut., Sebastian Wolf.   *2d Lieut.*, Lucas Sholly.
Ensign, Charles Rehrick.   *Ensign*, Alexander Martin.

Second Company.

Captain, William Paine.
1st Lieut., Anthony Kelker.
2d Lieut., Jacob Matti.
Ensign, vacancy.

Third Company.

Captain, Philip Weiser.
1st Lieut., Ludwig Shott.
2d Lieut., John Stone.
3d Lieut., John Thomas.

Fourth Company.

Captain, George Null.
1st Lieut., Jas. Mortersteel.
2d Lieut., Michael Minigh.
Ensign, George Meiser.

Sixth Company.

Captain, Leonard Immel.
1st Lieut., Mich'l Diffenbaugh.
2d Lieut., Peter Berry.
Ensign, Michael Spengler.

Seventh Company.

Captain, Valentine Shouffler.
1st Lieut., Matthew Henning.
2d Lieut., John Gossert.
Ensign, Peter Basehore.

Eighth Company.

Captain, Henry Sheaffer.
1st Lieut., Philip Wolfersberger.
2d Lieut., Nicholas Zollinger.
Ensign, George Frank.

Ninth Company.

Captain, Daniel Oldenbruck.
1st Lieut., Abraham Smith.
2d Lieut., John Rewalt.
Ensign, Peter Heckert.

Second Battalion.

Colonel, James Watson.
Lieut. Col., James Porter.
Major, Dorrington Wilson.

First Company.

Captain, John Scott.
1st Lieut., Jonn Cunningham.
2d Lieut., John Duncan.
Ensign, Dan'l Carmichael.

Fifth Company.

Captain, James Morrison.
1st Lieut., Robert King.
2d Lieut., Thomas Neil.
Ensign, William Nelson.

Second Company.

Captain, Joshua Anderson.
1st Lieut., Robert Miller.
2d Lieut., Alex. Hason.
Ensign, John Andrews.

Sixth Company.

Captain, Joshua Allison.
1st Lieut., James Patterson.
2d Lieut., Samuel Jamison.
Ensign, Robert Johnston.

Third Company.

Captain, John Johnston.
1st Lieut., Joshua Walker.
2d Lieut., Joshua Tweed.
Ensign, William Herd.

Seventh Company.

Captain, Patrick Marshall.
1st Lieut., John Caldwell.
2d Lieut., William Calhoun.
Ensign, William Bigham.

Fourth Company.

Captain, Thomas White.
1st Lieut., Thomas Clark.
2d Lieut., John Reed.
Ensign, Peter Simpson.

Eighth Company.

Captain, John Paxton.
1st Lieut., William Ramsey.
2d Lieut., John Shannon.
Ensign, William Brown.

Third Battalion.

(Commissioned July 1, 1777.)

Colonel, Alexander Lowry.
Lieut. Col., James Cunningham.
Major, Jacob Cooke.

First Company.

Captain, Robert McKee.
1st Lieut., James Scott.
2d Lieut., Hugh Hall.
Ensign, James Carothers.

Second Company.

Captain, Thos. Robinson.
1st Lieut., Rob't Robinson.
2d Lieut., James Miller.
Ensign, Robert Boal.

Third Company.

Captain, Joseph Work.
1st Lieut., William Wilson.
2d Lieut., James Cook.
Ensign, James Wilson.

Fourth Company.

Captain, David McQuown.
1st Lieut., Rob. McQuown.
2d Lieut., Matthew Hays.
Ensign, James Hays.

Fifth Company.

Captain, Robert Craig.
1st Lieut., John Cook
2d Lieut., Zach's Moore.
Ensign, Walter Bell.

Sixth Company.

Captain, Andrew Boggs.
1st Lieut., George Redsecker.
2d Lieut., Robert Jamison.
Ensign, William Meyers.

Seventh Company.

Captain, Abraham Scott.
1st Lieut., Michael Peters.
2d Lieut., John Bishop.
Ensign, Abraham Scott, Jr.

Eighth Company.

Captain, Hugh Pedan.
1st Lieut., Patrick Hays.
2d Lieut., Benjamin Mills.
Ensign, Arthur Hays.

Ninth Company—Aug. 16, 1777.

Captain, Abraham Forry.
1st Lieut., Noah Carey.
2d Lieut., Steven Wimer.
Ensign, John Dyer.

Tenth Company—Oct. 28, 1778

Captain, Chris. Earhart (or Martin Arehart).
1st Lieut., Noah Ceasey.
2d Lieut., Andras Shell.
3d Lieut., John Florey.

Fourth Battalion.

Colonel, Robert Elder.
Lieut. Col., James Cowden.
Major, Stephen Forster.

First Company.

Captain, James Murray.
1st Lieut., George Cochran.
2d Lieut., George Bell.
Ensign, Peter Sturgeon.

Second Company.

Captain, James Collier.
1st Lieut., Henry McKen.
2d Lieut., Sam'l Hutchinson.
Ensign, Samuel Shearer.

Third Company.

Captain, John Rutherford.
1st Lieut., Thos. McArthur.
2d Lieut., Wm. Montgomery.
Ensign, Robert Gray.

Fourth Company.

Captain, James Crouch.
1st Lieut., Jonathan McClure.
2d Lieut., Fred'k Hubley.
Ensign, Daniel Dowdle.

Fifth Company.

Captain, James Clark.
1st Lieut., William Johnson.
2d Lieut., George Clark.
Ensign, Elisha Chambers.

Sixth Company.

Captain, Martin Weaver.
1st Lieut., Philip Newbecker.
2d Lieut., Philip Rausculp.
Ensign, John Scheesley.

Seventh Company.

Captain, Michael Whitley.
1st Lieut., Andrew Stewart.
2d Lieut., John Dickey.
Ensign, Joseph Simpson.

Eighth Company.

Captain, John Gilchrist.
1st Lieut., William Swan.
2d Lieut., Mat. Gilchrist.
Ensign, Andrew Berryhill.

19

Fifth Battalion.

Colonel, Jacob Clatz.

Lieut. Col., Philip Stouffer.

Major, Jacob Richard.

Captains, Mich'l App, Ja's Krug, John Graff, George Franciscus, Peter Shaffner, Ch'r Petrie, Wm. Devis, Adam Wilhelm.

1st Lieuts., Ludw. Heck, John Maurer, Peter Diffedorfer, Andrew Cunningham, George Bigler, Henry Shauffer.

2d Lieuts., Jacob Shaefer, Valentine Krug, Ch'r Mayer, George Leitaer, John Bredigam, John Griner.

Ensigns, George Stragly, Hen'r Giger, Philip Witzel, Henry Groff, Geo. Koch.

Sixth Battalion.

(Commissioned July 31, 1777.)

Colonel, John Rogers.

Lieut. Col., Robert Clark.

Major, William Brown.

First Company.

Captain, Thos. Kopenheffer.

1st Lieut., William Hill.

2d Lieut., John Barnett.

Ensign, John Armstrong.

Second Company.

Captain, Ambrose Crain.

1st Lieut., Isaac Hanna.

2d Lieut., James Stewart.

Ensign, John Bickel.

Fifth Company.

Captain, Patrick Hays.

1st Lieut., Samuel Weir.

2d Lieut., James Wallace.

Ensign, James Willson.

Sixth Company.

Captain, Joseph McClure.

1st Lieut., James Johnson.

2d Lieut., James Willson.

Ensign, Joseph Willson.

Third Company.

Captain, Jas. McCreight.
1st Lieut., Abr'm Latcha.
2d Lieut., John Strain.
Ensign, James Willson.

Fourth Company.

Captain, William McCullough.
1st Lieut., Wm. Young.
2d Lieut., George Beasor.
Ensign, John Thomson.

Seventh Company.

Captain, William Laird.
1st Lieut., John McFarland.
2d Lieut., Michael Rahn.
Ensign, Jacob Becker.

Eighth Company.

Captain, Michael Moyer.
1st Lieut., Abraham Allis.
2d Lieut., Michael Brown.
Ensign, Peter Lineaweaver.

Seventh Battalion.

Colonel, John Boyd.
Lieut. Col., George Stewart.
Major, James Mercer.

First Company.

(Strasburg Township.)
Captain, James Brown.
1st Lieut., Alex. Hunter.
2d Lieut., Alex. Campbell.
Ensign, Jas. Campbell.

Second Company.

(Saulsbury Township.)
Captain, David Whitehill.
1st Lieut., John Caldwell.
2d Lieut., Jas. Henderson.
Ensign, Jno. Whitehill, Jr.

Fifth Company.

(Stroudsburg Township.)
Captain, John Slaymaker.
1st Lieut., George McIlvain.
2d Lieut., Daniel Huston.
Ensign, Samuel Hawthorne.

Sixth Company.

(Saulsbury Township.)
Captain, William Brisben.
1st Lieut., John Hoffer.
2d Lieut., John McSawin.
Ensign, Samuel Hughes.

Third Company.

(Leacock Township.)
Captain, John Rowland.
1st Lieut., Jas. Hamilton.
2d Lieut., John Moore.
Ensign, Abram Line.

Seventh Company.

(Leacock Township.)
Captain, Robert McCurdy.
1st Lieut., James Woods.
2d Lieut., Jacob Herbert.
Ensign, Robert Young.

Fourth Company.

(Lampeter Township.)
Captain, Samuel Heans.
1st Lieut., James Davis.
2d Lieut., John Scott.
Ensign, John Slater.

Eighth Company.

(Lampeter Township.)
Captain, Henry Kendrick.
1st Lieut., John Carpenter.
2d Lieut., Geo. Diffenbaugh.
Ensign, Daniel Lemmon.

Eighth Battalion.

No record is given of this battalion except, under date of November 18, 1777, the announcement of the appointments of the following officers:

Captain, James Barber.
1st Lieut., Robert Barber, Jr.
2d Lieut., John Barber.
Ensign, James Patton.

Ninth Battalion.

Colonel, John Huber.
Lieut. Col., Samuel Jones.
Major, Adam Bower.

First Company.

Captain, John Gingrich.
1st Lieut., vacancy.

Fifth Company.

Captain, Joseph Gehr.
1st Lieut., vacancy.

2d Lieut., vacancy.   *2d Lieut.*, Peter Geistwite.
Ensign, Andrew Ehrman.   *Ensign*, Abraham Bower.

Second Company.

Captain, Bernard Gardner.
1st Lieut., Conrad Haase.
2d Lieut., John Senseman.
Ensign, Philip Beck.

Sixth Company.

Captain, Christian Hollinger.
1st Lieut., Michael Horner.
2d Lieut., Christian Garman.
Ensign, John Jones.

Third Company.

Captain, George Feather.
1st Lieut., Ludwick Hoffer.
2d Lieut., vacancy.
Ensign, vacancy.

Seventh Company.

Captain, John Smuller.
1st Lieut., John Moeller.
2d Lieut., John Hoffer.
Ensign, Andrew Ream.

Fourth Company.

Captain, Isaac Adam.
1st Lieut., Adam Eichholtz.
2d Lieut., John Bechthold.
Ensign, Philip Broadstone.

Eighth Company.

Captain, George Foulke.
1st Lieut., John Martin.
2d Lieut., Daniel Parry.
Ensign, Joseph Bemersderfer.

Tenth Battalion.

Colonel, David Jenkins.
Lieut. Col., Jacob Karpenter.
Major, Henry Mercle.

First Company.

Captain, John Lutts.
Lieut., Christopher Heft.
   "   Henry Wite.
Ensign, Peter Bleaser.

Fifth Company.

Captain, Joseph Jenkins.
Lieut., Thomas Elliott.
   "   Joseph Williams.
Ensign, James Patterson.

Second Company.

Captain, James Davies.
Lieut., Samuel Elliott.

Sixth Company

Captain, James Watson.
Lieut., John Kirkpatrick.
　　"　　Alex'r McIlvain.
Ensign, Thomas McMullen.

Third Company.

Captain, Martin Bowman.
Lieut., George Duck.
　　"　　John Ream.
Ensign, Jacob Swarts-
welder.

Seventh Company.

Captain, Eman'l Carpenter.
Lieut., Rudy Statfor.
　　"　　John Rudy.
Ensign, James Harber.

Fourth Company.

Captain, George Rees.
Lieut., Valentine Kinser.
　　"　　Jno. Diffenderffer.
Ensign, John Shiverly.

Eighth Company.

Captain, William Crawford.
Lieut., John Davies.
　　"　　James Wallace.
Sub. Lieut., Simon Snyder.
　　"　　"　　Christopher Graw-
ford.
Ensign, James Vogan.

BERKS COUNTY.

Berks county furnished the following battalions. The roster is under date of August 27, 1777.

First Battalion—August 5, 1777, to January 5, 1778.

(At Brandywine and Germantown and later.)

Colonel, Daniel Hunter.　　　*Lieut. Col.,* Jacob Boyer.
Major, Martin Kercher.

Captains, Conrad Geist, Joseph McMurray, Charles Krause, John Lesher, Jacob Whetstone, Christopher Foulke.

Second Battalion—August 5, 1777, to January 5, 1778.

(At Brandywine and Germantown and later.)

Colonel, Daniel Udree.   *Lieut. Col.,* John Guldin.

Captains, Stephen Krumrein, John Reitmeyer, George Battorf, John Eisington, Peter Smith, Conrad Minch.

The following battalions joined the army after the battle of Brandywine, serving until January 5, 1778.

Third Battalion.

Colonel, Michael Lindemuth.

Captains, Sebastian Leutz, Daniel Deturck, Jacob Rothermel, David Strouse, Sebastian Miller, Jacob Shartly, George Souter, George Beaver.

Fourth Battalion.

Colonel, Joseph Hiester.

Captains, Sebastian Emerick, Peter Nagle, George Grant, Conrad Weiser.

Fifth Battalion.

Lieut. Col., George Miller.

Captains, Michael Bretz, George Reihm.

Sixth Battalion.

Colonel, Henry Spyker.

Captains, Michael Vogge, Jacob Rhoads, Jacob Shappell, Henry Weaver, Conrad Eckert, Jacob Hill.

Seventh and Eighth Battalions.

Colonel, Jacob Weaver.   *Major,* John Cinte.

Captains, Daniel Reif, John Eagner, Ferdinand Ritter, Philip Creek, David Morgan, Jacob Kremer, Philip Filbert, Conrad Mingle.

NORTHAMPTON COUNTY.

The following battalions are given for Northampton county:

First Battalion—June, 1777.

Colonel, George Hubner.   *Lieut. Col.,* Peter Sayler.
Major, Philip Mixel.

Captains, Joseph Frey, Christopher Jonsson, George Groff, Edward Sheimer, John Roberts, Friedrich Cleinehautz, Francis Rhoads, Jacob Wagner.

Second Battalion—June, 1777.

Colonel, George Breinig.   *Lieut. Col.,* Stephen Bolliet.
Major, Frederick Limbuch.

Captains, William Sheffer, George Knappenberger, Peter Shuler, John Moritz, Peter Traxler, Jr., Henry Ritz, Christian Fisher, Daniel Shnyder.

Third Battalion—June, 1777.

Colonel, Michael Bobst.   *Lieut. Col.,* Michael Teibert.
Major, Philip Beninghoff.

Captains, Adam Staller, William Mayer, Christian Marburger, Jacob Horner, Conrad Reather, Matthias Probst, John Krom, Joseph Sigfriet.

Fourth Battalion—June, 1777.

Colonel, John Sigfrit. *Lieut. Col.,* Nicholas Kern.
Major, James Boyd.

Captains, John Gregory, George Edelman, Henry Bowman, William Kromer, Frederick Coons, John Balstone, George Rondebush, Paul Flick.

Fifth Battalion—June, 1777.

Colonel, Abraham Labar. *Lieut. Col.,* Isaac Sidman.
Major, Robert Traill.

Captains, William Roup, Jacob Weygandt, Henry Lawall, Michael Huber, John Deichman, Adam Sorwer, George Engle, John Santee.

Sixth Battalion—June, 1777.

Colonel, Jacob Stroud. *Lieut. Col.,* Abraham Miller.
Major, John Gaston.

Captains, Anthony Shymer, Alexander Forsman, John Nelson, Johannes Van Etten, Henry Sawitz, Patrick Campbell, Timothy Jayne, Samuel Hover.

Seventh Battalion—May 21, 1782.

Colonel, Christian Shouss.
Captain, George Smethers, July 11, 1781.
Captain, George Nolff, May 21, 1782.

The following imperfect data are given relative to Col. Brinigh's battalion (probably the Second battalion), while in service at Billingsport, November 5, 1777.

Col. Brinigh's Battalion.

Colonel, George Brinigh.
Captain, Christian Johnston, 13 men.
Captain, George Roudebush, 17 men.
Captain, ———— ————, 25 men.
Lieut., Benjamin ————, 20 men.
Captain, Jacob Weigand, 19 men.
Captain, George Kappenberger, 33 men.

On the list of officers mentioned as in service in 1777 are the following names:

Lieut. Col., Michael Probst, June, 1777.
Captain, Adam Stahler, June, 1777.
Captain, Joseph Kooken, June, 1777.
Captain, George Knappenberger, September, 1777.
Lieut., Joseph Lorish, September, 1777 (Second Bat.).

YORK COUNTY.

The only data given for York county are the following:

Col. James Thompson's Battalion.

As it stood at Wilmington, Del., September 3, 1777.

First Company, Captain William Dodds, 18 men.
Second Company, Captain Samuel Ferguson, 41 men.
Third Company, illegible, — men.
Fourth Company, Captain Thomas Latta, 31 men.
Fifth Company, Captain John Laird, 32 men.
Sixth Company, Captain Peter Ford, 27 men.
Seventh Company, Captain John Myers, 18 men.

First Battalion.

(As of October 1, 1777.)

Third Company.	*Fourth Company.*
Captain, Christ. Kauffman.	*Captain,* Daniel May.
1st Lieut., John Shafer.	*1st Lieut.,* Andrew Milhorn.
2d Lieut., Henry Smith.	*2d Lieut.,* Henry Yessler.
Ensign, Jacob Strehr.	*Ensign,* Frederick Spahr.

THE OLD COURT HOUSE AT YORK.

Second Battalion.

(As of October 1, 1777.)

Colonel, William Rankin.
Lieut. Col., John Ewing.
Major, John Morgan.

First Company.

Captain, William Ashton.
1st Lieut., Mal. Steahley.
2d Lieut., James Elliott.
Ensign, John Crull.

Second Company.

Captain, John Rankin.
1st Lieut., Joseph Hunter.
2d Lieut., John Ashton.
Ensign, Daniel McHenry.

Third Company.

Captain, Simon Copen-
   hafer.
1st Lieut., Mich'l Shriver.
2d Lieut., Andrew Smith.
Ensign, Jacob Gotwalt.

Fourth Company.

Captain, Philip Gartner.
1st Lieut., John Higher.

Fifth Company.

Captain, Emanuel Herman.
1st Lieut., William Momeyer.
2d Lieut., John Rothrock.

Sixth Company.

Captain, John Mausberger.
1st Lieut., Henry Matthias.
2d Lieut., George Meyer.
Ensign, Jacob Kepler.

Seventh Company.

Captain, Jost. Horbach.
1st Lieut., Peter Shultz.
2d Lieut., Baltzer Rudisill.
Ensign, Michael Ettinger.

Eighth Company.

Captain, —— Wallis.
1st Lieut., Henry Leepert.
2d Lieut., John Jordan.
Ensign, James Schultz, Jr.

The Main Street of York, Pennsylvania, where Congress Met, 1777–1778.

The campaign of 1778 began with the evacuation of Philadelphia by the British, followed, shortly after, by the battle of Monmouth. Determined to strike an effective blow against the enemy Washington asked to be reinforced by the Pennsylvania militia, which was done. From this time, until the close of the war, various battalions, or companies, were in active service, at sundry times and for sundry purposes. The organizations which contained a large percentage of Pennsylvania-Germans, as far as the records show, will be named.

Many companies, besides, were ordered on expeditions against the Indians on the frontiers, to which a separate chapter will be devoted.

PHILADELPHIA COUNTY.

Col. Wm. Bradford's Battalion.

As of Nov. 2, 1778.   Commissioned Sept. 14, 1778.

Captains, John Linton, Isaac Cooper, Jeremiah Fisher, Henry Meyers (Lieut. Commanding), Joshua Humphreys, James Hood.

Col. Wm. Dean's Fourth Battalion.

As of Dec. 22, 1778.   Commissioned Dec. 8–11, 1778.

Captains, Samuel Hines, Philip Hahn, Jacob Peterman.

Col. Wm. Bradford's Battalion.

(First Regiment of Foot.)

Captain, Edw. Paschall, commission August 21, 1779, muster roll at Fort Mifflin, October 18, 1779.

Captain, Ezekiel Letts, commission August 25, 1779, muster roll at Billingsport, October 18, 1779.

Artillery Regiment—Col. Jehn Eyre.

Captain, Andrew Summers, Fifth Company, commission August 13, 1779, muster at Fort Mifflin and Billingsport, October 18, 1779.

Col. Benj. G. Eyre's Second Battalion.

Commissioned Aug. 10, 1780—Muster at Trenton, N. J., Aug. 31, 1780.

Captains, Elijah Weed, John Kling, John Hewson.

Artillery.

Commissioned Aug. 10, 1780—Muster at Trenton, N. J., Aug. 31, 1780.

Captains, Joseph Watkins, John Ogborn.

Col. William Will's Battalion.

(Third Regiment of Foot.)

Commissioned Aug. 10, 1780—Muster at Trenton, N. J., Aug. 31, 1780.

Captains, Andrew Burkhard, Michael Gilbert.

Major Richard Salter's Battalion.

Commissioned Feb. 4, 1781.

Captain, Christian Shaffer, muster of February 5, 1781.
Captain, John Geyer, muster of February 9, 1781.
Captain, William Bower, muster of March 5, 1781.

Major David Reese's Battalion.

Commissioned July 2, 1781—Muster of July 4, 1781.
Captains, Samuel McLane, Conrad Rush, James Hood.

Commissioned Sept. 1, 1781—Muster of Sept. 3, 1781.

Captains, Warwick Coats, Jr., George Taylor.

Capt. Philip Waggoner's Company.

Commissioned Nov. 1, 1781—Muster of Nov. 3, 1781.

LANCASTER COUNTY.

All returns as of August 26, 1780.

First Battalion.

Lieut. Col., George Stewart.

Captains, John Slater, Enoch Hastings, Alex. White, William Skyles, William Smith, ——— ———, ——— ———, William Brisben.

Third Battalion.

Lieut. Col., Jacob Bower.

Captains, Philip Dock, Andrew Ream, George Reist, Joseph Gehr, Jacob Vanderslice, Philip Peck, ——— ———, John Smuller.

Fourth Battalion.

Lieut. Col., Ludwig Meyer.

Captains, Frederick Rodfong, Jacob Brand, Jacob Metzger, Christian Doman, Alex. Scott, Jr., Joseph Wright, James Patton, James Beard.

Fifth Battalion.

Lieut. Col., Jacob Carpenter.

Captains, William Crawford, Samuel Elliot, Alexander McIlvaine, Joseph Jenkins, John Lutz, Martin Bowman, Randolph Statler, Martin Holman.

Sixth Battalion.

Lieut. Col., James Taylor.

Captains, John Caldwell, Robert Campbell, John Duncan, Robert Miller, James Clark, Joseph Walker, John Patton, Thomas Gormley.

Seventh Battalion.

Lieut. Col., Alexander Lowrey.

Captains, Andrew Boggs, Abraham Scott, Thomas Robinson, David McQuown, Noah Keesey, William Willson, Robert McKee, Hugh Pedan.

Eighth Battalion.

Commissions dated May 10, 1780.

Lieut. Col., James Ross.

Captains, John Hubley, John Ewing, Joseph Hubley, William Wirtz, Samuel Boyd, John Miller, James Davis, Jacob Wilhelm.

Ninth Battalion.

Lieut. Col., John Rogers.

Captains, William Allen, Patrick Hays, Ambrose Crain, John Harkensider, James McCreight, James Willson, Daniel Bradley, William Laird.

Tenth Battalion.

Lieut. Col., Robert Elder.

Captains, James Murray, George McMillen, William Johnston, Hugh Robinson, Andrew Stewart, Samuel Cochran, Martin Weaver, Jonathan McClure.

20

Second Battalion.

As of December 15, 1781.

Colonel, Thomas Edwards.

Captains, Baltzar Orth, Michael Holderbaum, Casper Stoever, David Krause, John Moore, John Stein, Matthias Henning.

BERKS COUNTY.

The active service records are given of but two battalions:

Third Battalion.

Marched August 11, 1780.

Lieut. Col., Jonathan Jones.

Captains, David Weidner, Thomas Hamilton, Adam Beard, George Graul, George Ax, John Ludwig.

Sixth Battalion.

In service from Aug. 10, 1780, to Sept. 9, 1780.

Lieut. Col., Joseph Hiester.

Captains, Charles Gobin, Ferdinand Ritter, Conrad Shirman, John Ludwig, Jacob Baldy, Henry Strouch.

Guards for Prisoners of War.

Captains, Peter Nagel, Conrad Geist.

Guarding Prisoners of War.

Captain, Charles Krause, August 13, 1781.

In Service at Newtown, October 1, 1781.

Captain, John Robinson.

YORK COUNTY.

Guarding Prisoners, November to December, 1781.

Captain, Andrew Forman, commissioned October 10, 1781.

PASTORAL SCENE IN YORK COUNTY.

CHAPTER XIII.

On the Frontiers Against the Indians.

THE employment of the savage during the Revolutionary War, by the British government, was, unquestionably, a most barbarous act, unworthy of a civilized power, and it is much to the credit of the Americans that they themselves, on the contrary, refused to take advantage of this alluring temptation. It is probably unfair, to some extent at least, that we should view this transaction through our twentieth century glasses, when making our criticism. One hundred and fifty years ago the Indian was a welcome and necessary ally against the encroachments of the French, and it was not altogether unnatural that the English should again turn to him in their time of need, some twenty years later. In doing so, however, they overlooked the fact that conditions had entirely changed, that the scene of hostilities was then far removed from the haunts of the savage, that the employment of such an inhuman ally could be of no material advantage to them, or their cause, that it meant only the unnecessary shedding of the blood of those who were their own brethren, with that of their helpless wives and children, and that, above all, their adversaries, realizing the facts just mentioned, had refused to employ the same means, as no longer within the pale of civilization. It is for these reasons the American people look, with just horror and reproach, upon the terrible atrocities which their ancestors were called upon to suffer through the acts of the barbarous ally whom the British authorities enlisted under their banner.

Various tribes of Indians were stirred to unrest by the continuance of the Revolutionary War, but the Six

Nations of New York were those largely employed by the British in their marauding expeditions along the frontiers. With the surrender of Burgoyne, and consequent weakening of the British force in New York, the aid of the

savage became especially welcome and necessary in the operations as there carried on.

Taking advantage of the absence at the front, in the Continental service, of nearly all the able-bodied men of the vicinity, on July 3, 1778, the eve of the second anniversary of the adoption of the Declaration of Independence, the British troops, composed of Sir John Johnson's Royal Greens (Tory), Tory Rangers and Indians, fell upon and massacred the helpless people of the Wyoming Valley.

Although not a few Pennsylvania-Germans were among the victims of the massacres which took place at that time yet it is not so much with this sad, but familiar, tale we have to do as with the vengeance which followed in its footsteps.

The various bodies of rangers, in constant service, proving inadequate to check the ravages of the Indians, it was wisely decided to have a body of regular troops carry the war into their own villages, drive them away or exterminate them, and to utterly destroy their homes, their crops and their substance, thus rendering them entirely helpless and powerless.

The first expedition sent out was that under command of Col. William Butler, consisting of a part of the Fourth Pennsylvania Continental Regiment, a part of Morgan's Rifle Corps, and some militia, in number about 260. In the Fourth regiment was Capt. Scull's company, largely Pennsylvania-German, with a considerable percentage in the rest of the organization, and in Morgan's Rifle Corps were also many Pennsylvania-Germans.

Shortly after the battle of Monmouth (June 26, 1778), Col. Butler was ordered to Schoharie, New York, to prevent the depredations of the savages. There a punitive expedition was fitted out, which, on Friday, October 2, 1778, started from Fort Defiance (a short distance south of the present town of Middleburg), and marched the first day to Mattises Grist Mill; thence, the second day, to Isaac Sawyer's, near the head of the West Branch of the Delaware River; thence to Wills' Mill (in the neighborhood of the present town of Delhi); thence, by two marches, crossed over to the Susquehanna River at Unadilla, which Indian town they found evacuated.

For the remaining operations we quote from the letter of Capt. William Gray (4th Penn.), dated Schoharie, October 28, 1778:

" From thence [Unadilla] we Marched Down the River Susquehanna for Ononaughquaga the Chief Indian town [just above the present town of Windsor—Ed.] where we thought to Start a Party of Savages & torys By Surprise, but we Happened Unluckily to be Discovered by Some Scouting Savages who made the best of their way & as they knew the path Better than we Did & had Got the start So far we Could not Come up with them though our Scouting Party traveled all Night, to no purpose. We Got to Ononaughquaga on Thursday the 8th Ult. [Oct. 8th] About 10 o'Clock at Night which we found Evacuated, Also in Greatest Disorder, Everything Seemed as if they had fled in the Greatest Haste. Next Morning we set the town (which Consisted of About 30 or forty good Houses) in flames Destroying therein Great Quantitys of Household Furniture & Indian Corn. After the Burning of the town two men of our party went out to Sarch for some Horses that were Lost, & not minding to take their Arms with them were fired on from a thicket by some Lurking Indians who wounded one of them (that is Since Dead of the wound) on which Col. Butler ordered Capt. Parr with a party of Rifel men to Go in Sarch of them but they Could not Come up with them though they Marched five or six miles Down the River Seting fier to a very Large Indian Council house on their Return. The same Day About 2 o'Clock we marched from Ononaughquaga. up the River too another Town Called Cunahunta [about

near Bainbridge—Ed.], burning Some Indian Houses & Corn on the Road, from thence we Marched Next morning Early Leaving it in flames, but that Night & the Day Raining so terrably that it Rendered Every small Run both Difficult & Dangerous in Crossing, but when we Came to the River below Unendilla it was Dreadful to see so Large a stream to the Mens Breasts & very Rappid & Rising at the Rate of one Inch P Minet, but by the Pressing Desire of the men to Get over & the Deligence of the Officers with their owne & the Pack Horses they were all Got over Safe which if we had been but one houre Longer we Could not have Crossed & God only knows what would have been the Dreadfull consequences.

"We Marched that Evening up the East side of the River as far as the Scotch Settlement [mouth of

MASSACRE OF WYOMING, JULY, 1778.

Ouleout Creek—Ed.] burning all as we went along that Could be of any use to the Enimy. We Could not March thence on Sunday by Reason of the Great Rains. On Munday we Marched, burning some Tory Houses before we Set out & Encamped in the wood that Night [along the Ouleout Creek—Ed.]. Marched Early next morning but when we Came to Delaware we Could not Cross it but was obliged to March up the N. W. Side of the River & the Pilot not knowing the Road & Night Coming on we Lost our Road about five or six miles & had to March over two very Large Hills Before we Could Get to the River again. However the Party Got Home on Saturday the 16th Ult. [Oct. 16] in Good spirits After a march of Near 300 miles in Such Terrable Weather, Almost bairfooted & Naked, we suffered a good Deal for want of Bread as we had not any of that very useful Article for four Days. You Doubtless may see a more Particular Acct of this at Head Quarters but I have Endeavored to Give it as True as I Could. Present My Best Compliments to Capt. Scull & the Rest of the Party & Let them See this."

The second expedition was that of April, 1779, to Onondaga, in which a company of the Fourth Pennsylvania and a company of Morgan's Rifle Corps participated. They left Fort Defiance on April 6 and proceeded to Fort Herkimer, where they joined Capt. Bleeker's company, from Col. Gansevort's regiment, Capt. Fowler's company, from Col. Livingstone's regiment, and Capt. Lane's company, from Col. Alden's regiment. In charge of Capt. Bleeker the whole party next marched to Fort Schuyler, where they were reinforced by three companies from Col. Van Schaick's regiment, who then took command.

Embarking in batteaux, with a high wind, they succeeded in reaching, with difficulty, the Onondaga landing at the farther end of the lake, about 3 P. M., April 19.

The proceedings of April 21 are now given as narrated

by Lieut. Erkwries Beatty, of the Fourth Pennsylvania regiment, in his journal.

"This morning set of about Day Break on the same line of march and went about 6 miles when we halted. Capt. Graham with his Compy, was sent forward as an advance party, then proceeded on to the Onondaga lake about 8 miles in length & 4 in Breadth, waded an arm of it about 4 foot deep and 200 yards wide and came to Onondaga creek, small but deep, had to cross it on a log. Capt. Graham's Co. Just as he had crossed this creek caught an Indian who was shooting Pidgeons & made him prisoner, And we got some Information from him, then proceeded on till we come within about one Mile of the Town when we Rec'd word from Capt. Graham that he had caught one Squaw and Killed one and had taken two or three Children and one White man, and one or two made their escape and alarmed the town. The Col. Immediately sent me forward to order him on as quick as possible and make as many prisoners as he could & he would support him with the main body. I overtook him at the first town and delivered my orders and he Immediately pushed on about two miles to the Next town where he made a small halt and took a great many prisoners. Soon after, Magor Cochran with Capt. Gray's Compy, came up and ordered me to stay with the prisoners, and their two Compys to push on to the next town about one mile forward, which they did and made more prisoners and killed some particularly a Negro who was their Dr. They then plundered the houses of the most valuable things and set fire to them and Returned to the middle Town where I was. Capt. Bleeker's Compy. had come up by this time and left the main body at their first town, we then collected all our prisoners, plundered this town and sett fire to it then marched of to the main body which lay at the first town, we stayd there about 8 hours and killed some five horses and a Number of Hogs & plundered their houses and set fire to them and Marched of about 4 o'Clock in the same line of march as we came only the front changed and a Comp'y to guard the pris'rs, who was to march between they two Columns. Marched on about 2 Miles from the town down the Onand'ga creek, when about 20

Indians who Lay concealed on the opposite side of the Creek fird upon us, but the Rifle men soon Dispersed them killing one of them, we then march'd on and crossed the Onand'ga Creek in two places for fear the enemy should attack us but we met with no interruption, crossed the arm of the lake and encamped by the side of the lake about 8 miles from the town—We Killed about 15 took 34 Prisoners, burned about 30 or 40 Houses, took 2 stand of Coulors, and we had not one man Killed or wounded."

By April 29 the Pennsylvania detachments were back again safely at Fort Defiance, Schoharie.

The continued depredations of the Indians on the frontiers, however, demanded more aggressive action, on a larger scale, so the Commander-in-Chief ordered Gen. Sullivan to carry the war into the country of the Six Nations, there "to cut off their settlements, destroy their crops, and inflict upon them every other mischief which time and circumstances would permit." To that end Sullivan repaired to Easton, as his headquarters, there to organize his forces. The German Continental Regiment, the Eleventh (new Eleventh) Pennsylvania Continental Regiment, and Capt. Schott's company with Armand's Cavalry Corps, arrived in April, 1779. They were accompanied by a detachment of Proctor's Artillery, and followed by various troops from New Jersey, New Hampshire, etc. Their tents were pitched along the Delaware and Lehigh rivers, and up the Bushkill creek. Of these bodies the German regiment, and Schott's company with Armand's cavalry corps, were entirely Pennsylvania-German. Proctor's artillery contained many of the same descent, and the Eleventh Pennsylvania regiment a considerable proportion.

The troops, consisting of 2,500 men, with 2,000 pack-horses and 120 boats, took up their line of march on the morning of June 18, 1779.

Their route lay by way of Fort Penn (present town of Stroudsburg), into the Great Swamp, which, with its thick trees and dense darkness, was appropriately named the " Shades of Death," and through which the wretched survivors of the Wyoming massacre had miserably toiled to their place of refuge at Fort Penn, its gateway.

On June 23, distant now only seven miles from Wyoming, they passed the spot where Capt. Davis and Lieut. Jones, with a corporal and four privates, were scalped, tomahawked and speared by the savages; two boards marked where the officers fell, the one at Lieut. Jones' grave being besmeared with his own blood. As the troops passed by Col. Proctor's musicians played an appropriate dirge to the tune of " Roslin Castle."

The next day they reached Wyoming where they met Col. Zebulon Butler, the hero of the past year, and one of the few survivors of the massacre. Being St. John's Day, a number of Free Masons met in the tent of Col. Proctor where the Rev. William Rogers, D.D., Chaplain of Gen. Hand's brigade, read a sermon to them.

From this time until the end of July the General was busily engaged in providing supplies for his troops and getting in readiness for a further advance. Constant reports were received of the inhuman acts perpetrated at various points by different parties of savages. One of an especially unfortunate character occurred on July 22, at a place called Lackawack, above the Minisink (near Stroudsburg), where a force of one hundred and forty militia, stationed on the Delaware, were drawn into an ambuscade, and some forty or fifty were killed or taken prisoners.

The following are the details of this sad episode:

Early in June, 1779, Captain Joseph Brant,[1] the half-breed Indian Chief, left the Susquehanna with some four hundred warriors to make an incursion into the Delaware valley. The settlers received due notice of this movement and threw out scouts to watch him. The wily Indians, however, turned a short corner, struck for the upper Delaware, crossed near Mast Hope, at a place known as Grassy Brook, clambered over the mountains, and by forced marches reached the little town of Minisink, where the town of Port Jervis now stands. The inhabitants fled, and the place was sacked and destroyed. Flushed with success the invaders moved slowly up the Delaware with their plunder, on the York State side. In the meantime the people of Orange County raised about one hundred and fifty men who started on the trail of the savages. On the night of July 21 the Indians encamped at the mouth of Beaver brook, whilst their pursuers lay four or five miles further down. On the fatal morning of the twenty-second both parties were early in motion. Brant had reached the ford at the mouth of the Lackawaxen and a good part of the plunder was safe in Pike County. The whites held a short consultation at the Indian encampment, where the more prudent urged a

[1] It is not generally known that Capt. Joseph Brant (Thayendanegea the Mohawk Indian) was a man of considerable culture and education. He was a religious man and a consistent Freemason, having been initiated at London, April 26, 1776. His certificate was signed by James Heseltine, Gr. Sec'y. He let no opportunity pass of saving the life or liberty of any Brother Mason if within his power. The case of the American Major Wood is a matter of history. In 1783, after the Revolution, Brant, with the loyal Mohawks, settled in Canada, where Capt. Joseph Brant built the first Protestant Church in either upper or lower Canada.— Julius F. Sachse.

THAYENDANEGEA (JOSEPH BRANT) SAVING THE LIFE OF
CAPT. JOHN McKINSTREY, A BROTHER FREEMASON.

FROM A CONTEMPORARY FRENCH PRINT.

return. All further deliberation, however, was cut short by a Captain Meeker, who boldly stepped to the front exclaiming, "Let brave men follow me," whereupon nearly the whole party once more started in pursuit. Two short miles brought them to the ford, where a large body of the enemy could be seen on the opposite shore. A few shots were fired and one Indian was seen to roll down the bank towards the river. About this time a heavy volley was fired into the whites from the high hills in the rear, which immediately awoke them to a sense of their danger and the mistake they had made in leaving their only avenue of escape in the hands of the enemy. The officers in command ordered a rush to be made for the high ground. The Indians fell back, and chose their position; the pursued recrossed the river, and the brave but doomed band of patriotic whites were cut off from the water and surrounded by their merciless foes. During the whole of that day the battle raged. As night was closing in, some twenty or thirty, who survived, made a dash for the river, headed by Major Wood, who, through mistake, made the grand masonic hailing sign of distress as he approached the spot where Brant was standing. The Indian, true to his obligation, allowed the party to pass. They swam the river and made their escape into the wilds of Pike County. A few more escaped under cover of darkness, and the rest slept the sleep which knows no waking on this earth. In the year 1822 the bones of friend and foe alike were gathered together, transported to Goshen, in Orange County, where they were decently interred and a beautiful monument erected over them by a public-spirited citizen of the place.

At 1:00 P. M., on Saturday, July 31, the whole army began its march from Wyoming. Agreeable to general

The Wyoming Valley, from Prospect Rock.
From an old print.

orders, the light corps, in advance, were to march in three columns, which were arranged by Gen. Hand as follows: "Eleventh Pennsylvania regt. and Capt. Spalding's independent company advanced by platoons from the center of a line formed by them, and constituted a column to proceed on the main road. The German regiment and Capt. Schott's independent corps from the right of the said regiment, formed a column and marched on the right of the Eleventh, having their right flank covered by one third of the light infantry of the Eleventh and Schott's riflemen in Indian file. Two thirds of the light infantry of the Eleventh and Capt. Spalding's riflemen marched in Indian file on the left flank, and answered the purpose of a third column; each column and flanking party had, proportioned to their strength respectively, a small party advanced in front, the same to be observed if possible until our arrival at Tioga."

On Thursday, August 5, the light troops reached the remains of Wyalusing, a town inhabited by Moravian Indians, which had been destroyed partly by the Americans, partly by the Indians. Not a vestige of what had been a most flourishing settlement remained standing.

On Thursday, August 12, a large detachment, under command of Sullivan himself, left the encampment to surprise the Indians at Chemung, but, unfortunately, found the town abandoned. It was well-built and beautifully situated on the banks of the Tioga branch. The whole was immediately destroyed. At his own request Gen. Hand was allowed to proceed towards Newtown (the site of the present city of Elmira, N. Y.), on his promise to return to Tioga the next morning, while Gen. Sullivan, with the rest of the troops started back to camp.

Gen. Hand's corps had proceeded but a short distance

21

when they reached a high hill on their right, and were given a very sharp volley by the Indians, who had there secreted themselves. A sergeant and some privates were killed, while Capt. Franklin, Adjutant Hinton and a few others were wounded. The Eleventh Pennsylvania at

once pushed rapidly up the hill, where the savages delivered another volley and fled. The light troops pursued for some distance, intending to push on to Newtown, but Gen. Sullivan, arriving at that moment, thought it best for them to return and destroy the crops of the enemy. As Gen. Poor's brigade were destroying an upper field they were fired upon and lost one man killed, with two or three wounded. The total loss of the Eleventh Pennsylvania was six killed and eight wounded; that of the main body, one killed and a few wounded.

On Saturday, August 14, the six killed, of Col. Hubley's Eleventh Pennsylvania, were solemly interred, the Rev. Dr. Rogers pronouncing a funeral oration.

On Monday, August 16, nine hundred picked men, under command of Gens. Poor and Hand, marched off to meet the troops, and boats, under command of Gen. Clinton, who were ordered to proceed from Schoharie to reinforce Sullivan's army.

This force consisted of the Fourth Pennsylvania Regiment and Morgan's Rifle Corps, which left Schoharie on Friday, June 11, 1779, were joined, at Conojoharie, by Col. Gansevort's Regiment, also by Col. Dubois' Regiment, with two pieces of artillery, at Springfield, on the twenty-sixth, and, on the twenty-ninth, at the same place, by the "flying hospital." On Saturday, July 3, Col. Wisenfill's Regiment joined them at the lower end of the lake (Otsego). Gen. Clinton and staff arrived on July 1, at which time he took command. On July 5, Col. Alden's Regiment came over with the last of the provisions and stores.

On Monday, August 9, the troops took up their line of march and reached the ruins of the Scotch Settlement, at the mouth of Ouleaut creek on the twelfth. On the fourteenth they arrived at the ruins of Ononaughquaga. Leaving that place on the seventeenth they came, on the same day, to the Tuscarora town of Shawhiaughto, which they destroyed, and, twelve miles further, to the town of Ingaren, which was also destroyed.

On Thursday, the nineteenth, Clinton's force fell in with that of Gen. Poor, and the combined bodies safely joined the main army, at the mouth of the Tioga, on Sunday, the twenty-second, where they were welcomed by Gen. Hand's brigade under arms, with the band of music and drums and fifes playing alternately, and saluted by thirteen pieces of cannon. The Fourth Pennsylvania and Morgan's Rifle Corps were then annexed to Hand's brigade.

Leaving Col. Shreve, with a garrison of two hundred and fifty men, at Wyoming, on Friday, the twenty-seventh, the army started on its final campaign. They found the enemy on Sunday, August 29, near Newtown (Elmira, N. Y.), strongly entrenched behind a breastwork of logs, dirt, brush, etc., their front protected by a large morass and brook. While Hand's brigade and the Rifle Corps kept up a brisk fire in front, Gens. Clinton and Poor were sent to turn their left flank and take a position in their rear. After the latter were gone for about half an hour, Gen. Hand advanced in line of battle, with the artillery in the center, and, by a heavy fire drove the enemy out of their entrenchments. As they retreated, in great disorder, they received a volley from Poor's brigade, which drove them around his right flank, by the river, which he had not yet had time to secure, whereby they made their escape. After pursuing them for some distance the army returned to its camp, with a loss of about forty killed and wounded. The loss of the enemy was very heavy, but could not be ascertained definitely. They consisted of about 400 Indians and 300 Tories, led by Col. John Butler, with Brant and other Indian chiefs under him.

On August 31, the army proceeded to Newtown, which they found to be a town of between twenty and thirty houses, well built but much scattered, which was destroyed.

Monday, Sepember 6, found the army at Kandaia, about one half mile from Cayuga Lake, where they succeeded in retaking one of their men who had been cap-

tured at Wyoming the previous summer.   This town, and
another on the lake, were likewise destroyed.

Proceeding along Lake Cayuga they destroyed Kana-
dasago, the chief town of the Senecas, and a smaller place,
called Kushay, on the seventh and eighth.   On the tenth

Philip Schuyler Esqr

they came to a small lake called "Kanandaqua," and
destroyed the town of the same name.   On the eleventh
Hanyaye met the same fate, and, on the twelfth, another
place about as large.

Monday, the thirteenth, found them at the town of
Adjutse.   Here a sad misfortune befell Lieut. Boyd, who,

with a party of eighteen riflemen and eight musketmen from the Fourth Pennsylvania, had been sent out, the previous day, to reconnoitre the next town. They reached the place, without interruption, and found it evacuated. Hiding themselves, in the hope of securing some prisoners, they succeeded in killing and wounding several Indians, but, finding a larger number about than had been anticipated, the Lieutenant decided to rejoin the army. Falling in with some of the enemy he pursued them slowly, but, suddenly, found himself surrounded by a large force, which made prisoners of or killed the whole party save four or five who managed to escape.

A great abundance of supplies was destroyed on the fourteenth, when the troops crossed over a branch of the Genesee river and came to Genesee town, the largest they had yet seen. Here they found the bodies of Lieut. Boyd and a rifleman, most horribly mutilated, and buried them with the honors of war. Everything in sight was then destroyed, including crops of all descriptions as well as the town itself.

On the twentieth, a detachment, under Col. Smith, went up to Kushe, and a little above, to destroy the locality; another, consisting of some 500 or 600 men, under Col. Butler, was sent to Lake Cayuga to complete the destruction in that vicinity; and a detachment, under Col. Gansevort, went to Albany to bring on the officers' baggage.

On the twenty-first, Col. Deerborn was likewise sent to the Cayuga Lake on a mission of destruction, and returned, on the twenty-sixth, having destroyed five Indian towns and a great quantity of corn. On the twenty-eighth, Col. Butler returned from his errand and reported the destruction, on the east side of the lake, of three capital towns, a great number of scattering houses, and a vast amount of corn.

On Thursday, October 7, the army was once more at Wyoming, where, on the ninth, Gen. Sullivan set out for Easton, leaving Gen. Clinton in command.

Sunday, the tenth, saw the army on the move. They entered the Great Swamp on the twelfth, and arrived at Larnard's Tavern on the thirteenth, which the narrator, in his journal, is pleased to call "the beginning of the settlement of a Christian Country, which appeared to me very strange here." They arrived at Easton about 3 P. M., on Friday, October 15, after a most remarkable and successful campaign, during which the savages had been dealt a blow such as they had never experienced before, and from which they never recovered.

The German Regiment remained on duty along the frontiers. On June 20, 1780, it consisted of about 100 men, of whom 33 were posted at Fort Jenkins, 30 at Bosley's Mill, 24 at Fort Bunner, the residue at headquarters at the town of Northumberland.

An interesting connection with the tale of Sullivan's Expedition is Fort Penn, at the present town of Stroudsburg, then in Northampton county, and especially so because of its Pennsylvania-German origin and garrison.

There is nothing on record to show when it was built, nor what was its appearance, but it probably came into existence during the earlier part of the war, and, doubtless, was a stockade of ordinary character. Its commanding officer was Col. Stroud, during its entire history, of the Sixth battalion of Northampton county militia.

It was to this place of refuge the miserable survivors of Wyoming fled, in 1778, and, as they emerged from "the shades of death," it must truly have appeared a haven of peace and beauty to their anxious eyes.

It was mercifully spared the attack of Brant, and his force of Tories and Indians, in the summer of 1779, who had approached within a short distance and was only turned back because of Sullivan's threatened invasion of his own country.

Fort Penn became the storehouse of supplies for Gen. Sullivan, and it was past its gates his army marched both when going and upon their victorious return.

It was the refuge for all the distressed settlers when threatened by the enemy.

The fort was located back from the present Main Street of Stroudsburg, at the curve just west of Chestnut Street, opposite the M. E. Church.

Besides the regular troops, of which detailed mention has been made, many companies of Frontier Rangers were in active service at all times. Even after the blow struck by Gen. Sullivan predatory parties of savages were constantly in motion, committing outrages here and there, which needed unwearied watching. This condition of affairs kept up until the close of the war, if not longer.

Most of these companies came from counties containing but few Pennsylvania-Germans, so few, in many cases, as not to warrant, for our purpose, the space required to mention them. Those which the records in existence show to have been Pennsylvania-German will now be given.

BERKS COUNTY.

Captains, Jacob Ladick, Jacob Rhorer, Fred. Miller, James Gleaves, George Rheem, Charles Krause, John Robinson, and *Lieut.,* Daniel Stroud, Commanding.

GEN. JOHN SULLIVAN.

B. FEBRUARY 17, 1740. D. JULY 23, 1795.

MONONGAHELA COUNTY.

Captain, John Wetzel, "ranging in Monongahela and Ohio county, from April 22 to July 25, 1778, under Col. Daniel McFarland."

WESTMORELAND COUNTY.

Captains, Jno. Kreps, John Crisp, Jno. Kilps, Christopher Truby, James Leech.

YORK COUNTY.

Captain, Andrew Forman, guarding prisoners at Camp Security, November to December, 1781.

NORTHUMBERLAND COUNTY.

Captains, Joseph Green, Casper Huntsacher, George Overmier, John Moll, Jno. Waggoner, Nicholas Bittinger, George Swartz, George Obermier, William Wyrick, Michael Weaver, Michael Motze.

First Battalion—May 1, 1778.

Colonel, John Kelly.

Captains, John Forster, 55 men; James Thompson, 44 men; George Overmier, 51 men; Samuel Fisher, 55 men; Samuel Young, 51 men; Abraham Piatt, 53 men; William Irvin, 53 men; William Gray, 44 men.

Second Battalion—May 1, 1778.

Colonel, James Murray.

Captains, Thomas Gaskins, 61 men; John Nelson, 60 men; David Hayes, 63 men; Arthur Taggart, 66 men; James McMahon, 57 men; Robert Reynolds, 43 men; John Chatham, 49 men; John Clingman, 73 men.

Third Battalion—May 1, 1778.

Colonel, Peter Hosterman.

Captains, Casper Reed, 34 men; Michael Weaver, 63 men; Samuel Harris, 54 men; John Mull, 55 men; John Black, 49 men; William Wyrick, 56 men; Adam Shaffer, 82 men; Michael Motze, 46 men.

Fourth Battalion—May 1, 1778.

Colonel, Cookson Long.

Captains, Thomas Wilson, 48 men; Simon Cole, 42 men; Joseph Newman, 43 men; Thomas Kemplin, 46 men; William Hepburn, 45 men; Alexander Hamilton, 41 men.

NORTHAMPTON COUNTY.

Captains, Peter Rothe, Jno. Jacoby, Jno. Gregory, Lewis Stocker, George Smith, Frederick Shuler, Jno. Van Etten, Jno. Deiter, George Shriver, Henry Shoemaker, Benj. Shanover, Peter Keippord, Paul Flick, Philip Shrawder (Feb. 10, 1781 to June 1, 1782), Philip Knause, Richard Shaw, Henry Geiger, Jno. Wyand, William Myers, Cassimir Greensmire, Lewis Stocker (July 30, 1784), Jacob Heller, John Lyles, Christian Rood (Lieut. Commanding), Charles Myers, Henry Ritts, John Ritter, Peter Strowell, Adam Dell, George Wolf, Adam Stocker, Adam Stahler, Jno. Gregory, Samuel Hoover.

Members of Fifth Battalion, ordered to march July 30, 1778, from companies of Captains Buss, Wyand, Lawald, Reeser, Deichman, Heimer, Engle, Sentee.

Members of First Battalion, Col. Balliot, ordered July 22, 1781, commanded by Capt. Henry Reitz.

From companies of Captains Zerfass, Jacoby, ———,

George Strine, Jo. Kooken, Trexler, Greenmayer, Reitz.

Sixth class, First Battalion, Lieut. Col. Henry Geiger, ordered November 15, 1781, commanded by Capt. Casper Greenmayer.

First class, Col. Christian Shaus, September 22, 1781, Captain Adam Serfoos.

Fifth and Sixth Battalions, Col. Nicholas Kern, service at Wyoming, July 30, 1784, Captains Lewis Stecher, John Van Etten.

Muster Roll of
Capt. Van Etten's Volunteer Company.

Commissioned June 15, 1780, mustered at Fort Penn, January 15, 1781, by Jacob Stroud, Lieut. Col.

Captain, Johannes Van Etten.
1st Lieut., John Fish.
2d Lieut., John Myer.
Ensigns, Henry Bush, James Scoby, commissioned September 1, 1780, taken prisoner September 11, 1780.

Sergeants.

Thomas Johnston.
Samuel Hellet.
James Scoby, promoted ensign September 1, 1780.
Frederick Everhart.
Joseph Gable, August 30.
George Price.

Corporals.

Lewis Holmes.
Thomas Gay.

Samuel Bond, killed September 11.
Adam Hicker.

Privates.

Samuel Vandermark.
Daniel McDale.
John Morhart.
John Kouts, killed Sept. 11.
Rudolph Smith.
Abraham Clider (Klader),
killed Sept. 11.
Daniel Smith.
George Gongaware.
John Myer.
Peter Apler.
John Weaver.
Daniel France.
Laurence Miller.
George Pigg.
John Robenholt.
Leonerd Pack.
John Sack.
Job Stout.
George Ripsher.
Peter Snyder.
Peter Lasher.
Jacob Cryder.
Coanrode Kowler.
John Napsnyder.
Adam Teel.
Voluntine Nicolas.
George Hikman.
John Smith.
John Wetherstone.
Christian Haller.

Peter Croom, killed Sept.
11.
Johannes Snyder.
Andrew Mourer.
Adam Lung.
George Shilhamer, killed
Sept. 11.
Paul Neely, killed Sept. 11.
Abraham Smith, killed
Sept. 11.
John Lyn, absent, sick.
Jacob Arndt, killed Sept.
11.
Samuel Summeny.
Jacob Collens.
Henry Davis.
Philip George, killed Sept.
11.
Peter McCoy.
John Hunn.
Abraham Wisner.
Uriah Tippy.
Paul Reeser.
Ballser Wever.
George Heater.
John Smith, Jr.
Christian Wood.
John Morgan.
Henry France.
Bond Heive.
John Hain.

Jacob Houser.

Peter Siner.

Peter Tubalt Coans, prisoner Sept. 11.

Philip George Shilhamer.

Baltzer Snyder, killed Sept. 11.

Philip Bitten, deserted Nov. 10.

George Peter Renhart, killed Sept. 11.

Andrew Myer.

Peter Quick.

Thomas Van Sikkle.

Samuel Van Garden.

Joseph Gable, to sergeant, Aug. 30.

Michael Yerty.

Adam Brunthaver.

Antony Bishop.

John Snider.

Peter Daniel.

Peter Simonton.

John Dayley.

Henry Van Garden.

Abraham Westfall.

Cornelius Devoor.

Casper Clutter.

Solomon Huff.

Thomas Heive.

James McGraw, killed Sept. 11.

Jacob Row, killed Sept. 11.

The date of death of the above members of Capt. Van Etten's company, September 11, the same day and month as that of the battle of Brandywine, has led various historians carelessly to state the fact that this company was at Brandywine and there lost heavily. Such was not the case, and it is well that this error should now be corrected. A mere glance will show the reader that the year is 1780 and not 1777.

The tragic death of these Pennsylvania-German volunteers, however, is a tale of its own, well worth the relating. The occurrence is more generally known as

THE SUGAR LOAF MASSACRE.

The regions of Pennsylvania to the north of the Blue Mountains, including what is generally known as the

Wyoming Valley, contained many tory sympathizers with and adherents to the cause of Great Britain. Those who took up arms openly against their brethren were bad enough, with their heartless and merciless methods of warfare, but, in one sense, those who acted secretly as spies, to convey information of American movements, were still worse, because so much the more difficult to guard against.

It was these latter who enabled the savages and tories to successfully, and with immunity, swoop down upon their victims; it was they who kept watch on Sullivan's movements, and those of all other expeditions. After Sullivan's victorious return they were the more moved, by a desire for revenge, to carry on their nefarious work. To such an extent was this done that Col. Hunter, in command at Fort Augusta (Sunbury) decided upon aggressive action and resolved to put an end to their transactions, as well as those of his enemies who were openly in the field. Captain D. Klader, of Northampton county, with a detachment of Captain John Van Etten's company, was ordered forward to join the enterprise. Unfortunately for them, the tory spies learned of the movement and imparted their knowledge to the enemy under the following circumstances.

On September 6, 1780, a body of tories and Indians, numbering some 250 or 300, appeared before Fort Rice, in Lewis township of Northumberland county, on the headwaters of the Chilisquake, some seventeen miles from Fort Augusta, and made a vigorous attack upon it. This, however, was gallantly repulsed by Capt. Rice's company of the German Continental Regiment. Reinforcements were at once ordered to their relief by Col. Hunter, and the inhabitants warned of their danger. The arrival of these

additional troops caused the enemy to break up into
smaller bodies and retreat in different directions, destroying everything in their way.

To one of these parties, numbering about forty, was
announced the coming of Capt. Klader's small force.
They immediately proceeded to the site of the present
town of Berwick, where they crossed over the river and
followed the path leading from the Susquehanna to
Northampton, a distance of about seven miles from
Nescopeck. Here, in Sugar Loaf Valley, southwestern
part of Luzerne county, they lay in ambush, and awaited
the arrival of their unsuspecting victims.

In the meanwhile, Capt. Klader, after toiling labori-
ously to the summit of the Buck Mountain, had taken the
path leading by the "old toll-house," thence down the
side of the mountain, through a ravine, over the farm of
N. Wagner and across the creek below, until they came
to what had been a Scotch settlement, but now, because
of the border troubles, wholly deserted. To their great
delight they saw before them open and cleared fields,
covered with a luxuriant growth of grass, and beautiful
with wild flowers. Weary as they were with the fatigue
and hardship of their long march, when, for days, they
had been tearing their way through the thickets and
bushes, and clambering over logs and stones, they seemed
to have entered upon a veritable paradise.

It was noontide of September 11, 1780, knapsacks
were immediately unslung, and they entered upon the
enjoyment of the hour. The very beauty of their surroundings lulled to rest all thought of danger. No one
seemed to realize the necessity for watchful care. Each
roamed about as best suited his fancy. Their guns were
scattered here and there, some stacked, some leaning

against stumps of logs, others lying flat on the ground. The position of the men resembled that of their fire arms. Some were on the ground indulging in a smoke, one man was leaning against a tree with his shoes off, cleaning them out, others had gone for grapes, which grew there in abundance, of which party one had climbed a tree and was picking and eating the grapes from the vine which entwined it.

Suddenly, while in this condition, a volley of musketry was poured in upon them from an unseen foe, and, with it, rang out the terrible war-whoop of the savages, who, in a moment more, were in their midst, hewing down their victims with the murderous tomahawk. Some escaped, and one or two were taken prisoners, but most of

AUTOGRAPH OF GENERAL SCHUYLER.

them were killed. A great-uncle of the Engle brothers, recently living in Hazleton and vicinity, escaped over the Nescopec Mountain; Abram Klader, brother of the officer in command, concealed himself in Little Nescopec Creek, by clinging to a tree that had fallen across the stream, and keeping his face only above the water until the enemy had disappeared, when he emerged from his concealment and succeeded in reaching home; Frederick

Shickler also escaped on Buck Mountain by avoiding the Indian trail, leaving it to his right, and keeping out of sight of the Indians, whose yells he could hear as they followed on in pursuit. Lieut. Myer, Ensign Scoby, and private Peter Tubalt Coans were taken prisoners; the lieutenant escaped, while the other two were taken through to Niagara.

The man in the tree after grapes was shot and fell heavily to the ground beneath. Some were killed in one place and some in another, as they fled and were overtaken by their merciless foes. One soldier whose name cannot be designated, escaped part way up the ravine down which the troops had marched, and there hid himself, but, unfortunately, was betrayed by the barking of his too faithful little dog that had followed him, and was slain. A comrade, secreted in a tree top near by, witnessed the scene. Capt. Klader, himself, did not succumb until after performing deeds of valor which caused his name to be remembered with feelings akin to veneration. He is said, by some, to have killed four, and, by others, seven of the enemy, before they finally slew and scalped him.

In time, the mutilated bodies of the dead were gathered by Van Campen, under directions of Col. Hunter, and decently interred.

Mr. C. F. Hill, of Hazleton, to whom I am under obligations for the material contained in this sketch, says the body of Capt. Klader lies buried on the farm of Samuel Wagner, about half a mile from Conyngham, but no trace of the grave can now be seen. The oak tree, under whose branches he lay, and upon which were cut the initials of his name—D. K.—was sacrilegiously cut

22

down some thirty years ago, and even the stump is decayed and gone.

The names of those killed and captured will be noticed on Captain Van Etten's roll, just given, but, as there are a couple inaccuracies, they will be again mentioned.

Killed.

Captain, D. Klader, John Weaver, Baltzer Snyder, Samuel Bond, *Corporal,* John Kouts, George Peter Reinhart, Peter Croom, George Shilhamer, Paul Neely, Abraham Smith, Jacob Arndt, Philip George, James McGraw, Jacob Row, 14 persons.

Abraham Clider (Klader), marked incorrectly as killed, escaped as described.

Prisoners.

John Meyer, *Second Lieutenant,* acting as commander after Klader's death, was captured but escaped.

James Scoby, *Ensign.*

Peter Tubalt Coons.

This massacre so thoroughly aroused the authorities that they decided to clear out the tory settlement. It will be readily understood that, under the nature of things, this could not be done by force of arms. By a trick, however, the inhabitants were inveigled into confessing their guilt, whereupon they were haled before Col. Hunter, and, upon pledging themselves to leave the frontier settlements, not returning until after the close of the war, they were permitted to peacefully depart.

CHAPTER XIV.

OUR NON-COMBATANT PATRIOTS.

THE Pennsylvania-German non-combatants have never received the praise to which they are entitled for their noble deeds during the Revolution.

By this term we do not mean, alone, those who, by chance, failed to be among the many who bore arms, but, especially, those whose religious principles forbade them to resist force by means of force, and to whom military service became a sin against their religion, and, as they believed, contrary to the Word of God.

Persecuted and maligned, because of their belief, accused even of being traitors to their country and of aiding, abetting and harboring its enemies, they pursued, unmoved, their course, and by deed, instead of word, by example rather than precept, have proven to this generation, if none other, the pureness of the motives by which they were actuated, and the unexcelled depth of their patriotism.

There is no grander tale of the war than that which relates the sacrifices made by the Pennsylvania-German Moravians and Mystics in caring for the sick and wounded soldiers who were placed in their hospitals. It is not only grand but it is unique, for we hear of no similar occurrence elsewhere.

This chapter, then, is a story of the Pennsylvania-German hospitals of the Revolution.

In 1776 the general hospital of the American army had been established at Morristown, N. J., and eventually contained over one thousand sick and wounded soldiers. With the defeat at Long Island, the capture of Fort Washington, and the active operations in New Jersey, which followed, it became necessary to transfer these helpless ones to a safer place. The interior of Pennsylvania was selected, and, whether with good or evil intent, Bethlehem became the exact spot.

On December 3, 1776, Dr. Cornelius Baldwin, of the New Jersey Line, rode up to the clergy house and handed the astonished pastor, Rev. John Ettwein, an order from Gen. Washington stating that "the General Hospital of the Army is removed to Bethlehem, and you will do the greatest Act of humanity by immediately providing proper buildings for their reception; the largest and most capacious will be most convenient." He was followed, the same evening, by Drs. Warren and William Shippen, and, say the Moravian records, "we assured them that we would do all we could for them." The population of Bethlehem, at that time, numbered about five hundred souls, and it is difficult to imagine what such an order meant to them.

Because of the willing disposition thus shown they were told that, of the one thousand inmates of the hospital

at Morristown, some five hundred would be taken to Easton (where they were largely placed in the German Reformed Church), and Allentown, while about one hundred and fifty would be brought to Bethlehem.

A portion of the Brethren's House having been vacated and prepared for the purpose, on December 5 the first instalment of invalids began to arrive, followed, the next day, by crowds, whose sufferings from lack of care, aggravated by the cold weather, made them pitiable objects to behold, two dying while waiting to be removed from the wagons. Many more would have speedily perished had not the Moravians, moved to pity, promptly supplied their needs, as the stores for the hospital did not come until three days later.

As two more of the sick died on December 7 a burying place became necessary, and a piece of ground was selected on the bluff across the Monocacy, back of the Indian House. There, subsequently, hundreds of graves were filled by the bodies of unnumbered and unregistered patriot dead.

On December 8, two dwellings were hurriedly cleared, to make room for the sick coming from Trenton, of whom a detachment arrived after dinner and remained on the opposite side of the river for two days.

Rev. Ettwein began his self-assumed duties as Chaplain on December 10, making, as regularly as possible, semi-weekly visits to all the wards, praying beside the rude pallets of suffering and dying men, "comforting the hearts of those who were professors of the Christian faith, pointing those who were not to the Friend of sinners, and statedly preaching sermons, as the circumstances permitted." On New Year's Day, 1777, he visited each inmate and wished him God's blessing.

Towards the end of February the small-pox was brought to the town by some soldiers, but, through prompt action, its spread was averted. Still, disease, with the effects of exposure and hardship, was working sad

BETHLEHEM, SHOWING CHURCH AND THE OLD HOSPITAL.

havoc among the sufferers in the hospital, and, by the twenty-seventh of March, 1777, when the hospital doors, as such, were closed for the first time, the number who succumbed had reached one hundred and ten. During all this time many attentions had been extended to the sick by the single brethren who remained in the house, by members of the congregation, and by the sisters who prepared lint and bandages. Furthermore, the Moravian carpenters made the coffins and dug the graves of those who died. " Charitable offices," says Dr. Jordan, " which are not unworthy the remembrance of posterity."

Following the battle of Brandywine, for the second time Bethlehem was called upon to be an asylum for the sick and wounded. On September 19, 1777, the authorities received the following communication from Dr. Shippen, Director-General of the Continental Hospital:

" *My D'r Sir.*—It gives me pain to be obliged by Order of Congress to send my sick and wounded to your peaceable village, but so it is. Your large buildings must be appropriated to their use. We will want room for two thousand at Bethlehem, Easton, Northampton, &c., and you may expect them Saturday or Sunday. . . . These are dreadful times, consequences of unnatural wars. I am truly concerned for your Society and wish sincerely this stroke could be averted, but 'tis impossible. . . ."

The next day, September 20, the single men vacated their house. Some of them were given quarters in various dwelling houses of the village, others removed to the Brethren's House at Christian's Spring and to Gnadenthal and Nazareth. By Sunday morning the building was all cleared save the kitchen, cellar and saddler's shop, which were to be occupied by a few of the single brethren who were to remain.

The wounded soldiers began to arrive on September 21, and, day by day, they continued to pour in. By Monday, September 25, the hospital was filled and tents were erected for those who could not be accommodated in the building. The demand for room became so great that it was proposed to utilize, in addition, the Widows' House, or a part of the Sisters' House, but this great hardship was averted by the presence, in Bethlehem, of many refugee members of Congress, who, after inspection and consultation, issued an order which set at rest the question and removed all danger of seizure from these buildings.

Brandywine was followed by Germantown, and, on October 7, its wounded began to come, still further augmenting the already great crowd of sufferers. On October 14 orders were received for the collection of clothing to

NAZARETH, PENNSYLVANIA, DURING THE REVOLUTIONARY PERIOD.

go to the needy soldiers in the army, and, says the Moravian diarist: "We made several collections of blankets for the destitute soldiers, also shoes, stockings, and breeches for the convalescents in the hospitals, many of whom had come here attired in rags swarming with vermin, while others during their stay had been deprived of their all by their comrades."

By October 22, there were over four hundred in the Brethren's House alone, fifty in tents in the rear of it, besides numerous sick officers in other buildings, so, when a final train of wagons arrived, with their groaning sufferers, the surgeons refused to receive them, and they had to be sent to Easton.

Early in December great numbers of sick soldiers were transferred from the hospitals in New Jersey to Bethlehem. They came in open wagons, often amid snow and rain, with clothing insufficient to cover their fevered bodies from the piercing cold, and, between Christmas and New Year, upwards of seven hundred were reported in the Single Brethren's House alone.

The condition of affairs in the hospital became appalling. The number of patients had increased beyond the facilities of the surgeons to care for them. Some, as has been said, were forced to continue on to Easton, many dying on the way; some were so near their end they could be taken no further; with no room in the building some were crowded into open tents; others, of the newly-arrived, were even denied this shelter and were laid on the ground, in the rain, to die; seventy were conveyed, on November 3, to the Geissinger farm, up the river. And yet, from lack of knowledge and management, those who were forwarding the sick continued to pour them into Bethlehem, where, if every building and house in the village had been turned into a hospital, the lack of provisions and everything else needed for their care would have subjected them to almost the same degree of privation as right on the field of battle.

This terrible situation could not fail to bring forth its harvest. "The Brethren's House, especially the crowded and unventilated attic floor, had become a reeking hole of indescribable filth. The intolerable stench polluted the air to some distance around it. A malignant putrid fever broke out and spread its contagion from ward to ward. The physicians were helpless and the situation became demoralized. Men died at the rate of five, six or even a dozen, during one day or night. The carpenters and laborers of Bethlehem were not asked to make coffins and help bury the dead, as in the previous winter. This was now done by the soldiers as quickly and secretly as possible. At last no coffins were made. Now and then, at dawn

LITITZ, PENNSYLVANIA.
From an old print.

of day, a cart piled full of dead bodies would be seen hurrying away from the door of the hospital to the trenches on the hill-side across the Monocacy. Statistics of the mortality were not procurable. Unnamed and un-numbered they were laid, side by side, in those trenches." (Jordan.)

Rev. Ettwein, who, above all others, could best tell, estimated the total deaths at Bethlehem to be some five hundred, of whom, horrible as it may seem, the names of but ten are known or ever will be known.

One of the surgeons at Bethlehem inquired of Dr. Tilton if he were acquainted with Col. Gibson's fine Virginia Volunteer Regiment. He then went on to say that forty of them had come to his hospital, and asked how many he supposed would ever rejoin their regiment. Dr. Tilton guessed a third or fourth part of the whole number, whereupon the surgeon solemnly declared that not even three would ever return, as that number was all that remained alive, and, of these, one had gone back to his command, another was convalescent and might recover, but the third was then in the last stages of the colliquative flux and must die. To this incident, related by Dr. Tilton, he adds "many similar melancholy instances might be adduced while the hospital was at Ephrata."

"Such was the pitiable condition of the hospital, and could its walls repeat the dreadful sounds and sights that they have heard and witnessed," said James M. Beck, in his beautiful oration on the subject, "what a tale of immeasurable sorrow could they not tell! Only He, who counteth all our sorrows, can ever know the infinite sorrow which these walls have witnessed. It is impossible to picture the scene in all its ghastly horror. The narrow rooms, the dirty pallets of straw, the half-naked soldiers, the fetid atmosphere, the heart-rending groans, the death rattle of the dying, all these were once where now the merry laughter of youth resounds. In one of the rooms was a painting of the crucifixion. It had been there for many years. In 1751 some Indians were shown through the building, and as they gazed upon the picture one of their number said, ' Behold how many wounds He has, and how they bleed! ' One can imagine the dying Continental, sorrowful unto death, and with death-sweat like unto great drops of blood, gazing upon the picture and gaining courage to descend into the valley of the shadow from the inspiring example of the great Martyr."

Here was a field for Christian benevolence which the Moravians cheerfully entered, and Mr. Ettwein, with his assistant, the Rev. Jacob Fries, were indefatigable in their attentions. They braved the pestilence in its stronghold, smoothing the pillows of the dying and imparting the consolation of religion.

The plague spread from the building to the town, among the single men first, who were brought more closely in contact with it, and then among others. It carried off seven of the single men in a short time, of which number was the estimable son, John, of that noble man, Rev. Ettwein. It even invaded the boarding-school and claimed as its victim one of the girls, Hannah Dean, who had fled thence from Philadelphia for safety.

At last, on March 22, 1778, definite information was received that the hospital was to be removed, but the joy occasioned by this news was greatly tempered by the announcement that it was to be established at the other Moravian village of Lititz. Bishop Matthew Hehl, on behalf of the congregation at Lititz, petitioned Dr. Shippen not to locate there, but the necessity for this step was deemed to be imperative, and it had to be submitted to.

The removal of the sick at Bethlehem began on Palm Sunday, April 12, and was completed by Tuesday, April 14, 1778. The building which had harbored so much suffering, wretchedness and squalor, was closed and left standing, gloomy and silent, in battered, feculent desolation, until June 1, when the army authorities released it back to its owners.

For upwards of eight months the little village of Lititz, in Lancaster county, with a population less than half that of Bethlehem, but with the usual collection of substantial

THE WHITEFIELD HOUSE, NAZARETH.

and commodious buildings, became the seat of a hospital.

On December 14, 1777, Dr. Samuel Kennedy, formerly surgeon of Wayne's battalion, armed with a written order from Washington for the quartering of two hundred and fifty men, appeared at Lititz and selected the building of the single men for the purpose.

The first sick, about eighty, arrived on December 19, and, the following day, fifteen additional wagon loads, which filled all the rooms and halls of the house. In a few days putrid fever broke out to an alarming extent, and both doctors were attacked by it. Their place was taken by the village physician, Dr. Adolph Meyer, until relieved by a doctor who was a German from Saxony, "name unknown." On the last day of the year a wagonload of sick arrived from Reading. Seven deaths were reported in ten days, all from the fever.

During January the fever became epidemic and five of the Moravians, who had volunteered as nurses, together with the assistant pastor of the congregation, the Rev. John J. Schmick, died of the malady.

As already mentioned, on March 22 it was decided to establish a general hospital at Lititz, which would have necessitated the practical abandonment of the place by its inhabitants.

Fortunately, the necessity for this step passed away, but the sick continued to be sent from Bethlehem, Easton, Allentown and Reading. From February 1 to April 20, 1778, "264 wounded and sick soldiers had been admitted to the Hospital; 142 had been discharged and sent to camp; 83 had died and deserted, and 39 were under treatment." It was also reported, "This is a convenient and pleasant place for a Hospital, and is so near Lancaster, that the same officer and surgeons may attend both. The hospitals at Schaefferstown (Lebanon) and Ephrata should be removed here, as both are very inconvenient."

On August 28 the remaining sixty-six patients were removed to Lancaster and the Yellow Springs. During the occupation of the " Brethren's House " (eight months and ten days), one hundred and twenty soldiers died, and were buried about a quarter of a mile to the east of the village.

Besides Bethlehem and Lititz hospitals were established at Easton, Allentown, Reading, Lebanon, Schaefferstown, Lancaster and Yellow Springs. Immediately after the battle of Germantown the Lutheran Church at Trappe was used as a field hospital. To a less degree than Bethlehem and Lititz, probably, the, experiences of the sick and wounded were similar at all places, and, in every instance, the Pennsylvania-Germans, among whom they were located, never failed in their duty to their suffering fellow-beings.

At Reading the hospitals were established in the Trinity Lutheran Church, First Reformed Church, Friends' Meeting House, also in the Court House, in the, so-called, Brick House, and in the Potter's Shop. Ten years ago a document came to light, which proved to be a most interesting relic of the time. It gave a list of the soldiers in these three latter buildings on November 17, 1777, and the names of their nurses. It is probable the nurses were relatives, doubtless wives, in most cases, of the soldiers. They were as follows:

A LIST OF SOLDIERS IN THE COURT HOUSE HOSPITAL AT READING, NOVEMBER 17, 1777

Cornelius Buck, Sergt.,	4th Virginia.
John McCuluga,	do.

Edward Tidus,	4th Virginia.
Daniel McKenna,	do.
John Barber,	3d Maryland.
Charles Chamberlain,	2d Pennsylvania.
Henry Tom,	Col. Hildner.
James Smith,	5th Pennsylvania.
Goldman Harris,	6th North Carolina.
William Noble,	do.
Edward Homes,	11th Virginia.
Andrew Drake,	do.
Nicholas Nichols,	5th Maryland.
Wm. Jeffries,	do.
Joseph Juba,	Congress, Penna.
William Donaldson,	7th Maryland.
Francis Mitchel,	do.
William Cofferoth,	do.
Charles Major,	do.
Conrad Cofferoth,	do.
John Doherty,	6th Virginia.
John Mefford,	4th Pennsylvania.
Nicholas Forster,	1st Virginia.
Philip Harrison,	7th Virginia.
Thomas Smith,	12th Virginia.
William West,	Prisoner of war.
Christopher Irwin,	5th Virginia.
James Stoffr,	do.
John Tucker,	2d Virginia.
John Coppage,	3d Virginia.
John Winn,	16th Virginia.
Robert Doyl,	3d Virginia.
Christopher Reed,	7th Maryland.
Thomas Young,	do.
Joseph Chambers,	7th Pennsylvania.

William Southerland,	3d Virginia.
William Marknalsh,	7th Maryland.
Joel Shelton,	2d Virginia.
Sarah Buck,	Nurse.
Ann Chamberlain,	do.
Martha Mitchel,	do.
Catherine West,	do.
Ann Doyle,	do.
Elisab. Southerland,	do.

A LIST OF SOLDIERS IN THE BRICK HOUSE HOSPITAL AT READING, NOVEMBER 17, 1777.

Stephen Lyon,	Cong^r. Penn.
John Hunt,	6th Maryland.
Samuel Huggins,	do.
John Delena,	State Virginia.
Mark Warren,	Col. McCoy.
William Holly,	Prisoner of war.
Abraham Best,	6th Pennsylvania.
Daniel Robertson,	11th Virginia.
Isaac Fowler,	4th New Jersey.
Joseph Spencer,	4th Pennsylvania.
Dennis McCarty,	12th Virginia.
Charles Lenix,	3d Virginia.
James Burns,	12th Pennsylvania.
James Gallant,	do.
Adam Trip,	4th Virginia.
Andrew Pinkenton,	Of Pennsylvania.
Arthur Corben,	7th North Carolina.
Elijah Pamer,	New England.
Thomas Kelly,	3d Virginia.
John Crooks,	do.
Margaret Lenix,	Nurse.
Hannah Crooks,	do.

A LIST OF THE SICK IN THE POTTER'S SHOP AT
READING, NOVEMBER 19.

Gilbert Allen,	5th Maryland.
Zadock Woods,	do.
Sam'l Kennedy,	do.
Thomas Tenibree and wife,	do.
Wm. Pinkfield and wife,	do.
Thomas Oliphant,	do.
David Kelly and wife,	do.
Henry Ollard,	15th Virginia.
James Jones,	3d Virginia.

There still remains the narrative of Ephrata, in many respects the most interesting of all because of the peculiar manners and habits of those into whose care the sick were placed.

In their search after solitude the German mystics and hermits of the Wissahickon wandered towards the wilderness of the interior, during the early part of the century, and, where the beautiful town of Ephrata now lies nestled along the banks of the picturesque Cocalico, there they stopped. In time they decided upon taking up a monastic and conventional life, and, one after another, gradually appeared their Kedar and Zion places of worship, their Saron, or Sister House, their Bethania, or Brother House, with their Kammers, or cells, for the little sleep they took, and adjoining Saals, or assembly rooms, for worship and love feasts. Here amidst their grand surroundings, the white-robed German Protestant monks and nuns wandered, labored, prayed and sang, doing such labors as the world little dreamed of, and singing such music as has, at this day, excited the wonder and admiration of the listener.

But the echoes of Brandywine's field of battle one day rudely broke in upon the peace of this quiet Theosophic community. It was to Washington himself, who, from personal acquaintance with Prior Jaebetz (Peter Miller),

BETHANIA, THE SINGLE BRETHREN HOUSE, EPHRATA.

knew his devotion to the patriot cause, that the idea came of sending some of his sick and wounded soldiers to this quiet and God-fearing community on the banks of the Cocalico, where he felt assured its pious men and women would tenderly care for them.

It was on the third day after the battle that the wagons began to arrive, not the comfortable ambulance of our day, but open and springless farm vehicles, in which the sufferer was laid on straw, and, in some instances, arranged to have two tiers of wounded, one above the other. Both Kammers and Saal were soon filled from the almost endless, as it seemed, stream of wagons which came, and, in less than a week, Kedar and Zion had their hundred of suffering patriots.

"The halls and corridors which, but a short time ago, had reëchoed the sweet music of the choirs, as it alternated with the fervent prayers of the mystic Theosophist, were now filled with the groans of the sick and the moans of the dying. The devout Brotherhood no longer formed into nocturnal processions, chanting their mystic incantations to the divine Sophia, nor assembled at the matins in the Saal to salute the first rays of the sun as they flooded the room with its roseate light; but now, as they noiselessly stepped from sufferer to sufferer, who occupied their cells, they whispered words of hope to one, attended to the wants of others, and, when necessary, prayed with such as needed it. What is true of the Brotherhood is also true of the Sisters. Many a brave lad from a far-off province who lay here sick and wounded, and now rests upon Zion hill in an unknown grave, had his last moments cheered by one of the Sisterhood of Saron, who took a mother's place and soothed the dying moments of the young patriot. The whole story is one of self-denial and devotion in the interest of humanity." (Sachse.)

Shortly after, the dreaded malignant typhus broke out in both Kedar and Zion, which spared neither soldier nor attendant. It was then, though even the chief doctor fell a victim to his zeal, that neither the Brothers nor Sisters, well advanced in years as they were, flinched from their duty, but continued to nurse the sick, soothe their dying moments, and, when all was over, give them a Christian burial in the consecrated ground of Zion Hill.

When Dr. Harris (or Harrison) was stricken with the deadly fever he was removed to one of the smaller houses in the valley, where he was tenderly cared for by Brother Joannes Anguas. Notwithstanding this care and attention bestowed upon him the surgeon succumbed to the disease, only to be followed, on March 4, 1778, by his faithful nurse.

Just how many more of these humble heroes and patriots became martyrs to the cause, and gave up their

SINGLE SISTER HOUSE, AND SAAL, AT EPHRATA.

lives for it, or else passed their remaining years on earth as invalids, will never be known. The community never recovered from the blow it then received. With much labor Dr. Sachse has gathered and preserved these few names:

Brother Martin Funk, the younger, October 5, 1777; Brother Johann Bentz; Sister Margaretha; Brother Johannes Koch; Brother Casper Walter, the younger. 1778— Sister Anna Maria Huber, January 19; Widow Gertraut Millinger, February 3; Henrich Miller, who kept the tavern, January 12; Brother Adam Kimmel, January 27; Brother Joannes Anguas, March 4.

To these must be added the names of John Bear, a Mennonite preacher, and his wife, who voluntarily entered the hospital as nurses, and who both caught the infection, the latter dying March 20, 1778, and the former April 15 following.

And here, besides their faithful nurses, died one after another of the soldiers, who were then laid in their graves on Zion Hill, until they numbered several hundred. Just how many there await the blast of the great trumpet, whose call all shall obey to arise and appear in final judgment, may perhaps never be known. The rude inscription placed over their common grave by Prior Jaebetz probably tells the tale better than any that could be devised. It merely reads, "Here rest the remains of many soldiers."

Not only did the community sacrifice their time and lives to the service of the hospitals, but their quilts and blankets were seized for the convalescent soldiers, their stores of grain were sent to replenish the commissary of the main army while encamped on the bleak hills of Valley Forge, and even their hymn books, their prayer books, and the unbound sheets of their great Martyr Book, were carried away to be made into cartridges, for all of which not a shilling was ever asked or received by them.

To such an extent were Kedar and Zion polluted by the scourge of typhus that they became unfit for habitation and had to be demolished.

CHAPTER XV.

SOME PENNSYLVANIA-GERMANS IN MILITARY SERVICE.

THE mere fact that the Pennsylvania-German was alien in language, blood and habits to the ruling element of the country, prevented him from attaining, to any great extent, that prominence in military station to which his patriotic deeds would, otherwise, have entitled him.

The names, which here follow, are those of but a few of our ancestors who became elevated somewhat above the level plane of the mass. It is trusted this list may prove the starting-point from which, as when a pebble is cast into the water, will radiate many efforts resulting in much new data.

MONTGOMERY COUNTY.

Maj. Gen. Peter Muhlenberg.

John Peter Gabriel Muhlenberg, the eldest son of the Lutheran Patriarch, Henry Melchior Muhlenberg, D.D.,

MAJ.-GEN. PETER MUHLENBERG.

B. TRAPPE, PA., OCTOBER 1, 1746.   D. OCTOBER 1, 1807.

was born at the Trappe, Montgomery Co., Pa., on October 1, 1746, near midnight; married November 6, 1770, Anna Barbara Meyer (1751–1806) ; died October 1, 1807.

At the age of sixteen, with his two younger brothers, he was sent to Halle, Germany, for his education. Not taking kindly to the strict discipline of the institution he ran away, and, foolishly, enlisted in a German regiment which chanced to be in the vicinity. From this predicament he was happily rescued through the efforts of an English officer, who was a friend of the family, and who happened to see him in the garb of a common soldier. In later years he was wont to relate how this same regiment of dragoons, dismounted at the time, were opposed to his brigade at the battle of Brandywine. As, in the thick of the fight, they saw his prominent figure advancing, at the head of his men, mounted on a white horse, some of the older soldiers (German enlistments being for life) recognized him, and the cry ran along their astonished ranks, "Hier kommt teufel Piet!" (Here comes Devil Pete!)

At the completion of his home education he was licensed to preach, June 20, 1769, and, for a couple years, served the congregations on the Raritan, in New Jersey.

Having received a call to the Lutheran congregation at Woodstock, Virginia, which, under the law of that province, necessitated Episcopal ordination, in company with the late Bishop White, he went to England for that purpose, and was ordained, April 23, 1772, at the Royal Chapel of St. James, the Bishop of London officiating.

At Woodstock, Dunmore Co., Virginia, he promptly took an interest in the progress of public matters. He became an active Whig and was sent as a delegate to the House of Burgesses, where he made the acquaintance of Washington, Patrick Henry and others. It was at the earnest solicitation of the former, who soon recognized his worth, that he consented to raise and command the Eighth Virginia Regiment, when the war broke out.

He took leave of his congregation in a most striking and impressive manner. One Sunday, about the middle of January, 1776, after preaching an eloquent sermon upon the duties which men owe their country, in the course of which he told his hearers, "there was a time for all things—a time to preach and a time to fight—and that now was the time to fight," he completed the service and pronounced the benediction. Then, removing his clerical gown, amidst the breathless silence of his congregation, he revealed himself in the uniform of his new rank, and immediately ordered the drums to beat for recruits. Three hundred of his parishioners joined at once, and his command, which became known as the "German Regiment," had its ranks filled in the very briefest time.

He promptly marched to the relief of Suffolk, and, later, under General Lee, to North Carolina, thence to Charleston, S. C., where they participated in the battle at Sullivan's Island. During the entire Southern campaign the regiment won many laurels for their gallantry and efficiency.

Col. Muhlenberg was promoted to Brigadier-General on February 21, 1777, and ordered north. At the battle of Brandywine, September 11, 1777, his brigade, with that of Weedon, bore the brunt of the action. On October 8, at Germantown, having advanced into the town further than any other troops, a British officer seized a musket and fired at him; while in the act of reloading and ordering his soldiers to "pick him off," the General, drawing a pistol, shot him dead on the spot. At Monmouth, June 28, 1778, his brigade received the praise of the English officers, opposed to them, for their gallantry.

He commanded the reserve at Stony Point; when Leslie invaded Virginia, in 1780, he was opposed to him, with the chief command; he acted, under Baron Steuben, against Benedict Arnold, and, when Cornwallis entered Virginia, was next in command to La Fayette. At the siege of Yorktown he commanded the First Brigade of Light Infantry, which furnished the American Division of the troops that carried the British redoubts by assault, he leading them.

He was promoted to Major General on September 30, 1783. Some months after, when the army was formally disbanded, he returned to his family at Woodstock, but soon removed to Pennsylvania.

He was immediately elected a member of the Supreme Executive Council of Pennsylvania. In 1785 he was chosen Vice President of the Commonwealth, and was reëlected to the same office the two following years. He was a member of the First Congress of the United States, 1789–1791, the Third Congress, 1793–1795, the Sixth Congress, 1799–1801; elected U. S. Senator February 18, 1801, but resigned, at the end of a few months, to accept the appointment tendered him by President Jefferson, June 30, 1801, of Supervisor of Internal Revenue for Pennsylvania; appointed Collector of the Port of Philadelphia, July, 1802, which position he held until his death.

He is one of the two Pennsylvanians who was honored by a statue in the Capitol at Washington, D. C.

His remains lie buried beside those of his father in the peaceful graveyard of the Augustus Lutheran Church, at the Trappe, and are marked by a simple stone, on which is cut:

> He was brave in the field,
> Faithful in the cabinet,
> Honorable in all his transactions,
> A sincere friend,
> And an honest man.

General Daniel Hiester.

Daniel Hiester was born in Upper Salford township, Montgomery Co., Pa., June 25, 1747, son of Daniel Hiester (1713–1795), son of John Hiester, from Elsoff, province of Westphalia, Germany. He married, about 1770, Rosanna Hager (1752–1810), daughter of Capt. Jonathan Hager, the founder of Hagerstown, Md.

For several years he devoted himself to the cultivation of his farm, to the business of the tannery, and to looking after the interests of the Hager estate in Maryland.

Upon the organization of the Philadelphia County Militia, in 1777, he was commissioned Colonel and was present at Brandywine, also during the subsequent operations of the army until the encampment at Valley Forge. On May 23, 1782, he was promoted to Brigadier-General; in 1784 elected to the Supreme Executive Council of Pennsylvania, and, in 1787, a Commissioner of the Connecticut Land Claims; returned to Berks County and elected a member of the First, Second, Third and Fourth Congresses; removed to Hagerstown, Md., and elected a member of the Seventh and Eighth Congresses, from that State; died in Washington, D. C., March 7, 1804, while in attendance upon the Eighth Congress, and buried at Hagerstown.

Captain Philip Hahn.

Philip Hahn, of New Hanover township, Montgomery Co., Pa., born March 31, 1736, died April 16, 1821, married, May 23, 1761, Anna Margaretha Hiester (1743–1820), sister of General Daniel Hiester.

Captain Hahn was in command of the Fourth company, Fourth battalion, Philadelphia County Militia, 1777, Col. Frederick Antes commanding; in 1778, Fourth battalion, Col. William Dean; 1779, Sixth battalion, Major Peter Richards.

Colonel Frederick Antes.

The Antes family came from Feinshein, in the Palatinate, Germany.

Philip Frederick Antes was the son of Henry and Christiana Antes, and was born in Frederick township, Montgomery Co., Pa., July 5, 1730.

He was a member of the Convention which met at Carpenter's Hall, Philadelphia, June, 1776, also a member of the General Assembly in 1776, and held many other responsible positions.

Col. Antes had command of the Fourth battalion, Philadelphia County Militia in 1777, his commission being dated May 6. On September 11, 1777, his battalion was ordered to rendezvous at Swedes' Ford, and served faithfully during the operations which followed.

Because of his open and active patriotism a price of £200 was set upon his head by Gen. Howe and several efforts made to capture him. In 1779 he emigrated to Northumberland county.

In 1780 he became the purchasing agent for the county, with stations at Sunbury and Wyoming. In 1783 he was appointed County Treasurer. In 1784 he resigned his position as Presiding Judge of the Court of Common Pleas, of the Quarter Sessions of the Peace and of the Orphans' Court, to take his seat in the Assembly, to which he had just been elected. He was reëlected to the Assembly in 1785, and elected Treasurer in 1789.

His daughter Catharine married (his second wife) Simon Snyder, later Governor of Pennsylvania.

Lieut. Col. Jacob Reed.

Eldest son of Johann Philip and Veronica (Bergey) Reed (Rieth), who emigrated to this country from Mannheim, Germany, in the summer of 1727. He located in Salford township, Montgomery Co., Pa., where Jacob was born on June 30, 1730, died, in New Britain township, Bucks Co., Pa., on November 2, 1820, married, in 1755, Magdalene Leidy.

He served, at different times during the Revolution, as Major and Lieutenant Colonel of a battalion of Philadelphia County Militia. His uniform and accoutrements were in the possession of the family until recently, when they became scattered.

A very interesting letter from his son, relative to his service, is in existence, and is here given:

"Sugar Creek Township,
"Stark County, Ohio, May 27, 1834.

"*To You Much Beloved Brother:*

". . . And you desire to know of father in reference to his Revolutionary service. I proceed to inform you that he was present at the battle of Brandywine, at the battle of White Horse and at the battle of Germantown. This was his first tour. His Major General was Armstrong. His Brigadier General was Potter. Hiester (Daniel) was Colonel, father was Lieutenant Colonel, and one Moore was Major. His second tour was at (after) Burgoyne's surrender (taking up the convention troops at Sherrard's Ferry, on the Delaware), thence to Taneytown (brother) Philip accompanied father, which is all Philip was in the army. Father's first tour was two months, but I do not remember how long a tour that was when he went to Taneytown in Maryland. I myself was out with the militia, going to Trenton, New Jersey, in 1780. . . .

"Your Faithful Brother

"JACOB RIEDT."

"To Andrew Riedt,
"Hilltown Township, Bucks County, Penn'a."

Because of his patriotism an attempt was made to capture him, one winter night in 1778, by the tories, but his assailants were driven off by the Colonel, after a gallant fight within the doorway of his house. One of them was traced by the drops of blood from his wound, captured by the neighbors and hanged.

At the close of the war he was appointed to various positions of trust, which he held, for a number of years, with much credit.

Lieut. Col. George Peter Richards.

Son of Matthias Richards (1719–1775), whose father, John Frederick Reichert, emigrated to America, in 1700 or 1703, from Augsburg, Germany, and settled in New Hanover township, Montgomery Co., Pa.

He was born, July 22, 1755, died, at Pottstown, October 21, 1822, married Magdalena, daughter of Henry and Catharine Schneider, of the Swamp.

During the war he was Major, April 3, 1779, of the Sixth battalion, Philadelphia County Militia, and, on October 4, 1779, was chosen, by the General Assembly, a Sub-lieutenant of Philadelphia County, and commissioned, as such, with the rank of Lieut. Colonel.

He was a prominent and influential man, an ironmaster, and a justice of the peace.

PHILADELPHIA.

Capt. John Markland.

Capt. John Markland was born in Philadelphia, August 12, 1755, died February 23, 1837, and is buried in Christ Church ground. He married, first, January 25, 1798, Christiana Heisz (1777–1804), and, second, Sophia ———— (1768–1843). He was one of the original members of the Society of the Cincinnati.

With his parents he removed to New York, where, as early as 1775, he began his military career as an active member of a uniformed company of Minute Men, commanded by Capt. Stockholm and attached to Col. Lasher's Regiment of New York Volunteers.

His regiment went into regular service in 1776, and was warmly engaged in the battle of Long Island, also in the Trenton and Princeton campaign. With the reorganization of the army in 1777 he entered the Continental service, in Captain Jacob Bower's company, of the Sixth Pennsylvania regiment, Col. Bicker, for the war, as Ensign. In the battle of Short Hills, New Jersey, June, 1777, he was captured by a detachment of Lord Rawdon's Horse, but escaped immediately after. At the same time he was fired upon by one of the troopers and nearly killed, so close being his assailant that the mark of the powder remained visible all his life under the left ear. On September 11, 1777, he was engaged, with

Conway's brigade, in the battle of Brandywine, and was with the first troops to encounter the British forces at Germantown on October 4. While attacking Chew's House one of his men, a worthy Pennsylvania-German from Reading, named Philip Ludwig, observing a handsome British musket leaning against the fence, turned to Markland and cheerfully said, "I will make an exchange; this is much better than mine." Shortly after, this brave fellow, immediately in the front, received a ball in his forehead and fell dead. It was during the height of this attack that Markland, himself, was shot in the right arm near the shoulder, severely shattering it. This wound was never fully healed and constantly caused him great pain and inconvenience.

In April, 1778, he rejoined the army at Valley Forge, though not fit for service. In 1779 he was with the army in New Jersey, and, in 1780, served in La Fayette's picked division of Light Infantry.

In the early part of 1781 Markland was engaged in recruiting at Lancaster, Lebanon and other places. He then went south and was present at the surrender of Cornwallis. The balance of his service was with the troops in the southern campaign which followed. During this time he was closely associated with Kosciusko.

He retired from the service, at the close of the war, with the brevet rank of Captain. In 1823 he was elected one of the County Commissioners of Philadelphia.

Christopher Ludwig, Baker-General.

Christopher Ludwig (or Ludwick) was born of Lutheran parents, October 17, 1720, at Giessen, Hesse-Darmstadt, Germany. His father was a baker, and the son was instructed in the same trade.

24

At the age of seventeen he enlisted as a private soldier, and participated in the war between Austria and Turkey (1737 and 1740).   He returned to Vienna and thence went to Prague, where he endured all the distresses of a seventeen weeks' siege, and, after its surrender to the French, in November, 1741, he enlisted in the Prussian army.

He made various voyages, as a baker or common sailor, to Holland, Ireland, the East and West Indies, finally settling down in Philadelphia, in 1754, as a gingerbread baker in Letitia Court, where he prospered.

He became an ardent patriot and was elected one of the Provincial Deputies, July 15, 1774; a delegate to the Provincial Convention of January 23–28, 1775, and to the Provincial Conference of June 18, 1776, which met in Carpenter's Hall.   In one of these conventions it was proposed, by General Mifflin, to open a private subscription for the purchase of fire-arms.   Considerable opposition was made to the proposition, whereupon Mr. Ludwig addressed the chair in the following laconic speech, which he delivered in broken English: " Mr. President, I am but a poor gingerbread baker, but put my name down for two hundred pounds."

In the summer of 1776 he entered the army as a volunteer, and was sent to the Flying Camp.   With the consent of his commanding officer he visited the camp of the Hessian contingent on Staten Island, in the character of a deserter, and was instrumental in inducing some of the soldiers to desert by his alluring description of the affluence and independence of their former countrymen in the German counties of Pennsylvania.   He escaped from the camp without detection or suspicion.

In the spring of 1777 he was appointed, by Congress, Baker-General of the army:

In Congress, May 30, 1777.

"*Resolved,* That Christopher Ludwick be, and is hereby appointed Superintendent of Bakers and Director of Baking in the army of the United States, and that he shall have power to engage, and by permission of the Commander-in-Chief, or officer commanding at any principal post, all persons to be employed in his business, and to regulate their pay, making proper report of his proceedings, and using his best endeavors to rectify all abuses in the article of bread.

"That no person be permitted to exercise the trade of baker in the said army without such license; and that he receive for his services herein, an allowance of 75 dollars a month and two rations a day."

When notified of his appointment by the Committee of Congress they proposed that, for every pound of flour, he should furnish the army with a pound of bread. "No, gentlemen," said he, "I will not accept of your commission upon any such terms. I do not wish to grow rich by the war; I have money enough. I will furnish one hundred and thirty-five pounds of bread for every hundred pounds of flour you put into my hands." The committee were ignorant of the increase of weight which flour acquires by the addition of water and leaven.

Finding some difficulty in obtaining a number of journeymen bakers, owing to many of them being in the militia service, on June 23, 1777, Congress ordered:

"That Mr. Ludwig apply to the Supreme Executive Council of the State of Pennsylvania, and that it be recommended to the said Council to furnish him with such a number of journeymen bakers out of the Militia employed in the service of the Continent as he may want."

From the date of his appointment all complaints ceased with regard to the bad quality of bread, nor was any movement delayed from the want of that necessary article of food.

In June, 1779, he went on from Easton to Wyoming, in advance of Sullivan's Expedition. Here, by his activity, a bake-house was built in eleven days, and a large quantity of bread ready for the army upon its arrival.

After the capitulation of Lord Cornwallis he baked six thousand pounds of bread to supply the needs of the British troops.

In his intercourse with the officers he was blunt but never offensive. His eccentric turns of thought and expression, his pleasant anecdotes, and, above all, a general conviction of the ardor and sincerity of his patriotism, always made him a welcome visitor.

At the close of the war he returned and settled on his farm at Germantown, which had been greatly plundered by the enemy. In his parlor hung, conspicuously, a framed certificate from General Washington, praising him for the services he had rendered his country.

He died in Philadelphia, June 17, 1801, and is buried in the Lutheran graveyard at Germantown.

CHESTER COUNTY.

Gen. John Hiester.

Brother of Gen. Daniel Hiester, of Montgomery county. Born April 9, 1745, died October 15, 1821, married Hannah Pawling (1747–1822). During the war he was Captain First Company, Fourth Battalion, Col. William Evans, 1777; Captain First Battalion, Chester County Militia, 1777; after the war, Major General of Militia; State Senator from Chester County, 1802–1806; Member of Congress, 1807–1809.

Dr. Branson Van Leer.

Son of Dr. Bernhardus von Loehr (the centenarian), who came to America from Hesse-Darmstadt, Germany, about 1698, and settled in Chester county, Pa.

Dr. Van Leer served as a member of the Committee of Observation for Chester County Associators, 1774, and as a surgeon of the Seventh Battalion of Militia, 1779.

Capt. Samuel Van Leer.

Likewise a son of Dr. Bernhardus von Loehr. He married Hannah Wayne, a sister of Gen. Anthony Wayne.

He was Captain of the Seventh Company, Fifth Battalion, Chester County Militia, 1777; also Lieutenant of the Chester County Light Horse in 1780–1781.

He became the owner of the old Reading furnace in Warwick township.

Dr. Jacob Ehrenzeller.

He was born about September 1, 1757, the son of Jacob Ehrenzeller, a native of Switzerland who came to America and engaged in business in Philadelphia, where the subject of this sketch was born.

Dr. Ehrenzeller was a classical scholar. Under whom he studied medicine is not known, but he was a medical apprentice in the Pennsylvania Hospital from 1773 to 1778.

Because of a certificate of qualification which he received from Drs. Kuhn and Shippen he was enabled to procure a commission as Assistant Surgeon in the army during the Revolution.

He was on duty at the battle of Monmouth, and in other engagements, always conducting himself with much credit.

Towards the close of the war he left the army and settled in the township of Goshen, Chester county, subsequently removing to West Chester, where he remained until his death, July 18, 1838, enjoying a lucrative practice and commanding, to a great degree, the confidence of the community. He married his cousin, Elizabeth Hankee, and was a most ardent patriot.

Major Peter Hartman.

Son of John Hartman, a native of Schwerin, Hesse-Cassel, Germany, who emigrated to America in 1753, and settled in the vicinity of Yellow Springs, Chester county.

Peter was placed in Philadelphia, with a wealthy German acquaintance, to learn the sugar-refining business, but soon abandoned it to join the army, in which he served as an officer. He was an ardent and active patriot.

His son George, when sixteen years of age, was taught, at the instance of his father, to beat the drum, and became so proficient as to receive the appointment of drum-major. He was taken, by his father, through his military campaign, and was, at different periods during the war, stationed at Fort Bergen, Billingsport, and other places.

A few days before the battle of Brandywine, George was taken sick with the camp fever at Chad's Ford, and removed by litter, at night, to his father's residence, six-teen miles distant. As Major Hartman wore the American uniform the son was in constant danger of capture, to avoid which he had to be carried from place to place, and was often concealed in the cellar at night.

Capt. William Van Lear.

It seems most probable that Capt. Van Lear was of the family of Dr. Bernhardus Van Leer, of Chester county.

He was Second Lieutenant, Ninth Pennsylvania Continental Regiment, promoted to Capt. Lieutenant January 27, 1779; to Captain October 10, 1779; to Brigade Major, First Pennsylvania Brigade; transferred to Fifth Pennsylvania, January 17, 1781; retired from the service January 1, 1783.

(OLD) NORTHAMPTON COUNTY.

Major Jacob Arndt.

Major Jacob Arndt, of Northampton county, a native of Baumholder, Upper Silesia, Germany, the son of Bernhardt Arndt, was born March 24, 1725, emigrated to Pennsylvania in 1731, and settled in Bucks county. At the breaking out of the French and Indian War he raised a company of volunteers, and was stationed on the frontiers. In 1755 he was in command at Gnadenhütten; April 19, 1756, commissioned Captain in the First Battalion of the Pennsylvania Regiment, and for a couple years stationed at Forts Norris and Allen, respectively; promoted to Major, June 2, 1758, and stationed at Fort Augusta. In 1760 he removed to Northampton county near Easton. During the Indian marauds of 1763 he was captain of an independent company raised in the vicinity for its defense.

Major Arndt was chosen a member of the Provincial
Conference, held at Philadelphia, July 15, 1774, and that
of January 23, 1775. He served as a member of the Constitutional Convention of July, 1776; of the First Assembly under the new Constitution; of the Committee of
Safety, October 17, 1777, and was elected a member of
the Supreme Executive Council, November 5, 1777, serving until October 14, 1780. He was appointed Commissioner of Excise for Northampton county, April 5, 1779,
a position which he held for several years. From 1782
to 1784 he again served in the General Assembly. For
half a century Major Arndt was in active life. He died
at Easton in the year 1805.

Capt. John Arndt.

Son of Major Jacob Arndt, was born June 5, 1748.
When New York was threatened he became Captain of
the company from Easton in Col. Kichlein's Battalion of
the Flying Camp, which was practically annihilated at
Long Island and Fort Washington. In the former battle
Capt. Arndt was severely wounded, by a cannon ball, in
the left arm, and ever after deprived of the use of his
elbow joint. He was also taken prisoner. Upon his
release, September, 1780, he returned to Easton, and,
with David Deshler, was appointed a Commissary for the
care of sick and disabled soldiers and their dependents.

In 1777 he was appointed Register of Wills, Recorder
of Deeds, Clerk of the Orphans' Court, and was an efficient member of the Committee of Safety. In 1783, he
was elected a representative in the Council of the Censors,
to propose amendments to the Constitution of Pennsylvania. The same year, when Dickinson College became

incorporated, he was made a Trustee. He died, in 1814, without a stain upon his character as a soldier and citizen.

Capt. Peter Burkhalter.

He settled in Egypt, Whitehall township, now Lehigh Co., Pa., in 1740. He was one of the Commissioners for the county of Northampton in 1776; a member of the Constitutional Convention of July 15, 1776; a member of the Assembly during that and the following year; appointed Sub-lieutenant of the county March 30, 1780. From 1784 to 1788 he again represented Northampton in the General Assembly, and, from 1791 to 1794, in the House of Representatives. He was captain of a company of Northampton Associators in active service in the Jerseys. He died in 1806, and lies buried in the old walled Union Church graveyard in Whitehall township, Lehigh county.

Capt. Abraham Miller.

He was a native of Northampton county, born about 1740. During the French and Indian War he was a non-commissioned officer, and was wounded in an engagement with the Indians.

He was a member of the Committee of Northampton County in December, 1774; and, in June, 1775, was chosen recruiting officer for raising half a company to go to Boston. Subsequently, a full company was raised and he was commissioned Captain, June 20, 1775, in Col. Thompson's Rifle Regiment. He resigned in the fall of the same year, and was succeeded by Thomas Craig, who, later, rose to be Lieut. Colonel of the Line. Capt. Miller afterwards commanded a company of Associators during the Long Island campaign of 1776. He was a member of the Constitutional Convention of July 15, 1776, and remained an active partisan till the close of the war. He died in 1821.

Col. Peter Kichlein.

Col. Kichlein was born in Heidelberg, Germany, October 8, 1722, and received a liberal education in that university town. In 1742 he emigrated, with his father, John Peter Kichlein, and, by 1749, was settled within the forks of the Delaware, afterwards the site of Easton.

In December, 1774, he was elected a member of the Committee of Safety for the county. He commanded the battalion of Northampton County Flying Camp at Long Island, who, by their bravery, saved the army from disaster, at which time Col. Kichlein was taken prisoner. He became Lieutenant of the county, and, on April 11, 1780, was directed by the Supreme Executive Council to order out the militia for duty on the frontiers against the Indians.

Lieut. Peter Kichlein.

Son of Col. Peter Kichlein; served as Second Lieutenant in Captain Arndt's company of Flying Camp Associators at Long Island, and was one of the thirty-three survivors of the company who managed to rendezvous after their disasters at Long Island and Fort Washington.

Sergeant John Herster.

Removed to Easton from Pottstown, Montgomery county, about 1750. As Capt. Arndt's company of Associators mustered in the Public Square of Easton to march for Long Island, amongst them was his son, John, then but eighteen years old. As the father saw him about to go, parental solicitation and affection prompted him to say: " John, give me your musket! You are too young for the camp; stay and take care of your mother and the children, and I will take your place!" He shouldered his son's musket, and marched off never to return. He was taken prisoner at Long Island and confined on the prison ship *Jersey,* where he miserably died about the following Christmas and was interred on the adjoining shore.

BERKS COUNTY.

Governor Joseph Hiester.

Gov. Hiester was born November 18, 1752, died June 10, 1832, married, 1771, Elizabeth Witman (1750–1825), daughter of Adam Witman of Reading, Pa.

He was the son of John Hiester, and grandson of John Hiester who came to America in 1732, from Elsoff, province of Westphalia, Germany, and settled in Bern township, Berks county, Pa.

He was a member of the Convention which met in Carpenter's Hall, Philadelphia, June 18, 1776; Captain in Lutz's Third Battalion, Flying Camp, and was taken prisoner at the battle of Long Island; during his captivity promoted to Major, and, on May 17, 1777, commissioned Lieut. Colonel Fourth Battalion, Berks County Militia; engaged in the battle of Germantown and subsequent operations; Commissioner of Exchange in 1779; on active duty with his battalion in 1780; member of the Assembly 1780–1790; member of Convention on Federal Constitution, 1787, also that of 1789 on State Constitution; State Senator, 1790–1794; Presidential Elector, 1792 and 1796; member of Congress from Berks county, 1797–1807, also 1815–1820; Governor of Pennsylvania, 1820–1823. His remains now rest, with those of his wife, in the Charles Evans Cemetery, Reading, Pa.

Capt. Conrad Eckert.

Son of John Eckert, who came to America in 1738, from Hanover, Germany, and settled in Heidelberg township of Berks county.

Served in the Revolution as follows: In 1776 with Col. Henry Haller's Battalion at Trenton; at Germantown, and subsequent operations, in 1777, in Sixth Company, Fourth Battalion, Lieut. Col. Joseph Hiester; 1778, in Sixth Company, Fourth Battalion, Col. Joseph Hiester; 1780, Sixth Battalion, Col. Joseph Hiester, all Berks County Militia.

Col. Valentine Eckert.

An older brother of the above Capt. Conrad Eckert, was a member of the Provincial Conference of June 18, 1776; of the Constitutional Convention of July 15, 1776, and of the Assembly during 1776 and 1779. He commanded a company of cavalry at Germantown, where he was wounded; Sub-lieutenant of Berks county, March 21, 1777; Lieutenant of the county, June 6, 1781; Commissioner for purchase of provisions for the army in 1778; Judge of the Berks County Court of Common Pleas in 1784; Brigade Inspector of Berks County, April 11, 1793, for twenty years.

Major Gabriel Hiester.

Son of Daniel Hiester and Catherine Schuler, and the brother of Gen. Daniel Hiester, of Montgomery county, Col. John Hiester, of Chester county, and Governor Joseph Hiester, of Berks county.

He was born June 17, 1749, died September 1, 1824, married, about 1773, Elizabeth Bausman (1751–1832), and resided on the ancestral farm in Bern township of Berks county.

He was chosen a member of the Constitutional Convention of July 15, 1776, and, from that time, was almost continuously in public life. He served as a Major of Militia in the campaign of 1776–1777; was appointed one of the Justices of the Court of Common Pleas, April 24, 1778, and served as a member of the Assembly, with the exception of a couple years, from 1778 to 1790. He was chosen a member of the House of Representatives in 1791, and again from 1802 to 1804; elected Senator, for the district comprising Berks and Dauphin counties, in 1795 and 1796, and from 1805 to 1812; in 1801 he was one of the Presidential electors from Pennsylvania.

William Hiester.

A younger brother of Major Gabriel Hiester, born June 10, 1757, died July 13, 1822, married, March 18, 1784, Anna Maria Myer (1758–1822), daughter of Isaac Meier, founder of Myerstown, Pa.

He served in one campaign of the Revolution, in Capt. George Will's company of the battalion of his brother, Major Gabriel Hiester, in 1777.

Capt. Jacob Yoder.

Rupp has this interesting record with regard to him:

"Captain Jacob Yoder was born in Reading, 1758. To him belongs the honor of having descended the Mississippi in the first Flat Boat—and if no other powers than those of time, and wind, and storm shall assail the *tablet*, of which an account is given below, which will preserve the fact recorded in deep indentations upon it, through a series of years to come.

"The iron tablet was cast by Hanks & Niles, of Cincinnati, in 1834, and now marks the spot where remains the bones of Captain Yoder. It is one of the first of the kind ever executed west of the Alleghanies. It has this inscription:

JACOB YODER

WAS BORN IN READING, PENNSYLVANIA,
AUGUST 11TH, 1755;
AND WAS A SOLDIER IN THE REVOLUTIONARY ARMY
IN 1777 AND 1778;
HE EMIGRATED TO THE WEST IN 1780, AND IN MAY
1782, FROM FORT REDSTONE, ON THE
MONONGAHELA RIVER,
IN THE
FIRST FLAT BOAT
THAT EVER DESCENDED THE MISSISSIPPI.
HE LANDED AT NEW ORLEANS WITH A CARGO OF
PRODUCE.
HE DIED APRIL 7, 1832, AT HIS FARM IN SPENCER
COUNTY, KENTUCKY, AND LIES HERE
INTERRED BENEATH THIS TABLET.

Major Matthias Richards.

Major Richards was born in Falkner Swamp, Montgomery county, Pa., on February 26, 1758, died August 4, 1830, married, May 8, 1782 (his second wife), Maria Salome Muhlenberg (1766–1827), youngest daughter of Henry Melchior Muhlenberg, D.D. His father was Matthias Richards, and his grandfather John Frederick Reichert, who emigrated to America from Augsburg, Germany, 1700 or 1703.

In 1777 he volunteered in Col. Daniel Udree's Second Battalion, Berks County Militia, and was present at the battles of Brandywine, Germantown, and in subsequent operations. In 1780 he was Major of the Fourth Battalion, Philadelphia County Militia, Lieut. Col. Anthony Bitting.

He removed to Berks county in 1788, having been appointed Justice of the Peace for that county, which office he held for forty years, at various times together. Associate Judge of the Berks County Courts, 1791–1797; Inspector of Customs, 1801–1802, at which time he moved to Reading; Member of Congress for the counties of Berks, Lancaster, etc., 1807, and reëlected 1809–1811; Collector of Revenue, 1812; Clerk of the Orphans' Court for Berks County, 1823; after that appointed Associate Judge of Berks County Courts by Gov. Shulze.

Capt. Jacob Bower.

Jacob Bower, of Reading, was born in 1757. He entered the service, in June, 1775, as Sergeant of Capt. George Nagel's Company, from Reading (First Defenders), in Col. Thompson's Battalion of Riflemen; promoted to Quartermaster; First Lieutenant January 18, 1776, in Capt. Benjamin Weiser's Company of the German Regiment, raised in Heidelberg township of Berks county, near the town of Womelsdorf; "served as Captain in Flying Camp;" Captain Sixth Pennsylvania Continental Regiment, February 15, 1777; transferred to Second Pennsylvania, January 1, 1783; died at Womelsdorf, August 3, 1818.

At the close of the war he settled at Reading, and became a prominent county official. He first filled the office of Sheriff for one term, 1788–1790; then County Commissioner, 1790–1793; Recorder, Register and Clerk of the Orphans' Court, 1792–1798; County Auditor, 1799 and 1800.

He was the son of Conrad Bower, innkeeper, of Reading, who died in 1765, and whose widow became the second wife of Michael Bright.

Capt. Bower served faithfully during the entire war and was a most gallant officer.

Capt. Henry Christ, Jr.

A man of prominence in Reading who showed a proper enthusiasm in the first movement at the outbreak of the Revolution. He was appointed, by Edward Biddle, as one of the Committee on Correspondence. On March 9, 1776, he was commissioned Captain in Col. Samuel Miles' Pennsylvania Rifle Regiment, participated in the battle of Long Island, and other operations of that splendid organization, until March 19, 1777, when he resigned.

In 1777 he was placed on the Committee to collect arms, etc. Upon his return from the army he was appointed a Justice of the Peace for Reading, and, in 1784, reappointed for another term of seven years. He also served as Recorder, Register, and Clerk of the Orphans' Court, from 1777 to 1789; he was also Clerk of the Quarter Sessions for 1789.

He died at Reading, in August, 1789, and left a large estate.

Capt. Peter Decker.

Capt. Decker was a retired gentleman at Reading in 1768. He was commissioned as Captain, January 5, 1776, and raised a company as a part of Lutz's Battalion of the Flying Camp. The county quota being already filled, on May 26, 1776, the company was mustered into Col. Magaw's Fifth Pennsylvania Battalion, with which they participated in the battles of Long Island and Fort Washington. In the latter engagement all the survivors of the company were taken prisoners, November 16, 1776. Capt. Decker resigned from the service on February 1, 1777. In 1779 he was a resident of Cumru township, where he kept an inn until his death in 1784.

Col. Balser Geehr.

He was born of German parentage at Germantown, on January 22, 1740, and removed to Amity township, Berks county, when a young man. By 1767 he was living in Oley township, employed as a gunsmith, where he married Catharine Hunter (Iaeger or Yeager), a sister of Col. Daniel Hunter. In 1771 he purchased a large plantation, of 500 acres, in Bern township, and moved upon it in 1772.

Upon the outbreak of the Revolution he became a member of the Standing Committee of Observation, in 1774. He took an active part in the formation of the County Militia, and was made Colonel of the Fourth Battalion, which marched to join Washington's army, passing through Bethlehem on Sunday, September 1, 1776, where they attended divine service.

He officiated as Judge of the County Courts from 1775 to 1784, and represented the County in the General Assembly for the years 1782 and 1786, and from 1792 to 1799. He died June 19, 1801.

25

Col. Henry Haller.

Henry Haller was a tailor at Reading in 1765, and, in 1775, was engaged as an innkeeper, by which time he had become a man of much influence.

He was chosen to command what is ordinarily known as Lutz's Battalion of the Flying Camp, in 1776, but was detained to complete the organization of the militia, and, in that way, prevented from participating, with his command, in the Long Island Campaign. In January, 1777, his battalion, of which Gabriel Hiester was Major, was on active duty at Newtown.

He took a prominent part in all the work pertaining to the war. He was a delegate to the Provincial Conference of June 18, 1776; a member of the Committee of Safety, the Committee on Attainder, and the Committee to Collect Arms, etc.; a member of the Assembly from 1776 to 1781. During the years 1778, 1779 and 1780 he was wagon-master of Berks county, and, during 1779–1780, wagon-master-general for the army.

After the Revolution he moved up the Schuylkill Valley, beyond the Blue Mountains, in Brunswick township, where he died in September, 1793.

Capt. Jacob Livingood.

Jacob Livingood was born in Tulpehocken township, Berks county, on January 26, 1752. His grandfather, of the same name, came with the German colony, from New York Province, in 1729.

On October 2, 1781, he was commissioned as Captain to raise a company of riflemen for service on the frontier, until January 1, 1782. He took such pride in his uniform that he died with it on him, and was thus laid to rest, in accordance with his wish, in the burying ground of the Lutheran Church near Stouchsburg.

Col. Nicholas Lutz.

He was born February 20, 1740, in the German Palatinate, and came to Pennsylvania when a young man. Some time previous to the Revolution he located at Reading, and became the owner of two mills at the mouth of the Wyomissing creek.

In 1775 he was selected as Chairman of the Standing Committee of Observation. He served as delegate to the Provincial Conference of June 18, 1776, and, upon his return, began at once to enlist men for his battalion. He was commissioned as Lieut. Colonel, and participated in the battle of Long Island where he was taken prisoner and exchanged on September 10, 1779.

In 1780 he was appointed Commissioner of Forage, and, as such, purchased supplies for the army until the close of the war. He was a member of the General Assembly from 1784 to 1786, and, again, from 1790 to 1794; and he filled the office of Associate Judge of the county from 1795 to 1806. He died November 28, 1807.

Capt. John Ludwig.

John Ludwig was born in Heidelberg township, of Berks county, the son of Daniel Ludwig.

He was in command of a company in Lutz's Battalion of the Flying Camp, at Long Island. He also was Captain of a company in Col. Joseph Hiester's Battalion, August, 1780, in New Jersey.

He was commissioned Justice of the Peace in 1777, and, again, in 1784; delegate to the Pennsylvania Convention to ratify the Federal Constitution in 1787; served in the General Assembly in 1782–1783, and, again, in 1788–1790; also served as a member of the Pennsylvania House of Representatives, from 1790 to 1793. In 1795 Gov. Mifflin appointed him a Justice of the Peace, which office he held at the time of his death, in July, 1802.

Col. George Nagel.

His father, Joachim Nagel, was born February 21, 1706, at Eisenberg, three miles from Coblentz, Germany. George, the eldest son came to Pennsylvania in 1748, and was followed by the family in 1751.

They settled in Douglass township of Berks county, and erected a grist mill which was operated by the father until his death, July 26, 1795.

George was born at Eisenberg, about 1728. He located in Reading, Pa., about 1755, and engaged in the work of a blacksmith. He served during the French and Indian War as an Ensign, being stationed, for a time, at Fort Augusta. At the outbreak of the Revolution he raised a company of volunteers which became the First Defenders of that war. They were attached to Col. Thompson's Battalion of Riflemen. His commission was dated June 25, 1775; promoted to Major of Fifth Battalion, Col. Robert Magaw, January 5, 1776; to Lieut. Colonel Ninth Pennsylvania Continentals, October 25, 1776, to rank from August 21, 1776; to Colonel of Tenth Pennsylvania Continentals, February 17, 1778; became supernumerary July 1, 1778.

Upon his return to Reading he carried on the mercantile business until his death in March, 1789.

Capt. Peter Nagel.

Brother of Col. George Nagel, was born October 31, 1750, at Eisenberg, Germany, emigrating, with his father, in 1751, to Douglass township, Berks county. When a young man he moved to Reading, and became a hatter.

He was prominently identified with the County Militia during the war, his name appearing as a captain in the returns from 1777 to 1783. In 1777 he commanded the Fourth Company of Lieut. Colonel Joseph Hiester's Battalion, which was engaged at Germantown, and in later operations. In 1778 he was a Captain in Col. Joseph Hiester's Fourth Battalion, which was then again in active service. In 1780 he is also reported in Col. Joseph Hiester's Sixth Battalion. His company was on duty guarding prisoners at Reading, 1781–1782.

In 1793 he was appointed a Justice of the Peace for Berks County, and served continuously until his decease; officiated as Coroner from 1781 to 1787, and Treasurer of Reading, from 1815 to 1828. He died November 30, 1834.

Dr. Bodo Otto.

Dr. Bodo Otto was born in Hanover, Germany, 1709, and obtained his christian name in honor of Baron Bodo, his sponsor in baptism. He was the son of Christopher and Marie Magdalena Otto. He received his education as a surgeon in the University of Göttingen, and was made a member of the College of Surgeons at Lueneberg, and had charge of prisoners in the Fortress Kaleberg and the Invalides.

In 1755 he emigrated to America, locating at Reading in 1773. He was chosen a delegate to the Provincial Conference of June 18, 1776. As an evidence of his patriotism he tendered his services to the Government as a Surgeon, which were gratefully accepted. During the gloomiest period of the war, he, with his two sons, were in charge of the camp hospital at Valley Forge. After the disastrous battle of Brandywine, September 11, 1777, Trinity Lutheran Church at Reading was used for hospital purposes, with the consent of the congregation, and possibly under the direction of Dr. Otto.

At the close of the war Dr. Otto returned to Reading, resumed his practice, and took a prominent part in the administration of local affairs. He died June 13, 1787, and his remains were interred in Trinity Lutheran church-yard.

The following complimentary certificate was furnished him at the close of his service:

"This is to certify that Dr. Bodo Otto served in the capacity of a senior surgeon in the Hospitals of United States in the year 1776, and when the new arrangement, in April, 1777, took place, he was continued in that station until the subsequent arrangement of September, 1780, when he was appointed hospital physician and surgeon, in which capacity he officiated until a reduction of the number of the officers of said department, in January, 1782, was made. During the whole of the time he acted in the above stations he discharged his duty with great faithfulness, care and attention. The humanity, for which he was distinguished, towards the brave American soldiery, claims the thanks of every lover of his country, and the success attending his practice will be a sufficient recommendation of his abilities in his profession.

"Given under my hand, the 26th day of January, 1782.
"JOHN COCHRAN,
        "*Director of the Military Hospitals.*"

Dr. John A. Otto.

John Augustus Otto, son of Dr. Bodo Otto, was born in Hanover, Germany, on July 30, 1751, and came to Philadelphia, with his father, in 1755, where he was given a thorough education, and especially prepared to practice medicine and surgery. He accompanied his father to Reading when he removed thence in 1773.

During the Revolution he assisted his father in surgical operations, and in attending the military hospitals. After the war he established a large practice at Reading, and was recognized as an eminent physician. He served as a Justice of the Peace from 1785 to 1789, and, in 1790, filled the office of Prothonotary.

He married Catharine Hitner, of Montgomery county, and died December 14, 1834.

Capt. John Soder.

John Soder was born in Bern township, Berks county, where his father, Nicholas Soder, settled, having emigrated from Berne, Switzerland, in 1735, and was brought up to farming, which occupation he pursued until his decease.

He was in command of a company of Berks County Militia during the summer of 1776; in 1777 he was Captain of Fifth Company, Third Battalion, Col. Michael Lindemuth. The record of his enlistments, obtained from the Pension Office of the United States, shows that he served as a Captain four different times during the war, each time for a period of sixty days, in different years.

He died in April, 1817, possessed of a considerable estate.

Capt. John Spohn.

John Spohn was born in Cumru township, Berks county, on January 19, 1754, son of John Spohn an early settler in that district. He was brought up as a farmer, and died as such, April 19, 1822.

He recruited one of the early companies in Reading. On January 5, 1776, he was commissioned Captain, and his command attached to Col. Robert Magaw's Fifth Pennsylvania Battalion. He participated in the movements of the army about New York until November 4, 1776, when he resigned.

He was married to Maria Beidler, daughter of Conrad Beidler, a prominent miller of Robeson township, who owned, and carried on for a long time, the large mill at the mouth of the Allegheny creek.

Col. Henry Spyker.

He was the son of Peter Spyker, Judge of the County Courts.

He officiated as Paymaster of the Militia of Berks County, from August, 1777, to the close of the war.

In 1777 he was Colonel of the Sixth Battalion of Berks County, participated in the battle of Germantown, and further operations of the year.

He continued at the head of the Sixth Battalion for 1778, and subsequent years of the war.

He represented the county in the General Assembly for the years 1785–1786.

Col. Daniel Udree.

Daniel Udree was born at Philadelphia on August 5, 1751. About the year 1768 he resided on the Moselem

Forge property in Richmond township, along the Onte-
launee creek, in the employ of his uncle, Jacob Winey,
of Philadelphia, who was largely interested in the iron
industries of Berks county. In 1778 he had become part
owner of the Oley Furnace, and, subsequently, became
its sole owner, as well as of the Rockland Forges, with a
landed estate embracing, altogether, 2,700 acres in one
connected tract.

In 1777 he was chosen Colonel of the Second Battalion,
Berks County Militia, and, with the First Battalion, Col.
Daniel Hunter, took part in the battles of Brandywine,
Germantown, etc. It is said that, in the former engage-
ment, he had a horse shot from under him.

He was again elected Colonel of the same battalion
in 1778, and, for many years, was prominently identified
with the militia of the county and state.

In the War of 1812–1815 he was Major-General of
the Sixth Division, which included the two battalions that
constituted the Second Brigade.

Col. Udree represented Berks county in the General
Assembly from 1799 to 1803, and also in 1805. He
also represented the county in the National Congress for
two terms, from 1813 to 1815, and from 1823 to 1825.

He died suddenly, from a stroke of apoplexy, at his
home on the Oley Furnace property, on July 15, 1828.

Capt. Benjamin Weiser.

Benjamin Weiser, the youngest son of Col. Conrad
Weiser, was born August 12, 1744, in Heidelberg township of Berks county.

On July 8, 1776, he was commissioned Captain in the
German Continental Regiment, but left the service Oc-

tober 31, 1776. He removed to the vicinity of Selinsgrove in Northumberland county, and served as Captain of a Northumberland County Militia Company, at Philadelphia, January 30, 1777.

On January 1, 1778, he was appointed Justice of the Peace for Northumberland County (now Snyder).

He was pursued by the phantom of recovering on his grandfather's possessions in New York State, and made various efforts to that end.

Lieut. Peter Weiser.

Peter Weiser, according to a notation in the Pennsylvania Archives, was a "son of Conrad Weiser." It is needless to say that this is an unauthorized interpolation to the original record. It has caused much trouble to genealogists.

The Rev. J. W. Early, of Reading, Pa., has just discovered his will, and kindly placed its contents at the disposal of the writer.

He was commissioned a Second Lieutenant in the First Pennsylvania Continental Regiment, doubtless about the time of its organization, say in June, 1776. Just prior to the battle of Long Island, on August 12, 1776, the will was written. In it he leaves practically all his property to his brothers Jabez and Conrad. He seems to have participated in the services of his splendid regiment until the battle of Germantown, where he was severely wounded and captured. A letter of Henry Melchior Muhlenberg, dated Philadelphia, November 5, 1777, says: "Peter Weiser is still alive." Fearing that his wound might prove fatal, on November 16, 1777, he added a codicil to the will bequeathing to Adolph Gillman, in whose house on

Market Street, Philadelphia, he was cared for, such a sum of money as might be necessary to defray the expenses which had been incurred.

This establishes the fact that he was the second son of Philip Weiser (September 7, 1722–March 27, 1761), who was the eldest son of Col. Conrad Weiser. Peter was born April 26, 1751, and died about February, 1785, his will being proved at Reading, Pa., on February 23, 1785.

Lieut. William Witman.

He was, most likely, a son of Christopher Witman of Reading.

In February, 1777, he was commissioned a Second Lieutenant in the Ninth Pennsylvania Continental Regiment; shot through the body with a musket ball at Germantown; captured and paroled; left off the roll in the arrangement of 1778; resided in Berks county in 1789; died October 12, 1806.

Capt. Daniel De Turk.

His ancestor was Isaac De Turck, a French Huguenot, who fled to the Palatinate of Germany, emigrated to Esopus, New York, and, from thence, to Oley township of Berks county, between 1704 and 1712.

It was in a barn of this family, in Oley township, that the first Indian converts of the Moravians were baptized.

He was commissioned a Captain of the Flying Camp, and, with his company, passed through Bethlehem, August 26, 1776, on his way to the front.

Capt. George Will.

He was a shoemaker of Berks county, and a native of Stettin, Germany. His father, when a young man, had lived at the Moravian settlement of Herrnhut.

He, also, was in command of a company of the Flying Camp, attached to Major Gabriel Hiester's First Battalion. He passed through Bethlehem, on his way to the front, August 23, 1776, where the company attended divine service.

Capt. George May.

Capt. George May, of Reading, was from Langendiebach, in the Wetterau, Germany, and had once worked at Herrnhaag, the abandoned Moravian settlement of that region.

He was a Captain in Lutz's Battalion of the Flying Camp, at the battle of Long Island.

LEBANON COUNTY.

Gen. John Philip De Haas.

Son of John Nicholas De Haas, was born about 1735; said to have come from Holland but was probably German; emigrated to America, and, on March 28, 1739, settled in Lebanon county.

He served in the French and Indian War as Ensign, December, 1757; Adjutant, Col. Armstrong's Battalion, April 30, 1758; Captain, Col. Burd's Battalion, April 28, 1760; Major, June 9, 1764. He was with Bouquet in the expedition of 1763. In June, 1764, Major De Haas was in command at Fort Henry. From 1765 to 1775 he resided at Lebanon, where he was a Justice of the Peace and an iron-master.

At the outbreak of the Revolution he was on the Committee of Observation for Lebanon Township. On February 22, 1775, he was made Colonel of the First Pennsylvania Battalion, to rank from January 22. His regiment was in the Northern Campaign of 1777 and partook of all the privations of that unfortunate expedition to Canada. His battalion became the nucleus of the Second Pennsylvania Continental Regiment, of which he was commissioned Colonel October 25, 1776. On February 21, 1777, he was promoted to Brigadier General and seems to have been in continuous service until 1778, when he appears to have left the service.

He removed to Philadelphia in 1779, and died in that city on June 3, 1786, leaving a son, John Philip, who served as an Ensign in his father's regiment.

Col. Abram Doebler.

The son of Anthony Doebler, was born March 17, 1765, in Lebanon Co., Pa.

In 1777, when but twelve years of age, he was a member of Col. Grubb's Battalion of Associators, and in active service at Brandywine and Germantown.

After the Revolution, upon the organization of the militia, under Act of Congress, he was made a Brigade inspector of Pennsylvania troops. He assisted in enrolling the volunteers for the Whiskey Insurrection of 1794. He died in Lebanon, August 17, 1849.

Col. John Gloninger.

Son of Philip and Anna Barbara Gloninger; he was born in Lebanon, September 19, 1758.

When the Revolution broke out he served as a subaltern in the Associators. Towards the close of the war he was in command of a battalion of the militia.

Upon the organization of Dauphin county he was appointed County Lieutenant, May 6, 1785. He was a representative to the General Assembly in 1790, resigning to accept the position of State Senator. Upon the erection of the county of Lebanon, in 1813, he was commissioned an Associate Judge, an office he filled for many years.

He died at Lebanon, on January 22, 1836.

Col. Philip Greenawalt.

Philip Lorenz Greenawalt was born June 10, 1725, in Hassloch, in Boehl, Germany. He came to America in 1749, located at first in Lancaster county, then removed to Lebanon.

He was commissioned Colonel of the First Battalion, Lancaster County Associators, and was with Washington at Trenton and Princeton. His battalion was at Brandywine and Germantown, and the conduct of Col. Greenawalt during the former engagement received the commendation of the Commander-in-Chief, especially with regard to his protection of the Continental supplies.

On May 6, 1778, he was appointed one of the agents for forfeited estates. The Assembly of the State made him one of the commissioners to take subscriptions for the Continental Loan, December 16, 1777, and, during the darkest period of the war, he did effective service in collecting blankets, food and forage for the needy troops at Valley Forge, for most of which he was never recompensed.

He died, February 28, 1802, at Lebanon.

Col. Nicholas Haussegger.

Nicholas Haussegger came to America, as a subaltern officer, during the early struggle between England and

France, about 1744. He was a native of Hanover, Germany. He subsequently resigned and came to Pennsylvania, where we find him, during the French and Indian War as Lieutenant of Capt. Atlee's Company of the Pennsylvania Regiment, commissioned May 6, 1760. It is probable that he was in the previous campaign under Gen. Forbes. On November 11, 1763, he was commissioned Captain in the First Battalion of the Pennsylvania Regiment, having distinguished himself in the battle of Bushy Run, in the expedition under Bouquet. During the summer of 1764 he was stationed on the frontiers in Heidelberg township of Lebanon county.

Prior to the Revolution he purchased a farm near Lebanon, where he lived, and on which he ended his days.

At the beginning of the war he was commissioned Major of the Fourth Pennsylvania Battalion, Col. Anthony Wayne, January 4, 1776, and, until the eighteenth of September following, shared in the fortunes and privations of that command at Three Rivers and in the Canada campaign. He was commissioned Colonel of the German Regiment, to rank from July 17, 1776. The regiment was at Trenton and Princeton, and, in May, 1777, was in Debore's Brigade of Sullivan's Division. The statement has been made that Col. Haussegger "deserted to the British after the battle of Monmouth, and nothing can be ascertained of his subsequent history." This is evidently false as he returned to his home .at Lebanon, where he died in July, 1786. His heirs participated in the donation land-grants, awarded by the State of Pennsylvania to its meritorious and brave officers and soldiers of the Revolution, which would not have been the case were he a traitor. It is more probable that, on account of his age, he became sick and incapacitated from active duty, and was given a lengthy furlough, which he spent at his Lebanon home.

Capt. Anthony Kelker.

Anthony Kelker, son of Henry Kelker and Regina Braetscher, was a native of Herrliberg, near Zurich, Switzerland, born December 30, 1733. In 1743 his parents emigrated to America, and settled four miles north of Lebanon, Pa.

August 28, 1775, he was commissioned Second Lieutenant of the Lancaster County Associators, being in active service during the campaign of 1776. In 1777 he was at Brandywine and Germantown. On January 19, 1778, appointed wagon-master of Col. Greenawalt's Battalion, and, the same year, was sent on a secret expedition to Virginia and Maryland. Until the close of the war Capt. Kelker was an active participant.

He was Deputy Sheriff of Lancaster County, 1781–1782; first Sheriff of Dauphin County, in 1785, serving till 1788; member of the House of Representatives, 1793–1794. He died at Lebanon, March 10, 1812.

Capt. David Krause.

Son of John Krause of the Palatinate, Germany, born about 1750 in Lebanon county, and a farmer by occupation.

He commanded a Company of Associators in the Jersey campaign of 1776, and in the campaign around Philadelphia in 1777, subsequently Commissary of Col. Greenawalt's Battalion.

Elected a member of the Assembly from Dauphin

County in 1785; House of Representatives, 1797-1799; Commissioner of Dauphin County, 1795-1797; subsequently, Associate Judge of Lebanon County until his death in 1822.

Major Philip Marstellar.

He was born January 4, 1742; son of Frederick Ludwig Marstellar, and wife Barbara, in New Providence township, Montgomery Co., Pa.

At the outbreak of the Revolution he resided in Lebanon. He was of the earliest Associators, and assisted in raising the troops in 1775 and 1776 for the service. He was a member of the Constitutional Convention of July 15, 1776, and, during that and the following year, of the Assembly. He was appointed Paymaster of the Militia, August 20, 1777; Agent to superintend the purchase of flour for the French fleet, July 13, 1779, and Assistant Forage-master, April 5, 1780. So well done was this latter service that Gen. Washington sent Major Marstellar a letter thanking him for the faithful and prompt performance of his duty.

He removed to Virginia in 1803, not far from Alexandria, where he died about 1809.

Col. Adam Orth.

The eldest son of Balthaser Orth, he was born about 1718 in the Palatinate, Germany. He came, with his parents, to America in 1725. During the French and Indian War he commanded the Lebanon Township Company in Rev. John Elder's rangers. In 1769 he was one of the Commissioners of the County.

During the Revolution he was well advanced in years, but, nevertheless, became early identified with the move-

26

ment, assisted in the organization of the associated battalions, and was appointed Sub-lieutenant of the County, March 12, 1777. He served as a representative in the General Assembly, from Dauphin County, in 1789 and 1790. For a long period he operated and owned New Market Forge. He died at Lebanon, November 15, 1794.

George Holstein.

Son of Leonard Holstein, who emigrated from New York Province into Pennsylvania, settling at Millbach, Lebanon county, in 1728, having originally come from the German Palatinate to England, and from thence to New York in 1710.

George Holstein served in Capt. Hudson's Company during the Revolution.

Michael Holstein.

Brother of George Holstein, who afterwards changed his name to Stoner, was a companion of Daniel Boone, and, at one time, the only white man in Kentucky. He took part in the battle of King's Mountain, the capture of Vincennes, and was wounded at the siege of Boone's Fort and the massacre of Blue Licks.

Capt. Henry Shaeffer.

Henry Shaeffer, son of Alexander Shaeffer and Anna Engle, was born about 1738, in Heidelberg township, Lebanon Co., Pa.

On March 26, 1776, he was commissioned Captain in the Second Battalion, Lancaster County Associators, and was in active service during the campaign of that year; Justice of the Peace, 1777; Judge of the Court of Common Pleas, Dauphin County, 1785 and 1790, until his death, October 12, 1803.

Col. Valentine Shouffler.

He was born April 7, 1752, in Bethel township, Lebanon county. His parents, John George Shouffler and Francisca Bendel, came from Switzerland.

He volunteered, as sergeant, in one of the first companies at the beginning of the Revolution, and was taken prisoner, but managed to escape. He was, subsequently, a Captain in the Flying Camp, and wounded in the skirmish at Chestnut Hill, in December, 1778. He served at Trenton, Brandywine and Germantown, and came out of the Revolution with the rank of Major of the Associated Battalions. In the interval of peace which followed he was a Colonel of Volunteer Militia. He represented the county of Dauphin in the Legislature, 1794–1796. He died at his residence in Jonestown, Lebanon county, August 7, 1845.

Capt. John Weidman.

John Weidman was born June 4, 1756, in Lancaster Co., Pa.

At the commencement of the war he became an officer in one of the Associated Battalions, and, upon the organization of the German Regiment, was commissioned an Ensign, July 12, 1776; promoted First Lieutenant, May 14, 1777, and served in the battles of Long Island, Brandywine, Germantown, White Plains, Monmouth, Trenton, Princeton, Newtown, and was with Sullivan in his expedition against the Indians, 1779. He was adjutant of the regiment that year, and retired the service January 1, 1781. He was a brave and gallant officer.

At the close of the war Capt. Weidman entered mercantile life at Philadelphia, thence removed to Lancaster county, and, afterwards, to Lebanon, where, in 1800, he purchased, from Robert Coleman, the Union Forge estate. He was one of the Associate Judges of Lebanon from 1821 to 1830. He died at Lebanon, on June 6, 1830.

Col. Philip Wolfersberger.

Son of Adam and Margaret Wolfersberger, born February 14, 1739, in Heidelberg township, Lebanon Co., Pa.

In the French and Indian War he saw active service, and was with Bouquet in his campaign of 1763. During the Revolution he was an officer in the Associated Battalions, and, later lieutenant under Col. Curtis Grubb, in the Flying Camp and Long Island campaign of 1776. He was also a participant in the subsequent campaigns in and around Philadelphia.

After the Revolution, when Congress directed the organization of the Provisional Army, he rose to be Major and Lieut. Colonel of the Militia. He died at Campbelltown, Lebanon county, on July 14, 1824.

Jacob Weirick.

He was born in Bethel township, Lebanon county, in 1754, the son of Christian and Margaret Weirick.

He served as a non-commissioned officer in Col. Greenawalt's Battalion, was taken prisoner at Long Island, but shortly after paroled.

He was elected Sheriff of Dauphin County, in 1790; member of the Legislature, from 1795 to 1797, and from 1802 to 1806. About 1807 he removed to Canton township, Washington county, where he died, September 17, 1822.

Francis Wenrick.

His family came from Germany and settled in Lebanon Co., Pa.

He was at the battles of Brandywine and Germantown, and on the frontiers against the Indians subsequent to the massacre of Wyoming. He removed to near Linglestown, Dauphin county, where he died about 1785.

LANCASTER COUNTY.

Capt. Abraham De Huff.

Commissioned March 15, 1776, a captain in Atlee's Musketry Battalion; taken prisoner at Fort Washington, November 16, 1776; exchanged April 20, 1778. In April, 1777, Miles' Rifle Regiment and Atlee's Musketry Battalion were consolidated into the State Regiment of Foot, under Col. John Bull, in which Capt. De Huff's company retained its organization.

Michael Whisler.

Was born near the Trappe, Montgomery Co., Pa., in 1756. In May, 1776, he enlisted for twenty months in Capt. Henry Christ's Company of Miles' Rifle Regiment. He was at Long Island, where the regiment lost heavily, at White Plains, Trenton, Princeton, Brandywine and Germantown, and discharged at Valley Forge, January 1, 1778. He was twice wounded.

He enlisted to serve during the Whiskey Insurrection, 1794, and was so impressed with the beautiful surroundings of Columbia, Lancaster county, that he removed thence, and died there September 14, 1824.

Major David Ziegler.

Born in Heidelberg, Germany, in 1748; served in the Russian campaign against the Turks, under the Empress Catharine; settled in Lancaster, Pa.; June 25, 1775, Adjutant of Col. Thompson's Battalion of Riflemen; First Lieutenant, January 16, 1777, First Pennsylvania Continental Regiment; promoted Captain, December 8, 1778; resigned and went to Cincinnati, Ohio, became its first Mayor and died there, September 24, 1811.

Major John Hubley.

Was born in Lancaster, December 25, 1747; member of the Constitutional Convention of July 15, 1776; member Committee of Safety from July 24, 1776, to March 13, 1777; Commissary of Continental Stores, with rank of Major, January 11, 1777; Prothonotary of Lancaster County, March 22, 1777; member of Supreme Executive Council, but resigned in the spring of 1777, became engaged in superintending the erection of a powder house and store house; commissioned Justice of the Peace, August 12, 1777; appointed Register of Wills and Recorder, October 11, 1777, to fill a vacancy; Commissioner to regulate price of commodities in the Colonies, met at New Haven, Connecticut, November 22, 1777; Commissioner to take subscriptions for Continental Loan, December 16, 1777; committee to supply army with blankets, 1778; Captain in Col. James Ross' Battalion in 1778; member of Constitutional Convention of 1787, and of subsequent convention on Constitution of Pennsylvania; member of State Constitutional Convention of 1789–1790; Prothonotary of Lancaster County, August 17, 1791; for many years Trustee of Franklin College; died at Lancaster on January 21, 1821.

Lieut. Col. Francis Mentges.

An officer in the Swiss and German armies.

On March 22, 1776, Adjutant Atlee's Musketry Battalion; promoted First Lieutenant, August 9, 1776; Major Eleventh Pennsylvania Continental Regiment, October 7, 1776; Lieut. Colonel Fifth Pennsylvania Continental Regiment, October 9, 1778; retired January 1, 1783; later appointed the first Inspector-General of the United States Army.

YORK COUNTY.

Dr. John Gottlieb Morris.

He was born in the village of Redekin, near Magdeburg, Prussia, in March, of 1754. He studied "medicine and surgery" and was granted a diploma to practice. "After finishing my professional studies," he writes in his journal, "I came to this country late in 1776, and served the United States as an army surgeon, with general approbation."

In 1777, after an examination by the State Board of Physicians, Dr. Morris was granted a certificate to serve as "surgeon in the Continental Army." He was appointed Surgeon's Mate of Armand's First Partisan Legion, organized May, 1777, and served with it both in the Northern Department of the army, and when it went south; promoted to surgeon after the battle of Camden, where he lost all his private papers. After the surrender of Cornwallis the Legion was ordered to York, Pa., and mustered out of service. At this time he received most complimentary testimonials from his commanding officer, Col. Armand, Marquis de la Rouerie, also one from Dr. Warren.

In 1783 Dr. Morris became a member of the Cincinnati. After the war he settled in York, and established an extensive practice.

He was married, in June, 1784, to Barbara Myers of York, and died in 1808.

Col. Michael Swope.

Son of George Swope, one of the Commissioners to lay off York county, and one of the first German settlers west of the Susquehanna.

Col. Swope commanded the First Battalion of Associators from York County in the Flying Camp. His battalion of four hundred men suffered severely at Long Island and Fort Washington, where, with fourteen of his officers, he fell into the hands of the British.

Capt. Gerhart Graeff.

Commanded the Second Company in Col. Swope's First Battalion of Associators. At the battle of Long Island the casualties in this company were very heavy, but eighteen men returning to join it after the fight was over.

Ensign Jacob Barnitz.

In Capt. Christian Stake's Fourth Company of Col. Swope's First Battalion of York County Associators. He was wounded and captured at the battle of Long Island, and lay in prison for fifteen months.

CUMBERLAND COUNTY.

Molly Pitcher.

Molly Pitcher, the female gunner at the battle of Monmouth, about whom so much has been said and written, was a pure-blooded Pennsylvania-German.

Among those who settled in Carlisle, about 1763, was a hardy young soldier named William Irvine, who, in time, became Colonel of the Sixth Pennsylvania Battalion, then of the Seventh Pennsylvania Continental Regiment, and, subsequently, promoted to Brigadier General.

In the Irvine household, at the outbreak of the war, was employed, in domestic service, a young woman, named Mary Ludwig, of pure Teutonic descent. She was neither noticeable for her beauty of person, nor for her refinement of manner, but, in kindliness of disposition and faithfulness to duty, she had no superior. Near her master's residence was an attractive young man, John Casper Hayes, who plied his trade as a barber, also sometimes neglected it to hold intercourse with Mary, the inevitable result of which was a wedding on July 24, 1769.

Her husband first enlisted December, 1775, in Col. Proctor's First Pennsylvania Artillery. Upon the expiration of his term of enlistment, December, 1776, he again entered the service, this time in the Seventh Pennsylvania Continental Regiment of Col. Irvine, in whose household his wife had served.

Strong and robust, Molly accompanied her husband in the campaign, to serve as a nurse to the wounded. At the battle of Monmouth the Seventh Pennsylvania greatly distinguished itself. Her husband had dropped his musket and taken temporary charge of a cannon when the grand charge of the British troops was made. In the thick of the engagement he was wounded (from which he subsequently recovered). Molly, who had been carrying water to the suffering soldiers, seeing her husband fall, just as she was approaching him, at once took his place at the gun, and, according to the story of some, fired several rounds at the enemy, but, according to others, only one round, when she was forced to retire although vehemently insisting upon remaining at her post. It is further said that Washington saw her at this service and gave her an appointment as sergeant by brevet.

As a further indication of her self-confidence and tenderness, it is related that, beside her husband, was a friend of hers wounded, so seriously that he was believed to have died, and was, accordingly, cast into a pit for burial, but was discovered by Molly to be alive and carried by her to a place of safety, where she took care of him until his convalescence.

She was called "Molly Pitcher" by the soldiers in grateful remembrance of her service to them in carrying water during the battle.

She remained with the army until the close of the war, then returned to Carlisle with her husband, where, shortly after, he died.

Unfortunately for herself, she did not remain single but married one John McKally, a worthless fellow who had been an army companion of her first husband.

On February 21, 1822, she was granted a pension of $40 per annum "for her services during the Revolutionary War."

She died on January 22, 1832. In 1876 the citizens of Carlisle erected a modest monument to mark the spot where the heroine of Monmouth sleeps her last sleep.

NORTHUMBERLAND COUNTY.

Col. John Henry Antes.

Born October 5, 1736, the son of Henry and Christiana Antes, who emigrated to America from Freinsheim in Rhenish Bavaria, in the early part of the century, and who wielded a great influence for good in the affairs of Pennsylvania between the years 1725 and 1755, being especially identified with the work of the Moravians.

Col. Antes was married, on May 11, 1756, to Anna Maria Pawling. In 1772 he removed, with his father, to Northumberland county from Frederick, Montgomery county. In the Revolution he became Captain of the First Company, Second Battalion, Northumberland County Associators, Col. William Plunkett. Before long, however, Col. Plunkett dropped out of service, when Capt. Antes was promoted to Lieut. Colonel, with command of the forces on the extreme frontier, and with headquarters at the stockade called Antes' Fort. Here he was constantly engaged in resisting the attacks and encroachments of the Indians, and here he died July 13, 1820.

Capt. Bernard Hubley.

Capt. Hubley was commissioned August 15, 1776, a First Lieutenant in the German Regiment; promoted to Captain on February 24, 1778. He participated, with his regiment, in the battles of Trenton, Princeton, Brandywine, Germantown, Monmouth, Sullivan's expedition against the Indians in 1779, and was retired in 1781. He was made Brigade Inspector of Northumberland County, etc., in 1807, and died in 1808.

Capt. Charles Gobin.

He was in command of a company in Lieut. Col. Joseph Hiester's Sixth Battalion, Berks County Militia, in the Jersey campaign of August and September, 1780. Later, he was on the Northumberland county frontier in command of a company of militia to protect the settlers from a threatened invasion of the Indians, Tories and British from New York.

BEDFORD COUNTY.

Chaplain Joseph Powell.

The son of Joseph Powell, a Moravian clergyman, was born in Bethlehem township, Northampton Co., Pa., about 1750. He was educated for the ministry, and was located in Bedford county at the beginning of the Revolution.

He served as Chaplain to the Bedford County Battalion of Associators in 1776; was a member of the Constitutional Convention of July 15, 1776; member of the General Assembly in 1779 and 1780; member of the Constitutional Convention of 1789–1790.

He died in November, 1804, in Southampton township, Bedford county.

The sketches just completed embrace those of whom we have some extended knowledge, however slight, beyond the mere name. It would be an act of much injustice were we to confine ourselves to them alone that it is now proposed to complete this chapter by mentioning the names, at least, of such Pennsylvania-German commissioned officers as are known to have been attached to the several battalions and regiments of Pennsylvania troops in regular service. Even this, by force of circumstances, can be but partial in character.

PARTIAL LIST OF PENNSYLVANIA-GERMAN COMMISSIONED OFFICERS IN REGULAR SERVICE.

Col. Thompson's Battalion of Riflemen.

Adjutant, David Ziegler.

Quartermasters, Frederick Hubley, Jacob Bower, of

Reading; served afterwards as Captain in the Flying Camp, and promoted to Sixth Pennsylvania.

Surgeon's Mate, Christian Reinick, of Lancaster.

Wagon-master, Adam Egle, of Lancaster, promoted from Capt. Ross' company.

Captains, Michael Doudel, resigned on account of ill health soon after the company reached Cambridge; from near Gettysburg, Pa. Abraham Miller, Northampton county (Mount Bethel), June 25, 1775; resigned November 9, 1775.

3d Lieut., Peter Weiser, January 5, 1776, Berks county.

Captain, George Nagel, Reading, June 25, 1775; Major Fifth Battalion, January 5, 1776.

1st Lieut., Jacob Zanck, Lancaster county.

2d Lieut., Frederick Hubley, Lancaster.

3d Lieut., David Ziegler, Lancaster county.

First Pennsylvania Battalion.

Colonel, John Philip De Haas, Lebanon, January 22, 1776.

1st Lieuts., Adam Hubley, Lancaster, October 27, 1775; Major, of Additional Regiment, 1776; Lieut. Col., Tenth Pennsylvania. Frederick Blankenberg, October 27, 1775. Roger Staynor, Jr., from 2d Lieut., January 19, 1776; Captain Second Pennsylvania. Christian Staddel, from 2d Lieut., May 4, 1776; Captain Second Pennsylvania.

2d Lieuts., Roger Staynor, Jr., October 27, 1775; promoted 1st Lieut. Christian Staddel, October 27, 1775; promoted 1st Lieut. Peter Gossner, January 15, 1776; 1st Lieut. Second Pennsylvania. Philip Clumberg, Jr., from Ensign, January 15, 1776; 1st Lieut. Second

Pennsylvania.   Jacob Ziegler, from Ensign, January
15, 1776; 1st Lieut. Second Pennsylvania.

Ensigns, Philip Clumberg, Jr., October 27, 1775; promoted 2d Lieut.   Jacob Ziegler, October 27, 1775;
promoted 2d Lieut.

Ensign, John Philip De Haas, Jr., appointed by Gen.
Gates, August 6, 1776, *vice* John Low, deceased; reappointed to Second Pennsylvania, but never joined the
regiment; died at Beech Creek, Clinton Co., Pa., on
September 22, 1826.

Second Pennsylvania Battalion.

Captain, Rudolph Bunner.

1st Lieut., Andrew Kachlein, January 5, 1776; discharged
June 21, 1776.

Ensign, Abraham Dull, October 25, 1776.

2d Lieut., Charles Seitz, January 5, 1776; dropped September 20, 1776.

Ensign, George Hoffner, July 4, 1776; promoted November 11, 1776.

2d Lieut., George Hoffner, from Ensign, November 11,
1776.

Ensign, Henry Eppley, January 5, 1776; Lieut. Capt.
Watson's Company, November 11, 1776.

Third Pennsylvania Battalion.

Major, Henry Bicker, January 4, 1776; transferred to
Tenth Pennsylvania, October 25, 1776.

Adjutant, Walter Bicker, January 11, 1776.

Captain, Joseph Hubley, January 5, 1776.

1st Lieut., John David Woelpper, January 6, 1776; a
German by birth who had served in the Virginia cam-

paign under Washington, and recommended by him for a company in the German Regiment, July 8, 1776.

2d Lieuts., Walter Bicker, January 8, 1776; Adjutant January 11; captured November 16, 1776; resided in New York City in 1815. Henry Bicker, Jr., January 8, 1776; captured November 11, 1776; promoted Fourth Pennsylvania. Herman Stout, from Ensign, June 13, 1776; 1st Lieut. Tenth Pennsylvania, December 4, 1776.

Ensigns, Herman Stout, January 8, 1776; 2d Lieut. June 13, 1776. Samuel Shriver, January 8, 1776; reported unfit for duty October 4, 1776; absent at Philadelphia.

Fourth Pennsylvania Battalion.

Major, Nicholas Haussegger, January 4, 1776; Colonel German Regiment, July 17, 1776; ordered to Philadelphia, September 18, 1776.

Ensign, Jacob Funk, January 8, 1776.

Fifth Pennsylvania Battalion.

Major, George Nagel, January 5, 1776; Lieut. Col. Ninth Pennsylvania.

Captain, John Miller, of Germantown, Pa., January 5, 1776; mortally wounded November 16, 1776; left a wife and six small children.

2d Lieut., Andrew Dover, Germantown, Pa., January 8, 1776; captured November 16, 1776; 1st Lieut. March 4, 1776; Captain June 1, 1778; exchanged October 25, 1780; residing in Philadelphia in June, 1817.

Captain, John Spohn, of Reading, January 5, 1776; resigned November 4, 1776.

Ensign, John Gansel, January 8, 1776.

Captain, Nathaniel Vansandt, of Bethlehem, January 5, 1776; taken November 16, 1776; exchanged November 20, 1778.

Ensign, Edward Hovenden, of Newtown, Bucks Co., January 8, 1776; taken November 16, 1776.

Captain, Peter Decker, of Reading, January 5, 1776; taken November 16, 1776; broke his parole; resigned February 1, 1777.

Sixth Pennsylvania Battalion.

1st Lieut., Barnet Eichelberger, of York Co., January 9, 1776; resigned February 5, 1776.

Miles' Rifle Regiment.

Surgeon, Jacob Rieger, of Lancaster Co., March 22, 1776.

Sergeant Major, First Battalion, George Hoffner, afterwards Adjutant Procter's Artillery.

Captain, Philip Albright, of York Co., March 19, 1776; resigned January 23, 1777.

3d Lieut., Jacob Stake, subsequently Captain Tenth Pennsylvania.

1st Lieut., George Wert, taken August 27, 1776; died in captivity, leaving a widow, Mary.

2d Lieut., Yost Driesbach, March 10, 1776; captured August 27, 1776.

Captain, Casper Weitzel, of Sunbury, March 9, 1776.

Captain, Henry Christ, Jr., of Berks Co., March 9, 1776; resigned March 19, 1777.

2d Lieut., Jacob Maess, March 16, 1776.

3d Lieut., George Gyger, from Sergeant, October 24, 1776.

Atlee's Musketry Battalion.

Adjutant, Francis Mentges, March 22, 1776; 1st Lieut. August 9, 1776; Lieut. Col. Fifth Pennsylvania.

Quartermaster, Jacob Eicholtz, from Sergeant in De Huff's Company.

Captain, Abraham De Huff, of Lancaster Co., March 15, 1776; captured at Fort Washington, November 16, 1776; exchanged April 20, 1778.

Lieuts., Peter Schaffner, March 20, 1776. Francis Mentges (supernumerary).

Ensign, Michael App, March 20, 1776; taken prisoner August 27, 1776; exchanged December 9, 1776, for Ensign Thomas.

Captain, John Nice, March 15, 1776; captured August 27, 1776; exchanged December 9, 1776, for Capt. Gordon.

Lieut., Matthias Weidman, March 20, 1776; captured November 16, 1776; exchanged August 26, 1778.

State Regiment of Foot.

Surgeon, William Lisener.

1st Lieut., Jacob Maess.

Captain, John Nice.

1st Lieut., George Gyger.

1st Lieut., Jacob Snyder.

Ensign, Abraham Boemper, April 28, 1777.

1st Lieut., George Hoffner.

First Pennsylvania Regiment.

Captain, David Ziegler, from 1st Lieut., December 8, 1778; died at Cincinnati, Ohio, September 24, 1811.

1st Lieuts., Jacob Zanck, resigned October 1, 1776; rc-

sided in Lancaster Co., 1814. Frederick Hubley, from
2d Lieut.; died at Harrisburg, December 23, 1822.
David Ziegler, January 16, 1777; Captain December
8, 1778.

2d Lieuts., Peter Weiser, September 25, 1776; wounded
and captured at Germantown. Michael Hoffman, from
Ensign October 1, 1779; died in service, July 18, 1780.

Ensign, Michael Hoffman, May 28, 1779; Lieut. *vice*
Hughes, October 1, 1779.

Adjutant, David Ziegler, wounded August 27, 1776.

Quartermaster, Frederick Hubley.

Surgeon's Mates, Christian Reinick, March 1, 1776; killed
at Paoli, September 21, 1777. His daughter, Catharine, a Pennsylvania pensioner, resided in Lancaster,
1791. John Hilsdorph.

Second Pennsylvania Regiment.

Colonels, John Philip De Haas, from First Battalion;
Brigadier General, February 21, 1777. Henry Bicker,
from Lieut. Col. of Sixth Pennsylvania, June 6, 1777;
became supernumerary July 1, 1778.

Captains, Jacob Ashmead, September 6, 1776; resigned
May 16, 1780. Roger Stayner, from Lieut. First Battalion; taken prisoner in Philadelphia in September,
1777; exchanged October 25, 1780; died near Aca-
demia, Juniata Co., in 1839. Christian Staddel, from
1st Lieut. of First Battalion. Peter Gosner, from 1st
Lieut., January 1, 1778; retired January 1, 1781.

Capt. Lieut., John Stoy, from 1st Lieut., May 16, 1780;
retired January 1, 1781.

1st Lieuts., Peter Gosner, promoted Captain January 1,
1778. Philip Clumberg, Jr., resigned January 1, 1777.

Jacob Ziegler, resigned. Major Walbron, from Ensign of De Haas; killed at Paoli, September 20, 1777. John Stoy, promoted Capt. Lieut., May 16, 1780. Henry Waggoner, from 2d Lieut., March 11, 1779; resigned May 3, 1779. Jacob M. De Hart, from Ensign, May 16, 1780, *vice* Stoy promoted; died of his wounds July 25, 1780.

2d Lieuts., John Philip De Haas, Jr., from First Battalion; absent from November 3, 1776; died at Beech Creek, Clinton Co., August, 1826. Benjamin Boyer. Henry Waggoner, promoted 1st Lieut., March 11, 1779.

2d Lieuts., John Stricker, from Ensign, October 1, 1777; promoted 1st Lieut., May 1, 1779. Abel Morris, of Berks Co., from Lieut. of Flying Camp, 1777; became supernumerary.

Ensigns, Peter Dietrick, February 5, 1777; killed in action, May 18, 1780, at Paramus. Jacob Morris De Hart, June 2, 1778; 1st Lieut., May 16, 1780.

Adjutant, Benjamin Boyer, April 10, 1779; applied for captaincy in marines.

Third Pennsylvania Regiment.

Lieut. Col., Rudolph Bunner, from Major, August 1, 1777; killed at Monmouth, June 28, 1778.

Major, Rudolph Bunner, January 6, 1777; promoted Lieut. Colonel, August 1, 1777.

Captain, Rudolph Bunner, January 5, 1776; Major, January 6, 1777.

1st Lieuts., George Hoffner, paid from January 1, 1777. Andrew Engle, from 2d Lieut., December 20, 1778; retired January 1, 1781.

2d Lieuts., George Hoffner, from November 11, 1776; 1st Lieut., January 1, 1777. Andrew Engle, from Twelfth Pennsylvania; promoted Lieut., December 20, 1778.

Ensigns, James Engle, from September 20, 1776. Henry Brower, from August 25, 1779.

Fourth Pennsylvania Regiment.

Captain, Henry Bicker, Jr., from Third Battalion, May 15, 1778; joined after his exchange.

Fifth Pennsylvania Regiment.

Lieut. Col., Francis Mentges, from Major Eleventh Pennsylvania, October 9, 1778; retired January 1, 1783.

Captain, William Van Lear, of the Ninth Pennsylvania, ranking from October 10, 1779; retired from the service January 1, 1783.

Sixth Pennsylvania Regiment.

Lieut. Col., Henry Bicker, from Major Tenth Pennsylvania, December 5, 1776; Colonel Second Pennsylvania, June 6, 1777.

Captains, John Spohn. Peter Decker, prisoner of war. Jacob Bower, of Col. Thompson's Rifles, February 15, 1777; transferred to Second Pennsylvania, January 1, 1783. Jacob Moser, February 15, 1777. John Nice, from Thirteenth Pennsylvania, June 15, 1776.

1st Lieut., George Will, February 15, 1777; resigned October 17, 1777; he had been eleven years in Prussian and English service.

2d Lieut., John Rudolph, prisoner; exchanged October 25, 1780.

Ensigns, Herman Leitheiser, of Reading, February, 1777;
died in Berks Co., February 11, 1829, aged seventy-
seven. Philip Snyder, August 21, 1777; supernumerary, June 21, 1778.
Adjutant, George Will, February 15, 1777.

Eighth Pennsylvania Regiment.

Captains, Van Swearingen, August 9, 1776; he had been
in command of an independent company, in the pay of
the State, from February until August 11, 1776, in
defense of the frontiers in Westmoreland Co. Eliezer
Miers. Michael Huffnagle, died December 31, 1819,
in Allegheny Co., aged sixty-six.
Adjutant, Michael Huffnagle, September 7, 1776.

Ninth Pennsylvania Regiment.

Lieut. Col., George Nagel, from Major Fifth Battalion,
October 25, 1776, to rank from August 21, 1776;
Colonel Tenth Pennsylvania, February 17, 1778.
Captain, William Van Lear, from Capt. Lieut., October
10, 1779; Brigade Major First Pennsylvania Brigade;
transferred to Fifth Pennsylvania, January 17, 1781.
Capt. Lieut., William Van Lear, from 2d Lieut., January
29, 1779; Captain, *vice* Grant deceased, August 10,
1779.
2d Lieuts., William Van Lear, promoted to Capt. Lieut.,
January 27, 1779. William Witman, February, 1777;
shot through the body with a musket ball at Germantown; taken and paroled; left out in arrangement of
1778; resided in Berks Co. in 1789; died October 12,
1808.

Tenth Pennsylvania Regiment.

Colonel, George Nagel, from Lieut. Col. Ninth Pennsylvania, February 7, 1778; became supernumerary July 1, 1778.

Lieut. Col., Adam Hubley, Jr., from Major, March 12, 1777, ranking from October 4, 1776; Lieut. Col. commandant of the New Eleventh Pennsylvania, June 5, 1779, to rank from February 13, 1779.

Majors, Henry Bicker, from Major Third Battalion, October 25, 1776; Lieut. Col. Sixth Pennsylvania, December 5, 1776. Adam Hubley, Jr., from First Battalion, December 6, 1776; transferred to one of the additional regiments, then promoted Lieut. Col. March 12, 1777.

Captains, William Wirtz, December 4, 1776; resigned March, 1778. Harman Stout, from 1st Lieut., February 12, 1777; resigned March 1, 1780. David Schrack, from 1st Lieut., October 17, 1777; supernumerary July 1, 1778. Jacob Weaver, January 13, 1777; captured; exchanged December 22, 1780; retired January 1, 1781. This was an independent company to guard British prisoners and public stores at Lancaster; on the removal of the prisoners it was ordered to join the main army.

1st Lieuts., Harman Stout, from Third Battalion, December 4, 1776; Captain, February 12, 1777. David Schrack, of New Providence (Montgomery Co.), December 4, 1776; Captain, October 17, 1777. Jacob Stake, from Miles' Rifle Regiment, December 4, 1776; Captain, November 12, 1777. William Feltman, from Ensign, November 7, 1777; transferred to First Pennsylvania, January 17, 1781. Michael Everly, from

Ensign, April 1, 1780; transferred to First Pennsylvania, January 17, 1781.

Ensigns, William Feltman, December 4, 1776; 1st Lieut., November 7, 1777. Michael Everly, from Sergeant, October, 1779; 1st Lieut., April 1, 1781.

Paymaster, William Feltman, lieutenant and paymaster.

(Old) Eleventh Pennsylvania Regiment.

Major, Francis Mentges, from Atlee's Battalion, October 7, 1776; Lieut. Col. Fifth Pennsylvania, October 9, 1778.

Captain, Adolph William Hedrick, November 13, 1776.

1st Lieut., Jacob Fiss, from Ensign; supernumerary, July 1, 1778.

2d Lieut., Henry Boogh, September 30, 1776.

Ensigns, Jacob Fiss, promoted Lieutenant. ——— Fricker, resigned, October, 1777.

Twelfth Pennsylvania Regiment.

Captain, Nicholas Miller, of Northumberland county, October 4, 1776; supernumerary July 1, 1778; died in Northampton county in 179–.

1st Lieut., Christopher Gettig, of Sunbury, October 14, 1776; wounded at Piscataway, New Jersey, May 11, 1777; taken prisoner and had his leg amputated; died at Sunbury, July 2, 1790.

2d Lieut., Andrew Engle, from Ensign; transferred to Third Pennsylvania.

Ensign, Andrew Engle, October 16, 1776; promoted 2d Lieut.

Thirteenth Pennsylvania Regiment.

Captain, John Nice, transferred to Sixth Pennsylvania, July 1, 1778.

1st Lieut., Jacob Mehs. George Hoffner. Jacob Snyder. George Gyger, supernumerary, 1778.

Col. Hartley's Additional Regiment.

Lieut., Martin Eichelberger, September 19, 1777.

Col. Patton's Additional Regiment.

Ensign, Jacob Weitzel, from April 2, 1779; transferred to New Eleventh.

(New) Eleventh Pennsylvania Regiment.

Lieut. Col. Commanding, Adam Hubley, February 13, 1779; retired January 1, 1781; appointed one of auctioneers of Philadelphia, and died there of yellow fever, in 1793.

Lieut., Jacob Weitzel, March 11, 1780.

Ensign, Jacob Weitzel, of Patton's Regiment, April 2, 1779; promoted Lieutenant, March 11, 1780.

German Regiment.

(Roster has already been given in full.)

Von Ottendorff's Corps.

Captain, Count Nicholas Von Ottendorff, promoted to Major.

Lieut., Henry Bedkin.

Captain, Yost Dreisbach, of Northampton county, February 22, 1777.

2d Lieut., Jacob Glaeton.

Captain, Anthony Selin, December 10, 1776; died in Selinsgrove, Snyder county, in 1792.

Lieuts., Laurence Myers, of Maryland, April 8, 1777. Christian Froelich.

Captain, John Paul Schott, September 7, 1776; captured at Short Hill, June 22, 1777; died in Philadelphia, June 18, 1829, aged eighty-five.

1st Lieut., Christian Mancke.

2d Lieut., George Shaffner.

Captain, Jacob Bauer, April 8, 1777.

1st Lieut., Baron Lewis Augustus de Uechtritz, April 29, 1777; captured at the head of Elk, September 2, 1777, and remained a prisoner till 1780; promoted Captain in Armand's in 1781, and served until end of war.

2d Lieut., John Sharf, of Philadelphia, applied for captaincy in 1778.

Armand's Legion.

Major, George Shaffner.

Surgeon, Gottlieb Morris.

Lieut., Godfried Swartz.

Cornet, Henry Reidel.

Pulaski's Legion.

Quartermaster, John Shrader.

Von Heer's Dragoons.

Captain, Bartholomew Von Heer, of Reading, from Captain in Procter's Artillery, January 1, 1778.

1st Lieut., Jacob Mytinger.

2d Lieut., Philip Strubing.

Procter's Pennsylvania Artillery.

Lieut. Col., John Martin Strobagh, May 13, 1776; appointed June 28, 1776, 3d Lieutenant from Lieutenant of Marines on board the *Hornet;* to Captain, October

5, 1776; to Lieut. Col., March 3, 1777; died in service, December 2, 1778.

Captain, Bartholomew Von Heer, March 3, 1777; appointed Captain of Provost Guard, June 1, 1778.

Adjutant, George Hoffner, April 14, 1777, from Sergeant Major of Miles' Regiment.

THE LAST SURVIVOR OF THE REVOLUTION.

CHAPTER XVI.

SOME OF OUR PATRIOTS IN PUBLIC LIFE.

FOLLOWING the plan outlined in the preceding chapter, it is proposed, in this, to mention some of our ancestors who attained more or less prominence in public life in connection with the Revolutionary period.

This list does not include all, however, who attained any degree of prominence, but merely a partial list of those with whom we are most familiarly acquainted.

MONTGOMERY COUNTY.

Henry Melchior Muhlenberg, D.D.

Henry Melchior Muhlenberg, the patriarch of the Lutheran Church in America, was born at Eimbeck, Hanover, Germany, on September 6, 1711, died October 7, 1787, married, April 22, 1745, Anna Maria Weiser, daughter of Col. Conrad Weiser (1727–1802).

He was one of the first students in the University of Göttingen, 1735. After graduation he received an appointment as teacher in the Orphan House at Halle, upon which duties he entered after a further course in the University of Jena.

It was decided to prepare him as a missionary to the East Indies, but, providentially, this plan was disarranged, and, eventually, he departed for America, reaching its shores, near Charleston, S. C., on September 23, 1742, and arriving at Philadelphia on November 25, 1742.

Here he began his work of organizing and upbuilding the Lutheran Church, the fruit of which is apparent to this day.

So great was his patriotism during the Revolution that he became a marked man, and was obliged to flee from Philadelphia to his home at the Trappe when the British entered it after the battle of Brandywine. Here he was in constant communication with the American leaders, and in the midst of all the important operations then going on.

His sons and sons-in-law were noted for their services to their country.

Frederick Augustus Conrad Muhlenberg.

The third child and second son of Henry Melchior Muhlenberg was born at the Trappe, Montgomery Co., Pa., on January 2, 1750, in the early morning, died June 5, 1801, married, October 15, 1771, Catharine Schafer (1750–1835).

With his two brothers he went to the Halle Institution, Germany, for his education, and was ordained a Lutheran clergyman on October 25, 1770. His first charge was the vicinity of the present city of Lebanon, Pa. In 1774 he became pastor of the Christ Lutheran congregation in New York city.

As an ardent and outspoken patriot he was forced to flee from that city when the British occupied it. He went to the Trappe for safety, and became pastor of the Swamp Lutheran Church, whence he removed.

The unsettled condition of the country at this time, filled as it was with military camps, made ministerial work of but little avail, and, before he entered his thirtieth year, he sat himself down to seriously consider whether his life vocation should not be given a different turn. The wanton destruction of his father-in-law's property by the British, necessitated a removal to the country. Frederick's small home was overrun with fugitives. This, with the proximity of his brother, Peter, whose camp at Valley Forge he frequently visited, had doubtless much to do in deciding him to seek public office. Despite his father's counsel and wishes, he finally made up his mind to abandon the ministry and to accept the candidacy offered him as a member of Congress. On March 2, 1779, he was accordingly selected by the Assembly of Pennsylvania to fill one of the three vacancies existing in that body.

From this time his successful and honorable career upward continued without intermission.

While still a member of the National House of Representatives he was elected, October 10, 1780, a member of the General Assembly of Pennsylvania, and, on November 3, 1780, chosen as its speaker. To this responsible position he was called by the two succeeding Assemblies.

For several years after he seemed to feel a desire to avoid public life, and refused a reëlection to the As-

sembly. He served as a justice of the peace in Montgomery county from March 19, 1784, until January 14,
1789, and was appointed, by the Assembly, as the first
county register of wills and recorder of deeds, September
21, 1784. He presided at its first court held September
28, 1784.

The time arrived when it became necessary to replace
the Articles of Confederation, no longer sufficient, by
the Constitution, and this paper Congress was now presenting to the several states for ratification. When elected
to the Convention which Pennsylvania called for that
purpose he knew he could not decline. Of this body he
was made the presiding officer and labored faithfully
for ratification.

The Constitution being adopted, he, with his brother
Peter, became two of the eight representatives in Congress to which Pennsylvania became entitled. On April 1,
1789, the First Congress met and organized. Such was
the prestige of Muhlenberg's name that he was chosen
as its presiding officer, and thus Frederick Augustus
Conrad Muhlenberg became speaker of the first House
of Representatives of the United States.

He was also a member of the House of the Second,
Third and Fourth Congresses, being again elected speaker
in the Third Congress. With the adjournment of the
Fourth Congress ended his active political life.

He died, at Lancaster, Pa., in the prime of his life.

The activity and worth of Frederick Muhlenberg was
displayed in many other walks of life, outside of politics.
He was a trustee of the University of Pennsylvania from
1779 till 1786; founder of the Hartwick Seminary, of
New York, under the will of the Rev. John Christian

Hartwig; president of the German Society of Pennsylvania.

Of him, and his brother Peter, John Adams querulously says: "These two Germans, who had been long in public affairs and in high offices, were the great leaders and oracles of the whole German interest in Pennsylvania and the neighboring States. . . . The Muhlenbergs turned the whole body of the Germans, great numbers of the Irish, and many of the English, and in this manner introduced the total change that followed in both Houses of the Legislature, and in all the executive departments of the national government. Upon such slender threads did our elections then depend."

Henry Ernest Muhlenberg, D.D.

Gottlieb Henry Ernest Muhlenberg, the youngest son of Henry Melchior Muhlenberg, was born at the Trappe, Montgomery Co., Pa., November 17, 1753, died May 23, 1815, married, July 26, 1774, Mary Catharine Hall (1756–1841).

Educated at Halle, with his brother Frederick, he was ordained to the Lutheran ministry October 25, 1770, and served as his father's assistant in Philadelphia.

Of a more quiet nature than his brothers he was none the less patriotic. The whole Muhlenberg family were marked for tory vengeance when the opportunity might occur. He remained in Philadelphia until after it had been occupied by the British, when safety imperatively demanded his flight. Disguised as an Indian, robed in a blanket and with a gun on his shoulder, he departed. Even then the treachery of a tory innkeeper might have resulted in his detection had it not been for the friendly warning of a Whig occupant of the building.

Having reached the Trappe he devoted the time of his enforced leisure to a study of botany, or, rather, to a practical application of the knowledge he already possessed, until the evacuation of the British troops, June, 1778, enabled him to return to his field of labor in Philadelphia. He succeeded his brother Frederick at New Hanover in 1779, and, in 1780, was called to Lancaster, Pa., to the pastorate of Trinity Lutheran congregation, which he served to the day of his death.

He became eminent as a botanist, and has been denominated (by Dr. Baldwin) as "The American Linnæus." He was also prominent in educational matters, especially in connection with the founding of Franklin College, Lancaster, in 1787. He received his degree of D.D. from the University of Pennsylvania, in 1780.

William Antes.

William Antes, brother of Col. Frederick Antes, and son of Henry and Christiana Antes, was born in Limerick township, Montgomery Co., Pa., on November 21, 1731, and married Christiana, daughter of Jacob and Barbara Markley.

During the Revolution he was Sub-lieutenant of the county. After the active operations of the war, in his locality, he removed to Northumberland county, where, in 1780, he became one of the commissioners to the Assembly, also a commissioner on estates.

When, by treaty with the Indians, the Genesee country in New York state, was opened to settlers, William, with his brother, Col. Henry Antes, and others, hastened there, in 1795, to take up fertile tracts of land. There he remained until his death, in 1810. His body lies in the cemetery at Canandaigua.

MICHAEL HILLEGASS.

B. PHILADELPHIA, 1728. D. 1804.

PHILADELPHIA.

Michael Hillegas.

Michael Hillegas, the first treasurer of the United States, was born in the city of Philadelphia, April 22, 1728–1729, the son of Michael and Margaret Hillegas, who came to this country from German Alsace-Lorraine early in the first quarter of the eighteenth century.

Possessed of ample means his devotion to the interests of his country stamps him as a pure patriot. He early took an interest in political affairs. In 1762 he was appointed one of the commissioners to select the site and erect a fort (Mifflin) for the protection of Philadelphia. From 1765 to 1775 he was a member of the Provincial Assembly. In 1771 he was a member of the board of commissioners to improve the navigation of the Delaware. In 1774 he was a member of the committee of observation of Philadelphia. In 1775 he became a member of the Pennsylvania Committee of Safety; and, in the same year, was chosen treasurer of the United Colonies, serving continuously in this capacity until the treasury department was established by Act of Congress, September 2, 1789, when Hillegas retired to make place for Samuel Meredith. While the Revolution was in progress the Journals of Congress constantly refer to him under the title of "Treasurer of the United States." Although nearly a year prior to the Declaration of Independence, Congress had created the office of "Joint Treasurer of the United Colonies," and Hillegas, together with George Clymer, had been named to fill it, yet this lasted only a little more than a year when Clymer retired and the entire duties of the office fell upon him. When the war had been in progress for six years Robert Morris was made super-

28

intendent of finance, but the position of Treasurer of the United States was continued and, shortly after, Hillegas was reëlected to it, on motion of Roger Sherman.

His services were during the darkest period in the history of this country, a time which required many sacrifices from him, both of time and money, all of which were cheerfully rendered, and yet, strange as it may seem, his name is but seldom mentioned and his praise still less.

He died at Philadelphia, September 29, 1804, and was buried in the hallowed ground of Christ Church, beside the remains of his wife, Henrietta Boude.

David Rittenhouse.

He was born near Germantown, Pa., April 8, 1732, the son of Matthias Rittenhouse, who came from the borders of Holland and settled on the Wissahickon.

He was brought up on his father's farm for which his mechanical genius entirely unfitted him. In his eighteenth year he built a workshop by the public road, and set up the business of a clock and mathematical instrument maker. At twenty-three he planned and made an orrery, by which he represented the revolution of the heavenly bodies more completely than had ever been done before. On the third of June, 1769, he was one of the committee of the American Philosophical Society to observe the transit of Venus, and, on the ninth of November, the transit of Mercury, his report of which events gave him a great reputation.

He was a member of the Constitutional Convention of July 15, 1776; member of the Pennsylvania Board of War, March 14, 1777; and treasurer of the state from 1777 to 1789. In 1792 he was appointed director of the mint of the United States, in which he continued until 1795, when he resigned on account of ill health. He was elected a member of the American Academy of Arts and Sciences at Boston, in 1782, and of the Royal Society of London in 1795. In 1791 he succeeded Dr. Franklin as president of the American Philosophical Society, which office he held until his death.

He died in Philadelphia, June 27, 1796, and lies buried in the graveyard of the Pine Street Presbyterian Church.

George Schlosser.

George Schlosser, of the city of Philadelphia, son of Rev. George Schlosser and Sophia Joannetta Ellwester, was born at St. Arnnal, Saarbruck, Nassau, Germany, in 1714. He came to America, with his parents, in 1751, and located at Philadelphia, where he became a successful merchant.

He was a deputy to the Provincial Convention of July 15, 1774, and that of January 23, 1775; member of the Provincial Conference that met at Carpenter's Hall, June 18, 1775; and of the Constitutional Convention of July 15, 1776. He was one of the Committee of Observation for the city of Philadelphia, August 16, 1775. In 1778 Mr. Schlosser advanced the state £2,000, to provide for the great wants of the army. During the yellow fever epidemic of 1793 he, with Stephen Girard, and Peter Helm, were volunteer workers in the hospital.

He was a true patriot, and died at Philadelphia in February, 1802.

Frederick Kuhl.

Frederick Kuhl was a native of Philadelphia and died in that city.

He was chosen a member of the Committee of Inspection, August 16, 1775, his district embracing from the south side of Vine Street to the north side of Arch Street. In the spring of 1776 he was nominated for the Assembly, but was defeated by a few votes, owing to the success of the conservative party. He was chosen a member of the Constitutional Convention of July 15, 1776, and, by that body, appointed a justice of the peace. He served faithfully as a member of the Council of Safety, and Marshall speaks of him as an active citizen. In 1784 he was elected to the General Assembly, and, in 1791, was one of the trustees of the University of Pennsylvania.

(OLD) NORTHAMPTON COUNTY.

Simon Driesbach.

A native of Witgenstein, Germany, he was born February 18, 1730.

He came to America about 1754, and settled on a large farm in what is Lehigh township, Northampton county.

He was a member of the Constitutional Convention of July 15, 1776; of the Assembly from 1776 to 1780; one of the commissioners appointed by the Pennsylvania war office to collect blankets for the continental troops, May 2, 1777; member of the Council of Censors, October 20, 1783. During the war he rendered efficient service in organizing and maintaining the militia of the county. Two of his sons were in the army. He was a member of the House of Representatives, 1793–1794. He died on his farm, near the present town of Weaversville, Northampton county, December 17, 1806.

Peter Rhoads.

Was the son of Peter Rhoads, or Roth, a Lutheran clergyman and a native of Germany. He was born 1730, came to America, with his parents in early life, and settled in Allentown.

He was a member of the Constitutional Convention of July 15, 1776, and member of Assembly from 1777 to 1780; member of the Committee of Safety, July 24, 1776; judge of the court of common pleas in 1777; justice of the peace, December 4, 1783; member of the Convention of 1789–1790; and, under that constitution, commissioned an associate judge, August 17, 1791. He died at his residence, in Allentown, in 1801.

BERKS COUNTY.

Daniel Hunter.

Daniel Hunter, of Berks county, was born in Oley township, about 1729; his parents were emigrants from Germany, and originally named Yeager.

Upon the formation of the Berks County Committee, at the beginning of the Revolution, Mr. Hunter took an active part in public affairs; he was a member of the Provincial Conference of June 18, 1776, and of the Constitutional Convention of July 15, 1776. He was appointed, by the Pennsylvania war office, one of the commissioners to procure blankets for the continental army, May, 1777, and paymaster of the militia, August 25, 1777. He was elected to the General Assembly in 1782, and, while in attendance on that body, was taken ill, returned home, and died in the latter part of February, 1783.

John Lesher.

John Lesher, of Berks county, a native of Germany, was born January 5, 1711, emigrated to Pennsylvania in 1734, at first located among "the Brethren" of Northampton county, but subsequently removed to Oley township, of Berks county, where he established, at an early day, an iron furnace.

He was a member of the Constitutional Convention of July 15, 1776, and served in the General Assembly from 1776 to 1782. On January 20, 1778, Mr. Lesher was appointed, by the Supreme Executive Council, one of the commissioners for purchasing provisions for the continental army. He died in Oley township on April 5, 1794.

Charles Shoemaker.

Was born at Germantown, Pa., about 1745. His ancestors came to America with Pastorius. He located in Windsor township, Berks county, at an early date. He was a member of the Provincial Conference of June 18, 1776, and of the Constitutional Convention of July 15, 1776; justice of the peace, July 25, 1777; appointed, by the Assembly, December 16, 1777, to take subscriptions for the continental loan; one of the commissioners who met at New Haven, Conn., November 22, 1777, to regulate the price of commodities in the colonies. On October 9, 1784, he was commissioned a judge of the court of common pleas, under the Constitution of 1776. He served as a member of the House of Representatives, from 1791 to 1802, and, again in 1812–1813; subsequently state senator, 1813–1816. He died at his residence in Windsor township in April, 1820, having been, for almost half a century, a gentleman of great prominence and influence in Berks county—reliable, upright, conscientious.

Michael Bright.

He was born, November 24, 1732, near Sheridan, Lebanon Co., Pa., and located at Reading about 1755. His father, Michael Brecht, emigrated from Schriesheim, in the Palatinate, to Pennsylvania, in 1726, when twenty years old.

Mr. Bright carried on the trade of saddler until 1762 when he became an innkeeper, and owner of the Farmers' Inn, northwest corner of Fifth and Washington Streets, still standing but somewhat altered.

In 1774 he was elected county commissioner, and served three years. He became a member of the Standing Committee of Observation for the county, in December, 1774. He died at Reading, in August, 1814.

George Ege.

George Ege was born March 9, 1784, and settled in Berks county about the year 1774, when he became the sole owner of the Charming Forge, a prominent industry on the Tulpehocken Creek, in Tulpehocken (now Marion) township, of Berks county.

During the Revolution he was an ardent patriot, and supplied the government with large quantities of cannon balls. He was a member of the General Assembly for 1779-1780 and 1782; upon the adoption of the state constitution of 1790, he was made associate judge in 1791, and served continuously until 1818.

He became owner of other iron industries, a large land-holder and very wealthy. He died at his home in the Charming Forge, December 14, 1829.

Sebastian Levan.

Was born in Maxatawney township, Berks county. He was son of Jacob Levan, one of the first judges of the county, 1752–1762.

At the breaking out of the Revolution he represented his district on the Standing Committee of Observation in 1774. Subsequently, he served in the State Assembly during 1779 and 1780, and as a Councillor in the Supreme Executive Council, from 1782 to 1784. He was also active in the county militia, being colonel of a battalion. He died in August, 1794.

Christian Lower (Lauer).

The name of his father, Christian, appears in the list of those who emigrated from Schoharie, in New York, to Tulpehocken, in 1723.

He was born in Tulpehocken township, Berks county, and taught the trade of a blacksmith. He took an active part in the Revolution.

In August, 1775, he was selected as one of the colonels of the Associated Battalions, and attended the convention at Philadelphia. He officiated as a county commissioner in 1777, 1778 and 1779; served as a sub-lieutenant, in supplying the quota of troops, from 1780 to the close of the war, and represented the county in the General Assembly for the years 1779, 1782 to 1785, 1793, 1794 and 1796. He died in January, 1807.

Christopher Schultz.

He was one of the Mennonite family of that name in Hereford township of Berks county, where they settled at an early period.

He was much interested in the movement for independence. He attended the first public meeting at Reading, on July 2, 1774, and was appointed on the Committee of Correspondence. On December 5, following, he was placed on the Committee of Observation. He also officiated as justice of the peace from 1777 to 1784, and died September 28, 1789.

Jacob Shoemaker.

Jacob Shoemaker, an elder brother of Charles Shoemaker, was born at Germantown. He became a resident of Reading some time before 1768. In that year he was elected sheriff of Berks county, and commissioned for three years. In December, 1774, he was made a member of the Committee of Observation. He died at Reading in September, 1783.

Benjamin Spyker.

Born in the Palatinate, about 1723. His father, John Peter Spyker, emigrated to Pennsylvania in 1738, and settled in Tulpehocken township of Berks county.

During the French and Indian War he was a close neighbor to Col. Conrad Weiser, and actively aided him in his efforts of defense against the savages, especially in the early part of that war, when his home was, on various occasions, used as a place of rendezvous.

At the beginning of the Revolution he assisted in organizing the Associators of the county, and preparing them for active military service. He represented Berks county in the Provincial Conference of June 18, 1776, and in the Constitutional Convention of July 15, 1776. He served as a justice of the peace for many years. His death occurred in September, 1802.

Peter Spyker.

Peter Spyker, a brother of Benjamin Spyker, also located in Tulpehocken township of Berks county, shortly after his landing at Philadelphia in 1738. He was a farmer.

He was appointed one of the judges of the county in 1763, and continued in that office until his death in August, 1789.

He was especially appointed as president of the courts in 1780. He was the principal judicial officer of the county during the Revolution, and served as a justice of the peace, for the Tulpehocken district, from 1777.

Henry Vanderslice.

Henry Vanderslice, son of Anthony Vanderslice and Martha Pannebecker, was born March 9, 1726, in Providence township of Montgomery county, where he was brought up as a miller. About 1760 he removed to Exeter township of Berks county.

In 1774 he was elected sheriff of Berks county, and held that position for three years. During the Revolutionary War he bore a prominent part in the military affairs of the county; when Congress directed a Declaration of Independence to be read publicly on July 8, 1776, he, as sheriff, performed that distinguished service at the court house in Reading.

On November 19, 1789, he was appointed a deputy surveyor. He died at Reading, February 10, 1797.

Christopher Witman.

He was a shoemaker at Reading in 1756. In 1774 he became an innkeeper, his public house being situated on the southwest corner of Penn Square and Fourth Street.

In December, 1774, he was selected as one of the Committee on Observation, and officiated as county treasurer from 1775 to 1778.

LANCASTER COUNTY.

Prior Jaebez.

Prior Jaebez, or Peter Miller, of the Ephrata Community, one of the most erudite men of his time in Pennsylvania, turned his learning to a most patriotic purpose during the Revolution, for which a more extended credit should be given than has been done in the past.

At the outbreak of the war Congress was in constant receipt of communications from various foreign powers, and, at times, were at great loss to find some one who could not only translate them into English but would also be able to turn the English language into that of the correspondent. Many of the professors and scholars of the academy, who might have been competent, were either fugitives or suspected of toryism. At this juncture Charles Thomson bethought himself of the quiet recluse at Ephrata, Prior Jaebez. The offer to do this work was made to him, and promptly accepted with the proviso, tradition says, that he was not to receive a penny for his services. That this was accepted appears by the records of Congress.

On April 8, 1768, Peter Miller (Prior Jaebez) was elected a member of the American Philosophical Society.

WESTMORELAND COUNTY.

Christopher Lobengiere.

The son of Christopher Lobengiere, a native of Wittenburg, Germany, was born in Dauphin Co., Pa., in the year 1740. He removed, in the spring of 1772, to Mt. Pleasant township, Westmoreland county. He served on the Committee of Correspondence, 1775–1776; a member of the Constitutional Convention of July 15, 1776; member of the House of Representatives, 1791–1793. He died July 4, 1798.

BEDFORD COUNTY.

Henry Rhoads.

Henry Rhoads was a native of Amity township, Berks Co., Pa., of German parentage and education, born about 1740. He settled in Bedford county prior to 1770, and took up a large tract of land, on which he resided until the close of his life, March, 1794.

He was a member of the Constitutional Convention of July 15, 1776; and, on February 27, 1778, appointed a justice of the peace.

MARKET SQUARE IN GERMANTOWN.

CHAPTER XVII.

WASHINGTON'S STOREHOUSE AND SUPPLY DEPOT.

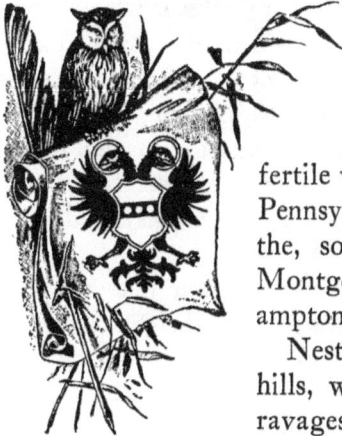

T HERE is no more beautiful sight in the world than that which greets the eye of the traveler, who may pass through the rich and fertile valleys of that part of eastern Pennsylvania which is made up of the, so-called, German counties of Montgomery, Berks, Lehigh, Northampton, Lebanon and Lancaster.

Nestling between the surrounding hills, which protect them from the ravages of the tempest, and furnish them with a never-failing supply of water, stand the substantial Pennsylvania-German farmhouses, adjoining barns which are bursting with plenty, and encircled by acres of waving grain or green fields. Beneath his feet the Pennsylvania-German treads upon other acres of mineral wealth, which keep in operation the never-ceasing wheels of industries that supply the world with its needed iron or fuel.

Today the interior of eastern Pennsylvania stands un-equalled for its home-like beauty, its fertile and highly cultivated fields, its agricultural and mineral wealth, and for its multitudinous industries.

While not to the same extent, yet to the same degree this truth held good during the Revolutionary War, and was fully appreciated by the commander-in-chief of the American army, and by the Congress of the United States.

It matters not how brave the soldiers of an army may be, nor how excellent the arms with which they carry on their warfare, if they be without food, clothing and munitions, their efforts are of no avail. It was the great need of these which prolonged the War for Independence; the lack of them would have caused ignominious defeat.

There was but one colony of the thirteen, which strove to cast off the yoke of Great Britain, that was so situated as to enable it to furnish, in sufficient quantity and variety, all the supplies needed by the troops, and that colony was Pennsylvania; and there was but one part of this colony from which these supplies could be adequately secured, and that was the part occupied by its Pennsylvania-German citizens.

Had they been even luke-warm in their patriotism, or had they utterly refused to part with their hard-earned possessions, as, with the example of others before their eyes, they might well have done, nothing but dire disaster would have been the result. The effort to attain inde-pendence would have been an utter and speedy failure.

Because the Pennsylvania-Germans did open wide their hearts, homes and hands, generally without reward or recompense, without thanks, without praise, without even a suitable acknowledgment of their deeds in the histories which their own descendants are taught in their own schools, we are what we are today, the greatest republic on the face of the earth, or in the history of the world.

The darkest days of the Revolution came in the years 1776, 1777, and 1778, with the defeat at Long Island, the capture of Fort Washington, the defeat at Brandywine, the capture of Philadelphia, and the miscarriage of all plans at Germantown. It was then that our noble forefathers, without food and starving, without clothing and freezing, still clung to the cause for which they were willing to lay down their lives; it was then that Washington, with the feeble remnant of his army, while chased about like the hunted hare, watched his opportunity to strike a feeble blow here and there; it was then that men were dying, by the score, on the bleak hills of Valley Forge; and it was during these dark days of these dark years that the American army found its refuge on the borders of the Pennsylvania-German counties of our state, from which it drew its supplies of all characters, and to which it sent its sick and wounded to be nursed back to life.

Not only were these supplies, which could have been obtained from no other source, given, at that time, cheerfully and unsparingly, but, at all times of the war, the same good work was kept up in the same manner, even though under different conditions.

The crucial, and most constantly active, period of the Revolution, was that from the winter of 1776 to the summer of 1778, when, in connection with the operations relating to the capture and evacuation of Philadelphia, the American army was tramping up and down the Schuylkill valley, or operating in its near vicinity.

Its camps were almost constantly on Pennsylvania-German farms, and when the troops disappeared from one camp to occupy another, with them disappeared everything which represented months of weary toil on the part of the Pennsylvania-German owners, whether crops already harvested in the barns, or those still in the field; whether grain and vegetables for food, hay for forage, or straw for bedding. And this was not because soldiers, in all wars, are accustomed to prey upon the property of others, but because the soldiers of the Revolution, and the horses of the Revolution, were hungry men and hungry animals, without even, at times, the necessities of life.

Worse even than the pangs of hunger were the sufferings of half-naked and bare-footed men, when exposed to the pitiless cold, and it is not to be wondered at that, as her husband lost the fruits of his labor in the field, so was the Pennsylvania-German matron called upon to sacrifice the fruits of her labor at the loom, in the form of blankets and clothing.

The plague of locusts was but a trifle to the visitation of the American army. The former left something, but the latter nothing, and it was no small sacrifice which the Pennsylvania-Germans made when they thus sustained the soldiers of Washington's army during the summer and fall of 1777.

This service, however, fell but to the few, and gave but a temporary relief to those in need. A systematic effort became necessary for continued sustenance. To that end committees were appointed, which were on continual duty during 1777 and part of 1778, some to collect blankets and clothing, others to gather forage, and still others to procure food supplies. Almost literally from door to door went their emissaries throughout the German counties, accompanied by wagons into which the donations were loaded and, as filled, forwarded to the army.

Beyond these came the regular supplies for the troops, procured in the regular way by purchase, even if paid for in a depreciated and almost worthless currency. Of these the flour came from the Pennsylvania-German mills, and the cannon, with their cannon-balls, largely from Pennsylvania-German foundries and furnaces.

As though all this were not sufficient, even the paper needed to make cartridges was furnished by the Pennsylvania-Germans, and it was no small sacrifice and loss to them, as well as ourselves at this day, when, for that purpose, the government seized the unbound leaves of the "Martyr Book," published by the theosophic community at Ephrata, at that time the greatest work of its kind ever attempted on this continent, and carried them off in two wagons guarded by six soldiers.

The extent of these sacrifices on the part of the Pennsylvania-Germans, and the actual quantity of material thus supplied by them, will never be known, but we do know that, by them, the army was kept together, and the independence of our country assured.

From the meager records in existence an attempt will now be made to produce some data, which is not intended to be a complete summary but merely a partial showing, tending to give an idea of the whole. The better to accomplish this end we will consider the subject under the separate head of the various counties.

CHESTER COUNTY.

One of the most interesting and valuable industries of Chester county, in connection with the Revolutionary War, was the Warwick Furnace, on its northern boundary, near the village of Coventry. So valuable, indeed, was its work as to give it a national reputation. It was here

29

that large quantities of cannon and cannon-balls were cast for the army, and, while the struggle for liberty was in progress, the furnace was in constant operation for the government.

A few days after the battle of Brandywine the American army retired from the neighborhood of Goshen,

Friends' Meeting House, where an expected battle was prevented by a rain storm, to the Warwick Furnace, where they procured a fresh supply of ammunition.

During the winter that followed, when the hardships encountered by the army at Valley Forge, filled the country with despair, the cannon at Warwick were in constant danger of seizure by the British, quartered at Philadelphia, within easy marching distance. One day the furnace bell sounded an alarm, and the peal summoned the loyal people in the vicinity to come and secrete the guns. They hid them in the stretch of meadow below the mill, and in front of the mansion house, and, tradition has it, that, after the interment, the fields were ploughed so that no trace of the excavations could be seen.

Buried cannon and shells are still discovered, probably those which contained imperfections. One of the shells, thus unearthed, was exceedingly heavy, about a foot in diameter and hollow, the thickness of the metal being about one inch.

During the year 1776 sixty cannon, of 12 and 18 pound caliber, were cast at Warwick for the continental forces. Col. Frederick Antes was appointed, by the State Council, to test these cannon and decide upon their acceptance. The first four-pounders cast in America were made here.

On March 15, 1736, an agreement was made between Samuel Nutt and William Branson, of the first part, and John Potts, of the second, to erect the " Reading Furnace," and carry on said business near Coventry.

The business relations of Nutt and Branson not proving entirely satisfactory, the former arranged for the erection of a second and near-by furnace, afterwards known by the name " Warwick." Both parties, however, appear to have retained some interest in the two furnaces.

Mr. Branson died in 1760, leaving his furnace property to his grandchildren. The interest of all these heirs was purchased by Rutter & Potts, then of the Warwick Furnace, by several conveyances in the years 1778 to 1783.

While it is true that the active managers and operators

of these furnaces were of English birth, yet their history is not disconnected from that of the Pennsylvania-Germans, and the especial point of interest to us, in this record, lies in the fact that, during the year 1777, at least, and possibly throughout the war, the grandchildren of William Branson were part owners. Of these, five were the children of his daughter Mary, who married Dr. Bernard Van Leer (known as "the centenarian"), an educated physician of pure German blood, from Isenburg in Rhenish Prussia.

Cannon and cannon-balls were not the only things needed to carry on the war. More difficult to obtain than most of the munitions of war was gunpowder. On February 7, 1776, Thomas Heimberger, a powder-maker, engaged to erect a mill in Chester county, about thirty-three miles from Philadelphia and a few miles from Yellow Springs, on a never-failing stream, provided the Committee on Safety would advance him one hundred and fifty pounds, and keep him employed for one year. On June 3, 1776, John Ladd Howell reported to the committee, respecting these works, as follows:

"Thomas Heinberger's Powder Mill on a Creek which empties into French Creek, about five miles above the aforesaid Mill & two miles from Young's Forge, 36 ft. × 30 ft. Water Wheel, 16 ft. Diameter, over Shot.

"Two Shafts, 22 ft. Length, to work 18 Stampers, each 9 ft. Long, 4½ Inches Square. Two Mortar Trees, 20 ft. Long, 9 Mortars, each of 12 Inches by 9, & 16 Inches Depth.

"One Drying House, 18 ft. by 20 ft., the Mill not floor'd, nor the Drying House Plaster'd, expects to begin Work in Ten Days. His Dwelling House not being yet in hand I cannot think he will begin so soon; he has received one Ton of Salt Petre but no Sulphur; has not began to build a refining House, what Salt Petre he has rec'd he refines in this City; he expects to make half a Ton of Powder ℔ Week."

Although the number of Germans who settled in Chester county was limited, and we may, therefore, hardly hope to find a record of many who were millers, and who produced the flour itself, yet we have the name of one who was, to a considerable extent, instrumental in the erection of these mills.

Zachary Rice (Reys or Reiss) came to this country from Germany about 1755, and settled on the Pickering Creek, near Pikeland Station. He was a mill-wright by trade. His first work of importance was the building of a mill for the separation of clover seed, which, without its machinery, was recently standing and used as a storehouse. A number of other mills followed after.

In 1757 he married Maria Appolonia Hartman, living in the vicinity. Their children were taught the same trade as the father.

As a carpenter he assisted in the erection of the hospital at the Yellow Springs in Pikeland, for the sick and wounded soldiers of 1776. While on visits of mercy to this place, carrying food and delicacies to its inmates, Mrs. Rice contracted the typhus fever, from the effects of which she never fully recovered.

MONTGOMERY COUNTY.

While not so largely occupied in producing material for the army, yet, because of its location, if nothing else, the old Valley Forge is sufficiently interesting to be worthy of mention. It was called "Mount Joy" by its first owners, when built about 1750. It stood on the lower (east) side of Valley Creek.

The works were purchased by John Potts, in 1757, and by him much improved. It was supplied with pig iron from the Warwick Furnace, which, when converted into bar iron, was hauled by team to Philadelphia. On May 10, 1768, the property was conveyed to Joseph, a son of John Potts, Sr., and embraced, "All that Iron Forge, called or known by the name of the Mount Joy Forge, saw-mill & grist-mill, and 3 tracts or parcels of land, thereunto belonging, one of them whereon the said forge and mills stand situate in Upper Merion Township, in the County of Philadelphia, it being part of the reputed Manor of Mount Joy." This, doubtless, embraced the building later used by Washington as his headquarters.

The grist mill was the scene of an exciting episode, shortly after the battle of Brandywine, when Alexander Hamilton, then a lieutenant-colonel, accompanied by Captain Lee ("Light Horse Harry"), came in haste, with a small party from the latter's troop, to destroy the stores of grain and flour, and, being hotly pressed by the British, barely escaped. The mill was burned down, in the spring of 1843, by a spark from a locomotive on the railroad.

In 1773 Joseph Potts, had conveyed to William Dewees an undivided moiety of Mount Joy Forge, and, as early as 1771, the latter appears to have resided at the mansion house belonging to these iron works, and to have aided in operating them. The Dewees family came to Germantown about the same time as Pastorius.

As the British army occupied that section, after their victory at Brandywine, they destroyed the old Valley Forge. We are told that a party of them entered the Dewees mansion for plunder, but Mrs. Dewees saved her valuables by gathering them together in one room and informing the soldiers that they could only enter over her dead body.

Prominent among the Pennsylvania-Germans, who were actively engaged in looking out for the needs of the army, was David Rittenhouse, the celebrated astronomer. Because of his mathematical knowledge he was sent to survey the shores of the Delaware, to ascertain what points it would be best to fortify in order to prevent a landing of the enemy. The Committee of Safety appointed him their engineer in October, 1775, and, in this capacity, he was called upon to arrange for casting cannon of iron and brass, to view a site for the erection of a continental powder mill, to conduct experiments for rifling cannon and muskets, to fix upon a method of fastening chain for the protection of the river, to superintend the manufacture of saltpeter, and to locate a magazine for military stores on the Wissahickon.

A full account has already been given of the splendid work done by Christopher Ludwig, the Pennsylvania-German Baker-general, in supplying the army with bread, during its campaign of 1777 in Montgomery county, and at Valley Forge, when Congress furnished him with sufficient flour to enable him to do so.

At and near Sumneytown a large number of mills were in existence, propelled by the waters of the Perkiomen river, Swamp creek, and Valley creek. Besides those for the making of flour, the manufacture of gunpowder was an important industry. It is said that a man, by the name of Fitzinger, first worked in powder at this place, about the year 1777, for the American army. Jacob Dast erected another powder-mill in 1780. It is probable that this was operated by Lorentz Jacoby, whose family records state that George Laurence Jacoby, commonly known by the name of Lorentz Jacoby, established the business in 1780. However this may be, the business was carried on by him successfully and developed to large proportions. He was born, in Germany, January 5, 1756, and died April 8, 1826.

Another most interesting and valuable mill was that commonly known as "Pennypacker's Mills," where the American army encamped on several occasions. It stands on the Perkiomen creek at the head of Skippack Road, and was originally named "Pawling's Mill," after John Pawling, its first owner. It passed over to his son, Henry Pawling, Jr., and, later, to Peter Pannebecker, who came there in 1747 and added a fulling mill to the grist mill. It then became "Pennypacker's Mills," and, as such, famous in our history. During the Revolution it was owned by Peter's son, Samuel. It is now in the possession of Samuel W. Pennypacker.

In December, 1777, the British general made a forward movement from Philadelphia, intending to attack Washington. The result was the battle of Edge Hill. During this maraud we are told the Hessians committed great outrages on the inhabitants, particularly at John Shoemaker's. He was a well-to-do farmer and miller, whose home and grist mill was beside the York road, near the present town of Ogontz.

The Dewees mill, on the Wissahickon, was built long before the Revolution. The first owner, after Farmar, was Peter Robeson, then his son, Jonathan Robeson, after whom it passed into the hands of the Dewees family who were its owners during the war.

On the Sandy Run, the largest tributary of the Wissahickon, is the mill built, in 1769, by Henry Scheetz, for a paper mill, and operated as such until comparatively

recent times. He erected an addition to it, shortly afterwards, for grinding grist and doing general country work,
for which purpose both buildings are now used. The
Scheetz family is descended from Dr. Johann Jacob
Schut (Scheetz), a native of Crefeld, Germany, and one
of the original purchasers from the Frankford Company
that settled Germantown. He never came to America,
but his son Henry emigrated and went, first, to Germantown, then, later, settled in Whitemarsh township of
Montgomery county.

There were three or four historic mills in Towamencin
township. The present Kriebel mill, on the Skippack,
formerly known as "Godshalk's," was in existence in
1767. The Kooker mill, on the Towamencin, was built
before the Revolution, at which time it was owned by
Johannes Springer. In 1776 Christopher Reinwalt had a
mill, which stood near the locality of the later Ander's
mill, a couple miles above the Kooker mill.

Among the mills near Philadelphia, which suffered
greatly from the depredations of the British, was that of
the Pennsylvania-German Paul family. In 1780 Robert
Paul owned a mill near Huntingdon Valley of Abington
township, and, in the same year, Andrew Keyser operated
a mill on the Tacony creek, near Abington Station, recently
the property of Daniel R. Rice.

Shoemaker's mill, called a "corn-grist water-mill" was
built in 1746, at Shoemakertown, in Cheltenham township,
and remained in the family until April 1, 1847.

On April 20, 1734, Joseph Groff (or Graff) obtained
a patent for 200 acres of land, on the west side of Perkiomen creek, in Frederick township, upon which he erected
a grist mill.

About 1735 Henry Antes erected a grist mill on his property in Frederick township, on Swamp creek.

In 1785 Frederick township had five grist mills within its limits, among them being Bertolet's mill, which succeeded Antes' mill but stood further down the stream.

The first grist mill on the Upper Perkiomen, in Upper Hanover township, was that of George Groner, on Macoby creek, who, on February 6, 1739, sold it to Frederick Hillegas.

The assessment of 1776, for Upper Salford township, shows that John Bergy owned 180 acres and a grist and saw mill; Jacob Graff, at Perkiomenville, 200 acres and a fulling mill; Ludwig Moyer, 50 acres and a grist mill; George Moyer, 50 acres and a grist and saw mill; Henry Deetz, 125 acres and a grist and saw mill; Jacob Kulp, 88 acres and a fulling mill.

In 1785 five grist mills are mentioned for Whitemarsh township.

Besides those already mentioned was Wertzner's mill, on Morris Road; Detwiler's, on the Wissahickon; several grist mills and a fulling mill on the Tacony, in Cheltenham; and several grist mills in Moreland township.

Even these constitute barely one half of the Pennsylvania-German grist and chopping mills which dotted, on every hand, the many streams of Montgomery county.

To transport the vast supplies which were received from these mills, and other sources, necessitated many vehicles. On the list of wagons ordered by Council, July 31, 1777, we find given 400 for Philadelphia county, all of which, without question, were received from what is now Montgomery county.

The teams of Col. Frederick Antes and Samuel Bertolet made constant trips to Valley Forge during the winter of

1777–1778, with such supplies as could be gathered in the community.

Many private teams were pressed into service. A family record, which has been preserved, is that of George Anders, a member of the Schwenkfelder sect, and his neighbor, Abraham Kriebel, whose fine horses, and a handsome new wagon, were confiscated for the use of the army. Fearing his pet animals might not be properly cared for, Anders sent his son, Abraham, a boy of eighteen, with them, as driver. After serving a while, and gaining the confidence of his officers, he was, at times, sent long distances for various commodities. On one of these occasions he attempted to escape, but was captured and brought back. To escape punishment he pleaded having lost his way, and, because of his youth, was forgiven. He continued to serve, with his team, until the operations of the army were transferred to other states.

In 1780 the records show that a call was made on Philadelphia county, which again meant our present Montgomery county, for 200 barrels of flour monthly, 1,000 bushels of oats, 20 wagons, 280 horses and 550 men.

BERKS COUNTY.

Among the furnaces of Berks county, which were operated by Pennsylvania-Germans during the Revolution, was the "Oley Furnace," on the Furnace creek, a branch of the Little Manatawney, in Oley township, a short distance north of Friedensburg. It was probably built by Dietrich Welcker, an iron-master of Skippack, about 1765. Becoming involved pecuniarily the property passed to Daniel Udree, who carried it on in connection with the Rockland Forges, located several miles to the northeast, till his death in 1828. It was recently owned by the Clymer Iron Co.

The Berkshire Furnace was situated on a branch of Spring creek, in Lower Heidelberg township, about two miles southwest from Wernersville. It was erected by William Bird, about 1760, and then called "Roxborough." From 1774, and during the Revolution, George Ege carried it on under a lease from Mr. Bird's widow, and, about 1790, purchased it, but abandoned it several years later. Many cannon-balls and shells were made here for the government. From an account, rendered by Mr. Ege, April 3, 1783, to the United States, it appears that he furnished, November 14, 1780, material to the value of £2,894, 11s., 6d., as follows:

Shells: 867, 10 in.; 714, 8 in.

Shot: 843, 24 pd.; 2,137, 18 pd.; 289, 12 pd.

The Oley Forge stood on the Manatawney creek, about ten miles from its confluence with the Schuylkill.

In 1744, John Ross, of Philadelphia, John Yoder and John Lesher, of Oley, entered into a partnership for the erection of this forge. In 1750, Yoder sold to Lesher his one third interest. The remaining partners operated it until the death of Ross, when litigation sprang up between Lesher and the Ross heirs. During this time, in 1784, Lesher sold his interest to his son, Jacob Lesher, and sons-in- law, John Potts, a miller, and Jacob Morgan, a merchant. In 1794, Frederick Spang, an iron-master of Oley, obtained an interest in the forge. It became known as the "Spang Forge," and was abandoned about 1870.

There were several forges known as "Spring Forge." The one pertaining to our narrative was situated on Pine creek, a branch of the Manatawney, in District (now

Pike) township. Its early history is unknown. In 1760 Rebecca Potts purchased a one sixth interest in it, at sheriff's sale, which, in 1773, her executors sold to John Old, an iron-master residing in District township. Old subsequently secured an increased interest in this industry, and, in 1778, sold a seventeen twenty-seventh part of it to Mark Bird. During its later history it was owned, successively, by William Schall, Jacob Deysher and Francis R. Heilig, the latter of whom abandoned it about 1865.

"Charming Forge" was located on the southeastern border of Tulpehocken township, on the Tulpehocken creek, several miles north of Womelsdorf. It was erected by John George Nikoll, a hammersmith, and Michael Miller, in 1749. Henry William Stiegel became the owner in 1763. It was then known as the "Tulpehocken Forge." By 1770 a half interest had passed into the hands of Charles Stedman, when it was first called "Charming Forge," although commonly known as such several years before because of its picturesque location. In 1773 the sheriff sold Stiegel's half interest to Paul Zensinger, a merchant of Lancaster, for £1,600, who, on February 9, 1774, the day he obtained his deed, conveyed it to George Ege. Nine years later Ege bought the Stedman interest and became sole owner, at a total cost of £2,402, 8s., 3d. In 1777 Ege improved the property by the erection of a mansion house, still standing. About the same time he hired, from the government, thirty-four Hessian prisoners to do laboring work. After his death, December, 1830, it passed through various hands, until, in 1855, it became vested in the Taylor family, who held and operated it for many years.

George Ege was most prominently identified with the material life of Berks county. From 1791 to 1818 he

was associate judge. In 1804 he built and operated the
" Schuylkill Forge," on the Little Schuylkill, a short distance north of Port Clinton. At this time he was, doubtless, the largest land holder in the county. His possessions
were: Charming Forge, with 4,000 acres; Reading
Furnace, with 6,000 acres; Schuylkill Forge, with 6,000
acres; also four large and valuable farms, in Heidelberg
and Tulpehocken townships, comprising, together, nearly
1,000 acres, and known, in the vicinity, as " Spring,"
" Sheaff," " Leiss," and " Richard " farms. In 1824 he
was forced to make an assignment. His debts and expenses amounted to over $300,000, but his estate proved
entirely solvent.

The " German," or " District " Furnace stood on Pine
creek, in District township, about one mile from the line
of Pike township. The time of its erection is not known.
It was owned by John Lesher previous to 1784. In 1793
he sold a one third interest to John Teysher (Deysher).
It was abandoned about 1797.

In Albany township, in the northern section of the
county, on a branch of the Maiden creek, called Pine
creek, there were two forges and a furnace. When
erected, or by whom, is unknown. In 1780, Arnold Billig
sold to Michael Brobst two tracts of land, 130 acres in
all, with the buildings, improvements, etc., for eleven
thousand pounds, which was probably the property in
question. In 1818 they were sold out by the sheriff.
They were, subsequently, known as " Union," and operated, for a number of years, by George Reagan.

Large quantities of powder, medicines, and other supplies, were constantly stored in Reading, especially during
1777 and 1778, doubtless in the storehouse at the corner
of Sixth and Franklin Streets. So large were these sup-

plies at times as to cause much uneasiness to the local authorities, and to necessitate the calling out of several companies of militia to guard them.

During the summer of 1777 Berks county furnished 350 wagons, in response to the requisition of the Council of Safety.

John Mears, of Reading, carried on the manufacture of saltpeter in 1776. He, subsequently, became Captain in the Fourth Pennsylvania Continental Regiment, but was retired May 26, 1778. On February 9, 1776, James Biddle, was directed to supply him with £100 for this business, saltpeter for said amount to be delivered within twelve months.

In the same year orders were drawn to pay John Reithmyer, John Deisler and Peter Brecht, for 300 cartridge boxes.

There were many gunsmiths in the country, prominent amongst whom was Col. Balser Geehr. In 1776 money was furnished, by the Council, to the amount of £1,000, to pay for guns which were extensively manufactured along the Wyomissing creek, in Cumru township, near Mohnsville.

In July, 1776, an order for £300 was drawn in favor of George Ege for 100 tons of cannon-balls, and, the same month, an order of £600 to pay for firelocks made in Berks county for the province.

During 1777 large quantities of cartridge boxes, canteens, blankets, muskets, flints, etc., were secured in the county.

The same year were furnished 4,000 bushels of grain for horse feed.

In 1778 Berks county was called upon to supply 8,000 barrels of flour.

During this year the supplies at Reading were again so large and valuable as to require the services of 200 militia for guard purposes, and to keep them secure against any sudden incursion of the enemy.

January 30, 1778, 50 wagons were ordered.

February 18, 1778, 32 wagons were required.

From February to May the wagons were constantly employed in carrying flour and forage to the Schuylkill, the articles being thence transported by water because of the bad condition of the roads.

September 27, 1778, 110 wagons were ordered from Berks county to carry provisions from Philadelphia to New Windsor.

June 11, 1779, a warrant was issued to the Wagon-master of Berks county to supply 60 wagons; and, on October 16 following, 30 wagons.

July 13, 1779, 500 barrels of flour were furnished.

April, 1780, 200 barrels of flour, 560 gallons of rum, 180 tons of hay, and 14,000 bushels of corn were taken from the supplies at Reading.

June, 1780, the commissioner of forage reported having secured, in Berks county, 40 tons of flour, 172 bushels of oats and 19 bags, 10 head of cattle and 40 sheep.

August 1, 1780, the county was required to furnish 600 barrels of flour monthly, 20 wagons, 280 horses, and 300 men.

Even the partial records in existence indicate that Berks county supplied 512 wagons and 48 teams of six horses each. As each team was in charge of two men we have a total of nearly 1,100 men in this service alone.

During August, 1780, a number of masts, for government vessels, were cut in the forests along the Schuylkill, thirty miles north of Reading.

It is to be regretted that no data seem to have ever been preserved with regard to the early grist mills of Berks county, every one of which, with hardly an exception, was owned and operated by Pennsylvania-Germans, and all of which so materially aided the patriotic cause during the Revolution. Some small idea may be gained of their number when we realize that the statistics for 1838 show one hundred and seven grain mills to have been in existence at that time.

In addition to the iron works, already mentioned in Berks county, were those in which the Pennsylvania-German Potts family were interested.

Wilhelm Potts, and wife, Gertrude, reached Philadelphia on September 12, 1734. He was an iron-master of means. He first settled at Germantown, but soon moved to Oley, Berks county, because of the rich deposits of iron ore which were there discovered.

It is asserted that he built the " German," or " District " Furnace, of which a brief account has been given, and that, from him, it descended to John Lesher, the brother-in-law of his grandson. Connected with it was the " District," or "Heilig" Forge. A short distance below the forge he built a stone grist mill, still standing. Still farther down the stream he put up a fulling mill, on the present site of Lobachsville, which, in 1745, he conveyed to his nephew, Peter Lobach, who added a dye-house, chair factory and turning mill, and, by his energy, developed the place into the thriving town which bears his name.

Wilhelm Potts died in 1767. His son, John, on December 23, 1755, married Maria Hoch, and was associated with his father in the iron and milling business. He died in 1804.

His son, John, born in Rockland township, Berks

30

county, January 16, 1759, was connected with his father
in the milling business, and with his brother-in-law, John
Lesher, in the iron business.   In 1786 he married Maria
Lesher, daughter of John Lesher.   Having disposed of
his Oley property in 1810, he moved to the present site
of Pottsville.   Here, in 1806, he had already purchased
the "Greenwood Furnace," which stood on the northwest
corner of the present Coal and Mauch Chunk Streets.
To this he added various works, and houses for his em-
ployees, which cluster of buildings was the beginning of
the city of Pottsville.

NORTHAMPTON COUNTY.

As in all the well-watered Pennsylvania-German counties of the state, so Northampton county was abundantly
supplied with grist mills in the early period of its history.

In 1762 Peter Kichline built a grist and saw mill on
the Bushkill creek, near Easton.   In recent years Michael
Buts was the proprietor of the grist mill, and erected
a planing mill on the same property; Adolph Groetzinger
recently owned the site of the saw mill, on the opposite
side of the creek.   Being the only mills then in the
vicinity they became speedily prosperous.

In 1743 the Moravians built their first grist mill at
Bethlehem, at the foot of the declivity above which the
original house of the settlement stood.   Henry Antes
undertook to superintend the construction, being assisted
by John Adam Schaus, the miller.   This was a great boon
to the settlers surrounding it.   It was replaced by another
mill in 1751.   The third mill on the spot continues to
turn the golden grain into flour, but by processes of which
the fathers never dreamed.

In 1747, under the wise planning of Henry Antes, a combined grist and saw mill was erected, by the Moravians, at Gnadenhütten, near the present town of Lehighton. This mill came to an untimely end with the Indian massacre of 1755. Immediately after the completion of the first a similar mill was built at Christian's Spring, up the Monocacy, which was started November 24, 1747, but, unfortunately, destroyed by fire December 6, 1749. It was replaced by a saw mill on April 17, 1750.

Feeling the need of additional facilities for grinding their grain the Moravians instructed Antes to erect another grist mill for them at Friedensthal, on the Bushkill creek a short distance northwest from Nazareth. This began operation on August 21, 1750, but, on April 20, 1771, it passed out of the hands of the Moravians into that of Samuel Huber, of Warwick township, Lancaster county, for $2,000, Pennsylvania currency. In 1791 the old mill gave place to a stone structure erected by John Eyerly.

The Hellertown flour mill, at Hellertown, on the bank of the Saucon creek, was deeded, by the Penns, to Blasius Beyer, December 13, 1767; by him to Joseph Jennings, February 10, 1768; to Jacob Overpeck, October 1, 1768; then to Christopher Wagner, October 20, 1772. It has since remained in the Wagner family.

Jacob Arndt owned and carried on one of the oldest mills in the Forks. It stood above the Kepler mill, on the Bushkill, and was built about 1763. It was destroyed by fire about 1865, but rebuilt by Jacob Walter, and did a thriving business. It was then known as Walter's lower mill. The upper one owned by him, in Palmer township, was built by Michael Messinger, about 1760.

Jacob Shoemaker's fulling mill, on the Bushkill, was

built and started prior to the Revolution. It was located two miles from Easton, opposite the mill recently owned by T. Kepler.

The " Rock Mill " is the first in Forks township above Easton, on the Bushkill. It is a very old site, and was in possession of George Messinger about the year 1756.

The first grist mill in Plainfield township was built by Adam Heller, about 1770, on land recently owned by John Stoppel.

In the year 1773 there were, in Lehigh township, three grist mills, of which two were owned by Jost Driesbach and George Driesbach, the last-named owning also a saw mill.

The first grist mill in Upper Mount Bethel township stood at a place about half a mile northwest of Williamsburg, some time probably prior to the Revolution. It was built of logs, and contained one run of stones. It was replaced by a substantial structure in 1840.

With the defeat at Brandywine came the flight of government officials from Philadelphia, and removal of stores. Many of these were taken to Bethlehem. Immediately after the battle John Okely, who served for a while as an assistant commissary in Northampton county, received an official letter from David Rittenhouse, member of the Board of War, communicating the instructions of General Washington to transfer the military stores to Bethlehem. With this message thirty-six wagons arrived from French Creek, laden with stores. They were followed, the next day, by thirty-eight wagons. These supplies were deposited at the lime-kilns near the Monocacy, a little to the north of the town, under a guard of forty soldiers. September 18, a continual train of army wagons came into the place. On the nineteenth

other wagons arrived, bringing more dangerous freight—
quantities of ammunition and material for the preparation of same—which was temporarily unloaded near the
oil mill. In the great variety of things, transported from
Philadelphia during those days, were the bells of Christ
Church, and other churches, but, especially, the now historic
State House bell that had pealed forth the announcement
of independence. These—at least some of them—were
conveyed, September 24, to Allentown, and secreted in
the cellar of Zion's Church. Somewhere in the open
square, in front of the Brethren's House, the wagon con-
veying the " Independence Bell " broke down, and this
already precious piece of freight had to be unloaded for
awhile.

On July 31, 1777, Northampton county was requi-
sitioned for 250 wagons. Frederick Beitel, the wagon-
master at Bethlehem, was, at this time, continually on the
road, now to transport sick officers, then official baggage
or continental stores, and, again, British prisoners of rank.

Sixty wagons were furnished by the county to equip
Sullivan's Expedition in 1779.

On June 22, 1776, Captain George Huebner contracted " to deliver to them (committee at Easton) 140
lbs. good gunpowder for every cwt. of saltpeter they shall
deliver to him, gross weight, he to be allowed at the rate
of £3 per cwt. for making and for the casks; he, the
said Huebner, delivering the powder at Easton and fetch-
ing the saltpeter, gratis."

At a meeting, August 5, 1776, the Township Committees were directed to buy all the blankets from the stores
and shops in their respective townships, and to ask " the
good people of their townships to spare from each family
as many as they possibly can, for the use of the Militia

and Flying Camp of this County, now preparing to march to New Brunswick for the defence of American liberty."

On August 1, 1780, Northampton county was required to furnish 500 barrels of flour monthly, 15 wagons, 160 horses.

In one respect, at least, the assistance, rendered by the county during the war, was unique. It was that which was afforded by the use of the "Durham" boats.

About 1727 the Durham Furnace was built ten miles below Easton. To provide a means for getting their

iron to Philadelphia, Robert Durham, the manager of the furnace, built this peculiar boat, nearly in the shape of an Indian canoe, with a wide board extending the entire length on either side, on which the men walked who propelled it with long poles, and with a short deck at either end. They were admirably adapted to the oft-times shallow waters of the upper Delaware, and soon became in general use.

They would carry 125 to 150 barrels of flour for a load, and float down the water to Philadelphia, being tediously poled back by hand. As early as 1758 they were used to transport flour from Van Campen's mill at Minisink (near Stroudsburg) to Philadelphia, and, when the Kichlines and Wageners built their mills on the Bushkill they found these same boats a ready means for taking their product to its market.

Old Squire Abel (Jacob Abel) was the first in Easton to own Durham boats, and take part in the traffic. On so small a thing as these Pennsylvania-German Durham boats hung, probably, the fate of our country in its struggle for independence. With the defeat at Long Island, and the subsequent disasters which followed in its footsteps, came the necessity for Washington to retreat, with his weakened and disheartened army, to Pennsylvania. To cross the Delaware, boats were necessary, but where were they to be found in sufficient number and of proper size? It was then that the Durham boats were brought to mind. With the valuable aid of Squire Abel, Col. Humpton, who was sent for that purpose, scoured the river and collected its boats together. There they were when needed to carry the American army to safety; there they were when Washington struck the blow at Trenton and Princeton which turned the tide of war, and which, without them, could not have been struck; and there they were, once more, to enable him to carry off the fruits of his hard-earned victory.

LEBANON COUNTY.

While, during the Revolution, still connected with Lancaster county, yet, having now a separate existence, it is but just that mention should be made, under this heading, of such data as are distinctively a part of its own history.

In 1772 the town of Lebanon had over two hundred houses. While small in size it occupied an important place during the war. It was a depot of supplies and storehouse for ammunition while Philadelphia was occupied by the British. A large number of gunsmiths were collected here at work for the continental army. Shoes, especially, were manufactured, and large quantities of leather tanned.

Not only was Lebanon a point of produce supply for the army, but quite a number of cannon were cast at Cornwall Furnace, near by, by its Pennsylvania-German workmen.

The magazine established here was in an old building on Tenth Street, a short distance west of the Quittapahilla creek. It was afterwards turned into a barracks, and the ammunition removed to Lancaster, being taken there by twenty wagons, which made from four to six trips each, showing that the quantity was large.

In Jackson township, on the Tulpehocken stream, a Mr. Kitzmiller had a grist mill (on the Hochstetter farm), the only one in the region.

Valentine Miller had his home on the Tulpehocken, near Myerstown, in 1750. His son, Valentine, for many years manufactured powder in a mill that occupied the present site of Miller's grist mill.

The first mill erected in Mill Creek township was that at Mühlbach, in 1778, by Philip Kalbach.

In Lebanon county was the "Elizabeth Furnace" of Baron Stiegel, who was a most interesting, and sometimes misunderstood, personage.

Henry William Stiegel, or Baron Stiegel, as he is generally called, was born near the city of Mannheim,

Germany, about the year 1733. Descended from a wealthy and noble family, he came to America in 1757, while in affluent circumstances, and settled on a tract of land in Lancaster county, where he laid out the present town of Manheim. Here he erected a mansion of an unusually imposing character, and lived in a style far surpassing anything to which his neighbors were accustomed. He also established a glass manufactory, which, for some reason, was not a success. However interesting it might be to do so, it does not pertain to this record to relate the causes which, eventually, led to his failure and bankruptcy, except to say that they were largely owing to the war. It is only intended to mention that he purchased a furnace, located six miles from Schaefferstown, in Lebanon county, which had been originally erected by John Huber, as early as 1755, and upon which he had inscribed this legend:

> "Johan Huber, der erste Deutsche mann
> Der das Eisewerk follfuren kann."

(Translation.)
> "John Huber the first German man
> Who to make iron-work can."

Some of the first stoves made in the country were manufactured by Stiegel. These were "jamb stoves," to be walled into the jamb of the kitchen fire-place.

Following Huber's example, he had cast upon the front of some of them this equally quaint inscription:

> "Baron Stiegel ist der mann
> Der die ofen gieszen kann."

(Translation.)

"Baron Stiegel is the man
Who to make the oven can."

At the Elizabeth Furnace, during the Revolution, were cast large quantities of shot and shell for the army, and even the cannon themselves.

LANCASTER COUNTY.

Early in the history of the war large stores of powder and lead were assembled at Lancaster. The following interesting record has been preserved of such stores delivered into the magazine:

May, 1775.

From the stores of Mathias Slough, Esquire—Powder, 3 quarter casks & 20 lbs., is 95 lbs.; Lead, 6 ct. 3 21, is 777 lbs.

From the store of Mr. Christian Wirtz—Powder, 5 quarter casks, is 125 lbs.; Lead, 2 ct. 0 0, is 224 lbs.

From the store of Mrs. Charles Hamilton—Powder, 26 quarter casks, is 650 lbs.; Lead, 9 ct. 0 22, is 1,130 lbs.

From the store of Messrs. Lauman & Hubley—Powder, 2 quarter casks, is 50 lbs.; Lead, 0 ct. 3 14, is 98 lbs.

From the store of Messrs. Simons & Levy—Powder, 2 quarter casks, is 50 lbs.; Lead, 2 ct. 2 0, is 280 lbs.

From the store of Messrs. Lockharts—Powder, 5 quarter casks, is 125 lbs.; Lead, 3 ct. 3 0, is 420 lbs.

From the store of Mr. John Hopson—Powder, 2 quarter casks, is 50 lbs.

From the store of Mr. George Graff—Powder, 20 lbs.; Lead, 0 ct. 1 0, is 28 lbs.

From the store of Mr. Michael Hubley—Powder, 15½ lbs.

From the store of Mr. John Ebberman—Powder, 20 lbs.; Lead, 50 lbs.

From the store of Mr. John Baker, of Leditz—Powder, 1 quarter cask, 25 lbs. March 15th, 1776.

From the store of Mr. Paul Zantzinger—Powder, 1 half barrel, 50 lbs.

Total Powder, 1,284½ lbs.; total Lead, 3,287 lbs.

Amount of Powder, Lead and Military Stores in the Magazine at Lancaster, the Fifteenth Day of March, 1776.
Powder, 27 quarter casks, 675 lbs.; Barr Lead, 1,539.
Loose powder, 16 lbs.; Bullits, 491 lbs.
Powder, 1 half barrel, 50 lbs.; Sheet Lead, 370.
Total Powder, 741 lbs.; total Lead, 2,400 lbs.

Account of the Powder and Lead expended and delivered out of the Magazine at Lancaster, before the Fifteenth of March, 1776, at the request of the Committee of Safety:

For the Treaty at Pittsburg—Powder, 8 quarter casks, 200 lbs.

For Northumberland—Powder, 8 quarter casks, 200 lbs.; Lead, 300 lbs.

Delivered out and used by the Rifle Companies of Capts. Smith & Ross—Powder, 65 lbs.; Lead, 250 lbs.

Used for cartridges— Powder, 22¼ lbs.; Lead, 49 lbs.

Used for prooving the Musket Barrels—Powder, 24 lbs.; Lead, 24 lbs.

Spared to different persons, viz't:

To Michael Nicholas— Powder, 2 lbs.

To John Henry, at different times—Powder, 24 lbs.
To Henry Zericher—Powder, 5 lbs.
To Peter Gonder—Lead, 10 lbs.
To Daniel Bard—Lead, 4 lbs.
To Sundry persons, to destroy mad dogs—Powder,
1¾ lbs.
Total—Powder, 545 lbs.; Lead, 637.

The requisition, made by the council, July 31, 1777,
for wagons, provided for 600 from Lancaster county.

In 1778, the assessment made and collected, of grain
and forage for the army, footed up 658 bushels of wheat
and 651 bushels of forage.

On August 1, 1780, the county was required to furnish
1,200 barrels of flour, monthly, 5,000 bushels of forage,
50 wagons, 400 horses, and 600 men.

A partial list of those providing horses, in compliance
with this demand, mentions the names of:

Benjamin Landis, Henry Landis, Christian Myer,
Samuel Myer, Jacob Kaufman, Henry Brubacker, Jacob
Peifer, John Kneisly, Jacob Kortz, Daniel Ruty, George
Bugh, Martin Myer, Christian Brubaker, Jacob Myer,
Abram Myer, Michael Shenck, Isaac Long, John Master,
Henry Lenn, Philip Boyer, Jacob Frick, John Frick,
John Leib, Jacob Rickseker, Benjamin Hershey, Christian
Binckly, Abram Hershey, Valentine Metzler, Peter Gre-
bill, George Huber, Abram Stoner, Peter Boughman,
Martin Weibrecht, Jacob Grub, Michael Rudysyl, Melcor
Snyder, Jacob Frick, Sebastian Graff, Andrew Billmyer,
Peter Swan.

Among those furnishing wagons were the following:

Michael Shriner, John Brubaker, Jacob Bare, John Myer, Abram Leib, Jacob Weidler, Peter Boughman, Christian Myer, Jacob Wilhelm.

Martic Furnace was built in 1751–1752, by Thomas Smith and his brother William, upon Furnace Run, in what is now Providence township, on the road leading from Lancaster to Burkholder's Ferry, upon the Susquehanna.

At the same time they also built Martic Forge, located on Pequea creek, about four miles below the furnace, whence they obtained their pig iron.

On December 8, 1777, Michael Hillegas secured a fourth interest in the forge property, and, during 1778, its owners became Michael Hillegas, Matthias Slough and George Ege.

The furnace went out of blast during the Revolutionary War, and was never again blown in.

The Windsor Forges were located on the eastern branch of the Conestoga creek, in Caernarvon township, about a mile south of Churchtown. They were built, about 1742, by William Branson, of Philadelphia. Like the Warwick Furnace, of Chester county, the property passed to his grandchildren, among whom were the five children of his daughter who married Dr. Bernard Van Leer. They were its owners during the Revolutionary period.

The Pool Forge was built by James Old, who returned from Reading to Caernarvon township in 1779. It stood about two miles west from Churchtown. He also built another forge, a mile farther down the creek.

Prior to the Revolution, Michael Withers built a forge on Octorara creek, Sadsbury township, between Christiana and Steeleville. Of this practically nothing remains.

For some time before the year 1754 the manufacturing of guns was carried on in Lancaster. Governor Pownall, who visited the place in that year, makes mention of the fact. When the war broke out these gunsmiths were busily employed. On October 7, 1775, the Committee of Safety took steps to expedite the work. The names of Christian Isch, Peter Reigart and Michael Withers are given, as engaged in the making of guns and bayonets, in November, 1775. Other gunsmiths, recorded for 1780, are:

Jacob Dickert, Frederick Fainot, Peter Gautec, Jacob Messersmith, and Peter Roeser.

Paul Zantzinger, of Lancaster, was largely engaged in the manufacture of clothing for the soldiers. His workshop, in which he must have employed quite a number of tailors, was on North Queen Street. In 1777, he furnished Anthony Wayne's men with 650 suits of uniforms. In April, 1778, he reported that, since the preceding November, he had supplied 550 coats, 200 waistcoats, 380 pairs of breeches, 380 pairs of stockings, about 100 pairs of shoes and several hundred hats.

In the borough of Manheim, nearly south of the present mill of E. B. Bomberger, was standing an old mill built by Peter Longenecker between 1763 and 1780.

In 1765, Felix Baughman purchased land in Bart township, about half a mile southeast from Georgetown, on the west branch of Octorara creek, where, later, a saw mill was erected, either by him or his son George, to which was added a small grinding mill.

On the Muddy creek, about a quarter of a mile south from Bowmansville, in Brecknock township, Christian Good (Guth), settled at an early date and erected a grist mill, where the large flouring mill of Mr. Von Nieda now stands.

During different periods of the war the following mills were in operation throughout Brecknock township:

Jacob Fonieda (Von Nieda), grist and saw mill.

Martin Frey, grist and saw mill.

Rudy Frey, saw mill.

Peter Good, saw and hemp mill.

Hans Good, grist mill.

Samuel Martin, grist and saw mill.

Von Nieda's mill was on the Muddy creek, about one mile south from Adamstown. He purchased it in 1785.

Martin Frey's mill was on the same creek, two miles farther down.

Dr. Samuel Martin's mill was also on the Muddy creek, in the southwestern part of the township.

Henry Nissly's mill was on the Chickies creek, below Sporting Hill, in Rapho township.

A frame grist mill was built, in pioneer days, on Middle creek, in Clay township, by Peter Wiland. Jacob Erb became its owner in 1787 and greatly improved it.

Christopher Weidman built a grist and saw mill on Middle creek, in 1755.

Jacob Eberly's stone grist mill, on Middle creek, was built in 1774.

The tax list, for East Cocalico township, shows the following mills in existence during the Revolutionary period:

Michael Bear, 2 mills.

Isaac Adams, 2 mills.

Henry Bear, 1 mill.

Mithe Kneisley, 1 mill.

John Musleman, 1 mill.

Abram Ream, Jr., 2 mills.

For West Cocalico township the same list shows:

John Flickinger, 2 mills. He lived near the present Reinhold's Station.

In 1730, John Mais erected a fulling mill on Little Chickies creek, about one and a half miles south of Mount Joy. It ran for one hundred years.

John Greider had a grist mill in Donegal township, prior to 1776.

Staufer's mill is quite old, and was built probably by Tobias Miller about 1770.

West Earl township boasts of having, within her bounds, one of the first, if not the first, mill erected in Lancaster county. It stood on the south side of the Conestoga, where it unites with the Cocalico. It was in existence in 1729. Hans Graaf, the first settler, was the builder and owner.

Millsville mill, on West Branch in the southern part of Eden township, is said to be the place where a grist mill was erected, by William Downing, in 1754, which furnished large quantities of material for the army.

Another old grist mill is that located on Hammer's creek, in Elizabeth township, supposed to have been built in 1776 by J. Stauffer.

The list of taxables for Ephrata township shows the following mills to have been in existence at the time of the Revolution:

Samuel Bowman, 1 mill.

George Harlacher, 2 mills.

In 1718 Hance Brubaker built a grist and saw mill on the west bank of Little Conestoga, in East Hempfield township, which was contemporaneous with the one erected by Dr. Neff, five miles further east upon Big Conestoga. He sold the mill to Christian Stoneman in 1729, and his daughter sold it to John Stoner in 1755, whose son John erected a new grist mill upon its site in 1767.

John Huber built a grist mill on Little Conestoga prior to the Revolution, which was destroyed by fire in 1797, and rebuilt by his son, Christian, in 1798.

In 1778 Jacob Neff put up a mill on Swarr's run in East Hempfield township, the work upon which was done by Hessian prisoners, from the barracks at Lancaster.

A short distance from Neff's mill Peter Swarr built a grist and corn mill, prior to 1750, which was rebuilt by John Swarr, a son, during the Revolution.

In West Hempfield township, about 1750, Ulrich Shellaberger built a grist and saw mill on Barber's (or Strickler's) run, two miles above its mouth.

Musselman's mill was built by Henry Musselman, on Big Chickies creek, about a mile south from Pedan's Tavern, prior to the Revolution.

John Hamaker built a grist and saw mill on Shawanese run, some two miles from its mouth.

In East Lampeter township Joseph Boughwalter, and his son, John, built a mill on Mill creek, about 1723, which remained in the family for eighty years.

Felix Binckley erected a mill in 1767, at Millport, on Mill creek, which similarly remained in the Binckley family until about 1820.

In 1717 Dr. Hans Neff erected a small grist and saw mill at the mouth of Boring Mill run, where it empties into Big Conestoga. It was sold, in 1750, by Abraham, his son, to Sebastian Graffe.

Francis Neff, a brother of Dr. Neff, built a grist and saw mill, in 1728, about a mile below his brother's location. This passed, in 1750, to John Christy, who sold it, in 1779, to John Witmer, Jr., and George Ross.

31

Peter Lemon, a Swiss Mennonite, settled, in 1717, on the Conestoga creek, in Lancaster township, where he built a grist and clover mill. This he gave to his stepson, Henry Light, who bequeathed it to his son, Jacob Light.

Theodorus Eby, a Swiss Mennonite, about 1725 erected a grist mill on Mill creek, a short distance south of Earl township line, which passed to his son, Peter, in 1730.

On the Mill creek, in Upper Leacock township, was the grist mill of Jacob Becker, on the Newport Road. Marcus Groff owned it during the war.

The following mills were in Manor township in 1780:

Christian Burkholder; Jacob Goodman; Rudolph Herr, oil mill; Christian Herr; John Keller; Christian Kauffman; Yost Musser, saw mill; Jacob Kauffman.

In Manheim township, Martin Myer, in 1756, had a grist and saw mill; Samuel Bare (Bear), a mill in 1779; Christian Buckley, a grist and saw mill in 1779; the same year, George Bugh, an oil mill; Jacob Kauffman and Martin Myers, grist and saw mills. At Oregon, Jacob Bear settled in 1717; he built the first mill on Carter's (now Lititz) creek, and another, half a mile above; it was known as " Bear's Mill" as late as 1865, and passed into the hands of Martin Myers in 1767.

In 1760, Frederick Wise, a German, built a small grist mill at the base of the Mine Hill, in Paradise township. He lived there fifty years and amassed a fortune.

Rohrer's mill, in the southwestern part of Paradise township, occupies one of the oldest mill sites in the county. Its early history is unknown, beyond the fact that a small mill was built there at an early period.

The returns from Providence township, of 1777, show the following:

George Hess, 2 mills.

Jacob Hoover, hemp mill.

Henry Kendrick, 1 mill.

The mill of B. D. Moyer, in Strasburg township, was erected between 1759 and 1769. On April 6, 1769, John Herr conveyed the mill and saw mill to his son Abraham. He held it until his death in 1800.

B. B. Herr's mill, in the same township, is another old mill, erected about 1750, but no data are in existence regarding it.

The Lititz saw and grist mill was erected, in 1756, by the Moravian Brethren, and started November 11. It was burned down in 1775, but immediately rebuilt. Its profits, in 1777, were $2,500.

In 1765 a fulling mill was built at Lititz. The first mill, in the township, was erected, between 1733 and 1760, by George Eby, at the junction of Hammer and Cocalico creeks.

CUMBERLAND COUNTY.

The distinction of producing what was probably the first wrought-iron cannon made in this country belongs to a Pennsylvania-German of this county.

At the beginning of the War for Independence a Westphalian journeyman blacksmith, named Wilhelm Döning, was employed in the iron-works at Middlesex, Cumberland Co., Pa. He proposed to his employer to make wrought-iron guns for the army, and actually finished two fine field-guns, one of which fell into the hands of the English at the battle of Brandywine. It is still preserved in the Tower of London as a great curiosity.

In the Mount Holly iron-works Döning began to make a third gun of heavier caliber, which, however, remained unfinished because he was unable to find an assistant who could endure the heat, which, it is said, was so great as to melt the leaden buttons on his clothes. This unfinished cannon remained for a time in Holly Forge and was afterwards conveyed to the barracks in Carlisle. It is not known what finally became of it.

The English offered a large reward to Döning if he would instruct them in the art of manufacturing these superior guns, but the German blacksmith could not be induced to become disloyal to his adopted country. He, and his fellow-journeyman, Michael Engle, joined the "Artificers' troops" of Captain Nicholas and served to the end of the war. Döning was pensioned under the law of 1818 and died at Mifflin, Pa., December 19, 1830, aged ninety-four years.

PLAN

Of Fort Mercer, at Red Bank, N. J.

REFERENCES.

A End of the fort at which the Hessians entered.
B Small ditch, cross embankment and location of the masked battery.
C Remains of the hickory-tree used during the battle as a flag-staff.
D Ruins of a brick wall in the middle of the artificial bank.—Gateway.
E Count Donop's grave.
F Louis Whitall's house.
G Monument, erected in 1829.
H Pleasure-house.
I Marks of the trenches in which the slain were deposited.
K Road the Hessians marched to the attack.—Reeve's old road.
L Tenant house.
M Road to Woodbury.
N Direction of Fort Mifflin.
O Farm road.

NOTE—The works represented extend about 350 yards in a right line.

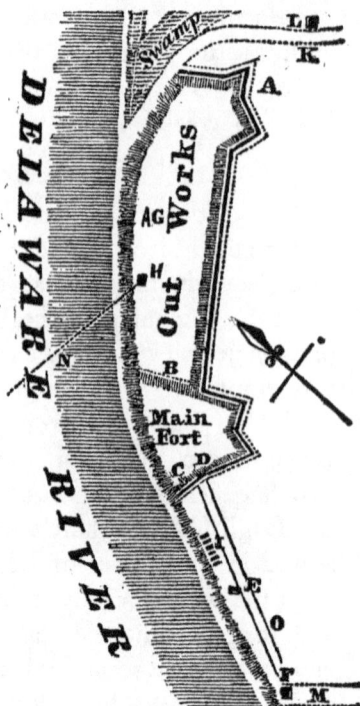

CHAPTER XVIII.

A Place of Safe Keeping and a Refuge.

WITHOUT even considering the many records which have already been laid before the reader, the true patriotism of the Pennsylvania-Germans, and the depth of their loyalty to the cause of independence, would be sufficiently shown by the fact that, at the most trying period of a most trying conflict, when others were plotting, some even turning traitors, and many openly disloyal, so much so that the brave and true men, who held firmly to the cause, were almost driven to despair, it was to the Pennsylvania-Germans they turned their eyes, without a question as to their unswerving faithfulness, and it was to their safe-keeping they committed their own bodies, with the archives and property of the government. Not only were the Pennsylvania-German counties a place of refuge for the members of the Continental Congress, and other officials, when forced to flee from Philadelphia, but they were a veritable place of safe-keeping for the enemies of the country who had been made prisoners of war. There were no tories among the Pennsylvania-Germans, and the authorities knew it.

Early in the war, because of the character of their citizens, the advantage of the interior of Pennsylvania-German counties, as an excellent locality for the safe keeping of prisoners of war, was recognized. The places especially selected were Reading, Lebanon and Lancaster.

In addition to these places Bethlehem was also used for a short time. On September 2, 1777, a messenger from the Board of War appeared before the dismayed Brethren, and announced that 260 British prisoners were to be kept there under a strong guard. As a place of confinement for them the officials seized upon the " Family House," occupied by married people, and standing on what is now the Main Street, north of the " Brethren's House." The water-works became barracks for the guard. This obliged three families to vacate their apartments on the premises. viz.: the Administrator, de Schweinitz, who moved into the old " Community House " with the other clergy; Capt. Webb, often styled, " The Father of Methodism in America," a loyalist soldier-preacher, who was sent to Bethlehem from Philadelphia as a prisoner of war on parole, with his family of seven persons, who was placed in William Boehler's house; and old Thomas Bartow, who, like many others, had come to Bethlehem for rest, some time before, took the room over the store lately vacated by Col. Isaac Reed, of Virginia, who had arrived with the hospital caravan in the previous December, and, on June 22, 1777, was transferred to Philadelphia, where he died on August 21, greatly mourned.

On Sunday, September 7, at noon, 218 of these prisoners arrived, accompanied by a guard of one hundred Continentals. Of these prisoners some one hundred were the partisan Highlanders of Donald MacDonald, from the Cross Creek settlement, near Fayetteville, North Carolina.

A few days later occurred the disaster at Brandywine, then the flight of many government officials to Bethlehem, followed by the wagon-loads of wretched sufferers sent to the hospital again established, until the long suffering and overburdened patient citizens of the little town were at their wit's end. At the height of their misery and perplexity the members of Congress, who, fortunately, chanced to be with them, came to their relief, and, on September 25, 1777, the prisoners took their departure for Reading and Lancaster.

A most interesting connection with this subject is that which refers to Major André. He was first taken prisoner November 3, 1775, at St. John's, at the head of Lake Champlain, by Gen. Richard Montgomery, while on his way to Quebec. At first he was taken to Lancaster, where he became an inmate of the home of Caleb Cope, a Quaker. John Cope, the son, then but a boy, showed such marked talent in drawing that the Major volunteered to become his instructor, and thus the two soon became firm friends.

Interesting accounts exist of André's life at Lancaster, where he was speedily well known, because of his comely countenance, his refined and polished manner—all the marks of the educated gentleman. He was an admirer of the muses, a lover of art, an artist of no mean ability, and an accomplished player on the flute.

In the spring of 1776, with other British officers he was removed to York, where he was shown proper hospitality by the Rev. Dr. Andrews, rector of St. John's Episcopal Church from 1765 until 1772.

About the close of November, 1776, he was on his way from Carlisle to Philadelphia for exchange. On this journey he stopped, in December, at the Crooked Hill Tavern, now the Sanatoga Inn, kept by Henry Dering. The niece of the landlord, Anna Maria Krause, was then visiting his daughter, Kitty, and has left with us an account of this brief stay of an unfortunate man. She describes him as rather under the average stature, of a light, agile frame, active in his movements, and of sprightly conversation. She tells of his singing and performance on the flute, and adds that much of his time was taken up in writing his journal, examining and drawing maps and charts of the country. Among others, he was accompanied by Colonel North, and a young nobleman, a mere stripling.

To Reading were assigned a number of the Hessian prisoners captured at Trenton in 1776, together with many British, and the principal Scotch Loyalists who were subdued and captured in North Carolina.

These were stationed in a grove on the bank of the Schuylkill river, in the southern part of the borough. In the fall of 1776 they were removed to the hill, east of the town, now known as Mt. Penn, and the spot they occupied is called the "Hessian Camp" to this day. Not long since traces were still to be seen of the lines of their huts.

The officers, on parole, were, of course, allowed many liberties, and moved freely around the town. Alexander Graydon, who had been taken prisoner at New York, but, while on parole, visited his mother, who had removed her residence to Reading, gives some interesting reminiscences of his stay here in 1777.

He speaks of a couple subaltern officers, who were lacking in the instincts and behavior of gentlemen, but, otherwise, he says, "all the prisoners in Reading behaved with much decency." He has words of praise for the German officers, whom he calls "downright men," and gives the names of Major Stine, Captain Sobbe and Captain Wetherholt. He refers, especially, to one of the latter, named Graff, a Brunswick officer, who, under the patronage of Dr. Potts, had been introduced to the dancing parties, and was a general favorite, being "a young man of mild and pleasing manners, with urbanity enough to witness the little triumphs of party, without being incited to ill humor by them. Overhearing a dance called for, one evening, which we named 'Burgoyne's Surrender,' he observed to his partner that it was a very pretty dance, notwithstanding the name; and that General Burgoyne himself would be happy to dance it in such good company."

The following record of prisoners at Reading, October 11, 1776, was given to the Council of Safety of Pennsylvania by the local committee:

TAKEN AT ST. JOHN'S, NOVEMBER 3, 1775.

Of the 26th Regiment.

Major Charles Preston.

TAKEN ON THE RIVER ST. LAWRENCE, NOVEMBER 18.

Capt. Wm. Anstruther.	Capt. Rowland Swan.
Capt. John Crawford.	Doctor H. Beaumont.

1 Corporal, 1 Drummer and 8 Privates.

Taken on the River St. Lawrence, November 19.
Of the 47th Regiment.

Capt. Thomas Gamble, Asst. Q'r M'r Gen'l, and one private.

Taken at Chambly, October 19, 1775.
Of the Royal Fuzileers.

Lieut. Harner.

Taken on the River St. Lawrence, November 18.

Lieut. Cleveland, and 3 privates.

Taken at St. John's, November 3, 1775.
Of the Royal Artillery.

Lieut. Schalck.   Dr. James Gill.
Capt. John Marr, Engineer.

Taken at New York.
Of the 59th Regiment.

Ensign Wm. M'Leod.

Taken on the River St. Lawrence, November 19.
Of the Navy.

Mr. Ryal, master of ye Gaspee.

Taken at Point Levy, November 4.

Mr. M'Kenzie, Midshipman of the Hunter.

Taken on the River St. Lawrence, November 19.

Joseph Whitefield, cook of the Gaspee.
James Carr, Foremastman.

TAKEN AT JOHNSTOWN, JANUARY 18, 1776.

From Tryon County, New York.

Allen M'Donell.

Allen M'Donell, Jr.

Alexander M'Donell.

Archibald M'Donell.

Ronald M'Donell.

Wm. Falconer, taken Jan. 21.

From North Carolina.

Lieut. Col. Allen M'Donell, and his son Alexander M'Donell, taken March 5, 1776.

From Canada.

Mr. De lo Corne St. Luc, taken November 22, 1775.

Major Campbell, November 20, 1775.

Captain Fraser, November 25.

Mr. Hertel de Bourville, y'e father, January 16, 1776

Hertel de Bourville, y'e son, November 3, 1775.

Hertel de Braubassin, March 14, 1776.

Nich's Bazin, November 22, 1775.

Joseph Dejarlias, January 6, 1776.

Joseph Hetier, March 1.

Gabriel Hetier.

John Smith, November 20, 1775.

Duncan Cameron.

——— Sutherland, October.

Thomas Donoghue, October 17.

This list was largely augmented by the coming of the Hessians captured at Trenton, and still further increased upon the surrender of Burgoyne. In July, 1780, the prisoners at Reading numbered one hundred. On June 16, 1781, ten hundred and fifty prisoners, all German save sixty-three British, arrived in Reading under guard of York County Militia. By the following week the whole number was increased to near eleven hundred. They were encamped on the east bank of the Schuylkill. It is not known whether they were sent to the "Hessian Camp" on the hill.

During the winter of 1776–1777 there was much sickness among the prisoners, many of whom died and were buried in the "Potter's Field," on the west side of North Sixth Street, south of Walnut. The deaths were so numerous, at times, that it became necessary to bury two, and even three, in one grave.

Not only were the Hessian prisoners sent to the several Pennsylvania-German counties because these were places of safe keeping, but because the people spoke their language, and it was wisely considered that intercourse between the two parties would aid greatly in changing the wrong opinions which each had of the other. To such an extent did this indeed occur that the Pennsylvania-German farmers and people were largely instrumental in bringing about various desertions on the part of the Hessian soldiers, and, of those taken prisoners, it is a fact that not a few chose to remain in Pennsylvania rather than return to their own country, at the close of the war.

On July 8, 1776, the Executive Council passed a resolution authorizing the employment of Hessian prisoners of war, at Lancaster and Reading, in the furnaces of Chester, Lancaster and Berks counties, which were engaged in casting cannon or shot for the government. Many availed themselves of this privilege, as did also the millers and farmers, during the continuance of the labor scarcity caused by enlistments in the army.

After the victories at Trenton and Princeton, with the

surrender of Burgoyne, other prisoners, mostly Hessian, were taken to Lebanon. At first these were confined in the old Moravian Hebron Church, but recently torn down, standing between Lebanon and Avon. As their number increased, temporary barracks were erected adjoining the building, inclosed with a stockade and vigilantly guarded by the battalions of Col. Greenawalt and Col. Klotz, by turns. Later, this charge fell to Col. Hazen, commanding "The Congress Regiment."

While, for a period of ten months, in 1777–1778, the prisoners were quartered in the church at Hebron, its lower story was occupied by the pastor, Rev. C. F. Bader, and his family, who was, naturally, thrown much into contact with the Hessians, as many quaint entries in his church diary testify. One anecdote, translated by Bishop de Schweinitz, is here given:

"Today a rifleman from Anspach, and a corporal, visited Brother Bader. They related to him that Howe had written a letter to Washington containing merely the seventh chapter of the prophet Ezekiel, and that Washington had replied by copying, and sending to Howe, the fourth chapter of the book of Baruch."

Any one taking the trouble to read these two chapters will see the great tact displayed in selecting this Biblical reply to a Biblical despatch.

The daughter of Rev. Bader was one of the so-called "Moravian Nuns" of Bethlehem, who assisted in embroidering the banner of Count Pulaski.

Brother Bader's lot was not a happy one during this time. In addition to the annoyance caused by the presence of prisoners overhead, occupying his church, and interfering with the worship of his congregation, there was a constant intrusion upon his private life. At one time, on April 29, 1778, Major Watkins came to the building, with five men and a wagon-load of powder, broke open his door by force and placed the powder in his room. The next day he again came and advised the clergyman to leave the house, as he intended filling it with powder. As there was no other place for him to go his situation was certainly none too enviable.

Immediately after the battle of Trenton lists of the prisoners taken to Lancaster were made out by the Hessian officers, extracts from which are given herewith:

DETACHMENTS OF ARTILLERY CAPTURED DECEMBER 26, 1776

	Commissioned Officers.	Others.	Total.
Of the Regiment of Losberg........		18	18
Of the Regiment of Knyphausen....	1	18	19
Of the Regiment of Rall...........		3	3

LIST OF PRISONERS DECEMBER 27, 1776.

Philip Brand, Henrich Grebenteich, George Schade, Henrich Corel, Johan Boc, George Fleck, Martin Ludolph, Conrad Mestmacher, Kaspar Klenekerfus, Henric Eberdinck, Henric Berles, Friderick Becher, Henric Wagner, Carl Hartman, Wilhelm Harkenberg, Carl Falckman, Henric Keerl (chirurgeon, *i. e.,* surgeon), Carl Beckmejer (chirurgeon), Christian Mejier, Henric Woodman, Niclaus Henckel, Dieterich Thoma, Wilhelm Kock, Henric Hartwic, Gerhardt Hansfing, Johannes Roes, Anton Mocman, Jacob Fric, Johannes Ruhl, Wilhelm Rupe, Henric Rupe, Andreas Becher, Andreas Schoenewald, Rebecca Ahlhausen (woman), Shemes Malaede (Dori), Thomas Rerisohert (negro), Johannes Geisler, Andreas Ariacke, Frederic Liebe, Martin Wetloser (corporal),

Jacob Rohling, Henric Luders, William Brandson, Johannes Vestweber, Friderick Berker, Catharina Wetlosern, Elizabeth Sepwebein, William Saefer (negro), Johann Staude, Striftoph Hering, Frideric Rusmuller, Henrich Herbold, Conrad Schenck, Peter Mull, Cetlin Nellmejerin, Wilhelmina Clausin—total 56.

PRISONERS FROM REGIMENT OF LOSBERG.

	Commissioned Officers.	Others.	Total.
First Company	1	56	57
Lieut. Col. Scheffer	1	47	48
Captain von Altenbockum	1	36	37
Major von Harnstein..............	3	45	48
Vacant, Colonel	3	54	57
Middle and under staff..........			7

Names of Officers.

Lieut. Col. F. Scheffer.   Lieut. Moller.
Major von Harnstein.   Ensign von Hohe.
Captain Steding.   "   Graebe.
Lieut. Keller.   "   von Zengen.
   "   Piel.   "   Hendorff.

Killed in Trenton, December 26, 1776.

Capt. Rice.   Lieut. Kimm.
   "   von Benning.

Wounded and Remained at Trenton.

Capt. von Altenbockum.   Lieut. Zoll.
Lieut. Schwabe.

PRISONERS FROM REGIMENT OF KNYPHAUSEN.

	Commissioned Officers.	Others.	Total.
First Company	1	53	54
Col. von Borck....................	1	54	55
Lieut. Col. von Minigerode..........	2	69	71
Major von Dechow.................		52	52
Captain von Beisenrodt.............	2	60	62
Middle and under staff.........			3

Names of Officers.

Capt. von Biesenrodt.   Lieut. von Ferry.
   "   von Loewenstein.   Ensign Fuhner.
Lieut. Wiederhold.   "   von Drach.
   "   Sobbe.

Wounded in Newtown.

Major von Dechow, re-   Col. Imberger.
   mained at Trenton.   Lieut. Col. Krapp.
First Company, Bast, Jun'r.   Major Sohn.
Col. Kneise.   Capt. von Beisen, Jung.
   "   Corell.

PRISONERS FROM GRENADIER REGIMENT OF RALL.

	Commissioned Officers.	Others.	Total.
First Company	3	56	59
Lieut. Col. Kohler.................		56	56
Lieut. Col. Brethauer...............		51	51
Major Mateus		62	62
Captain Bocking	2	67	69
Middle and under staff.........			5

Names of Officers.

Lieut. Col. Brethauer.   Lieut. Kinen.
Major Mateus.   Ensign Fleck.
Capt. Brubach.   "   Kleinschmit.
Lieut. Salzmann.   "   Schroder.

Killed—Col. Rall, December 26, at Trenton.
Wounded—Lieut. Sternickel, December 26, at Trenton.
Missing—Ensign Kinen.

TRADESMEN AMONG HESSIAN PRISONERS AT LANCASTER, JANUARY 10, 1777.

Smiths	16	Stocking weavers	7
Carpenters	15	Musicians	2
Distiller	1	Combmaker	1
Bakers	6	Windowmakers	2
Weavers, linen and woolen	82	Nailsmiths	2
Wagonmakers	15	Gardener	1
Weavers of worsted shalloons, etc.	3	Tanners	2
		Coopers	4
Weavers of flowered linens	2	Barber	1
Shoemakers	38	Slater	1
Tailors	49	Thatcher	1
Butchers	9	Knifemaker	1
Masons	12	Horseshoer	1
Joiners	10	Bookbinders	2
Plasterers	7	Huntsman	1
Tilemaker	1	Breeches maker	1
Pipemakers	2	Dyers	2
Riflemaker	1	Locksmiths	4
Silversmith	1	Stone cutter	1
Lime burners	2		315
Millers	6		

PRISONERS AT LANCASTER, OF THE HESSIANS.

Artillery, 39 men; of the Regiment of Losberg, 234 men; of the Regiment of Knyphausen, 291 men; of the Ralischer Grenadiers, 266 men.

Total, 830 men and a few women and children, per Serjeant's returns.

The first prisoners arrived at Lancaster in the latter part of October, 1775, some being taken from vessels driven ashore on the New Jersey coast, and some captured

32

in November, 1775, at St. Johns, Canada, by Gen. Montgomery, while on his way to Quebec. The first of these latter arrived on December 9, 1775, and numbered 8 officers and 242 privates of the Seventh Royal Fusiliers, who were accompanied by 30 women and 30 children. About the same time, or soon after, came a party of prisoners, officers and soldiers of the Twenty-sixth British Regiment.

The officers were, in the beginning, lodged in one of the public houses, and the privates placed in the Lancaster barracks, which was, subsequently, inclosed by a strong stockade. Among the officers was Major André, of whom we have already spoken.

The number of prisoners at Lancaster was largely augmented by the arrival of the Hessians in January, 1777. It is stated that, during this year, as many as two thousand were held there at one time.

In July, 1777, when the British fleet was expected to attack Philadelphia, it was reported that the prisoners had threatened the destruction of Lancaster, so it was thought best, when their number was still further increased by the surrender of Burgoyne, on October 16, 1777, to forward quite a proportion of them to York, although very many were still left behind.

The Saratoga prisoners at Lancaster remained until December, 1778, when they were sent south. On March 3, 1781, Congress directed that the Convention prisoners should be removed back, from Virginia and Maryland, to Pennsylvania, the British to York Town and the Hessians to Lancaster, or such other place as the Council of Pennsylvania might direct. The prisoners held at Lancaster, at this time, were about eight hundred. They were principally Hessians, of the class termed "unconditional prisoners."

A daring plan was laid, by the British prisoners in the barracks for a general uprising on May 17, 1781, which fortunately was discovered and the plot spoiled.

At the beginning of the summer of that year the people of the borough were greatly alarmed by the appearance and rapid spread of a malignant fever among the prisoners, and this alarm was increased by the arrival of a body of "Convention prisoners" from the south, but, happily, the disease does not seem to have resulted as fatally as was anticipated.

In October, 1781, some of the "Convention prisoners" were removed to Easton and Philadelphia. For a year longer the prisoners remained at Lancaster, without the occurrence of any matters of moment. At last the British disappeared, as did also most of the Hessians, but many of these latter never returned to Europe or the British army, but settled in Lancaster or adjoining counties, where their descendants are still found.

To guard this number of prisoners, and to defeat their various attempts at escape, was no light matter. It was just as irksome a duty at Reading and Lebanon, but, as the numbers involved were greater at Lancaster, we will merely record the services of this character which were there performed, to give the reader some idea of what the Pennsylvania-Germans were called upon to do in this direction, a duty never pleasant and always without glory or reward.

In the beginning regular details of guards were appointed, from the militia, to serve on specific days. The first posting of guards seems to have taken place on October 25, 1775, and was as follows: Officer of the day, Capt. Paul Zantzinger; sergeant of the guard, Arnold Bombarger; corporal of the guard, Andrew Cunningham;

drummer, ——— Keisey; fifer, ——— Brooks; number of privates, sixteen. The detail averaged from twelve guards to about nineteen, up to March 6, 1776.

From December 30, 1775, to March, 1776, we have given the names of each officer of the day, and sergeant of the guard, which list is believed to be of sufficient interest to reproduce:

1775.	Officers of the day.	Sergeants.
Dec. 30.	Lieut. John Hubley.	John Messencope.
31.	Lieut. George Bickham.	Ludwick Heck.
1776.		
Jan. 1.	Lieut. John Offner.	Robert Lockhart.
2.	Capt. Samuel Boyd.	Isaac Solomon.
3.	Lieut. C. Crawford.	John Fleiger.
4.	Lieut. Ch. Hall.	John Fleiger.
5.	Capt. Hoofnagle.	Philip Wehmer.
6.	Lieut. Huttenstein.	John Slater.
7.	Lieut. Lightner.	Daniel Stricher.
8.	Ensign Franciscus.	Jacob Messencope.
9.	Capt. Musser.	John Snyder.
10.	Lieut. Moore.	John Weidley.
11.	Lieut. Trissler.	Godlieb Newman.
12.	Ensign Feltman.	John Blattenberger.
13.	Capt. Henry.	John Palmer.
14.	Lieut. Hyner.	Henry Maurer.
15.	Lieut. Keineck.	Peter Row.
16.	Capt. Graaff.	George Weiss.
Jan. 17.	Lieut. Graeff.	Henry Stouffer.
18.	Ensign Miller.	Andreas Geiss.
19.	Capt. Clatz.	George Eberly.
20.	Lieut. C. Shaffner.	Matthias Snyder.
21.	Lieut. P. Shaffner.	Andrew Truckenbide.
22.	Lieut. Baker.	Jacob Young.
23.	Ensign Petry.	George Strehley.
24.	Lieut. Dehuff.	Christopher Hager.
25.	Ensign Musser.	Christian Eberman.
26.	Ensign Fortine.	Henry Geiger.
27.	Lieut. Hubley.	Ludwick Keck.
28.	Lieut. Bickham.	John Messencope.
29.	Lieut. Ewing.	Robert Lockhart.

1775.	*Officers of the Day.*	*Sergeants.*
	30. Capt. Boyd.	Nicholas Bousman.
	31. Lieut. Crawford.	John Eppele.
Feb.	1. Lieut. Hall.	Isaac Solomon.
	2. Ensign Krug.	Jacob Heppele.
	3. Capt. Hoofnagle.	Philip Wehner.
	4. Lieut. Huttenstein.	John Slater.
	5. Lieut. Lightner.	Daniel Stricker.
	6. Ensign Franciscus.	Jacob Massencope.
	7. Capt. Mosser.	John Snyder.
	8. Lieut. Moore.	John Weidle.
	9. Lieut. Trissler.	Godlieb Newman.
	10. Ensign Feltman.	John Blattenberger.
	11. Capt. John Henry.	Henry Mourer.
	12. Lieut. Hyner.	Peter Kew.
	13. Capt. Graaff.	George Weiss.
	14. Lieut. Graeff.	Michael Gorb.
	15. Lieut. Graeff.	Henry Stouffer.
	16. Capt. Clatz.	George Eberly.
	17. Lieut. C. Shaffner.	Matthias Snyder.
	18. Lieut. Baker.	Andrew Trockenbide.
	19. Lieut. P. Shaffner.	Jacob Young.
	20. Capt. Yeates.	George Strehley.
	21. Lieut. Dehuff.	Henry Geiger.
	22. Lieut. Petry.	Frederick Mann.
	23. Ensign Musser.	Christopher Hager.
	24. Lieut. Hubley.	Arnold Bomberger.
	25. Lieut. Bickham.	John Messencope.
	26. Lieut Offner.	Francis Dailey.
	27. Lieut. Crawford.	Michael Crawford.
	28. Lieut. Hall.	Matthias Young.
	29. Capt. Boyd and Ensign Krug.	John Fleiger, John Eppele, & James Kain.
Mar.	1. Capt. Hoofnagle.	Philip Wehner.
	2. Lieut. Franciscus.	John Slater.
	3. Lieut. Graeff.	Daniel Stricker.
	4. Ensign Turbert.	Jacob Messencope.
	5. Capt. Musser.	John Snyder.
	6. Lieut. Moore.	John Weidle.

About this time the independent company of Capt.
Jacob Weaver, which had been raised in Lancaster for the
purpose of guarding the prisoners, was assigned to that

duty, in place of the militia. It was afterwards (January 13, 1777) attached to the Tenth Pennsylvania Continental Regiment.

On January 6, 1777, the Committee of Safety having ordered Col. Slough's battalion, and a part of Ross' battalion, to Philadelphia, and Capt. Weaver's company having departed, it became necessary to enroll a number of citizens who, because of age or otherwise, were unfit for active duty, into a company to guard the prisoners.

From that time until January, 1782, different classes of the militia were again in service on guard duty, when the situation became such as to make it necessary to supersede the militia guards with regular troops, and, accordingly, Col. Moses Hazen, with his regiment ("Congress' Own"), was ordered to Lancaster for that purpose, and remained until November, 1782, when again replaced by the militia.

Various attempts at escape had been made, some of which proved successful, and it was partly to prevent this in the future that Col. Hazen was detailed for the duty of guarding the prisoners. He promptly started in to ferret out the matter, and Capt. Lee, one of his officers, volunteered to assume the part of a prisoner and act as a spy. With much difficulty he succeeded in his purpose, and, unfortunately, implicated various people of the county, who, doubtless for the sake of gain, rather than because of disloyalty, had been base enough to allow themselves to be tempted into the performance of the wrong deeds in question. Their offence, however, does not seem to have been considered as heinous as might appear on the surface, because, later, a large part of the fine imposed upon them was remitted by the Court.

In May, 1781, a detachment of Col. Moylan's Dragoons had been stationed at Lancaster, to assist the militia in their guard duty. Before long, a most unfriendly feeling developed between the two, resulting in a sad occurrence.

One of the dragoons, for some offence, had been confined in the gaol house, whereupon his comrades threatened to release him by force. Armed with pistols and swords, they marched to the barracks, where they were halted by the militia sentinel. One, more daring than the others, advanced to the sentinel, cocked his pistol, presented it, and attempted to seize the arms of the guard, who, immediately, shot him dead. As the man fell his pistol went off and wounded another of his comrades. There was great alarm and commotion for a time, but, eventually, affairs resumed their normal state.

When, after the battle of Brandywine, it became evident that the British troops would soon occupy Philadelphia, hurried preparations were made for the removal of Congress and the government archives. Many of the members fled, for the time being, to Bethlehem, en route to Lancaster, and many effects were taken to that place.

When Congress actually adjourned, on September 18, 1777, it was to meet at Lancaster, and, for a while, it looked as though that place might be selected as the seat of government, but it was deemed advisable to cross the Susquehanna, and place said river between that body and its enemies, so, when it convened at Lancaster, on September 27, the same day that Gen. Howe entered Philadelphia, it held but one session in that town and adjourned to York, where the renewed session began on September 30, 1777, and continued until the British had again evacuated Philadelphia, in the following summer.

The State Government remained in Philadelphia until September 24 when it adjourned to Lancaster, the archives, etc., having previously been removed to Easton.

So favorably were the members of Congress impressed with the town of Bethlehem, and the character of its people, from the contact had with them on various occasions, that, at one time, the subject of making it the seat of our National Government was very seriously taken into consideration. This is a fact but little known. Through the courtesy of Dr. John W. Jordan, of the Historical Society of Pennsylvania, the following letters, gleaned by him from the Moravian Archives, are presented. They are most interesting and self-explanatory.

The first is from Lewis Weiss to the Rev. John Ettwein, and the second is his reply.

Lewis Weiss was born in Berlin on December 28, 1717. Emigrated to Pennsylvania in December, 1755, and settled in Philadelphia. For many years he was the attorney of the Moravian Church. He was one of the founders of the German Society, and its President in 1782. Commissioned Justice of the Court of Common Pleas for Philadelphia, May 26, 1786. He died October 22, 1796, and was buried in the Moravian cemetery at the corner of Franklin and Vine Streets.

The Rev. John Ettwein was a distinguished clergyman of the American Moravian Church, born in Friedenstadt, Germany. In 1754 he was consecrated bishop, and stood at the head of the church in Pennsylvania until his death in 1802.

PHILADELPHIA, 14 April, 1780.

"*Dear Sir*—I was yesterday spoken to by a friend of mine, a member of Congress, intimating that Congress had a mind to change their residence, and that it was proposed by some members Bethlehem would be a very proper place for making a Hague, like in Holland. I immediately exclaimed that Congress was mad! but was stopped when the gentleman declared that Congress would never enter upon the subject, if they should conceive this plan might put the Society at Bethlehem under greater inconvenience, as Congress *was* able to relieve them by the payment of money, and other advantages which would accrue to the trades of Bethlehem. I told him in my opinion it was impracticable, without ruining and eating up the Society; it was a question with me whether, if every soul was removed from Bethlehem, the houses built there was sufficient to contain Congress and the several departments belonging thereto; and if Congress had a mind to examine Mr. Edmonds, who happened to be in town, I believed he could give them information of the number of houses and inhabitants of Bethlehem and Nazareth, by which Congress would see the impossibility of putting that plan into execution.

"I had really stopped Bro. Edmonds, but was told this morning I might let him go home, and advised that I should write for a description of Bethlehem and perhaps Nazareth too, particularly the number of inhabitants of the several houses and cabins; and whenever the matter should come on the carpet, they would move the House to send for me for information. Indeed, I should be very sorry if Congress should come to reside even in your neighborhood, for it would spoil the morals of many of your people, and the markets for all of them.

" (Signed)   Lewis Weiss."

(*Reply.*)

"*Dear Sir*—As I have been informed that the honorable Congress intends to shift their residence from Philadelphia to some other place in this State; and that some inquiries have been made of you, whether that honorable body could not be accommodated here or at New York, I take this opportunity to inform you of the true state of Bethlehem, in regard to its dwelling houses and present inhabitants. You know our situation well enough, and that it would be impossible to receive them, if even they were willing to submit to many and great inconveniences.

"Bethlehem has about *thirty-six private dwelling houses,* which are inhabited by *sixty-one families,* with their different trade and workshops, so that many a family has but one single room for themselves and their all. You know the public buildings, as the meeting house, schools, the homes of the single brethren, single sisters, and widows, tavern and mills, are full of people; and I may, with truth, observe that no village or town in this State is so crowded with inhabitants as Bethlehem now is. Nazareth is not much better; and as it lies nine miles nigher to the Blue Mountains, that settlement is the first refuge of the settlers behind the mountains, as soon as they fear the least danger on account of the Indians. Some have already fled to Nazareth (a few days ago), and how many may follow them soon we cannot know.

"Yet if even the honorable Congress, and its appendages, could find the necessary accommodation here and in the neighborhood, which I know to be impossible, if they will not live in tents, it would, in my humble opinion, be a dangerous residence for them, as we are so nigh the mountains and the Big Swamp, from which an enemy could with ease walk in one night to Bethlehem.   And such a treasure as the Congress might be a great temptation for the Indians or their desperate associates to make a sudden attempt upon the place, if they were not covered by a considerable force.

" Dear Sir, I must beg the favor of you to be attentive in this matter, and if you find that there is really such a notion or motive, to make, in the name of the Brethren or in their behalf, a representation against it, and cause, at least, an inspection into our situation and circumstances, before Congress resolves to move into these parts.   We should be very sorry at the certain disappointment of the Congress in our (*unintelligible*) that they may not distress the inhabitants of this little place, disturb its happy constitution, and have nothing for it but trouble, exposure and disappointment.

" I am, dear Sir, with love and respect,
" JOHN ETTWEIN."

When Congress assembled in York on the last day of September, 1777, in the old Court House, which stood in Center Square, it beheld the chief cities of the country in the hands of the enemy, and a shattered and dispirited army retreating before a victorious foe.

It sat with closed doors.   None but its own members, with, occasionally, a few government officials, were allowed to hear the debates which took place on the momentous questions of the day.

In a building at one corner of Center Square, Michael Hillegas, Treasurer of the United States, kept the accounts of the government.   In the office of James Smith, on the west side of South George Street, John Adams presided over the Board of War, corresponding to our War De-

partment of today.   The President of Congress, John
Hancock, rented a house owned by Col. Michael Swope,
on the south side of West Market Street, near Center
Square.   As a man of means, and because of his position,
he lived in considerable style.   York was then a town of
286 houses, and contained about 1,500 inhabitants.   Mr.
Adams, in a letter of October 25, says: " This town is a
small one, not larger than Plymouth.   There are in it
two German churches, the one Lutheran, the other Calvin-
istical.   The congregations are pretty numerous, and their
attendance upon public worship is decent.   It is remarkable that the Germans wherever they are found are care-
ful to maintain the public worship, which is more than
can be said of the other denominations of Christians this
way . . . ," and, on October 28, wrote: " The people
of this country are chiefly Germans who have schools in
their own language, as well as prayers, psalms and sermons, so that multitudes are born, grow up and die here
without ever learning the English. . . ."

On November 4, 1777, Congress requested Gen. Washington to appoint Lafayette to the command of a division
in the Continental army, and commissioned him a Major-
General.

Having heard Col. Wilkinson announce, from its floor,
the glad tidings of the surrender of Burgoyne at Saratoga, on October 12, the same day the thanks of Congress
were presented to Gen. Gates, his officers and troops.

On the fifteenth of November the Articles of Confederation were adopted, after having been debated three
times a week for nearly seven months.

On November 27 a new Board of War was organized,
composed of General Mifflin, Joseph Trumbull, Richard

BARON FRIEDRICH VON STEUBEN.

B. MAGDEBURG, NOVEMBER 15, 1730.   D. STEUBENVILLE, N. Y., NOVEMBER 28, 1794.

Peters, Colonel Pickering and General Gates, of which the latter was made President.

Baron Steuben, and suite, arrived at York on February 5, 1778, and remained until February 19. Congress received him with every mark of distinction, and, at the solicitation of Washington, appointed him Inspector General of the army.

On March 28, 1778, Count Pulaski was appointed to the command of an independent corps of cavalry and infantry.

The Treaty of Alliance, between France and the United States, was ratified by Congress on May 4, and, two days after, the entire town showed its joy over the same by an illumination.

The death of Philip Livingstone, a delegate from New York, occurred on June 11, 1778, and his body was interred, on the evening of the twelfth, in the graveyard of the German Reformed Church.

When, at length, Philadelphia was evacuated by the enemy, Congress adjourned to that city on June 27.

The diary of the Rev. George Neisser, Moravian pastor, for this period, contains many interesting entries with regard to the events just mentioned, also concerning movements of troops and prisoners. Among them he narrates how Adam Orth and Christopher Kucker, came, on May 1, 1778, from Lebanon, as representatives of the Hebron congregation, to tell the authorities how Major Watkins had filled, with powder, the residence portion of their church, occupied by the Rev. Bader, and praying for relief. It is gratifying to know that, on May 4, the Board of War directed the powder to be removed, and other stores put in its place, which would not materially inconvenience Pastor Bader in his occupation of the building.

One of the memorable events which took place during the occupancy of York by Congress was the treasonable attempt to induce Washington to surrender his army to the British. It was made by the Rev. Jacob Duché, in a letter written from Philadelphia on October 8, 1777, wherein he rehearses the misfortunes which had overtaken the cause of independence, together with the sad condition of the country, and urges the Commander-in-chief to put an end to further attempts to gain that which is impossible of attainment, by entering into negotiations with Lord Howe looking towards the bringing about of peace. In other words, pleading with Washington to traitorously surrender the cause for which he was then fighting, for which thousands had suffered, and for which other thousands had already laid down their lives. It is needless to say this suggestion was indignantly spurned, and the whole correspondence immediately laid before Congress by Washington, on October 16, 1777, accompanied by an explanatory note.

Mr. Duché, formerly rector of Christ Church in Philadelphia, was a man of eloquence and piety, who had been appointed by Congress its first Chaplain, and whose prayer, upon the opening of the session, was pronounced to be not only eloquent but patriotic in the extreme.

But, beyond even this occurrence, came the now famous Conway Cabal.

There seems to be so much misunderstanding as to the meaning and derivation of this word that it may be well to say it comes from the French *cabale,* and the Hebrew *cabala,* signifying *secret knowledge.* One of the ministries of Charles II. (1670), was called a cabal from the accidental fact that the initials of its members' names formed that word.

The Conway Cabal was instigated by Thomas Conway, born in Ireland, February 27, 1733, and educated in France. He entered the French army, and, in 1777, had attained the rank of Colonel, with the decoration of St. Louis. On the recommendation of the American Minister, Silas Deane, he came to America, offered his services to the Continental Congress, and was made Brigadier General, May 13, 1777. He was present at the battles of Brandywine and Germantown.

We have seen under what discouragements Washington labored during the fall and winter of 1776, with only here and there a ray of sunshine to lighten the surrounding gloom. We know how, notwithstanding the best laid plans, these dark days were followed by those of Brandywine and Germantown, necessitating the evacuation of Philadelphia and flight to York. We have read, even though not in detail, of the terrible winter at Valley Forge. In the midst of these trials, and what was almost a period of despair, came the glorious tidings of Burgoyne's surrender. Is it to be wondered that weak human nature, no different then from what it is now, should be tempted, in not a few cases, to doubt the ability of Washington. Here was the golden opportunity for all malcontents to combine against him and accomplish his overthrow.

Embittered by the opposition of the Commander-in-chief to his promotion, a mere adventurer, over the heads of faithful and competent American officers, Conway gathered about him a band of congenial conspirators. Anonymous letters were written to prominent men, alleging the responsibility of Washington for recent disasters;

it has been even charged that the name of Washington
was forged by Conway to papers designed to further the
plans of the conspirators; various members of Congress
were gained over, and, through them, Conway was promoted to his coveted position of Major General; Gates
was invited to appear before Congress, where he was
given an ovation, and, on November 27, 1777, made
president of the newly organized Board of War, where
he was in a position to hamper Washington in every
possible way, and through which he hoped to be able to
supersede him in the chief command, either by the appointment of himself or General Charles Lee to that office.

In York he lived in sumptuous style, Mrs. Gates enter-
taining lavishly all her husband's friends. They first
occupied quarters in a hotel on the south side of West
Market Street near Center Square; later, they rented a
house on the north side of West Market, near Beaver
Street.

It mattered not that Washington was then at the front,
straining every nerve to save his country, and, by his absence, unable to defend himself; it mattered not that he
had just given an additional proof of the depth of his
patriotism by the way in which he spurned the suggestion
of Rev. Duché to become a traitor; it mattered not that
Gates was but a weak, and inefficient tool, who had reaped
the benefit of the work of other and better men whom
he had superseded; it mattered not that Conway was but
a selfish adventurer, who, in the course of a few brief
months, would be forced to leave the army against his
own free will; it mattered not that Lee had, doubtless,
even then, within his heart the embryo seeds of that
treason which was, later, to prove his ruin; nothing was

considered, and all were blinded to the truth by the glittering rays of the new star which had temporarily appeared above the horizon.

The scheme of Conway embraced an attempt to separate Lafayette from Washington. Accordingly, Gates planned an expedition to Canada, which was approved by Congress, and Lafayette was appointed to its command, without consultation with Washington. Fortunately, sober common sense was again beginning to assert its sway. Washington was now in possession of most of the facts in the case, and, upon his advice, Lafayette accepted the place tendered him, went to York for instructions, and called on Gates, whom he found surrounded by his friends at the table. Being invited to join them he determined to make his position unequivocal from the beginning, so, when the proper time came, he rose to his feet, and, in a toast, pledged "The Commander-in-Chief of the American Armies." The toast was drunk with coolness and in silence, but this incident was the commencement of the end, and, in a brief time, the Conway Cabal was but a matter of history.

Where now are the names of the men who took part in this conspiracy? Almost buried in oblivion, or else remembered with contempt, while he, whom they sought to ruin is, from day to day, becoming more greatly endeared to the nation whose independence he succeeded in gaining.

There is a lesson to be learned from all this. It is an example of the difference between patriotism and selfishness. It tells us what is meant by a *true* American. It is an instance of silent suffering and continued faithfulness, notwithstanding injustice, calumny and ingratitude.

It is also a proof of the eventual triumph of right over wrong.

So with our Pennsylvania-German ancestors. They were not perfect any more than was Washington. Indeed, among their number could doubtless have been found some who were far from being such. But, considering them as a whole, and overlooking the mere unimportant frailties of weak human nature incident to all peoples, whatever their nationality, we feel justified in asking where, in the history of the Revolution, are found those who have done more for their country, who have given more to their country, and who have undergone greater sacrifices of all descriptions? And this was done quietly, unostentatiously, and often amidst much calumny and persecution. They were true American patriots and truly unselfish. They did not seek for the "high places," but were content to take a "lower room" and wait until the time should come when their worth might be recognized, and they would be summoned to "go up higher." That time has already come, and if, in this imperfect and incomplete narrative, the author has aided, even to a small extent, in accomplishing this object, he will consider himself amply repaid for his labor.

hic finis laborum !

FINIS.

INDEX TO SURNAMES.

GENERAL INDEX.

Metalmark Books is a joint imprint of The Pennsylvania State University
Press and the Office of Digital Scholarly Publishing at The Pennsylvania State
University Libraries. The facsimile editions published under this
imprint are reproductions of out-of-print, public domain works that hold
a significant place in Pennsylvania's rich literary and cultural past.
Metalmark editions are primarily reproduced from the University Libraries'
extensive Pennsylvania collections and in cooperation with other
state libraries. These volumes are available to the public for viewing online
and can be ordered as print-on-demand paperbacks.

LIBRARY OF CONGRESS CATALOGING-IN-PUBLICATION DATA

Richards, Henry Melchior Muhlenberg, 1848–1935.
The Pennsylvania German in the Revolutionary War,
1775–1783 / Henry Melchior Muhlenberg Richards.
p.   cm.
Includes bibliographical references and index.
Summary: "Examines the achievements of the
Pennsylvania Germans during the Revolutionary War era,
in both civilian and military occupations. Originally
published by the Pennsylvania German Society in
1908"—Provided by publisher.
ISBN 978-0-271-05386-8 (pbk. : alk. paper)
1. Pennsylvania—History—Revolution, 1775–1783—
Participation, German American.
2. United States—History—Revolution, 1775–1783—
Participation, German American.
3. Pennsylvania Dutch—History—18th century.
I. Title.

E269.G3R54 2012
973.3'448—dc23
2011046808

Printed in the United States of America
Reprinted by The Pennsylvania State University Press, 2012
University Park, PA 16802-1003